DATE DUE			

Second Edition

CHORAL
MUSIC
EDUCATION

Paul F. Roe

North Texas State University

Prentice-Hall, Inc., Englewood Cliffs, New Jersey 07632

Library of Congress Cataloging in Publication Data

ROE, PAUL F.
  Choral music education.

  Bibliography: p.
  Includes index.
  1. Choral singing—Instruction and study. I. Title.
MT930.R65 1983   784.9'62   82-18546
ISBN   0-13-133322-4

Editorial/production supervision and
   interior design: Patricia V. Amoroso
Cover design: Karolina Harris
Manufacturing buyer: Raymond Keating

Printed in the United States of America

10 9 8 7 6 5 4 3 2 1

ISBN 0-13-133322-4

PRENTICE-HALL INTERNATIONAL, INC., *London*
PRENTICE-HALL OF AUSTRALIA PTY. LIMITED, *Sydney*
EDITORA PRENTICE-HALL DO BRASIL, LTDA., *Rio de Janeiro*
PRENTICE-HALL CANADA INC., *Toronto*
PRENTICE-HALL OF INDIA PRIVATE LIMITED, *New Delhi*
PRENTICE-HALL OF JAPAN, INC., *Tokyo*
PRENTICE-HALL OF SOUTHEAST ASIA PTE. LTD., *Singapore*
WHITEHALL BOOKS LIMITED, *Wellington, New Zealand*

Contents

Preface

This text may be used for a one-semester course or a two-semester course in secondary methods or conducting. If a one-semester course is necessary, the teacher will need to discuss three or four chapters in depth and skim the remainder (see the next paragraph for a suggested procedure). When the student becomes a teacher, the book will remain a source of many usable ideas and solutions to problems. The book should also prove to be very valuable to the in-service teacher who is striving to improve in teaching and directing, since it gives an unusually comprehensive look at the many facets of vocal music education. It is my sincere hope that the reader will find this book a practical and useful tool in accomplishing the development of skills and musical taste in the students.

The chapters in this book tend to fall into three natural divisions. Chapters 1, 2, and 3, the functional music program and music management procedures, investigate the practical administrative procedures that are necessary both in and out of the classroom. The next four chapters contain the very important areas of vocal fundamentals, sight-reading, general music, and middle school or junior high problems. The author has spent a great deal of time in the secondary methods class working with this subject matter. Chapters 8 through 11 form the third large area of emphasis. A class in conducting will spend most of its time on the chapter on conducting, with increasing time and attention, as its skill increases, to the other chapters on rehearsal techniques, style, and performances. If these matters are not covered well in conducting classes, they should be in the methods course.

The book begins with a discussion of public relations and student recruitment. Recommendations are made for middle school and junior and senior high school music curriculums. Ranges and tessituras, voice testing, and seating arrangements are presented in the chapter on the functional music program. The closely related area of management is treated in Chapter 3. The teacher must know how to handle budgets, music, supplies, equipment, records, and reports simply and efficiently. Some help is provided in the use of visual aids, student grading, lesson planning, and music selection.

Chapters 4 and 5 are two of the most important chapters in the book. They discuss in great detail how to obtain sound vocal fundamentals with large groups of students through the employment of various physical and psychological techniques. Time must be taken from each class period to teach sight-reading. Music is a nonverbal language, and living musical experiences with tone and pitch and rhythm are the only means by which sight-reading skills may be built. Chapter 6 tells how to investigate and deepen the students' sight-reading ability and how to build upon these abilities through rhythmic, melodic, harmonic, and ear training drills that grow from problems presented by interesting literature. A constant effort must be made to have the students gain the capacity to deal with several elements simultaneously and learn musicality in the process. Sight-reading literature and the sight-reading contest are also included. The junior high and middle school age tend to be somewhat neglected in books on the secondary school. Chapter 7 provides some basic information on the physical, psychological, and vocal problems of these students plus some suggestions concerning the teaching of the general music class.

Enough information on conducting is included in Chapter 8 to make this text usable for a college conducting class. A presentation is made of the preparatory beat, beat patterns, releases, the use of the left hand, and cueing. Important information is also given on ways to control pitches, vowel sounds and consonant closures, and dynamics. Carrying a phrase and influencing style through flexible beat patterns convey the very essence of musicianship. Class control in beginning and general classroom activities is attained through enthusiasm, creativity, musicianship, and good student-teacher rapport. A careful look at these processes is taken in Chapter 9. Then, an order of rehearsal and some rehearsal techniques are given. Methods of memorizing, ways of presenting a "whole" concept of a score to a choir, how to drill when necessary so as to use rehearsal time economically, and ways of teaching interpretation are some of the areas discussed. All the important aspects of music may be learned in a meaningful and interesting context when style and musical traditions are taught.

Chapter 10 gives some general understandings of dynamics, harmony, notation, melody, tempo, and tone quality typical of each period of musical history. Chronological listings of the composers and their large-form choral works are given. The concluding chapter discusses all aspects of performance from choosing and building the program to the final production. A work time-schedule for the performance is set up, with specific suggestions for tasks that should be taken care of during each period of time starting three months before and culminating in the program. The chapter concludes with suggestions for television studio productions and a pro and con discussion of the contest and festival.

As large as this book is, there were still some areas that were not developed. Very little was done with audio-visual, although it was discussed in general terms. The reader may be disappointed that lengthy lists of choral materials were not included. It is the author's firm conviction that conductors do not usually pick songs from a list in a book. Most of the songs they use they have experienced in high school, college, or graduate school *or* have heard at conventions, clinics, contests, or on recordings.

The author is grateful to the many people who have encouraged the writing of this book. Great appreciation goes to N.T.S.U. for permitting manuscript copies of the book to be used and improved in secondary methods and conducting classes. Special thanks are due the musicologists Dr. Dika Newlin and Dr. Cecil Adkins for their assistance in checking the accuracy of the chapter on style and musical tradition.

PAUL F. ROE

Introduction

The great task of education is to help students acquire more knowledge about themselves and their universe. All the major academic disciplines contribute to this knowledge. Music may take its rightful place as one of the major disciplines only when the main teaching emphasis is placed upon increasing students' knowledge of the innate qualities and subtle values of music.

Music cannot be taught for aesthetic insight unless the instructor carefully and regularly plans lessons with that goal in mind. The music selected must be well-constructed and expressive (see Chapter 3). It must be of a suitable difficulty for the age and experience of the students, spanning a gamut of complexity *from* some music that can be almost completely comprehended, *through* much music that will require a length of time to understand and master, *to* some numbers that are unreachable but stretch musical imaginations. The sequence of learning advocated by

Reimer[1] should be observed. Reimer says that all levels of classes should start with an *experience* with the music; then *study* should be pursued so that the students will *reexperience* the music with increased understanding and better technique.

The teacher of general music has an opportunity to teach the entire range of things musical to a class that is not bound by performance pressures. Singing, playing, composing, listening to, and sight-reading music are effective means for making clear how music operates. Bodily movements, analysis, discussion, evaluation, and reading are some other means for obtaining growing insight. Students must be constantly exposed to the musical elements (melody, harmony, rhythm, texture, tone color, form, and style) in a variety of carefully chosen music in a manner that will help develop musical sensitivity and understanding.

In the performance class, it is quite possible for a member of a fine choir to experience a thrill in a well-executed number, even when little insight has been provided. The modern music educator is increasingly being made aware that teaching for performance alone is not enough. Students who are involved in a cooperative analysis and improvement of interpretation, tone balance, and quality are creatively evolving higher standards of musicianship. Encourage these young singers to adjudicate their own performance; to decide whether the song was sung and interpreted as it should be; and to constructively criticize the spots that require attention. Students will be more excited about an interpretation or tone quality they have helped to create than about one produced by the teacher alone. Don't allow monotony in technical details to put out the fire of interest. Music that is taught so that the learner is given opportunities to taste and feel and obtain an intelligent grasp of style, texture, form, and all other musical elements provides numerous additional opportunities for an exciting experience to occur.

[1] Bennett Reimer, *A Philosophy of Music Education* (Englewood Cliffs, N.J.: Prentice-Hall, Inc., 1970).

PART ONE

1

Promotional Activities and Recommendations for Scheduling and Curriculum

A vocal teacher's unusually good musicianship and personality may result in a fine reputation in spite of piled-high desks and inattention to details. This accomplishment does not excuse the choral musician from providing the proper teaching-learning environment. Any accomplishments will be enhanced by quick and efficient ways of keeping records and getting things done.

The experienced teacher should have command of a good plan for the organization of classes, music files, student reports, programs, the class roll, seating arrangements, the appearance of the classroom, and fee collection. Since many of these details are routine procedures, the inexperienced teacher will need to plan ways to do them and should include them in the lesson plan until they become second nature.

The study of the functional music program consists of three major parts: promotional activities, recommendations for scheduling and curriculum, and student activities. The first two will be discussed in this chapter. Some ways to organize singers will be examined in Chapter 2.

WHEN THE BEGINNING INSTRUCTOR
IS AN ASSISTANT, NOT A HEAD TEACHER

Many teachers whose first teaching positions are in a city will find themselves assisting the principal teachers. Large schools or well-developed music departments in middle school, junior high, or high school employ assistants, and new instructors are most likely to start at that level in these kinds of schools. Do not expect to start as head music teachers in high schools until some years of successful experience have been completed. If you want to start as the *only* vocal teacher in a school, look for small schools (especially in remote areas of the state away from the population centers) or poorly developed vocal programs in larger schools.

If you are accepted as an assistant, realize that you will probably have the classes and tasks that the established teacher doesn't want. The general music classes where mainstreaming may have brought about the most difficult situations and performance ensembles other than the top ones will probably be your lot.

Undoubtedly you will assist or do team teaching in some of the principal teacher's classes, especially in top choral groups. You may be asked to work with small groups of students on remedial exercises and coach small ensembles and soloists for contest, and you may be asked to help within the class context by accompanying, vocalizing the choir, assisting with pitches, posture, improvisation, and anything that is required. Preparing bulletin board displays, checking attendance, putting material on the board, preparing slides for the overhead projector, mimeographing materials, and grading tests are other kinds of duties you may be asked to assume.

You will either assist or do the majority of the work of collecting fees, issuing books, gathering information, making seating charts, arranging equipment or furniture (particularly chairs or desks), unpackaging new equipment, music, or materials, obtaining supplies, inventorying and storing, studying cumulative records for student interests, competencies, and needs, and ordering music and films. Many of these activities may be needed at any time of the year, but most of them are required particularly at the beginning of a school term.

As quickly as possible become oriented to the school building, policies, regulations, and practices. Discover the resources that are available (library, guidance office, auditorium, and audio-visual equipment such as records, tape, videotape, film, and film strips). Obtain a copy of each textbook that will be used in your teaching and borrow each for your entire stay in the school. Collect all available material that will help you understand the school program and peruse it as quickly as possible. This material may include class schedules, statements of philosophy, department-wide syllabi, course outlines, and curriculum study reports.

The school handbook is perhaps the best source of information concerning school rules. Here you may learn about student clubs, organizations and activities sponsored by the school, the school's regulations for teachers and students, and the rules concerning school records, absences, tardiness, and violations of school regulations. Other helpful items of knowledge are the mores of the community, of the students, and of the school personnel.

Adjust to the situation as rapidly as you can, and do not upset established ways of doing things. After you have a track record of success you can begin to introduce some innovations. However, don't just copy the other instructor. Develop your own style of teaching. Use extra periods (if any) for planning, research, and conferences. Attend all faculty meetings, department-wide meetings, and extracurricular group practices. Be loyal to the school, students, co-workers, and administration.

If you need assistance with lesson planning, disciplinary problems, rehearsal procedures, background of students, or with any other area, don't hesitate to talk to the established teacher or the music supervisor. Either one will be glad to give you advice.[1]

PROMOTIONAL ACTIVITIES

Student Recruitment

Recruit constantly. There are many subjects and activities vying for the students' time.[2] Because of this, students with musical potential must receive assurance that they have ability and that the music teacher wants them as students.

Personal Contact

Wherever music is a required subject, a stimulating and knowledgeable teacher will influence students to register for elective classes, and no real recruitment problem will exist. Personal contact with students, brought about through team teaching of all the music from sixth grade through high school, has resulted in superior choral departments. Students in your church choir may be persuaded to join school groups. Close friends of school choir members should be invited to join, if they have musical ability. Recruit students from study halls. Audition students who have been recommended by music teachers. Also open the auditions to *anyone* who wishes to try out. Include at least a few of the most intelligent and most popular in the next year's music classes if they are qualified.

[1] Much of the foregoing information is equally applicable to the student teacher. For supplementary information see Joan Boney and Lois Rhea, *A Guide to Student Teaching in Music* (Englewood Cliffs, N.J.: Prentice-Hall, Inc., 1970).

[2] See "Scheduling Difficulties," p. 14, for a detailed listing of these problems.

Guidance Counselors

Make friends with the guidance counselors. They can make or break the music program. Make sure they are fully informed. Give the lists of recommended students to these officials (or, better yet, obtain permission to put a notation on each student's registration card).

Performances

Interesting, polished programs[3] sell the music department better than anything else. Programs presented to students at middle school or junior or senior high assemblies provide the greatest coverage and impact, but musical comedy shows presented for the community also have tremendous appeal for students and for their parents. Male groups and male soloists are enthusiastically accepted by audiences. Have the junior high choir sing a number with the high school choir and include the junior high in money-raising projects.

Community Singing

All choral directors should achieve at least some skill in community songleading. A good songleader may attract *some* members of the student body into the vocal groups; the conductor will be a good advertisement for excellent teaching abilities in music if students' fathers or mothers can be inspired in a professional club Sing-Song or both parents become interested in singing at a church party. Conversely, if the choral director is uninspiring, students will be discouraged from taking vocal music and parents will wonder if the new choral director at the high school really is any good. The successful songleader must be enthusiastic (a "musical cheerleader"), with the ability to inspire and create enthusiasm in the singers. A good sense of humor is an asset. A strong voice helps, but it is not a necessity.

In community songleading, follow the main accented beats and the main words, usually employing both hands with large motions. The directional beat pattern may be broken down when the conductor works with children or untrained adults while teaching by rote. A pitch pattern drawn in the air like this:

$$\begin{array}{cccc} & try & & Thee \\ My\ coun & & of & \\ & 'tis\text{--} & & \end{array}$$

will help singers visualize the pitches they are learning by ear.

A good pianist who accents heavily and overemphasizes the rhythmic swing in the music is a great asset to an informal sing. This technique is

---

[3] See Chapter 11 for information on programs and shows.

necessary in order to pull a group of casual singers along and bolster their confidence enough to cause even off-key singers to feel that they can sing out and no one will pay attention to them. The pianist who can do a skillful job of filling in chord spaces with inverted chords should do it, but it is more important to play musically and strongly.

Songleading Techniques

Some of the techniques and songs used in general music classes, such as chanting, rounds, vocal chording, sound effects, and changed rhythms, lend themselves beautifully to community singing (see Chapter 6). Be sure to have the entire group sing the melody until they know it before dividing them for singing parts. Be sure the directions given to the singers specify exactly who is to sing in what group, when they are to begin singing, and how many times the round or song is to be sung.

Put the chords in close harmony.

For example: Assign one section to the low part, one to the middle, etc. Indicate chord changes by finger signals whenever the melody requires the chord to change. Have the melody sung by a soloist or by one section. The singers will enjoy actually making harmony in a creative manner. A group will welcome the fun of following a conductor who challenges them. Use a variation in tempos, diversify the dynamics, hold fermatas, and make the group sing phrases, words, and songs "musically." The musical experience of singing Malotte's "The Lord's Prayer" like members of a fine choir will thrill untrained singers.

Public Relations

In order to keep public relations A-OK with your administrators, observe the "chain of command." Always go to the person immediately over you (supervisor, etc.) or to the principal. Don't go to the superintendent if you can help it. Get reports and details that are asked for by the administration in on time. Be careful to attend all faculty meetings. Do extracurricular work for the school, such as selling football tickets or sponsoring dances. Remain optimistic when things go wrong. Above all, don't complain to other teachers about your administrators (or about how much you have to do). Put all requests for materials and supplies in writing (what is wanted, cost, reasons for needing it, where to buy it, and type needed).

Be a good citizen in the community. Assume leadership in community and church music groups. It is usually desirable to become active in professional and social organizations so the people of the community may become acquainted with you. Well-prepared soloists, small ensembles, and musical demonstrations freely proffered will help the public know about the excellent vocal music department at their school. Parents need to be kept informed of the progress their children are making. Cooperate with private music teachers so that they feel the music department is promoting more students for them to teach instead of taking money from their pockets. Professional musicians must be reassured that the music department is not competing with them. Share students and do favors for the teachers and custodians, for the time will come when it will be necessary to enlist their active help and support. Students are the strongest medium of all for good public relations. Know their names. Make a special effort to show interest in them and in the things that they and their families do. According to Dr. Earle Wiltse,[4] the five most important words in human relations are, "I am proud of you"; the four most important are, "What is your opinion"; the two most important are, "Thank you"; and the least effective word is "I."[5]

RECOMMENDATIONS FOR SCHEDULING AND CURRICULUM

The MENC (Music Educators National Conference) has described basic standards and quality standards for the curriculum in its 1974 publication, *The School Music Program: Description and Standards.* Virtually all of the recommendations are identical for grades 6–9 and 10–12. The only real difference is one of degree. As might be expected, more meeting time per week and a greater variety of instructional settings is suggested for grades 10–12. Ideally, music classes will meet for as many minutes as regular academic offerings.

Every student, regardless of talent, should have opportunities to participate in music. Select choirs (male, female, and mixed) must be available to offer enriching experiences to the more talented. Small-ensemble and individualized instruction should be offered at beginning, intermediate, and advanced levels. In grades 6–9 folk instruments, listening, composition, electronic music, keyboard, and interdisciplinary studies will usually be taught in the general music class, although there could be separate courses in any of these areas. All courses should have these elements as part of the class content. If the geographic area has an indigenous musical idiom (Indian, etc.), it should receive special emphasis.

In the small high school, the offerings are necessarily very modest.

---

[4] Dr. Wiltse was a professor in school administration at Northern Illinois University, De Kalb, Illinois.

[5] *See* Joan Gaines, *Approaches to Public Relations for the Music Educator* (Washington, D.C.: Music Educators National Conference, 1968).

Swing choir probably will be added and general music deleted from the above recommendations for grades 6–9. In the large school, the course selections might include some or all of the following: Basic Musicianship, Music Literature, Music History, Music Theory, Composition, Electronic Music, Non-Western Music, Interdisciplinary Studies, Specialized Ensembles such as Swiss Hand Bells or Afro-American Ensembles, Music Theater, and Class Instruction in Voice, Keyboard, or Guitar.

Basic music fundamentals combined with some meaningful integration with history, art, and literature need to be an integral part of the learning in any performance group, but when schools do not have the necessary personnel or numbers of students to schedule classes in harmony, theory, ear training, and so on, these subjects must be taught within the framework of the choir rehearsal. The performance group will profit because the students will become better readers, performers, and musicians.

General Music

Many schools have no provision for the student who likes music but is *not good* at it. Considering the aims of music education, and particularly the musical needs of students, the general music class is a neglected area. Music teachers as a whole have been trained to direct instrumental and vocal groups and often lack specific training for general music teaching.

There has been a great deal of national emphasis and thought for several years on "general music." Educators finally realized that the music teachers in the secondary schools were teaching "performance," not "music," and many were settling for second-rate music. The Music Educators National Conference began strongly emphasizing general music in publications and in regional and national conventions. The very fine publication, *Music in General Education*, printed in 1965 by the MENC, gives a great deal of insight into teaching for musicianship. It discusses experiences all music classes should provide, special experiences for nonselective music classes, and special experiences for instrumental and vocal music classes. Every teacher, especially every teacher of general music classes, should own this inexpensive paperback book.

Consult the Bibliography in this book at the end of Chapter 7 for many other excellent books on General Education (Andrews, Monsour and Perry, Hughes, Metz, Regelski, Hughes and Kjelson, and others). Also, the chapters on Sight-Reading and The General Music Class And Some Junior High Problems (Chapters 6 and 7) should be quite helpful.

Small Ensembles and Solo Voice Class

One goal of a vocal teacher might very well be to give every student who is truly interested an opportunity to become involved with small ensemble and solo work. It is a goal that can never be reached, for a music instructor's time is always too limited to allow everyone's participation. If you have never honestly given students a chance to sing in small ensembles, it will amaze you how many students are interested and willing to spend a great deal of time on the chance that they may ultimately perform for programs (including men's and women's clubs, professional clubs, etc.) or in contests.

In extracurricular small ensembles, there are three contrasting plans of action that may be adopted (although there may be any combination of these three): (1) A *once-a-week meeting with each small ensemble*, year-round to check its work and help it progress, with the expectation that it will meet two or more additional times per week on its own. (See Chapter 3 for a suggested way to keep attendance.) Ten to fifteen small ensembles *can* be organized and kept moving with this plan. (2) One to five small ensembles *meeting multiple times per week* with the instructor all year long. This will involve all of the teacher's available time. (3) *Small Ensembles organized just before a contest*. Usually the groups are picked out of the large vocal groups after a tryout. The groups may or may not continue after the contest for the remainder of the school year.

The best choral program is one built upon small ensembles. The more active ensembles there are in the choir, the better the choir should be, for small ensemble members will learn to blend and to read better, and will be more interested in the whole music program because of the experience. If talent permits, organize the small ensembles according to grade levels (sophomore sextet, etc.) and with students who are, or who are likely to be, compatible. With this arrangement, students will practice because they like to be together anyway. Small ensemble members will be graduated at the same time, so there won't be remaining members who will lose their previous year's repertoire while gambling on the blending ability and likability of any new members that are chosen. All-senior small ensembles are greatly in demand for senior graduation events.

Small ensembles may be organized for credit during the school day. One of the best solutions is the voice class, in which the small ensemble works as a group part of the time and members also improve their voices on solo literature. If a voice class cannot be offered for credit, it would be wise to organize one that meets regularly outside school.

The voice class that is part of the curriculum should be at least a one-year course for the ultimate good of the student. There are many advantages that a voice class even has over private lessons. For instance, the school will usually have good recording equipment, so that students can record their voices at the beginning and end of each semester to recognize progress made. Recording equipment will be available during the middle of the semester to solve voice problems on the spot. Another advantage is the ready-made audience in the class, so the singer can become accustomed to singing in front of people. Many vocal principles may be demonstrated and practiced as a group, so there is the inspiration of others practicing at the same time. Individual vocal literature should be studied (suited to each voice and special abilities) in addition to learning some unison numbers. Tryouts for soloists for the oratorio, school programs, opera, contest, etc. may be coached, encouraged (even forced and enforced) through voice class.

The national organization, Modern Music Masters, is still another excellent way to encourage solo and small ensemble, musicianship, and interest in music. Modern Music Masters is a national music honor society for junior and senior high schools. Its chief aims are to foster greater interest in choral, orchestral, and band performances; to challenge students to greater efforts; to encourage solo and ensemble performances; to recognize personal musical achievements; to promote better public relations; and to inspire students to higher ideals and to service to the school, churches, and community through music. This organization is especially fine for stimulating a strong solo and small ensemble program.

The selection of students for membership is based upon ability and scholarship in musical and academic subjects. Although Modern Music Masters is basically an honorary society, most chapters have regular meetings and an active program (special speakers, small ensembles, a Music Masters choir, a special study of some phase of music, a service organization for community musical functions, etc.). Information on organizing a chapter may be obtained from the national office: Modern Music Masters, P.O. Box 347, Park Ridge, Illinois, 60068.

Swing Choirs

Special vocal ensembles singing popular music as part or all of their repertoire are not a new development. Even madrigals sometimes included some popular music on their programs.

What *is* new is the movement that has developed as a result of the legitimization of jazz and the organization of the National Association of Jazz Educators under the auspices of the MENC in 1968. Out of the NAJE has come the flowering of the Swing Choirs. The NAJE publications described techniques for the development of vocal swing groups, and music arrangements quickly became available and were cited in the newsletters.

The swing choir employs instrumental accompaniment, and usually choreography is present much of the time. Styles of presentation vary in different sections of the country. The pure 'jazz' choir may be content to express itself through the music only. *The Scat Singing Method* by Scott Fredrickson is an excellent introduction to vocal jazz.

The director must decide on a style and construct a choir and instrumental ensemble and use music that is appropriate. Get help from a director who has been successful in the medium. Contests are available if you wish to go to them and see what other swing choirs are doing.

Mixed Choirs versus Women's and Men's Choruses

In recent years there has been a strong interest in mixed vocal classes, at the expense of separate women's and men's groups. The top performing group is almost invariably a mixed choir. The richness of literature available and the greater variety of colors and voice ranges explain this preference. However, men's and women's choruses offer interesting challenges and sounds that make their inclusion in a music program desirable. All-male groups, especially in junior high, will appeal to manliness and lessen vocal embarassment. Obtaining enough young men to maintain a good program is always a major problem, but their recruitment is especially easy when they are offered a chance to sing manly music with other young men. The SSA and SSAA music of a female chorus and the TTBB of a male chorus is superior training ground for later independent singing of eight-part music in the mixed choir. Music written for women's chorus today is an improvement over some of the music of the past, much of which concerned moons and robins.

Much of the foregoing information about general music, small ensembles, Modern Music Masters, and choirs applies to the middle school and the junior high as well as the high school.

Summer Music Classes

Many choral music educators are using summers to enrich their students' musical experiences. Provide this training free, if possible, because even a minimal charge will keep many students out.

The following summer programs may suggest a class you would like to promote: a music camp conducted by the local university; a choir rehearsed occasionally for fun; operetta classes in the morning; a Swing Choir; afternoon voice classes three times weekly, with individual voice lessons for members of voice classes; one lesson a week for seven weeks, voice classes at no charge, open to anyone grades 9–12; a music program sponsored by the city recreation department using school rehearsal room and equipment; individual vocal lessons for six weeks; a clinic chorus; a six-week summer school chorus held in a centrally located school, choirs two evenings per week for seven weeks; and two six-week voice classes (one for young men, one for young women), meeting daily for a 50-minute session.

Curriculum Planning

If possible, the music curriculum should be planned with the cooperation of the music teachers and administrative officer(s). Mutual decisions should be made that affect the operation of the schedule in the following areas:

How performance groups are arranged.   Will performance groups be arranged according to "grade," "ability," "grade and ability," or will they be "completely open to everyone"? It is easier for administrators to schedule classes of just one grade level; but if balance or ability are not present, more than one class level must be used.

What classes will be offered.   Will music courses be made available for everyone? Will the brilliant student and the dull student both be taken care of in the courses offered? The music teacher may need to remind the administrative officers that, according to research, the bright student who has an integral part in the social life of the school nearly always does better academic work than the student of equal ability who does not take part; and the educator should feel compelled to provide for the "very able" student the enriching experience of participation in the arts. At the other end, there are many things the dull adolescent cannot do musically because of mental limitations, but there are still many benefits to be derived from participation in music (experiences in social contacts, training in good uses of leisure time, emotional outlet, training in cooperation, etc.).

How much credit can be offered.

What classes may be offered:

1. In regular periods[6] (ordinarily the most desirable). The best class periods for vocal performance groups are the second and third morning periods and the second afternoon period.
2. Part in-school and part out-of-school.
3. On a rotation plan.
4. Outside regular school time but counted as a school period.
5. During extracurricular time (after school, at night, in the morning, at noon).
6. On modular scheduling.

What budget will be available   for music, supplies, and equipment. Discuss with the administrators any special problems and possible solutions or recommendations for the future.

---

[6] The increasing amount of knowledge the student must acquire has resulted in the addition of accelerated classes for college credit to an already overcrowded curriculum. Curiously, the school day has not been lengthened to accommodate these added classes. The six-period day is still the norm, although there is an encouraging trend toward a seven-period day and more flexible scheduling. To alleviate a crowded schedule and make room for music, students might take summer school classes in nonmusic subjects so that they have time for music during the school year; or the number of weekly rehearsals might be reduced from five to two and one-half or three, which would allow the good student the opportunity to take such courses as music theory, if there is a five-period block to devote to music.

Scheduling Difficulties

Major difficulties in getting students to register for music are academic subject conflicts caused by increasing scholastic requirements, multiple musical interests, physical education requirements, varsity athletic conflicts, unsympathetic counselors and administrators, guidance class requirements, lack of interest of student and parents, expense, curricular conflicts in scheduling with required solids, intramurals, and social climbing, which causes students to be too busy with clubs and parties. Some students may be tired of music after grade school or junior high, and some may be discouraged by a requirement that they must have an average of "C" to take music.

Find ways to solve these difficulties; for example, cooperation with other teachers in sharing a student's time or substitution of music for physical education credit.

2

Organizing the Singers

This chapter will discuss the operation of the testing program (especially voice testing), ranges and tessituras of junior high and senior high voices, classification of voices, the selection of personnel for music classes, the selection and use of student officers, and seating arrangements.

THE TESTING PROGRAM

Standardized Tests

According to surveys, very few secondary school teachers use standardized tests. As these tests become more precise, teachers of vocal music should give careful consideration to them as a means of obtaining additional information about their students. Standardized tests may be used to understand more about the weaknesses and strengths in students' musical ability; to place a student in a performance group according to ability; to help determine six-weeks or semester grades, especially when other information is not available; to aid in counseling, especially through use of the

Seashore test; to recruit for potential classes; to compare a student's or a class's rating against a standard norm; and to indicate advancement made in skills. For a good source of information on standardized testing, consult Paul R. Lehman's *Tests and Measurements in Music*, Englewood Cliffs, N.J.: Prentice-Hall, Inc., 1968.

Written Tests

Teachers are seeing an increasing need for some kind of written test to challenge their students' knowledge, even in performance classes. These tests may investigate students' comprehension of music theory materials, breathing fundamentals, proper tonal concepts, intonation problems, the correct singing of vowels and consonants, music appreciation materials, the class texts, song lyrics, Italian terms, basic attitudes and value patterns, and ear training materials by demonstrating their ability to take melodic and rhythmic dictation accurately.

Voice Testing

Most of the classes taught by the vocal teacher will be involved in some singing activities. Until the instructor determines individual voice ranges and tessituras,[1] music cannot be intelligently selected or the class vocalized. Depending upon the needs of the class, the teacher will test both easy and extreme voice ranges, ear keenness, rhythmic ability, sight-reading skills, and musical memory. A quick classification of voices may serve the purpose, but usually a more careful voice check will be necessary. Because of student insecurity, most teachers will test each student individually with no spectators. If time is a critical factor, or if a class grade is needed, the exam may be administered in small ensembles, with or without the class being present. The administrator of the test will be listening for special problems of musicality and vocal problems, but also for exceptionally talented students who should be encouraged to participate in solo and small ensemble work.

Junior High Ranges and Tessituras

Eighty to ninety-five percent of the junior high school female voices can maneuver within the soprano range. The upper range may extend to A or higher unless it is limited by self-consciousness and a growing fear of high notes.

---

[1] *Tessitura:* The prevailing or average position of the notes in relation to the compass of the voice, whether high, medium, or low; the heart of the range. Knowledge of a student's tessitura is particularly helpful to the director who is placing voices in the correct voice parts.

The most favorable tessitura for most of these voices is:

Do not confine these voices to the soprano part. Give them some experience in singing alto so they will learn to read.

The other five to twenty percent of female voices may lie higher or lower. The higher voices should stay on soprano, and the lower voices must remain on alto.

The typical seventh-grade voice quality will be somewhat breathy and thin. The impressionable eighth- and ninth-grade voices may very easily be pushed to a raucous, hard quality by the director who drives them too hard. Above all, be sure the quality remains "easy."

The boy's voice may start to change as early as in the fourth grade when he is around ten years old. However, in rare instances, the voice may not change until college or later life. The boy soprano's range and tessitura roughly correspond to that of the female soprano. The quality is usually clear and pure, although relatively thin compared to an adult soprano. When a young man's voice starts to lower, a celestial brilliancy forewarns the teacher that the change is coming.[2] From that time on there should be constant vigilance and reclassification of the changing voice whenever it is required. Most of these young men's voices will shift rather rapidly, within two or three weeks, to cambiata or baritone. At times, voices drop to a low bass.

This is the range of the cambiata[3] voice, according to Dr. Cooper.[4]

Actually, the cambiata should not even try to hit low F's and E's, although he can hit them by tightening his throat. When the pupil sings a part that goes lower than G, he must either omit the notes or sing them an octave higher. Treat this voice as a first tenor in a male quartet, where the voice will operate efficiently and easily. The tessitura will be:

[2] See Chapter 7 for a complete discussion of physiological and vocal warning signs.

[3] *Cambiata:* A word meaning "changing." The word was first applied to the voice by Irvin Cooper. The older concept of "alto-tenor" perceives this voice as having a more limited range.

[4] See Chapter 7 for other authorities on the boy's changing voice.

or even:

The color of the voice does not have warmth or richness to any extent. The cambiata tends to force into his quality a kind of strained viola timbre, which immediately becomes offensively obtrusive. His voice will blend with the changed tenor and other voices, but the tone quality will stand out when it is driven.

Keep the cambiata voice on tenor until a test shows that another part should be taken. Some of these voices will remain tenor, and the bottom range will extend while the tone remains light. Others will shift down to baritone or bass. Instruct the student to ask for a test whenever he feels the range is a strain. However, do not change him until he has been tested privately, for he is likely to want to sing lower (because it is more manly) before his voice has shifted. Remember, however, that a voice must be on the right part to sing in tune and have the right quality.

The newly changed "baritone" voice is likely to have this range, with a tessitura of:

Some voices will appear to have much smaller ranges and tessituras than these examples, but properly produced tones and confidence will quickly move them toward these ranges and tessituras.

Occasionally, the adolescent male voice will drop temporarily into a phenomenally low "bass," then move upward after a period of time. It is almost as though the voice were a rubber band which, when thrown downward by the voice change, stretched extra low and then moved back upward to its original resilient shape. Usually, the upper range of the voice will move up along with the rising lower range.

Once in awhile the male voice remains a "true bass" with this approximate range.

Sometimes the voice will move to a "changed tenor," with an approximate range of:

Straining for high tones probably starts along with difficulties in finding the proper pitch. The changing voice is apt to cause exaggeration of the wrinkled brow, the raised eyebrows, the "goose-neck," the pained look, etc.

Remember that unisons cannot be sung by cambiatas and junior high young women, since the only notes their tessituras have in common are:

For further information on middle school and junior high, see Chapter 7.

High School Ranges and Tessituras

The quality and tessitura of the junior high voice will still be found in immature high school singers. The following chart[5] will also apply to the singers in the average amateur adult choir as well as to relatively untrained high school voices.

| Voice | Easy Range | Tessitura |

Fuller, more dramatic than the first soprano.   Many mezzo voices in junior high and high school sing alto.

---

[5] Ranges and tessituras are provided through the courtesy of the American Academy of Teachers of Singing (ATTS) and the National Association of Teachers of Singing (NATS). They apply to the average amateur singer and not to the professional artist, and they refer only to *choral* music.

The alto has a heavier, deeper voice than the soprano, especially in the lower range. True altos are rare even at the high school age. Most of the young women who sing contralto in high school are really mezzos. The true alto voice is apt to be breathy in quality. Do not worry about it. Simply work this voice the same as the others, and when the young woman attains the age of nineteen or twenty (if proper vocal training has been followed), this voice will suddenly bloom into a mature alto sound.

There is the constant temptation to encourage young people to sing in the voice section that is weak and needs more voices for good balance. For example, the director is likely to assign the alto part to any young woman who can read music well, particularly in younger choirs. The singer assigned may be a soprano with good lower range. The ability to produce tones of low pitch does not necessarily make her a contralto, and real harm can be done to a soprano voice if it is kept too long exclusively in its lower portion. The preference of a student to sing alto because she wants to sit by her friend who sings alto or because she doesn't want to put forth the effort to sing high notes should not influence a teacher's decision about the type of the student's voice. The conductor who engages in the practice of using altos to bolster the tenor section needs to be extremely careful that these voices are shifted from number to number so that the young women have an opportunity to sing in the high part of their voices as well as in the low part. Altos singing exclusively in their lower mechanism will develop a large break in their voices if they are allowed to sing too heavily (which they will do when they attempt to match the tenor quality and are never vocalized in the upper range). A good alternative is to have the altos help on the high tenor notes only, which will be in the altos' comfortable tessitura and will strengthen the tenors' weak upper notes. Let the tenors sing their own lower pitches. The choral leader must restrain any ambition to produce a perfectly balanced organization and to have the group sing musical programs that are so overly ambitious that they will jeopardize the vocal welfare of the singers.

Light quality, but fuller in sound. (High baritones often sing this part.) Tenors rarely mature at high school age. Have them use head quality or falsetto, properly supported in the top notes. Be careful not to force or push this voice. Generally F or F ♯ is the highest note the high school tenor can sing without moving into head voice or falsetto. Don't be afraid to use falsetto, which is produced by vibration of the extreme outer edge of the vocal folds. It will help strengthen the feeling of correct placement for high tones and will protect against straining for high pitches. Falsetto is a "true" part of a man's voice and it should be strengthened and used. (Unless an issue is made of this, boys will not want to sing falsetto, because they want to sound manly, and falsetto sounds like a female voice to them.)

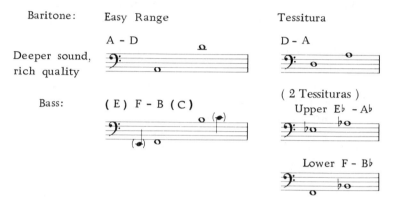

The bass has a heavier, darker, deeper quality, especially in the middle and lower ranges of the voice.

Quick Classification Through Testing

The speaking voice of a student may or may not indicate the true type of the singing voice. Poor speech habits can obscure the potential voice type; therefore, the teacher should use great discretion in evaluating evidence from this source. Nevertheless, many teachers have used this technique, with marked success, as a quick way to assign voices. It works with the most success at the junior high age, where the changing voice of the young man is easily distinguishable in his speaking voice. The young woman's voice quality may be more easily discovered at this time, also, because it will usually be untrained. *The rule:* Speaking range that is identified as normal will be approximately four steps above the bottom of the singer's lowest note. If the student speaks loudly—almost shouts—it is much easier to identify voice characteristics. Most students will mumble unless the instructor insists upon louder speaking.

A second means of voice classification is through a quick *range test.* The following procedure applies to high school but may be used in junior high by substituting the proper ranges and tessituras (see pp. 16–19). Start on G above middle C for women, top space G in the bass clef for men, and move downward. As voices drop out, assign the parts (according to the range charts). The singer who can sing an easy and resonant low F or lower is likely to be a second alto or a second bass; the one who can sing A♭ is likely to be an alto or a baritone; etc. Then start on G and move upward, assigning voices according to the easy tones at the top of the range (first soprano should hit an easy G or higher, second soprano E♭ -G, first tenor an easy F or higher, second tenor an easy E♭ or higher). The range charts will give the extreme range and tessitura that may be expected in each voice and the basic sound of the quality for each voice. These should be described to the students. Be sure to use easy sound and good quality as the gauge, and not just how high or low the students can manage to squeak or gargle. Let the students decide where they belong, but remind them that they will all be tested individually later and reassigned to the correct part if they are not in the correct voice section. This means that the student might have to relearn a part and be moved from the place to which he or she had become accustomed. Under these circumstances, most students will judge as correctly as they are capable of judging.

A third way to test voices quickly is to *use a familiar tune* such as "America" for groups of students to sing. It will probably be wise to start testing the basses first, since they will be the most restless. Move it into various keys, and group the students according to those who find it easiest to sing in F, in high B♭, in low B♭, etc. The fact that "America" has less than an octave range will work advantageously for the voice of the alto-tenor or the new baritone. These divisions will work out into the various voice parts. Another good song to use as a check is "Love's Old Sweet Song." Have the students sing only the words "Just a song at twilight/ When the lights are low." Altos and basses should sing in the key of E♭ (melody starts on low B♭), sopranos and tenors in the key of B♭ (melody starts on F).

In any of the above three ways to test voices, the instructor may wish to have the students remember their part by finger signals. (The students do not need to know what the signal means.)

Finger Signals:
    1—soprano
    2—alto
    3—tenor
    4—bass
    Thumb—ineligible
    All 5—a retest is indicated.

Additional information may be obtained about individuals in the choir, without embarrassing them, by having everyone sing, then having particular ones *stop* singing as the director points to them. It is quite revealing when the ensemble sounds better or worse without the singer. Another way to obtain this information is by having only two or three singers sing, but this is more likely to embarrass someone.

Individual Testing

Chatting informally with a singer before beginning the audition will help induce relaxation. Many inexperienced students will be so afraid of what the director thinks of their voices that it will be very difficult to make a valid judgment of their voices and abilities. Nervousness can be reduced by explaining what is being tested in the audition. Let the singers begin the audition by singing something they know well so that they can sing with confidence. Then vocalize the singers on arpeggios to check for the extreme ranges of their voices. With even these simple tests the director will be able to check for easy range, extreme ranges, best tessitura, voice quality, breath control, diction, posture, loose jaw, sense of rhythm, intonation, aggressiveness, and ambition.

If the director feels the need to examine the candidate even more completely, sight-reading, aural testing, musical memory testing, rhythm testing, and ear keenness testing may be added to the test.

The usual test for sight-reading, and an excellent one, is to select a song that contains sight-reading problems and use *it* as the test. Pick one of the following alternatives, placed in order of increasing difficulty, and have the candidate sing:

The melody; conductor plays full chords including the melody line.
The melody; conductor plays chords without melody line.
A part; conductor plays chords without the part.
The melody; a cappella.
A part; a cappella.

In the following test the student will read as far as possible, and that figure (5, etc.) will be the sight-reading score.

Various aural tests are used by teachers to determine voice type. They are based upon a change in the sound of the voice that is heard in certain points in the range. For one technique, have the student try singing a bright Ah (smiling lips) with a full voice. Start on middle C with the woman's voice, an octave lower than that for the man's. Have them sing upward until the voice "lift" or change in quality becomes apparent. Try it again, and have the singer change to Aw on that pitch. If it smooths out the lift, more than likely this is the lower lift in the voice. Contraltos, basses, and baritones will lift around E, the third note up. Tenors and sopranos will lift around G, the fifth note up. This method expertly used will do a superior job of identifying voice types. Other directors have used the following lifts with success: in first tenors and first sopranos tone lightens about C♯; in second tenors and second sopranos tone lightens about B–C♯; in first basses and first altos tone lightens about A–B; in second basses and second altos tone lightens about A down. See the table of "Voice Lifts" in Chapter 5.

A "memory" test is one of the most reliable ways to check for choir membership. A rating of "4" on the following test is good. Few people will sing all seven patterns accurately. Play each pattern just once, and have the singer repeat all tones accurately from memory (this tests the ear keenness of the students, also). The patterns become increasingly more difficult to remember and reproduce accurately. This test originated with Louis Diercks, former choral director at Ohio State University and Eastern New Mexico University.

The following keys will probably work best:

Key of A for Bass
Key of D for Tenor
Key of E for Soprano
Key of C for Baritone

The director may test for rhythm accuracy also, if the above tone drills are changed rhythmically. For example,[6]

---

[6] Louis Diercks, "A Prognostic Approach to the Choral Audition," *The Choral Journal* (November, 1962).

One of the best ways to test an applicant for the ability to carry a part alone against other parts is to use a small ensemble of good singers from the choir and have the contralto applicant sing in place of the choir contralto, etc. This test will be more accurate without a piano and, if possible, the part should be memorized. If she cannot hold her part, test by playing all parts on the piano except the one the student must read. If the student isn't strong enough to do this, play all parts and have the student read her part.[7]

The tape recorder may be used very effectively in the testing program. Start the recorder and have students sing in an ensemble or individually (carefully write down the names of the students as they sing). This gives the conductor the opportunity to play the tape back later and evaluate each student. If the conductor needs to hear a student again, the tape may be rerun as many times as is necessary for careful appraisal.

SELECTION OF PERFORMANCE GROUP PERSONNEL

Personnel for top performance groups is selected on the basis of:

    Recommendations
    Balance needed
    Grade level
    Tests
    Tryouts

Generally, the plan that gives a director the most information about the student is the "try-out" using some or all of the ways mentioned in the preceding paragraphs. Even in the select choir, the teacher should consider personality, dependability, and other qualities, as well as the student's talent. *Cooperation* is the most important quality in a singer. A good ear and musicianship are much more important than a good voice. The good voice may be developed *if* the singer is willing to work at it. Even if the record shows that a student has a "bad attitude," the teacher may occasionally wish to take this individual on a trial basis. (If this student is given a chance to be cooperative, but warned that he or she is "on trial," it is possible that the situation will change.) Most directors will take into consideration the recommendations of former music teachers, if these recom-

[7] See page 23 for other possibilities.

mendations are available. Since cooperation is such an important quality in a choral organization, previous interest and effort regardless of ability will need to be weighed carefully and may be reason enough to accept a student for a good group. Some instructors may wish to give some weight to a student's previous experience in the schools, and a few instructors might see some validity in the use of standardized tests as one measure of merit.

A fine choral organization will usually have some members who have not yet graduated, so the director must give consideration to the "balance" needed (for example, the choir may need only one soprano and six tenors, so even though the sopranos who try out are excellent and the tenors are poor, many good sopranos are left out of the choir and the weaker tenors get in).

STUDENT OFFICERS

Many of the organizational details of a music class will be accomplished more efficiently through the employment of student officers and committees. Students will have more interest and pride of membership in a class where they are guided into many opportunities for planning, sharing, discussing, evaluating activities, and assuming responsibility in various ways.

Duties

Librarian: To be in charge of the organization library of the class. This means assisting with any duties necessary to maintain an orderly library. Specifically, the librarian helps with music repair, takes music from folios, refiles the numbers, files music in envelopes, distributes music to folios, stamps music with the name of the school, counts octavo copies, collects the folios, issues the folios, fills out index cards, stamps music with folio numbers, and stamps music with the name of the organization. The librarian will be appointed by the director from student volunteers (it may be desirable to have more than one).

Secretary: To check attendance carefully at all class meetings and at all other rehearsals and performances. This officer will be appointive from volunteers.

Assistant Secretary: To take over the secretary's duties. Office appointive.

Accompanist: Most important student officer. The musicianship, the care with which music is prepared, and sharpness in following the conductor make a great deal of difference in the quality of the organization. This office is appointive through tryout.

Assistant Accompanist:	Becomes accompanist when the accompanist is absent. Is the second pianist on numbers requiring two pianists.
Student Director:	Takes over the warming-up exercises of the group each class period. Directs in the director's absence. Directs whenever required as "all the women, or all the men in sectional rehearsal, etc."
Section (Part) Leader:	Assumes the responsibility of his or her entire section, that all notes and markings are learned correctly; runs section rehearsals.
Section (Part) Pianist:	Plays for the section assigned whenever the section rehearses. Directs section in section leader's absence.

In addition to the above officers, many directors like to use a president (to conduct choir meetings), a vice-president (to assist the president and serve in the president's absence), and a treasurer (to handle organizational money) for each organization. A robe committee is a very good permanent committee. Use a committee to set up the rehearsal area. A standing committee to fix the bulletin board sometimes aids in arousing student enthusiasm. The reporter is usually appointed by the journalism department. When the journalism department sends the student for news every week, the music director must have some news ready. Additional committees may be appointed for each special occasion (See Chapter 11.)

SEATING ARRANGEMENTS

The choral performance group should be seated in an arrangement that will allow every singer to see the ictus of the director's beat pattern easily and that will enable the director to see the entire face of each singer. The most efficient way to seat singers is in the same places they will occupy when standing on risers in performance, if the amount and shape of the square footage in the room permit it. (Risers will allow more efficient utilization of the available space. They will also make it easier to arrange the choir so that all faces may be seen and voices heard.) Tapering the group's height in a uniform manner ($<$ $>$ or $\times$) will facilitate a good view of faces and good appearance in the rehearsal room and for an audience. The arrangement also must be one that will allow every singer to hear all the other parts and the piano. The director will probably need to adjust the basic seating chart, since other important factors, such as the balance and blend of parts, must be considered. Balance and blend will be affected by the number of singers on each part, the strength of individual voices, and the reading abilities of the singers. Another important factor is the voice quality of a singer; for example, a dramatic or mezzo-soprano will ordinarily dominate a group of lyric sopranos, who usually constitute the first soprano section in a junior or senior high choir, but will blend nicely with second sopranos. The acoustics in a rehearsal or performance hall may require a re-placement of voices so that certain parts may be heard either more clearly or not so loudly. Finally, the possibility of discipline problems must be taken into consideration when students are seated.

Seat strong singers at the rear (or middle) of the section. This way they are heard by the weaker singers in front of them, who may depend upon their help. It will also help to blend strong voices into the overall sound of the section. For some reason, sometimes placing a singer with a voice that 'sticks out' in the second or third seat in from the end of the second or third row will cause the voice to blend into the ensemble. Put mellow voices, sure of their pitches, in the front row. The quality of the choir is very much like the front row. Balance the section like a pyramid— so that the low voices are strongest and the high voices are lightest in tonal weight.

Balance is determined by:

1. Voice quality and degree of maturity
2. The range and tessitura in which voices are singing
3. The number of singers on each part
4. Harmonic aspects of the chord
5. Uniformity of vowel production
6. Relative importance of the various vocal lines (the melody needs to be brought out, etc.)
7. Dynamic levels
8. Voice placement in the choir

Blend is attained by:

1. Fusing various voice qualities into a united sound in a variety of vocal colors (poor breath control, voice production, and tremolo will be problems that must be corrected)
2. Uniformity of pitch
3. Uniformity and precision of phonetic sounds
4. Voice placement in the choir

5. Singers listening to themselves, to the accompaniment, to their section, and to the choir as a whole (humming may be helpful)
6. Having all singers sing in their correct ranges and tessituras
7. Uniform dynamics within a section and between sections, except when a part should be emphasized

Mens' voices at the junior or senior high school age tend to be more powerful than womens' voices, unless the women are well-trained. Because of this fact, a 50/50 arrangement in a large choral group will usually result in the female voices being overpowered. (In a madrigal, or smaller group, the voices might be picked and trained to balance with an equal number on each part.) Consequently, the balance of a mixed choir should ordinarily be 3/5 women to 2/5 men, or even 2/3 women to 1/3 men. Be sure this chorus has a solid foundation (the basses and altos—see the pyramids), and for best blend and balance taper to lighter qualities in the upper parts. Fortunately, it is not necessary to have many tenors with powerful voices to balance the chord quite well in either the mixed group or the male chorus. Good first tenors and second altos are quite rare, even in high school.

The dynamic range of a particular choral group depends upon the age level, physical maturity, and vocal development of the singers. Don't attempt to have junior high voices sound like adult voices. Attain effectiveness by dynamic contrast. *Don't allow vocal strain.*

Pitch is more easily maintained when every singer can hear all the other parts and the piano. It is quite possible to come very close to realizing this goal with the modified quartet seating arrangement, which will be described later. Unless a group is quite capable, it is impractical to place it permanently in this arrangement, however, although a "scrambled" arrangement will many times give better blend and balance to even a mediocre group, when it is used after a song has been thoroughly learned with each part in its own voice category. The arrangement of the group in "sections" is the usual solution.

Mixed Choir Sectional Seating

First soprano and second bass should be placed together in a mixed choir. Pitch is more easily maintained when the pitch extremes (the outer voices of the chord) can hear each other and tune up. Placing these two sections where they can't hear each other very well will result in the basses going flat and the sopranos going sharp. For the same reason, the second altos and the first tenors should be placed together. This placement of voices allows the second altos to help out for a short while if the first tenors need to be reinforced on a high solo. Using a line of women across the front (see below) will screen off the roughness of male voices. This may not be necessary if the quality of the male voices is excellent.

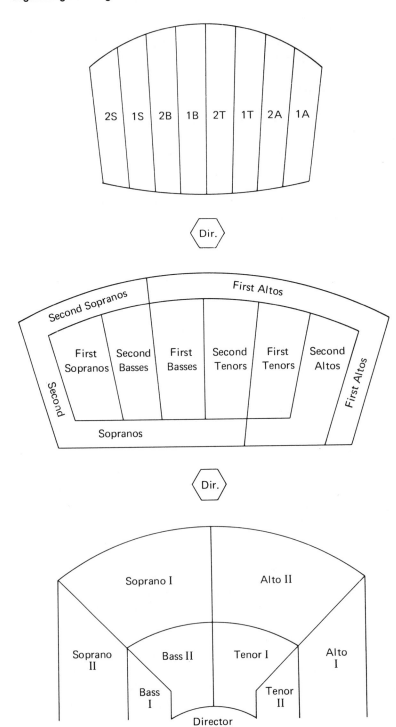

The female sections need to be joined either at the front or at the back of the choir (or both, as in the preceding illustration) for a feeling of unity, especially when singing as a women's choir (SSA or SSAA). Unless the men are unusually mature, *don't* put them across the back; they will not be able to hear the piano or the chord well enough and will pull the choir flat.[8]

Women's Chorus

In the *Women's Chorus* place the altos next to the first sopranos (see the suggested seating chart). This arrangement places the outside of the chord together and is very advantageous for the second sopranos. Second sopranos have the hardest notes to sing—nearly always a tone between the pitches of the altos and first sopranos. This process is somewhat easier if the seconds have only *one* strong part singing in their ears. With this arrangement the seconds will hear the firsts singing loudly and the altos only faintly. This gives them a chance to harmonize with the firsts (the natural harmonization) and become somewhat used to hearing that other part from a distance.

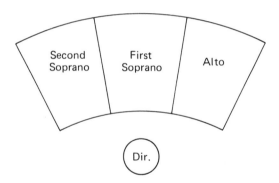

Some of the seconds will still slip to first soprano, a few to alto. As a practical tip, if they cannot learn to stay on their part *most* of the time by the end of a semester (provided much ear training has been done in class), in most cases everyone will be happier if they are reassigned to first soprano or alto, whichever part fits their voices best, and told to sing easily and even leave notes out if the part goes out of range. Unless these young women are moved, they will learn more and more to dislike singing, for their hearing isn't keen enough for them to ever be really successful in the second part. They won't be able to get into a highly selective group anyway, and they might as well sing melody and enjoy it. (Of course, the

---

[8] In the average junior high class or weak general music class in high school, put the young men in the front row so their uncertain voices can be helped with pitches and also so that the discipline problems may be dealt with more readily.

director always tries to obtain better musicianship and singing from the group.)

With an excellent, selective women's chorus all parts may be mixed ("muddled") so each singer hears her own voice and learns to sing her part independently. Even with a fair group, parts may be mixed after a number has been thoroughly learned.

In the next arrangement, the weak section may be placed closest to the piano and to the director so they may be given added assistance (and they will be closer to the audience so they may be heard). The strongest section may be placed farthest from the audience, which will help the group's balance. This section will be strong enough that the distance from the piano and not hearing the chord quite so well will not bother them too much. Also, every member of the chorus will be able to hear the full chord much better than they could in the previous arrangement. Some directors have used this arrangement with a core of good singers in the center of the chorus that can be used as a demonstration group. If, in a concert, the tonality of the entire group becomes shaky, a prearranged signal can tell the core group to "take over," while the rest drop out temporarily. Sectional cueing will need to be by *level* rather than by *direction*.

1 Soprano		1 Soprano
2 Soprano	(or)	Alto
1 Alto		2 Soprano
2 Alto		

Male Chorus

With the male chorus, either the second tenors or the first tenors may be placed next to the second basses. The first tenor part represents the outer edge of the chord, but the second tenor part is ordinarily the "lead" (melody), and the root of the chord (sung by the second basses) and the melody tune up together very well. It is frequently necessary to place the second tenors next to the basses because of height. There will usually be some mature men who are first tenors; but many first tenors are immature and small physically and may still be operating with alto-tenor (cambiata) voices even in high school. With a really selective male chorus, this group can also sing with a modified quartet seating plan (the same remarks are appropriate here that are made in connection with women's chorus and mixed choir).

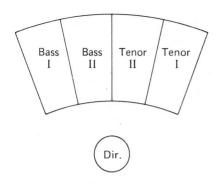

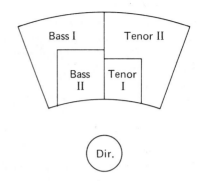

Modified Quartets

A modified quartet will:

1. Clear up flatting (because every voice can hear the entire chord all the time and stay tuned up).
2. Give a new and better blend (every voice must blend with the whole choir instead of each section blending with the others).
3. Give a superior balance (for example, each soprano will almost automatically sing a little louder if some strong sopranos are missing and the soprano part sounds weaker than usual).
4. Make students more independent in reading and singing (it definitely challenges the good student to become a still better musician).
5. Help the voice quality of students, because they will be able to hear more clearly how they sound. Weaker-voiced singers, even with good voices, cannot hear themselves sing when seated next to more powerful voices.
(Every student should be taught to sing, if possible, with the tone quality of a soloist but in balance with the group.)

One or two singers with strong voices can, and sometimes do, pull a whole section out of tune or to a wrong note. This can be disastrous for the entire choir, because the sense of tonality may be lost. With "scrambled" seating the other voices will sing correctly even though someone sings a wrong pitch, because singers can hear their own voices and the chord, and most important, have learned parts independently so they can sing it with confidence.

On page 34 is a suggested arrangement for a 75-voice mixed choir. The author realizes that the voicing will never be exactly like this and that heights and voice strengths need to be considered as well as the voices available. However, this basic seating plan was used satisfactorily by him for five years in a senior high school, and it was always possible to make a satisfactory adaptation of this arrangement. Please note that there are four choirs available to sing an SATB part (for an "echo," etc.). In addition, the left half is a complete choir; the two center sections are a complete choir;

and the two end sections are a complete eight-part choir. This gives a conductor great flexibility in rehearsal and in concert.

There are some logical reasons why students should *not* be seated in small ensembles. A male quartet, a female trio, or a mixed quartet seated together will sing as an ensemble, but the individuals in that group are likely to forget to listen to the rest of the choir. Their concern becomes the

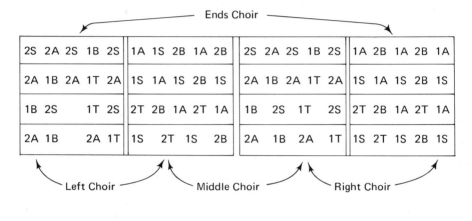

blend and balance within their own small ensemble instead of the blend and balance of the entire choir. When there are harmony parts missing in the small ensemble, this incomplete group will need to listen to the other singers to hear the remainder of the chord—and the tendency is to blend and balance with the whole choir.

The group that is insecure and weak should not use "mixed seating" daily; it will only tend to make the singers even more afraid to sing out. However, the weaker group can use a "scrambled" arrangement after a number has been thoroughly learned, and this will challenge the individuals to hold their parts. In fact, the group will be very likely to have better blend, balance, and intonation than it did in sections. It is actual "punishment" to a group who sings regularly in "mixed-up" seating to move it into sections, because singers cannot hear their own voices or the chord as well. The scrambled arrangement will work advantageously also for ensembles (even as small as a sextet) and male and female choruses. No attempt is made here to show a definite arrangement for these other groups, but the basic rules shown for the mixed choir would be followed in setting up the seating or standing arrangements for the choruses and ensembles.

Cueing might seem to be a problem with this arrangement. Actually, it may be accomplished very easily by designating a particular area as the place where a voice part will be cued. For example, cue "far left" for soprano, "far right" for alto, etc. The students will learn to look for their cue at a particular spot no matter where they are standing in the choir.

3

Extra-Class
Responsibilities
of the Teacher

The six basic areas of concentration in regard to efficient management procedures needed by music teachers are finance; business procedures; music, supplies, and equipment; records and reports; lesson planning; and music selection.

FINANCE

You must become familiar with the financial routine established for the school system where you are employed. With the principal or superintendent, go over budgets and the methods of requisitioning until you feel certain you understand everything.

Every school music budget is handled differently. Although educators feel that any expenses the music department incurs should be paid for by the school board as are other school subjects, many schools still need to finance their music program partially or totally through sources other than a budget. The simplest workable financial plan is to have the director approach the school official in charge of finance each time music, equipment, or other items are needed, and make out a purchase order for the expenditure. Although this plan works, the director never can be absolutely sure how much money will be allowed for the program. A definite long-range plan for purchases with an exact budget is much more businesslike and, therefore, is preferable.

Sources of funds other than a budget are concert receipts, opera or operetta, variety show, activity fund, fees, magazine sales or sales of foodstuffs, festival, parents' clubs, savings, and occasional checks from organizations at which programs were given.

BUSINESS PROCEDURES

Music teachers tend, many times rightfully, to get a reputation for being impractical and unbusinesslike in dealings with others. The music teacher who can answer the following questions affirmatively will soon gain the respect of others for being a good businessperson as well as a good musician.

Are you always prompt and reliable in your dealings so you don't inconvenience others? Is your correspondence prompt? Do you type your letters or do them legibly and neatly in longhand? Do you write them in correct form, with a letterhead that gives your name, position, and address? Do you keep a correspondence file? Do you keep an organized and extensive file of catalogues of books, music, instruments, robes, and other essential materials? Do you keep informed about available materials and sources of supply by having your name on the mailing lists of several publishers? Do you hand in all grades, reports, requisitions, and budgeting items on time? Do you give care and study when you recommend materials, equipment, and music for purchase, and inform the school board why you are selecting a certain article to be purchased instead of similar articles? In requisitioning instruments or equipment for bid do you list the exact instruments or equipment by name and not allow substitution unless the instruments or equipment are really "as good" and the change has the director's approval? Do you handle school accounts carefully and accurately, staying within your allotted budget and keeping your personal accounts separate from the school's? Do you refuse all commissions on materials or instruments purchased by the school or parents? Do you use the *Business Handbook of Music Education*, published by the MENC, as a guide for businesslike procedures in your dealings with the school and with the public?

MUSIC, SUPPLIES, AND EQUIPMENT

Music

When ordering music, avoid incorrect voice arrangements (for example, avoid getting SSA arrangements for SATB), delays in shipment, etc., through careful listing of quantity, title, publisher, composer and arranger, arrangement, octavo number, price if it is known, to whom the music is to be sent, and to whom it should be charged. The director must realize that the music may be out of stock or out of print, even when precautions are taken in ordering. A delay in shipment can prove embarrassing if the director has procrastinated in sending the order. The experienced director will anticipate probable delays by ordering music six months before it is needed in the rehearsal. Be careful to return "on approval" music in a salable condition and on time, or buy it.

Most music departments purchase one copy of music for two students. This traditional practice is open to question. Musicians strive to teach students to read well, accurately, speedily—then give two students one copy of music. Would educators assign one textbook to two students who have different reading speeds, differences in intelligence, and differences in eyesight? Yet music teachers do this because they cannot afford to buy much extra music. Not only are words read in vocal music, so are pitches, rhythms, and all the markings such as accents and dynamic levels. At the same time, the student must watch the conductor, follow exactly, and think of breathing, posture, and beautiful tone production. In addition, the chorister must read the parts of the other singers so that blending with the section and the choir can be accomplished efficiently. Can this extremely complicated process go on with the student sharing music with someone else? Music educators should buy a copy of music for each child, if there is enough money in the budget, at least on numbers that are studied for a period of time. This practice will also help discipline, since students do not have as much opportunity to whisper or engage in other distracting activities. If there is a limited budget, fewer numbers may be bought and more care exercised in filling in worthwhile music already in the library and in buying new music. Music may be borrowed from church libraries, state clinic organizations, and other such places as a temporary expedient. Within a few years, a fine library with enough copies can be built.

Of the most vital concern to the director is the way the music library is managed. If the music library is poorly handled, the unfortunate teacher will have music out of repair when it is needed (because the music was not mended properly when it was filed); there will not be enough copies (because the music was not inventoried and ordered when it should have been or because the music is mixed in with some other title through inaccurate sorting); the conductor will not be able to find a title at all if there has been no orderly way to file the music—problem heaps upon problem.

The simplest way to organize the library is to classify the compositions by arrangements, so the TTBB is in its section, SATB in its section, etc. Then alphabetize the music by title or composer. With a small library, it may be convenient to organize by title, composer, and subject on different colored cards; but it will take a prohibitive amount of time, more time than it will be worth, to catalogue a good-sized library into three colors. A few of the materials needed are legal-size filing cabinets for solo music and letter-size filing cabinets for octavo music (or specially made wooden cabinets for filing music), choral filing envelopes or cardboard filing boxes, filing cards, and a box for the filing cards.

The most efficient way to record octavo music is by a card file or music card. Fill out the choral inventory card with the title, composer, arranger, arrangement (TTBB, etc.), octavo number, publisher, a cappella or accompanied, and number of copies (in pencil so the number may be changed at inventory time). This is the minimum information needed.

Example:

```
┌──────────────────────────────────────────────────────────────────┐
│                                                                    │
│              ------------------------- Public Schools              │
│                     Vocal Music Division                           │
│                                                                    │
│   Title . . . . . . . . . . . . . . . . . . . . . . Octavo No. . . │
│                                                                    │
│   Composer . . . . . . . . . . . . . . . . . . . No. of copies . . │
│                                                                    │
│   Difficulty:                          Publication . . . . . . . . │
│                                                                    │
│            Piano . . . . . . . . . . . . . . . Voice . . . . . . . │
│                                                                    │
│   Remarks:  . . . . . . . . . . . . . . . . . . . . . . . . . . . . │
│                                                                    │
│             . . . . . . . . . . . . . . . . . . . . . . . . . . . . │
│                                                                    │
└──────────────────────────────────────────────────────────────────┘
```

Some directors will find it desirable to put other pertinent information on the cards, such as whether a number is sacred or secular, its file number (very essential if the filing is done by number), dates on which it has been used, whether it is seasonal and, if so, for what season, type, difficulty, date acquired, author of the text, mood, tonality, key, performance time, and price. A notebook with one copy of each number in the choral SATB library, SSA library, and TTBB library in correctly alphabetized order, is an excellent aid for the conductor to use for study purposes. It is also a quick way to obtain a record of the music. A penciled notation can be placed on each piece of music, telling the number of copies and other needed information.

Directors receive much sample material through the mails, and these samples may be very effectively used by separating this music into SATB, SAB, SSA, TTBB, etc., and then alphabetizing it by title and filing it for future reference. (Multiple identical copies may be paper-clipped together.) This is a teacher's *single copy reference library*. This material may be useful for small groups and soloists and is a source of new music to browse through when selecting numbers for programs and for a contest. Some directors inventory this single copy library, but this is a time-consuming task that is not essential to a well-organized department.

Vocal music departments are not likely to have solo music in the files. Usually, instructors supply soloists with copies from their personal libraries or have students order their own music. If the school has solo classes in the schedule, it should own solo music and class method books for the students. In this case, a card filing system should be set up for this sheet music. Arrangement according to voice classifications (baritone, etc.) is one of the most practical systems of organization. Classification according to type of song (sacred, art song, semi-classical, contest, etc.) can also be a helpful and usable scheme of arrangement.

The individual folio or envelope is used almost universally as the best way to distribute music. Folios usually will carry the names of the school and the organization. Folios should also be made up for permanently organized small ensembles. Some directors like to list the part on each folio and to number each folio or simply list the student's name.

Generally, choral leaders have the music handed out by monitors. Other means of getting the music to students may be more desirable. For example, where it is possible, permanently assign music to students. It speeds up the rehearsal to have the vocalists pick up the music from self-serve pigeonholed cabinets similar to those commonly in use by instrumental departments (ordinary pasteboard boxes numbered 1–10, etc. and placed on the floor may substitute for the cabinets). Placing music on seats ahead of the rehearsal is considered advantageous by other teachers.

Music is generally returned in the same manner it is distributed: monitors, music passed to the end of the row, students place the music in a cabinet or box, or music is left on the seat to be collected later.

All instructors will desire to keep a careful record of any music checked in or out by students. The teacher may personally check out the music, have a student monitor check it out, or have each student check out the music in some prearranged manner. Write the name of the student on a card that contains the music title and composer's name; write the title and composer of the music (or student's folio number) on the student's personal card or use a telephone index (or spindle) and have the student sign it and write down the title and composer (or folio number). Write in pencil so it can be erased when the music is returned (or throw the piece of paper away if a spindle is used).

A surprisingly large number of schools permit pieces of music to be removed from the folio for home practice. Music undoubtedly should be made available for home practice. However, it is much more satisfactory to check out the complete folder rather than to allow individual songs to be taken from it. Music is more likely to be lost, misplaced, and abused when separated from its folder. (Probably these teachers have two students sharing the same folder and feel they must allow music removal in order to give pupils free access to the numbers. There are three satisfactory solutions to this problem: the music folio may be checked out very efficiently on alternate nights, or the students may wish to check out the music and rehearse it together, or one student may assume responsibility for the folder and divide the music with a partner.)

Set aside two or three days a semester as "music repair" days. Fifteen minutes spent mending music on these days with the entire class assisting will save many hours of work by librarians and directors. Use "magic tape" which does not shrink, discolor, or glare.

Supplies

It is good business to plan and order supplies for the music department for the entire year. Supplies that most departments will need in some quantity are mending tape, masking tape, edging tape, filing envelopes or boxes, filing cards, music folios, tapes for the tape recorder and videotape machine, award certificates or their equivalent, red and blue pencils, and school stationery.

Equipment

Well-equipped schools will have most of the following: robes, jackets, or sweaters for choral groups; filing cabinets of legal and letter size or wooden cabinets for filing music; pigeonholed music folio cabinet; sorting racks; storage cabinets; built-in or portable risers (for a seated group) and portable standing risers; pianos; phonographs; records, recording equipment, videotape machine; portable blackboard, bulletin board, overhead projector; and chairs.

Robes and other uniform clothing owned by the school must be marked permanently in some manner. Most directors use sewed-in numbers. However, schools have used many other plans with success. Name or number written in India ink, tape with name, metal tags, paper tags, and stamped printed numbers have all been used. The clothing must also be marked in one of these ways according to size, so they may be assigned easily. Usually it seems best to have the school uniforms cleaned once a year, but it depends upon how much they are used and if they were soiled. If garments can be assigned permanently to a student, a successful plan is to make the student responsible for cleaning them. If students buy or make their own uniforms, of course, there is no reason to mark them.

In cataloging phonograph records, include the name of the composition, the composer, the medium (solo, chamber, chorus, band, orchestra, madrigal, etc.), and the type of composition (fugue, symphony, etc.). Note the catalogue number, the record company, and whether recorded at 33⅓, 45, or 78 rpm.

Use of Teaching Aids

The main purpose of *devices for vicarious experience* is to enrich the students' experiences in music and the fine arts. These devices include films, TV, micro-photographic film, film strips, videotapes, sound recordings, and books. Records may be used effectively to give a model of sound to students, to teach form in music, to sing with in order to learn a selection more quickly, and to teach music appreciation.

Music teachers at the secondary level tend to neglect the use of music films in their teaching. It is true that any time a film is used, the teacher must be sure that this is the most efficient way to teach that particular class. Nevertheless, with the wealth of material now available and the ease of securing it, the teacher must become acquainted with the many fine films. Put your name on some mailing lists when you go to state and national conventions.

Model devices are charts, models, mock-ups, demonstrations, and "sequential programs." These are teaching devices that help students understand the underlying structure of a phenomenon. They include: for music classes, listening charts; mock-ups of the body for vocal pedagogy; demonstrations of correct breathing, vowels sounds, conducting techniques, etc.

Usually, teachers take care of bulletin board displays. A student or a student committee, however, can do a beautiful job of this task if challenged by the instructor. The bulletin board may be used to stimulate and challenge the students, and its use is limited only by imagination. The teacher may efficiently use the bulletin board to inform students of coming musical events, to call articles of musical information and interest to the attention of the student musicians, to publicize good music books and magazines, to post robe lists, to post a new seating chart, and to post lists of new personnel of choirs. Musical cartoons, novel lettering, arrangements of material, and the like, will assist in keeping students interested enough to check the board regularly for new information and articles.

The chalkboard's important use is for illustration. It may be used very effectively for opening instructions and the order of music to be rehearsed. A less efficient use of the chalkboard (although a good one) is its use for a short written test.

The overhead projector can be invaluable as a replacement for the chalkboard and has excellent advantages: the instructor may face the class while writing instead of having to turn his back; slides are easily and quickly prepared and may be prepared in advance of the class period; overlays in various colors will effectively show successive steps in a process. Several companies are now competing for this market.

Unlike the overhead projector, the opaque projector must have the room in almost total darkness to function well. It is not as clear, even at its best, but has the advantage of needing less preparation (a book can simply be placed in the projector). Another advantage is that there is no danger of violating copyright laws, which there might be with the overhead projector.

Recording machines are excellent teaching aids. Students are fascinated by the prospect of hearing themselves sing. This puts the students in a very receptive frame of mind for learning. This, coupled with the fact that errors are magnified to some extent on recordings, helps the students to correct these mistakes more rapidly than they would ever do without the assistance of this device. The music teacher may expect the most aid from tape-recording in the following areas:

> Students are enabled to hear their tone color, pitch, etc. The soloist (or group) is enabled to criticize his efforts more objectively and can check progress that has been made.

> Many times, good accompanists are not available when the student has time to practice. Piano accompaniments may be recorded by the instructor to be used by the student. These recordings may even be used for performance when there are no pianos or accompanists available. Some companies are now selling piano and instrumental accompaniments for many standard numbers. There are distinct disadvantages to any of these recordings; for example, the soloist or group has no choice but to follow the speed of the accompaniment on the record. However, they are a viable alternative.

> Tape or disc recordings may be used to enable a women's chorus to hear the male chorus or vice versa—especially convenient when they are rehearsing separately for mixed chorus numbers.

> Some groups will tape their singing to use on radio programs. This gives the opportunity to correct mistakes and do a more nearly perfect job. It may be desirable to keep a permanent tape file of all performances.

> One of the most valuable uses of recordings is in testing. The director can listen to groups and individual students more objectively when there is leisure time to run and even rerun a tape for purposes of study and analysis.

Instant replay television (videotape) will do almost all of the things the recordings will do, with the added dimension of sight. The original cost of the machines is becoming more reasonable all the time, and many districts can afford to purchase one or more or apply for them on a grant. Tapes are quite expensive, but may be used thousands of times by simply rerecording in a process similar to that used in tape recording. Convenience, portability, and cost still remain the principal obstacles to extensive use of large sets. Portability at a moderate cost is available and is being increasingly used.

Dramatizing devices include such things as documentaries, and result in causing the student to identify more closely with an idea.

Automatizing devices are teaching machines to aid in teaching. Some of these machines should be made available to students to offer enriching materials. The texts on music fundamentals can save a great deal of teacher time and will teach this material as thoroughly as most teachers. Some of the machines and books designed to be used with tape or disc recordings can assist with ear training. Teaching machines or books are carefully designed by experts to follow an excellent learning sequence, moving logically step-by-step from simple to more complicated concepts. The student responds to a question; the machine or book answers instantaneously. If the student has answered correctly, the program will move to the next question in the sequence. If wrong, some machines or books simply repeat the question, others branch into a series of steps that reteach previously taught materials. The computer is becoming a big factor in music learning. The T.A.P. machine programs are excellent for rhythmic learning. A list of programmed music books can be found at the end of this chapter.

All of these devices may be used with success as long as they remain "teacher oriented"; that is, it is necessary for the teacher to motivate students to use, and continue to use, the machines or books. These devices furnish some basic information that may be obtained outside class. This saves class time and enables the teacher to move the students more rapidly during class periods. Remember, also, that most of the teaching machines and books were devised for college-age students, so some adaptions may need to be made when they are used with junior or senior high school students who may not have such firmly established vocational direction.

RECORDS AND REPORTS

Pupil Progress Reports

The universal type of student progress report is, of course, the report card. There are occasions when the music teacher will, in addition, send a letter or have a conference with parents. This is apt to be concerning some problem with the student (in all probability, a failing grade), but it is also a very effective way to discuss a pupil's ability and talent and the teacher's future hopes concerning them with the father and mother. Parents need to know if their child has excellent musical ability, and an A does not necessarily reveal this information. A few teachers keep practice records and send practice reports to parents. Most teachers feel that the great amount of extra bookkeeping that practice records involve outweighs the value derived.

William Burton states that extrinsic motivations operate as follows:

> Motivation by reward is generally preferable to motivation by failure. Marks, rewards, punishments operate as follows:
>
> Marks, rewards, and punishments not functionally related to the learning situation will beget learning, but it is learning soon lost and accompanied by detrimental concomitant learnings.
>
> The more closely the mark, reward, or punishment used as motive is a natural outcome of the learning process, the better effect it has. Learning is stimulated and undesirable concomitants are at a minimum.
>
> The more clearly the learner sees that the mark, reward, or punishment is an inherent aspect of the learning situation, not artificial and imposed, the better the learning which results.[1]

Some schools adopt a policy of giving everyone an A in music in order to attract enough students to start a good program. This coincides with the feeling that music and physical education should not count as academic grades when the honor roll is compiled. Since the grade is not important, what difference does it make whether it is A or D? Some administrators have decreed that it is not appropriate to compete for grades in art or music, that enjoyment is more important. Therefore, students are simply passed or failed, *or* high passed, passed, or failed.

There are problems attached to each of these systems of grading or nongrading. A policy of all A's is fraught with many dangers. The good student is not challenged and will also resent the poor student receiving the same grade, and therefore is likely to say, "What's the use?" and stop trying. The scholar may become the biggest discipline problem in the class. The poor learner realizes that everyone in the class is receiving an A; therefore there is no thrill or value in the unearned grade. When the weak learner and the rest of the students discover that A's are still received even when they do not cooperate in any way, is it likely they *will* cooperate?

The grade of "pass" or "fail" is better, but has its limitations. There is still no extrinsic reward for the good student; therefore, the lowest grade the student can receive, and still pass, looks as good on the report card as the grade of the best student. However, the possibility of failure may be used by the teacher as leverage for good behavior. The addition of "high pass" makes this system almost as desirable as the regular grading system. There is still no way to differentiate between the weak and medium quality students, since both of them receive the grade of "pass." This system does not count academically on the honor roll; therefore, the good scholar is likely to try harder to attain that extrinsic reward under the regular grading system of A, B, C, D, F than under the "high pass" system.

There are problems inherent in the regular grading system, too. In

[1] William H. Burton, "Basic Principles in a Good Teaching-Learning Situation," *Phi Delta Kappan* (March, 1958), p. 246.

any kind of beginning music class, it becomes a relatively simple matter to determine some degree of gradations of talent and amounts of student application to the subject area, although large class size may be an obstacle to overcome before the first grading period arrives. Usually the members of a beginning class will not expect an A or B unless it is earned. The exception is the straight A student who is a C or D in music because of a lack of musical talent. This student will not stay in music, no matter how enjoyable it is, if it means missing the honor roll. The parents will probably insist that their child drop, even if he or she wants to continue. The teacher who wants to try to keep this student may wish to allow the learner to do extra work for the betterment of the music department and self, and allow the extra grade credit for the effort.

In the advanced class, especially the choral class, the assumption should be that the grade will be an A or B because class members were selectively chosen. Only lack of effort or lack of cooperation will lower the grade below B. Work, and extra work, must be first-rate for an A. Without the A or B assumption, many students will be promoted to a more advanced choral group, do better work than they did while they received A's in the beginning chorus (from which they were promoted because they were doing superior work), and still drop to C's when in competition with the older and more experienced students in the advanced choir. It is difficult for students and their parents to understand this drop in grade, and even though these students may have the ability to obtain A's with more time, effort, and maturity, parents may insist on the students' withdrawals from class. If the students are kept aware of how much learning is occurring each day, the intrinsic values of the learning may overcome sufficiently the displeasure of lowered grades.

Grades in music will depend on the student's attitude and cooperation (enthusiasm and interest, general conduct and behavior, ability to follow instructions, and leadership and dependability) *and* on musical progress and ability (private practice and study, and the ability to sing an individual part accurately from memory after a suitable time). Give separate grades for voice production, effort, musicianship, class participation, absences, test grade average, and subject matter, and then average them into an overall grade. The teacher may wish to weigh some areas more heavily than others.

Student Information Forms

All instructors keep some information on students. Each instructor needs to decide how much information about a student is needed to be able to know the student and what musical ability is inherent. All directors should have at least the following information: name, address, telephone number, sex, age, parents' names, grade in school, homeroom number, semester schedule, voice part, voice range, previous instrumental and vocal experience, public appearances, interest in small ensembles, interest in solo, ability in rhythm and sight-reading, musical memory test score, attitude, and free time before and after school. It is difficult to do a good job as a director if any of the above information is missing. It may be desirable

Student Information Form

VOCAL MUSIC DATA SHEET

Name . . . . Parents . . . . Address . . . . Phone . . . .

Date . . . . . Year in school . . . . . Age . . . . . Height . . . . . Voice part . . . . .

Part-time work . . . . . . Hours . . . . Where . . . . Phone . . . .

Free time: Before school . . . . . . After school . . . . . . Homeroom no. . . . .

Musical Background:

Music performed in home? . . . . . . Describe . . . .

Other members of family in musical groups? . . . .

Piano lessons . . . . Years . . . . Still studying . . . . Teacher . . . .

Interested in accompanying? . . . . Experience . . . .

Interested in small ensemble? . . . . Experience . . . .

Other instruments . . . . Studying . . . . Teacher . . . .

Voice lessons . . . . Years . . . . . . Still studying . . . . Teachers . . . .

Interested in singing solos? . . . . . . School or church solo experience . . . . . .

Church choir (No. of years) . . . Member now . . . Plan to be a member . . .

Music in junior high (7) . . . . (8) . . . . (9) . . . .

Music in senior high (10) . . . . (11) . . . . (12) . . . .

Do not write below this line

Vocal Equipment:

Classification . . . . Range [ ] Tessitura . . . .

Quality . . . . Agility . . . . Pitch sense . . . . Rhythm . . . .

Posture . . . . Breath support . . . . Physical condition . . . .

Jaw . . . . . . Tongue . . . . . . Tone line . . . . . . Resonance . . . . . . Blend . . . . . .

Diction . . . . . Sight-reading . . . . . Section leader . . . . . Accompanist . . . . .

Secretary . . . . . . Librarian . . . . . . Choir position . . . . . . Committee . . . . . .

---

to know also the student's academic record, I.Q. score, special aptitude in allied fields (art, for example), if now active in a choir, and what church choir experience is in the student's background. On the previous page is an example of a student information form.

Awards

Most music departments use some type of award to motivate students. Educators may frown on this practice, but conductors have found it useful to recognize outstanding achievement. The types of award most frequently granted are sweater emblems, jewelry, certificates, or medals. Sweaters, disc or tape records of performance, loving cups, and pencils are other types of awards that are occasionally given.

Awards may be given on the basis of attendance at rehearsals and performances, yearly service, membership in the group for all four (or three) years, small ensemble service, good grades in music, maintenance of good grades in other subjects (as is done in athletics), solo performance, offices held, private music study or solo class, sectional leadership, concert promotion, and contest participation.

Many vocal directors have some kind of most valuable music student award. Some schools have a scholarship fund or monetary reward.

Most schools find it desirable to have an achievement, recognition, or honors day in music. This presentation may be made at an assembly, a final concert, a music banquet, or at a music dance. Any seniors receiving music scholarships to colleges should tell the music director or principal so that it will receive recognition at the senior class night.

Attendance Record

Directors usually delegate the responsibility of taking attendance to a reliable student so that the class may start immediately and all of the time may be used to its fullest extent. Some school officials will not permit a student to check roll for two reasons: the advent of IBM has made it even more imperative for the class attendance to be taken accurately, and in many states the average daily attendance determines the amount of money a school receives from the state.

Music Records

Most music educators completely inventory their music once a year. This procedure is the most businesslike approach, for it accurately keeps the record for the yearly report to the school system and protects the school on their insurance reports in case of fire or other catastrophes. The least amount of businesslike music inventory is: a full inventory taken biennially and in the alternate year a complete and careful inventory of all music the teacher plans to use during the year.

Miscellaneous

Before the teacher leaves a school at the end of the spring term, usually there will be a mandate to fill in the school inventory book. List robes, audio-visual equipment (unless under the auspices of the audio-visual department), chairs, records, and all equipment belonging to the music department, giving the number of items and the condition of the equipment. Also, as a matter of good business, receipt and file important items.

Annual Reports

Many musicians do not make an annual report to the superintendents of schools and the boards of education. This practice is required in many states. Music educators who keep their employers informed of plans and accomplishments will certainly have some advantages over the ones who do not, even though the reports are not required. The following areas may profitably be reported on in this annual report: accomplishments, what difficulties have been met and how they have been solved, problems ahead for the next year, recommendations for the future, and significant trends and events.

LESSON PLANNING

Good planning and organization go hand-in-hand with good teaching. While it is true that good planning cannot take the place of good teaching, good planning will result in better teaching from even a good teacher—and *much better* teaching from a weak or inexperienced teacher. The experienced teacher does not always write the daily lesson plan in detail, but always has a plan clearly in mind.

The experienced teacher usually will make long-range plans by course segments (called *units, projects,* or *programs*). Planning for a period of time ahead will allow the instructor to see each day's lesson or rehearsal in better perspective. Also, the assignments will make much more sense to the students, and they will cooperate more fully if they can see how the carrying through of the assignment will contribute toward the successful completion of the project or program. There are certain facts and information that the teacher must know before the course segment can be planned with any real insight.

The teacher must know what to expect psychologically, sociologically, and physiologically from each age group being taught. For example, the tessitura that a group can successfully handle will vary from choir to choir and from age to age. The lesson plans must reflect knowledge of the musical needs, abilities, and interests of the students in the way materials, songs, methods, and techniques are used.

The teacher must find out everything possible about the background of the student. Cumulative records about each student are available in the counselor's office of most schools. The instructor probably will want to have a personal record of each student for convenience.

Lesson plans must fit into (certainly *must not violate*) the general pattern of activity and procedure of the school. The teacher must become oriented to the school building; must learn policies, regulations, and practices; and should discover the resources that are available for teaching vocal music (library, guidance office, auditorium, and audio-visual equipment such as records, tape, film, and film strips). Obtain a copy of each textbook that might be used in teaching. Collect all available material that will help in understanding the school program and peruse it as quickly as possible. This material may be class schedules, statements of philosophy, department-wide syllabi, course outlines, and curriculum study reports. The school handbook is perhaps the best source of information concerning school rules. Here the teacher may learn about student clubs, organizations and activities sponsored by the school, the school's regulations for teachers and students, and the rules concerning school records, absences, tardiness, and violation of school regulations. It is helpful to know the mores of the community, the student population, and the school personnel.

The teacher must become well-acquainted with all the available music materials that might be used in the project. From this may be prepared a "song list" of music that is appropriate to the project, a "listening list" of available recordings, a "reading list," and a "materials list." Investigate the knowledge of the class by asking leading or open-ended questions of the group. Find out what songs and materials have been taught. Investigate their music-related skills. Give them an opportunity to tell you about their musical knowledge of key signatures, what *subito* means, and so forth. Don't insult them by assuming they can't do a musical skill or don't know the answer. Many times the teacher will be surprised at what they know and can do—or don't know and can't do. Make provision in planning to fill in whatever facts are missing and to deepen any knowledge students already have. Learning is usually related to the goals or purposes of the learners rather than to the purposes of teachers. Without "leading questions," the pupils may not become involved in the learning process at all. That is to say, don't expect much interest or cooperation from the students unless the music or activity is such that they feel their personal and social status (especially with their peers) will be improved as a result of learning it.

With this information as groundwork, block out some long-range plans that will fit into the time schedule available for the project, that are realistic, and that can be achieved in the length of time and with the skills and abilities of that particular class. Use creative imagination in planning.

Carefully choose a project in which the majority will be interested, but do provide for individual differences.[2] Allow for some individualization of instruction and if contracts are used, be careful to avoid the inherent disadvantages. Provide for the gifted and talented students and the culturally deprived. If the state administers a student competency testing program, be careful to cover the material in the test. The teacher's selection of excellent music and the insights given on style and form are other important phases of this program that strives ultimately to develop student musicianship.

Make definite plans for continual, comprehensive, and future evaluation of student work, so the students will be aware of progress made toward the goal. The plans must be flexible enough to allow for changes. Use the well-known 'systems' approach which involves a complete inventory of assets and liabilities, development of a flowchart, then implementation of the program with continuous feedback and adjustment (Renewal).

Form for Lesson Plan

Song or Activity	Source	Page	Procedure

Select the instructional objectives to be sought and explored during the lesson. List the music and materials and describe the particular teaching procedures that have been selected as the best ways to obtain the desired goals. Prepare for musical and other problems that will probably arise in the class.

Use some method of regular evaluation to determine the effectiveness of the selected teaching procedures in arriving at desired outcomes. Tape-recording a group is one means of evaluation. If tests are used, be sure *really important information* is asked for by the tests. Keep students informed about their progress (for example, Johnny can match some pitches today that he couldn't yesterday, some additional tone qualities of instruments can be distinguished by the class, a number is memorized, dynamics are improved in a song, a phrase can now be carried properly, and so on).

Plan to start the class promptly. Open with a song or a musical activity that will stimulate interest and participation. Simultaneously, have the class roll checked and music and materials issued and gathered in a routine manner. Insist that these items be handled quietly, carefully, and quickly. Plan a closing song or activity that students will remember and that will make them want to return to music class. If music or materials must be

---

[2] Chapters 6 and 9 describe some of the ways to provide for student differences.

passed in, end the class period with planned activities such as the musical game "hang-man," challenging follow-the-leader rhythmic drills with syncopations, or well-liked memorized songs. The body of the class period must follow a logical sequence that will contribute to the development of musical concepts, skills, and values in the student. The chapter on rehearsal procedures outlines an "order of rehearsal" to follow in a performance-oriented class. Note the discussion of lesson plans for middle school and junior high in Chapter 7.

Budget the time allowed for each activity. If too much time is spent on one area, skip to the other most important things to be accomplished during the period. With the exact time allowance stated in the lesson plan, for example:

vocalization
9:30–9:40

"The Peaceable Kingdom"
9:40–9:55

the teacher can glance at a clock and see immediately that activities or music must be adjusted to fit the remainder of the period.

A pitfall that must be avoided is the listing of activities, titles, sources, and page numbers to the exclusion of objectives, teaching procedures, and methods of evaluation. Lack of planning and the kind of planning that merely lists usually mean that the teacher must have the ability, musicianship, and quick wit to be able to somehow do and say the right things "on the spur of the moment." Even when the instructor is clever enough to succeed, a critical look at several class periods will reveal the repetitiousness of the instructions. The students will be denied an all-round development of musical concepts, skills, and values toward goals that good planning ensures.

Budget adequate time to ensure a clear understanding by the students of each new assignment. Make explanations definite and clear.

Provide for thorough teaching, but vary the teaching techniques and musical activities enough to avoid monotony. Drill and repetition that do not result in learning may result in students' dislike for the subject and even for the teacher. Morale goes down as monotony goes up. Rotate different methods of opening the class period to achieve spontaneity. Vary activities such as vocalizing to avoid monotony. If repetition is to result in learning, such other elements as interest, meaning, relatedness, and direction toward a goal must be present. Students must *understand* what a drill is accomplishing, why something is worth doing, and how an activity means something in terms of class goals. Some "class ritual" may add to the feeling of organization. If the same basic structure of vocalizing is retained for this purpose, vary the way it is done enough to retain some freshness and spark.

Design the period so that class members may be led to discover some things for themselves. Keep the entire class working as much of the time as possible, for while one section is being rehearsed for a lengthy period of time, the inactive part will become bored and restless and may start creating discipline problems. Talk little, have the group do much. Spending most of the period lecturing or on listening activities (although active participation by students can and should be involved even here) is dangerous. Students are impatient with inactivity, much talking by the teacher, and with faraway ideas that have no reality for them. Students like to be active and have exciting things to do, so plan the lesson accordingly.

Plan more than can be covered in one class period. This safeguards the inexperienced teacher against running out of ideas and doing poor teaching. Place it as an "addenda" immediately following the written lesson plan. Also, have at least one extra lesson plan available for emergencies, such as the record player going dead.

Arrive at the classroom in time to organize all books, materials, sheet music, and the lesson plan being used that period. The teacher must spread materials out, open books to the correct pages, use markers, do whatever is necessary to have the material organized and quickly available so that the class can be taught with dispatch and purpose all period.

Spend a moment at the conclusion of each class to evaluate the effectiveness of class activities. Incorporate unused activities into the next day's plans, and devise new teaching techniques or adapt old ones to reteach concepts or skills that were not taught successfully. These ideas will have to be jotted down hurriedly in the form of reminders that may be used in the written lesson plan.

MUSIC SELECTION

The selection of suitable music literature to achieve the goals set forth by the lesson plan is an immediate necessity before the lesson plan can be developed. A primary goal should be the teaching of musical taste to the students. When this is the goal, trashy literature is unthinkable, for musicality and aesthetic experiences cannot develop from contacts with the trite and the cheap. The only way students may be taught musical taste is through contacts with "authentic" music that is a good example of the style, country, or period in history it represents. The music should usually contain many of the characteristics of the period denoted so that the teacher can help the students recognize and perform music in the various styles. The teacher must select music that is an example of skillful writing in its genre, with good formal organization and expressive qualities. The music must say something and mean something intellectually and emotionally to both its listeners and its performers. Ordinarily, there will be one or more melodies that are worthwhile in themselves; there will be appealing harmony or counterpoint that has smooth voice leadings and other elements of good construction (this statement is not applicable to some contemporary music with wide voice leaps); and there will be interesting dynamic changes with good climaxes. Unique, unusual, or fresh rhythms will add to the interest. Music and text must fit and complement each other, with important words and parts of words falling on the agogic, tonic, metric, or dynamic accents. The text (with a few exceptions) must have literary value and significance. The students will enjoy doing some of the songs in the original language. When a translation is used, be sure it faithfully reproduces the original meanings while it maintains its own integrity and value. The conductor must attempt to select music that will arouse and inspire the singers to recreative action (if the teacher is not excited about the music, it is almost a certainty that the students will not be). Be sure that the ranges, the tessituras, and the difficulty of the music are intrinsically suited to the skill, age, and maturity of the performers.

Before proceeding further, the teacher should refer to Chapter 10, on style and musical traditions, unless already possessing an exceptionally solid background in musicology, to discover some of the typical elements of the style and period of the pieces to be taught to the class. Consult the Chapter 10 Bibliography for more detailed information. Select several pieces of music that promise to be good examples of the style. Then analyze these pieces, using multiple copies of an analysis sheet similar or identical to the following simple form.

Title _____   Publisher _____
Composer _____   Octavo pub. no. _____
Arranger_____   Voice arrangement (SATB, etc.)_____
Harmonic structure_____   Rhythm _____
Melodic style _____   Texture _____
Text_____   A cappella or accompanied_____
Form _____   Performance time _____
Evaluation of difficulty for this age and level of organization _____

Ranges
and
Tessituras

Additional help in analyzing the music will be obtained by using the following analytical outline, which shows some of the kinds of harmonic structures, texts, melodic styles, rhythmic complexities, and forms in music. Use only the one or two items that best describe the music under scrutiny.

Harmonic Structure

Kinds of intervals ordinarily used. Any impossibly difficult intervals?
Chord Structure:
   Use of triads, 7ths, 9ths, etc.
   Root positions or inversions

Non-tertian (4ths, 5ths, 2nds, heterogeneous)
Use of altered chords (diminished, augmented, etc.)

Progression
Diatonic or chromatic
Type of cadence structure
Consonant or dissonant
Canon, fugal, chorale, folk style, etc.
Contemporary (including jazz), Romantic, Classical, Galant, Baroque, or
  Renaissance style
Interesting dynamic changes; good climaxes
Interesting harmony
Harmony well-constructed

Texture

Monophonic—single line (linear music)
Homophonic—chordal
Polyphonic—contrapuntal
Hybrid—combinations
Tessitura
Special effects (antiphonal, unusual instruments used, etc.)
Thick or thin; delicate or rich

Tonality

Minor, major, modal, polytonal, atonal, etc.
Key scheme
A feeling of central tonality?
Frequent changes of key or tonality, many modulations

Harmony more important than the melody, rhythm, or text?

Text

Dramatic, narrative, descriptive, contemplative, sentimental, fun songs
Folk, art, sacred, secular, patriotic, spirtuals, holiday, seasonal
Classical, semi-classical, popular
Compatibility of music and text
Has emotional appeal
Has audience appeal
Stimulating or insipid
A good or poor translation

Text more important than the harmony, melody, or rhythm?

Melodic Style

Modal, pentatonic, folk style, based on whole tone scale, major, minor
Gregorian, plainsong, madrigal, motet, contemporary, etc.
Tonal, atonal
Many major arpeggios
Many, few, or no runs
Interesting dynamic changes; good climaxes
Legato and sustained; sweet, staccato, marcato
Phrases regular or irregular, long or short
Progression: Conjunct or disjunct

Diatonic or chromatic
Ornamentations or embellishments
Dimensions: Vertical—narrow or wide range.
                      Horizontal—long, continuous lines
General Qualities: Lyric or dramatic
                              Cantabile (singing) or instrumental (wide leaps)
                              Tunefulness—folksong quality

Melody more important than the harmony, rhythm, or text?

Rhythm

Meter: duple, triple, compound, irregular, or non-metric
Tempo: fast, medium, slow, changing (*allegro, moderato, andante,* etc.)
Rhythm: simple or complex
                 rigid or flexible (with *rubato*)
Frequent changes of rhythm
Syncopation
Waltz, samba, march, calypso, etc.

Rhythm more important than the harmony, melody, or text?

Form

ABA, ABC, etc.
Is it interesting? Does it have variety?
Is it repetitive? Is it monotonous?

Is form or the text more important?

Use the fives lines as a staff and draw the proper clef sign and key signature. Then place on the lines or spaces the notes of the *extremes* of range in each voice *and its tessitura* in this song. Make special note of any difficult tessituras or ranges.

When the analyses are complete, the director can confidently select the pieces that fit the group and provide the best examples of authenticity. The director must keep in mind that some music is for the small group, some is for the large choir. A conductor may select music for reasons other than style. The kind of music that should be selected for the development of sight-reading is thoroughly discussed in Chapter 6. Some of the music used for sight-reading and for the development of basic musicianship will need to be extremely elementary, for example, rounds and canons. When music must be selected for informal occasions, it must be familiar, whether it has good style or not. A conductor sometimes finds the same difficulty in seasonal music.

Whenever possible, the general interests of the singers should be considered, especially in the text. Students are interested in the people of other nations and how they live, and folksongs and other music of these countries will provide a good way to impart the information. The origin of life and life after death (religion) are important to teen-agers. Songs that have adult topics hold special interest for adolescents. Challenge them with music that makes them work to polish it. Strong rhythms in music (spirituals, folk music with dance origin, etc.) have special appeal. Songs of romance will interest these young adults.

READINGS IN ADMINISTRATION

BESSOM, M.E., A.M. TATARUNIS, and S.L. FORCUCCI, *Teaching Music in Today's Secondary Schools* (2nd ed.) New York: Holt, Rinehart and Winston. 1980.

BONEY, JOAN, and LOUIS RHEA, *A Guide to Student Teaching in Music,* Englewood Cliffs, N.J.: Prentice-Hall, Inc., 1970.

Business Handbook of Music Education (pamphlet). Reston, Va.: Music Educators National Conference. Obtain latest revision, free of cost.

COLWELL, RICHARD, *The Evaluation of Music Teaching and Learning.* Englewood Cliffs, N.J.: Prentice-Hall, Inc., 1970.

COMMITTEE ON MUSIC ROOMS AND EQUIPMENT OF MENC, *Music Buildings, Rooms, and Equipment.* Reston, Va.: Music Educators National Conference, 1966.

GAINES, JOAN, *Approaches to Public Relations for the Music Educator.* Reston, Va.: Music Educators National Conference, 1968.

GLENN, N.E., WM. B. McBRIDE, and GEORGE H. WILSON. *Secondary School Music.* Englewood Cliffs, N.J.: Prentice-Hall, Inc., 1970.

HARTLEY, HARRY J., *Educational Planning-Programming-Budgeting: A Systems Approach.* Englewood Cliffs, N.J.: Prentice-Hall, Inc., 1968.

HOFFER, CHARLES R., *Teaching Music in the Secondary Schools* (2nd ed.). Belmont, Calif.: Wadsworth Publishing Co., Inc., 1973.

JANKOWSKI, PAUL and FRANCES, *Accelerated programs for the Gifted Music Student.* West Nyack, N.Y.: Parker Publishing Co., Inc., 1976.

JIPSON, WAYNE R., *The High School Vocal Program.* West Nyack, N.Y.: Parker Publishing Co., Inc., 1972.

KLOTMAN, ROBERT H., *Scheduling Music Classes.* Reston, Va.: Music Educators National Conference, 1968.

——, *The School Music Administrator and Supervisor: Catalysts for Change in Music Education.* Englewood Cliffs, N.J.: Prentice-Hall, Inc., 1973.

LABUTA, JOSEPH A., *Guide to Accountability in Music Instruction.* West Nyack, N.Y.: Parker Publishing Co., Inc., 1974.

LEONARD, C., and ROBERT HOUSE, *Foundations and Principles of Music Education* (2nd ed.). New York: McGraw-Hill Book Company, 1972.

MOSES, HARRY E., *Developing and Administering a Comprehensive High School Music Program.* West Nyack, N.Y.: Parker Publishing Co., Inc., 1970.

NATIONAL COMMISSION ON INSTRUCTION, *The School Music Program: Description and Standards.* Reston, Va.: Music Educators National Conference, 1974.

NEIDIG, K.L. and J.W. JENNINGS, *Choral Director's Guide.* West Nyack, N.Y.: Parker Publishing Co., Inc., 1967.

PUBLIC RELATIONS WORKSHOP, *Public Relations and the Music Educator.* Austin, Texas: Texas Music Educators Association, 1979–1980.

SINGLETON, SIMON V., and IRA C. ANDERSON, *Music in the Secondary Schools* (2nd ed.). Boston: Allyn and Bacon, Inc., 1969.

SNYDER, K.D., *School Music Administration* (2nd ed.). Boston: Allyn and Bacon, Inc., 1965.

SUR, W.R., and C.F. SCHULLER, *Music for Teen-Agers*. New York: Harper and Row, Pub., 1966.

Your Key to Music Buying (pamphlet).   Los Angeles: Keynote Music Service, Inc. Free.

READINGS IN PROGRAMED MUSIC MATERIALS

ANDREWS, J.A., and J.F. WARDIAN, *Introduction to Music Fundamentals* (3rd ed.). New York: Appleton-Century-Crofts, 1972.

ASHFORD, T.H.A., *A Programed Introduction to the Fundamentals of Music* (2nd ed.). Dubuque, Iowa: William C. Brown Co., Publishers, 1975.

BOND, DOROTHY, and GORDON HARDY, *Enjoy Music More*. New York: Project Publications, Inc., 1968. (Cartoons and drawings are used to teach listening.)

CARLSEN, JAMES C., *Melodic Perception*. New York: McGraw-Hill Book Co., 1965. (With Demonstration Tapes.)

HARDER, PAUL O., *A Bridge to Twentieth-Century Music*. Boston: Allyn and Bacon, Inc., 1973.

_____, *Basic Materials in Music Theory* (3rd ed.). Boston: Allyn and Bacon, 1975.

HARGISS, GENEVIEVE, *Music for Elementary Teachers*. New York: Appleton-Century-Crofts, 1968. (Features keyboard and chording.)

HOFFER, CHARLES R., and DONALD K. ANDERSON, *Performing Music with Understanding–Orange*. Belmont, Calif.: Wadsworth Publishing Co., 1970.

_____, *Performing Music with Understanding—Green*. Belmont, Calif.: Wadsworth Publishing Co., 1971.

HORACEK, LEO, and GERALD LEFKOFF, Programmed Ear Training. New York: Harcourt, Brace and World, Inc., 1970. Four volumes with tapes.

MARTIN, GARY M., *Musical Beginnings: for Teachers and Students*. Belmont, Calif.: Wadsworth Publishing Co., 1975.

OTTMAN, ROBERT, and FRANK MAINOUS, *Programmed Rudiments of Music*. Englewood Cliffs, N.J.: Prentice-Hall, Inc., 1979.

SCHWARTZ, PAUL, *Hearing Music with Understanding*. Chicago: Educational Methods, Inc., 1968. With five reels of tape.

SHRADER, DAVID L., *The TAP Rhythm System*. Seattle, Wash.: Temporal Acuity Products, Inc., 1974–1975. Three programs and a tape machine.

SPOHN, CHARLES L., and B. WILLIAM POLAND, *Sounds of Music: Ascending Intervals*. Englewood Cliffs, N.J.: Prentice-Hall, Inc., 1967. With LP recording.

_____, *Sounds of Music: Descending Intervals*. Englewood Cliffs, N.J.: Prentice-Hall, Inc., 1967. With LP recording.

_____, *Sounds of Music: Harmonic Intervals*. Englewood Cliffs, N.J.: Prentice-Hall, Inc., 1967. With LP recording.

WARDIAN, JEANNE F., *The Language of Music*. New York: Appleton-Century-Crofts, 1967. With ten transparent plastic records.

WOELFLIN, L.E., *Classroom Melody Instruments: A Programmed Text*, Glenwood, Ill.: Scott, Foresman & Company, 1967.

PART TWO

4

Vocal Fundamentals

The conductor must realize that singing is only partly mechanics and techniques. *Making music is always the primary goal.* Begin with the music, *then* help the students acquire understandings and skills that will lead to a more skillful and knowledgeable rendition of the music when it is sung again. Do not become so involved in intricate detail that students aren't able to see how their increasing skills are contributing to the beauty of the music through a better tonal line, harmony, balance, and blend. Basic skills must be taught simply and effectively before much time can be spent on refinements. If the fundamentals are taught thoroughly, the choir will already be ninety percent of the way toward its goal of excellence.

This chapter contains many suggestions and techniques proposed for the teacher's consideration. However, before these techniques can be utilized, the choir must be convinced of the desirability of producing a good tone, always keeping excellent posture, singing with the jaw relaxed, breathing properly, phrasing correctly, and so on. It is only after the choir has been motivated to improve in an individual aspect of singing that it will follow the teacher's suggestion regarding a particular technique. Any teaching process introduced without motivation is almost certain to end in disaster.

Teach for concept learning. Students should be led to discover generalized concepts through the use of various behavioral ways of experiencing each concept. Thus, students may learn the correct concept of breath control while they are singing song phrases by doing some of the physical isometric actions that keep the chest naturally lifted and the ribs expanded. The breath control concept may be enlarged through a technique such as holding the hand in front of the mouth and singing so that warmth, not air, is felt (an act that must be accomplished through mental imagery), demonstrating the fact that good tone is produced mostly through breath pressure under the larynx rather than through spilled air. Gradually increasing volume when the breath support starts to fade will reinforce the previous two concepts, if it is pointed out that intensifying the tone keeps bodies expanded and breath pressure under the larynx. This learning process may be continued and expanded until the habits become fixed and a more generalized concept of breath control is formed by the singers. The teacher owes the students this kind of continuous learning to allow a growth in vocal skills and understandings that will keep pace with growing concepts of music.

Perhaps a discussion of vocal fundamentals should begin with the primary goal of the teacher—good singing. The characteristics of good singing are attractive tone quality, aesthetically satisfying interpretation, careful intonation, a satisfactory vocal range, flexibility and agility, superior breath control, relaxed jaw, and the singer's self-confidence. Tone quality is made attractive by brilliance (resonance), fullness (depth), hum-like placement (see pp. 99–100), a correct vibrato, "moving tone," and an even scale. Brilliance in a voice is brought about by the *forward placement* of tone and the overtones in the voice. It is this resonance that enables a voice, or voices, to carry to the back of a huge auditorium. The full, rich part of the voice originates from the spaces above the root of the tongue. This big sound may be demonstrated by instructing a section to talk or sing and yawn simultaneously. The resulting overtension of the pharynx and soft palate should be avoided, but some of the space must be retained.

Interpretation that is aesthetically satisfying reflects the following qualities: the attainment of empathy with the words and music, proper musical phrasing and style, errorless performance of musical notation, good vowel color, and crisply clicked consonants. Good singing originates from a powerful desire to sing within the individual. Notice how the canary's chest expands, then song bubbles out in a liquid, effortless torrent of melody. Precisely the same process needs to take place in the fine singer or inspired amateur choristers: the rolling (free) tone is released rather than driven; it is like water bubbling from a water fountain, not a fire hose under pressure.

Singers will find it impossible to construct or rehabilitate their voices because they *cannot hear their own tone quality.* Vocalists must judge their voices by what is heard through bone and muscle conduction to the inner ear plus *some* tone that is heard bouncing off walls. Singers' impressions of their voices tend to stem from this inner hearing reinforced by what friends and enemies have to say about their voices. Persons hearing their voices objectively for the first time, through the medium of a tape recording, will not recognize their voices, and will usually be chagrined and disappointed. Bone-conduction hearing will tend to fool them into thinking they possess much bigger, heavier tones than is the actuality. Throaty tones will sound much bigger to vocalists than well-produced tones simply because out-of-position tongues will shove much more sound back into throats where inner ears will hear the tones more loudly, while well-produced tones will be bounced out of mouths by properly placed, relaxed tongues.

Because a singer cannot hear one's own tone quality, a teacher must assume the responsibility in the voice building and mending procedure. Much of the time the voice instructor must act as the student's ears and tell the singer when good and bad tones are being produced. If the student is unwilling to accept the teacher's evaluation, the teacher may remove some resistance through use of the tape recorder. Even when the singer accepts the teacher's judgment without question, the wise teacher still will use a tape recorder. Students should have the opportunity to adjust to the way others hear their voices and to learn to associate certain tone sensations with good or bad tones. The voice coach still may have a real selling problem, however, if the student's goal is to sound like a "pop" singer instead of an opera star. If a recorder is not available, have the student cup hands behind the ears and sing into a corner. This will bounce more of the outside sound into the ear and will give the singer a more realistic concept of the sound others hear. Stopping up the ears with the fingertips will intensify the singing sensation and help singers have a better concept of their voices. Varying acoustics (hard walls vs. soft walls) may prove confusing to the inexperienced singer.

Even the poorest voice will grow with proper training. When any faculty is used, it will grow. When it isn't used, it will be lost. Be patient. Don't expect a voice to be mature at the beginning of training. Musicianship and the ability to hear mentally will grow *if* the teacher supplies the student with the proper materials to stimulate musical maturation.

Improper posture or muscle tension will result in poor tone quality. No sound can be better than the physical conditions in back of it. A collapsed body, a tight jaw, etc., must give bad sound. All bad sound is induced and can be removed unless the parts of the body involved in producing sound are diseased. Faulty habits in tone production are usually the result of *protective* impulses. For example, when a singer begins to sing higher than the singer is used to hearing, a listening tolerance must be developed to that sound; otherwise, the vocalist winces and backs away (particularly from high notes). When you start to remedy voices, listen with the *eyes* first for tensions and inhibitions. Realize that where there is the image of strain in a singer's mind, the tone will be strained. The conductor can *see* that the singer who is moving muscles up and down, lifting the eyebrows, wrinkling the forehead or scowling, singing with tight or pushed-out jaw, tensing the tongue so much it is pulled out of position on vowel sounds is in vocal difficulty. (Of course, the trained ear of a teacher soon learns to *hear* the strain and know what is happening physically without needing to look.)

Much of this "image of strain" can be erased eventually through psychological means. The teacher must convince the students that "the only thing that has pitch is pitch." (See the discussion on p. 72.) It is not difficult to get students to *think down* as they *go up* in pitch, to use the "jaw position tips" to open the jaw (the teacher should be watching to be sure the tip of the tongue stays relaxed and forward on all vowels), to use the "breath control tips" to fool the body into staying expanded, and so forth.

Teach the student a correct mental concept of how a good tone should sound. This may be accomplished through the teacher's personal demonstration of good and bad tone, through demonstrations by good student singers, or through recordings. Singing is almost more ear training than voice training. The singer who cannot mentally hear a good tone cannot produce a good tone. "Tonal imagery" is essential.

Why not concentrate on muscles to control them? The problem here is that anything that is done self-consciously tenses muscles. Try moving individual muscles while walking. Concentration on the walking process may end with a pedestrian flat on the floor because of a lack of coordination. Muscular management of the voice or forcing and pushing tone by breath can be injurious (even if the extent of the damage is only the difficulty of breaking down all these bad habits and replacing them with good habits at a later date). A teacher should remember that "muscles tend to relax when they are used." When singers have tense muscles, they should sing mostly on fast-moving songs and exercises until proper habits have been established.

It is not until the voice fundamentals function automatically that a singer can be artistic and concentrate upon interpretation. Move good habits into the subconscious so they function mechanically. Substituting good habits for bad is one of the most important functions of the voice teacher. Any student who has to think about what to do is still just an awkward amateur. A person who wants to be free in any skill must first have control.

There is a great deal of controversy concerning the age at which to start voice training. It seems useful to give the declaration by the American

Academy of Teachers of Singing, which is endorsed by the other eminent professional organization, the National Association of Teachers of Singing, Inc., of their views for the readers' information.

SOME PRINCIPLES IN THE CARE
AND DEVELOPMENT OF THE
HUMAN VOICE FROM CHILDHOOD
THROUGH ADOLESCENCE TO MATURITY[1]

Among teachers in charge of the training of the child and adolescent voice there is at present serious disagreement concerning the nature of the physical structure of the voice mechanism, its use, and its treatment during these periods.

The American Academy of Teachers of Singing presents the following beliefs regarding this important subject, which beliefs, in consultation with various authorities, have received definite substantiation.

WE BELIEVE that the functioning of the voice of the child, of the adolescent, and of the adult is governed by identical physical laws: that the principles governing the use of voice are the same in all three stages.

From childhood to maturity there is a development of the body structure but no change in position or muscular action.

WE BELIEVE that these principles demand a balance in the posture of the body, in the position of the vocal organs, and in their muscular activity, and a coordination of the whole. The ideal procedure is to teach the child correct habits in these matters during the early years. The habits of the early formative period then will carry through the various changes as the individual and the voice grow and mature. In any physical activity, golf, swimming, etc., correct form acquired in childhood is retained as the child matures.

WE BELIEVE that the principles of balance in the posture of the body, in the position of the vocal organs and in their muscular activity should be taken up in that order, as the first steps in formative training at any stage of the individual's development, whether child, adolescent or adult.

Such instruction might well be incorporated in the child's physical education.

WE BELIEVE that, notwithstanding the significance and benefits of mass singing and the need for it, the primary stress in the early years in vocal matters should be on the correct use of the voice. This will not necessarily be brought about by mass singing. In fact, all too often the con-

---

[1] Reprinted by permission of the American Academy of Teachers of Singing.

trary is true; the stress on effects from the group—with little regard to the use of the voice—generally proves antagonistic to the vocal welfare of the singer.

We submit that only through sufficient attention to the correct use of the voice may the joy of singing, the chief aim of mass singing, be fully realized. It is axiomatic to say that a certain degree of skill in any physical endeavor is necessary for any considerable degree of pleasure.

WE BELIEVE that the practice of inducing young people to sing in a way commonly and inaccurately described as "soft," which should be termed "devitalized," will result in the presence rather than in the absence of strain; therefore, children and adolescents should be taught the vitalization and coordination of the body in singing.

WE BELIEVE that the director of a choral group should know the technic of voice.

No dean of music or school principal would think of putting a choral conductor in charge of the training of an orchestra or band, but it is a common practice to place the choruses under the direction of a band leader, orchestra conductor, organist, or pianist who has no technical knowlege of the voice.

POSTURE

Simple logic places good posture close to the beginning of any consideration of fundamental vocal principles. Obviously, correct breathing is more important, but maintenance of good posture is the first and most important step toward correct breathing in singing and will tend to induce it.

One of the very first things a director must tell a new choir is, "Hold up your music." It is impossible to get consistently good posture and attention from a group unless books and music are held up in the proper position. Immediately demonstrate the way music should be held and insist that the choir consistently hold the music this way. One excellent way to hold music is to place one hand *under* the open music and place the other hand *on* the music to turn the pages and control the angle and height of the music. Each singer must see the director by shifing *only* the eyes, not the whole head. If there is only one copy of music to two singers, it is important that most of the music be held by the singer closest to the director.

The director can sell students on the idea of holding the music properly by explaining that if the music is held too high the audience and teacher cannot see the mouth and face and the sound is cut off to some extent. If the music is held too low, the head will be too low and will cause poor singing posture; the singer will not watch the director, since it is too much trouble to move the head up and down; sound will be directed toward the floor instead of toward the audience; and the audience will see the top of the singer's head instead of the eyes.

When the new choir slumps for the first time, a monologue such as the following makes very good sense to students: "The body is an instrument. It is the *only* instrument that is player and instrument combined. Since your body is the instrument you play, it is essential that this personal instrument be kept in good shape and free from dents so the tone will not deteriorate. If this personal instrument were a trumpet, what would happen to the tone quality if you took hold of the mouthpiece and bent the neck of the instrument over to a 45-degree angle? You *know* what kind of sound would come out of the *trumpet*, but you expect to be able to jut your jaw out of position, cross your legs, slump in your seat, and have beautiful sounds come out of your personal instrument. You wouldn't attempt to play a trumpet and chew gum simultaneously, for your intelligence tells you it would affect the tone quality of the instrument and cause the tongue to have less dexterity. Yet you jam gum into your personal instrument and unreasonably expect the tone to be beautiful, even though your tongue and jaw cannot function freely and the gum interferes with vocal resonance."

To show students that the entire body is used as a resonator, have each student put one hand on the forehead and say, "Hello, how are you?" Then have each one put a hand on the chest and repeat the question. Vibration will be felt in each area, which will enable the teacher to lead naturally into a discussion of the body as a musical instrument.

The Singing Movement[2] is an excellent technique that will quickly involve singers in a valid sensation of correct singing posture. It is also a very good way to introduce and demonstrate the "we expand to breathe; we do not breathe to expand" concept. Start with all singers standing, each having one knee relaxed, and hands down at the sides. Have them straighten and stiffen the fingers using downward pressure as though trying to reach the floor. While they keep their fingers stiffened, have them turn their palms slowly outward[3] until they feel their ribs and intercostals expand. Simultaneously, while the palms are being rotated, have the singers straighten their relaxed knees until all choir members are poised on the balls of their feet. At end of this simple exercise, the director will find that shoulders are down (pressure down on the fingers *keeps* them down), chests are expanded naturally, bodies are lifted out of the hips, and a full breath has been taken (be sure the students notice that the expanded body *caused* the breath to come in automatically). The one posture fault that still may be evident will be seen in the chin. The leader may wish to have the singers tuck in their chins a little as part of the exercise.[4] Ultimately, it

---

[2] E.J. Myer, *The Vocal Instructor* (Bryn Mawr, Penna.: Theodore Presser Company, 1918), pp. vii, viii.

[3] Right hand clockwise, left hand counter-clockwise.

[4] Every time this book mentions the "chin back over the chest" or the "chin needing to be tucked in," the position is one of freedom. The chin must be level, and tucked in just far enough that the student will feel his chest lift.

will be noticed also that backs are overly arched. The fifth of the "Additional Tips for Correct Posture" gives a way to correct this problem.

Warning: The director will need to check on all of the singers to be sure that their hands are turned about as far as they can turn them and that their fingers still remain tense and are pointed downward. Unless the director insists that these two things are done correctly, the singers may feel nothing, and lifted bodies with expanded chests and intercostals will not occur. The teacher will probably need to move over to some of the singers and turn their hands farther, while insisting that their fingers remain stiffened.

Once the proper position is attained with everyone, do the exercise again to obtain a fresh breath and sing a long phrase while maintaining the posture. As the group begins to run out of breath, suggest that they reach toward the floor even harder and turn the hands still more. This will assist the singers in keeping their ribs out, so that rib cages do not collapse on lungs and so that the singers will be able to carry a longer phrase with better sound. The lifting motion with the arms, described later under "Breath Control," may be added to help keep ribs out (but be sure to have the singers make a quarter-turn so arms do not collide, if this movement is used). Quickly point out that it is impractical to sing with arms tensed in this manner in concert, so, after their bodies are in position, have singers relax arms but keep bodies in position. However, it is profitable to occasionally return to the basic exercise position while singing.

Suggest to the singers that they "sit tall" or "stand tall" or "sit or stand with the body lifted out of the hips." When class members are allowed to sing with poor postures, incorrect vocal habits result and are strengthened. If singers cannot maintain good posture when they sit, the director must have them stand. Some directors prefer to have their choirs stand all period, and this is an acceptable procedure. However, the students can sing as well sitting as they can standing, *if* they sit correctly.

When sitting and singing, it is important that the students sit as far back on the chair seats as possible, sitting into the angle between the chair seats and the chair backs *or* on the front edges of the seats (any other places will promote slumping); that the singers' backs are straight, but not arched; and that the feet be in a position that requires *no shifting* when the students stand (it is especially important to practice this technique when preparing for a program like the *Messiah*, where shuffling feet will be annoying to the audience). Many times it is better to have the singers curl their feet under their chairs during rehearsal than to insist that the feet be flat on the floor.[5] The choir that is seated is likely to slump unless it is reminded constantly to "sit tall."

[5] The usual command, "Put your feet flat on the floor," can actually *cause* posture problems with singers of varying heights. "Feet flat" tends to throw bodies back in the chairs, whereas feet curled under the chairs makes it easier for the singers to sit upright without a feeling of strain or feeling out of balance.

Unfortunately, some students in your class may not be interested in becoming good singers. The director may be able to appeal to these non-singers with nonmusical, common-sense reasons for working to obtain good posture (with hope that involvement will eventually result in these students' musical interest). Make an appeal by statements such as, "An erect, alive body can be anyone's greatest asset. The first thing a woman notices about a new man she meets is his physical appearance. Most men are not likely to be attracted to a woman with slumpy posture, while the woman with excellent posture will usually draw a second appreciative glance. You students are now developing the bodies you will have to live with at age 25."

A professional model is taught to sit and stand with the body lifted out of the hips, chest lifted, ribs out, shoulders relaxed and down, and head and chin level. This is exactly what a singer needs to do in correct singing. The organization and the individual singers will appear much better if they use correct posture. (Since singers can increase their breath intake considerably by good posture, it is almost inevitable that they will *sound* much better also.)

Additional Tips for Correct Posture

Have the students do the following:

1. Interlace the fingers behind the upper part of the head. Swing the elbows back or to the front and up while pulling the chin gently *in*. Moving the elbows back will work better for most singers.
2. Stand as if hooks were pulling the tops of the backs of their heads, then relax a little. This device will straighten bodies and move chins back over chests, where they should be. Students may find it helpful to keep this in mind when walking.
3. Reach up for an imaginary high bar, then reach still a little more. Mentally touch the bottom of the ribs and then gently drop the arms but not the ribs (don't allow the students to slap their sides when the hands drop down), *or* bring hands down as though actually using the movement and strength involved in "chinning themselves" on the bar.
4. Move the head forward and up, neck free, and widen and lengthen the torso.
5. Stand with the back to a door. The heels should be against the door. The head is brought back against the door; the chin remains level (chin back over the chest). Some students will need to relax the head from the wall a little or the throat may be tense, while some will be able to keep the back of the head against the door. Square the shoulders against the door, but keep them relaxed. It is important that the hips be tightened and the small of the back moved against the door for strength and to release frontal muscles for freedom in breathing. The back must *not* be arched enough to cause the student to be swaybacked. The knees may have to be bent in order to allow the back to straighten; then the student should straighten the knees and keep the back *out* and *straight,* and the hips *tightened.*

Joyous enthusiasm tends to expand the body. Rouse the students to sing vigorously and with freedom.

Be careful that legs do not become "locked." The tension that results may cause fainting during a performance.

BREATHING

There are at least four schools of thought on breathing. The local effort school directs the attention of the student to how inhalation occurs and what certain organs do to perform that function. The prevocal school would have the singer watch diet and posture for quite a while before even starting to sing, and breathing will be automatic. The automatic school states that if the singer gets the tone right, the breathing will also be correct. The psychological school, as represented by Dunkley, presupposes that the singer becomes so absorbed in the song that enough breath will be automatically taken in to sing the phrase. It seems reasonable to believe that all of these schools have their good points, so we will assume an outlook that includes all of them.

Insist that all singers open their mouths to the first *vowel* sound of the song, even though the song may commence on a consonant. This enables the conductor to *see* if choir members are forming the correct vowels. It also enables the director to tell if students are alert and are breathing with the preparatory beat. *Do not permit students to breathe audibly!* Noisy breathing is caused by the incoming breath striking the soft palate and setting up a vibration between it and the pharynx behind it. Have the singers lift the soft palate out of the way by "opening the throat." Vocalists must always sing with a firm, open throat and relaxed neck muscles. The enlarged pharynx is essential to properly resonated tone. However, it is easy to enlarge the throat until it feels taut, and this condition is very dangerous (causing the throat to ache, causing swallowing muscles to be lifted, etc.). The singers may feel this throat tenseness by simply yawning and feeling how the throat feels at the peak of the yawn. In the complete yawn the pillars of the pharynx become very taut. *Avoid that feeling.*

Try one of the following suggestions to obtain the firm, open throat with relaxed neck muscles: (1) Imagine the way the throat feels just before you take a drink, and keep that open position while singing; (2) feel suddenly amazed, and the throat will open properly; (3) with mouth open, attempt to hear the slight sound of a pin dropping, and the throat will open; (4) sing with an inner smile; (5) feel "ecstasy"; (6) feel the beginning or end of a yawn. *The singer must always keep the throat firm and open with the neck muscles relaxed.*

When inhalation occurs, the abdominal muscles should be relaxed and the chest expanded, while, at the same time, the lower back muscles are kept relaxed. The belt-line *must* expand when the singer inhales. The ribs *must* be held out from the time the vocalist begins until the finish. It is relatively easy to keep the ribs out when inhaling, but it is difficult to keep the ribs expanded when the singer is about out of oxygen. There will be some contraction of the ribs when the performer has about exhausted his air supply, but the change in girth of the rib cage will not be noticeable to the observer *if* breathing is done properly. (Have the choristers open their mouths and bend over. Air will rush out unless the singers forcibly hold it by tightening their throats. The teacher should notice any throat tightening, if it occurs, and correct this condition. Next, have the choristers straighten up, and they will perceive that air has once again filled their bodies. This little exercise will demonstrate to the students that collapsing the ribs, which was done when they bent over, will squeeze the air from the lungs.) The ribs must be held out in order that the oxygen will not be crushed out of the lungs and intercostals by the pressure of collapsing ribs. Holding the ribs out allows the diaphragm and abdomen to function properly with no interference from outside pressures.

Mentally try to fit the expanded lungs in the left diagram below into the collapsed rib cage at the right.

To expel air and produce tone properly, keep the ribs out, the shoulders down and relaxed, and the throat firm and open with relaxed neck muscles, and pull gently in and up with the abdominal or stomach muscles. Some singers attempt to control the tone by hardening the diaphragm. Since the diaphragm is an involuntary muscle and cannot be directly controlled, the resultant effect is a locked, tight throat. If the singer gets ready to blow, then delays the action, the diaphragm feels as it should in good singing, firm, not hard. The diaphragm is the controlling muscle; the abdomen is the power. The diaphragm and abdomen react most favorably when the singer concentrates upon keeping the ribs out and the shoulders relaxed. This leaves the diaphragm and abdomen free to obey the commands of the mind without conflicting localized tensions.

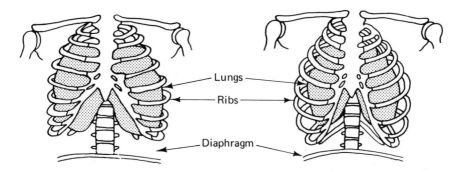

FIGURE 4-1 Diagrams of lungs, rib cage, and diaphragm expanded and collapsed.

Although breath pressure may be a factor, pitch is really controlled by the higher centers of the brain. Thus, a singer must mentally hear or think a pitch before a sound can be produced, and it is relatively as easy to think a high pitch as a low one. (However, if a singer tries to sing higher pitches than are usually used in speaking, a listening tolerance must be developed for those sounds. The singer will wince, back away, and tighten muscles, until those sounds are established. This need for ease of production is one of the important reasons for the use of falsetto with men.) Always think mentally on top of the pitch.

The thyroarytenoid nerve fibers (which extend from front to back in the larynx) and the aryvocalis nerve fibers (which run across and are interwoven with the longitudinal fibers) open the glottis with the aid of air pressure. The glottis closes partly through adductor tension; the rest of the closure is accomplished by suction caused by flowing air, which may be identified as the Bernoulli Effect.

The Bernoulli Effect may be demonstrated to students with two sheets of paper. When the instructor holds them close together in a parallel position, ‖ ‖, and blows between them, the sheets will be drawn together by the pressure. This phenomenon was first brought to our attention in 1957.[6] William Vennard, former president of the National Association of the Teachers of Singing, has been instrumental in further explanations and interpretations of this phenomenon. His article describes it as "a suction created when air is in motion, and which can draw the vocal cords together in a fraction of a second, provided they are *almost* approximated, *but not quite*, at the moment the breath flow begins."[7]

An article by Vennard written in collaboration with Nobuhiko Isshiki has this to say:

> There is a flow of breath for a quarter of a second before the tone begins, but the ear does not detect an aspirate sound because the rate is lower and the flow is smooth. This momentary flow sucks together the vocal folds so smartly that there is a sensation of the breath striking them. There is as much clarity in the beginning of the sound as in the case of most glottal plosives . . . However, both the sound and the sensation of the glottal plosive are decidedly different from those of the "imaginary h." Many teachers use plosive consonants to insure a good adjustment of the breath and the larynx. Indeed, for those students who may not have the patience to learn a good *coup de Glotte*, a plosive consonant (other than the glottal plosive, of course, in which the vocal folds are literally *exploded open* by the pressure) is a useful substitute. . . . The expression "imaginary h" or "imaginary aspirate" is recommended as pedagogically useful and accurately descriptive of the desirable attack.[8]

[6] Jan Willen Van den Berg, J.T. Zantema, and P. Doornenbal, "On the Air Resistance and the Bernoulli Effect of the Human Larynx," *Journal of the Acoustical Society of America*, XXIX, 5 (May, 1957), 626–31.

[7] William Vennard, "The Bernoulli Effect in Singing," *The NATS Bulletin*, XVII, 3 (February, 1961), 8–11.

[8] William Vennard and Nobuhiko Isshiki, "Coup de Glotte, A Misunderstood Expression," *The NATS Bulletin*, xx, 3 (February, 1964), 15–18.

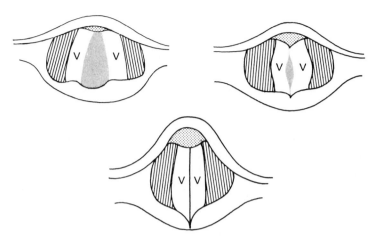

FIGURE 4-2

Vocal cords during act of respiration

Vocal cords during the act of singing a clear tone

Vocal cords singing a breathy tone

The attack may be learned by deliberately starting vowel sounds with the h sound (e.g., ha, ho, etc.). This gives the singers the sensation of starting the power and tone at the abdomen instead of in the throat. Tell the singers immediately, however, that the sound of the h and the wasting of breath caused by it must be reduced until only an "imaginary h" remains and only the *feeling* of singing on the breath is left.

The singer must concentrate upon using as little air as possible because the vocalist actually sings with air *pressure*, not air. Ask a good singer who smokes (there are a few) to inhale and then sing a tune. It will be noticeable that no smoke will appear until the smoker stops singing; then smoke will come in a gush. In other words, there is so little air used in good singing that no smoke is visible during the act of singing (see Figure 4-2).

According to a number of authorities, the vocal "lips" produce sound in a similar manner to that employed by a cornet player's lips in the production of sound. This initial "buzzing" sound is reinforced by the various resonance chambers until an amazing quality and volume can be obtained.

When babies and animals inhale, their diaphragms move downward. The viscera are pushed down, and the relaxed abdomen then expands (see Figure 4-1). Adults breathe properly when they are asleep but tend to keep their abdomens pulled in tightly while inhaling until they have been trained back into the natural method of breathing with relaxed abdomens. Our entire culture trains us to breathe improperly; tight garments force our waists to be smaller; even physical education departments train us to pull in our stomachs habitually. Students will, therefore, hold in their waistlines and breathe only with the upper lungs. As a consequence, the vocal instructor has a problem from the outset. Students must be taught to enlarge their waists when they inhale and to breathe down into their beltlines.

The voice coach can prove to the students that they will not look fat when they breathe correctly. Sing for the students and show them that when the shoulders are kept down and relaxed, the ribs are kept expanded, and breathing fills the whole body (including the back), onlookers will not be conscious of the singer's breathing. Audiences look at the upper part of the performer's body, not the waist, and when the upper part does not noticeably move, the audience (except for singers who are looking to see if breathing is done correctly) will not notice the breathing process at all. Now demonstrate incorrect breathing for the students. Allow chest and shoulders to heave, as they must in shallow breathing. It will be obvious to the students which way is going to make them appear the best when *they* sing. Point out, furthermore, that it is only for an instant that the abdomen is expanded and that, except for the instant inhalation, the stomach muscles are being pulled in and up (while the diaphragm resists and controls). Also, point out as a known fact that the process of relaxing and tightening the stomach muscles is recommended as one of the best, if not the very finest, ways to slim the waistline (isometrics).

To show the abdomen's power, the necessity for deep breathing, and the feeling of starting the breath properly when a tune is produced, have the group shout "Hey" loudly enough to make the voices ring. Warn the singers to keep their neck muscles relaxed, so the sound goes through without tensing these muscles. This is a good place for the teacher to talk about cheerleaders and the harm they can do to their voices unless they cheer the way they sing, with breath power and relaxed neck muscles. Too powerful shouting will cause the throat to constrict, but the shout produced through relaxed neck muscles will give the singer the correct direction of the "breath support muscles" and the feeling of power and strength needed for a correctly produced tone.

Try using the following procedure: Have the students hold their stomach muscles tight and breathe *only* with the upper chest. Still holding the stomach muscles tight, have this group shout. Have them breathe deeply, with their stomach muscles relaxed and *use* those abdominal muscles when they shout. This procedure will effectively demonstrate to the group the extra power and strength they may obtain through deep breathing. Then, have the singers shout "Hey," keeping the neck muscles relaxed. Without releasing the "Hey," keep the breath support coming and sustain the "Hey" on an easy pitch.

Two areas need to be considered when trying to attain correct breathing: correct *direction* (deep breathing) and *control*. Either of these two areas may be used as a starting point and intermingled at any time and in any way the instructor feels is the most meaningful to the singers. Following are exercises that will assist in the attainment of each.

Suggestions for Obtaining Deep Breathing

Have the students yawn. It is almost impossible not to take a deep breath. Have the students take breaths as if they intend to blow out candles in the distance.

The instructor can point out the sudden expansion of the abdomen that occurs when one is suddenly surprised or amazed (or has cold water thrown on the torso when taking a shower). Simulate these occurrences until the full supply of air may be gasped in quickly and silently through the open throat.

Have the singers stand and lean over until the body, from the hips up, is virtually parallel to the floor. Place the hands around the waist with the thumbs to the back and inhale and exhale until expansion is felt at the waist.

While the choir is seated, have each student place one hand at the waist, thumb at the back, to check the breathing, and the elbow of the other arm on the knee. Tell the students to lean forward, keeping their backs straight. Have them breathe in and out until the correct expansion and contraction is observed.

A psychological device that works well is suggested by Kortkamp.[9] Have the singers stand with their right hands on their abdomens, their left hands on their chests. As they *inhale*, have them move their right hands out about a foot and then try to make their stomachs go out that far also. As they *exhale*, the choir will place their right hands on their abdomens and pull in and up, and at the same time they will move their left hands out about a foot in front of their chest and try to make their chests reach their hands.

Suggest that the students imagine drinking the air in. The throats will open as though to take a drink, then the air is poured through that open throat. "Take a drink, but don't swallow." Swallowing muscles must never be engaged in the singing process.

Have the students put their elbows at their ribs, their arms straight out in front, with the hands cupped as if to hold water in the palms. Then have them open their mouths, keep their elbows in place at the ribs but move the right hands right and the left hands left horizontally, move their chins back toward their chests, and permit air to come into their bodies.[10] This movement is also very helpful in gaining breath control as well as proper direction.

[9] Ivan Kortkamp, *Advanced Choir* (rev. ed.; Tower, Minn.: Mohawk Publishing Company, 1969), p. 6.

[10] Myer, *The Vocal Instructor*, p. v.

Tell the students to blow all the air out of the lungs. They will still have air in their lungs, so have them pull their abdomens in as far as possible and blow still more air out. Have them relax their tense stomach muscles and simultaneously take breaths.[11]

Home Exercises for Students

Suggest to the students that they may be able to attain the correct sensation by lying prone on a bed in their homes and putting the heels of their hands against their nostrils as they breathe, almost completely stopping the intake of air, leaving their bodies relaxed, or that they might place a book on their stomachs while lying on their backs and make the book move up when the air is inhaled, down when exhaled.

Suggestions to Improve Breath Control

Have the singers position their hands, palms downward, about six inches in front of them at chest height, elbows out. Have them push firmly and strongly downward while singing up a scale or arpeggio. When the arms are fully extended, everyone will continue to push hard while completing the musical phrase. (Bodies will remain erect, backs straight, chests expanded, and chins level.) This exercise is excellent, for the downward movement of the hands (even the eyes should look downward) while the voice moves upward tends to psychologically remove strain and fear from the high notes, and the strength of the pushing hands will keep bodies expanded and permit tones to be free. Obviously, you should not use this exercise with untuned singers, who need all the help they can get to find the pitches.

Have everyone, while singing in a seated position, push against the tops of the chair seats or put hands under the chair seats and pull upward. This exercise will give strength to rib cages and will help in singing high notes or carrying long phrases. Students must not push or pull so hard that their throats tighten.

Have the students put their elbows at their ribs, their arms straight out in front, with the hands cupped as if to hold water in the palms. Then have them open their mouths, keep their elbows in place at the ribs but move their right hands right and their left hands left horizontally, move their chins back toward their chests, and permit air to come into their bodies. Keep the hands out with the elbows at the ribs through the entire phrase being sung. Go through the entire exercise at the beginning of each new phrase to obtain a fresh breath.

Have the students put their fists together at their chests and then pull outward horizontally as though to put fists into armpits while keeping

[11] Kortkamp, *Advanced Choir*, p. 8.

wrists straight. Have them inhale at the same time and tuck chins in toward chests. This position may be held while students sing a long phrase. (This movement works very efficiently also with the fists at the armpits just at the top of an arpeggio during vocalising, to give strength to the ribs on the high pitch.) Let the students notice that the movement opens the pharynx and gently lifts the soft palate. Point out that it also strengthens the chest and promotes proper chin position.[12]

Have the students place the backs of the hands together, arms extended full-length downward. Move them up the center of the body and up and out over the shoulders, the hands saying to the chest, "Follow me." The peak of the phrase or arpeggio is reached just as the hands move out over the shoulders.[13]

Have vocalists extend arms full-length downward, palms forward and fingers tense, and lift arms gradually upward and outward as the singers begin to run out of air. This exercise helps keep the ribs expanded. (Also use this exercise with the arms reaching the top just at the peak of an arpeggio. It makes the bodies strong on the high notes. A choir will need to turn their bodies a quarter-turn, however, to avoid a collision of arms.) See the Haywood Class voice books (F.H. Haywood, *Universal Song*, Vols. 1–3. New York: G. Schirmer, Inc., 1942) if you wish further information on this exercise. The Singing Movement, mentioned previously, is also a good basis for this movement. Notice the helpfulness of these kinds of movements to aid untuned singers psychologically and physically.

Have everyone interlock or cup fingers or clasp hands at the chest and pull hard while singing. This will work unbelievably well for a group that is singing softly, resulting in improved intonation and resonance. Students must not pull so hard that their throats tighten. Also, try having choir members interlock arms and pull (this works best with boys).

Have choir members put hands three or four inches in front of mouths and sing so that no air is felt, only warmth on hands (this will help hold the students' ribs out and help them hold back on the air, thus creating the pressure under the larynx that is needed for correct tone). If students wet index fingers and place them before mouths, the same sort of results should be accomplished.

Tell the choir to crescendo as it starts to lose its breath support. The extra pressure that is required helps keep the ribs strong so that they don't collapse on the lungs.

Vocalize with staccato exercises. It will help breath control and voice control. "Panting" will start a correct action going at the waists of the singers.

Have the class members sing $\overline{ee}$ in the middle lower register of their voices. Have the students listen for glisten or ring (resonance) in their

[12] Myer, *The Vocal Instructor*, pp. 19, 20.

[13] *Ibid.*, pp. vi, vii.

voices. Have them match that ring in the other vowel sounds. Use kee or hard g (gee) with the students, and tell them to allow the backs of their tongues to come down the slightest amount possible, making sure that the tips of their tongues are on the fleshy ridges at the bases of the lower teeth. Do the practicing mf only (e.g., Kee-ah-ee-ah-ee on F′; Kee-ay-ee-ay-ee on E′, etc.).

Discover, with the class, how long it is possible to hiss or blow through a small aperture in the mouth. Time it with a watch that has a second hand. Tell the students to concentrate upon hissing as smoothly and evenly as possible, keeping ribs out and shoulders relaxed and down, using the smallest amount of breath they are capable of using. Try for 25 seconds at first, eventually going 45 or 50 seconds. Very few students in junior high or senior high school will be able to go 25 seconds at the beginning. This exercise used regularly in class can do a great deal of good, for it gives students much the same sensation of the constantly expanded chest that is felt in correct singing. Also, the emphasis placed upon smoothness of release and using the smallest amount of breath possible trains young singers in habits that transfer directly to the singing act *if* the teacher helps them make the transfer. To assist in this transfer, after practicing longevity of hissing, have the singers hiss and move directly and powerfully to the Ah vowel, retaining carefully the feel that their chests had while the students were hissing. Move back and forth (SSSAHSSSSAHSS . . .) until some transfer occurs. Humming or other vowels may be used also, of course.

Mrs. Ann Bilger, who formerly taught at Richardson West Junior High School, Richardson, Texas, used the hissing exercise very effectively and uniquely with her junior high classes. She had the students bend forward to attain the deep breathing benefits mentioned in the previous section. The heads are in a downward position, eyes looking downward, elbows braced on the desks (or knees), and hands are placed like blinders on each side of the students' heads so they can see no one. A complete sequence of exercises is done (a student monitor counts while students breathe in and out):

EX. 1: IN, OUT, 2, OUT, 3, OUT, 4, OUT, 5, OUT . . . 25, OUT.
(Full inhalation on IN and full exhalation on OUT.)

EX. 2: IN 2345678910, HOLD IT 2345678910, OUT 2345678910. (Students take air in for 10 counts, hold for 10, and out for 10.)
2 2345, etc.
3 2345 etc.
to 10 2345678910, HOLD IT 2345678910, OUT 2345678910.

EX. 3: ALL IN, HOLD IT, EASY OUT 2345678910. (Quick IN, HOLD briefly, HISS OUT for 10 counts.) Do this ten times.

EX. 4: Before starting Ex. 4, go IN OUT, IN OUT, IN OUT (as in Ex. 1). Then: IN, HOLD IT, HISS AS LONG AS POSSIBLE.

The physical position maintained during this exercise is very advantageous, since each student's attention is focused upon the process of breathing, and the leaning-over position of the body almost *forces* deep breathing to occur. Since the student's peers are unable to watch there is no reason for self-consciousness.

Have the choir sing any vowel sound or hum as long as possible (time it with a second hand). Always insist that students sing or hum with free resonant quality to the very end, that they keep the ribs out and shoulders relaxed and down, and that they inhale silently.

Take any song and have the choir sing as long as possible without taking a breath, going across regular phrase marks. While they sing, have the choir members try to keep the same sensation of expansion at the waist and ribs that they had just after deep inhalation. Necks must stay relaxed.

Home Exercises for Students

Stand before a mirror or cold window pane (about 2–4 inches away) and sing so carefully that no moisture or fog collects on the glass.

Light a candle and sing so carefully that it does not flicker or go out.

Place a small strip of tissue paper against a wall and keep it there by blowing with a steady pressure through a small aperture in the mouth.

Have a friend put pressure on the ribs (be sure it's a friend!). This pressure should be applied just below the chest area and should be hard enough to force the singer to hold out the ribs or get hurt. (This exercise can be of great assistance to a voice teacher when he is working with private students and needs to get them to hold their ribs out. It will work in a class, but if it is used, be careful that girls' hands are on girls' bodies—watch out for horseplay!)

TRY lifting against a table while singing.

TRY pushing down firmly on the piano (or any object about waist high) while singing.

SUMMARY

Advise your students to avoid an initial expulsion of air. Remind them that after half their air has been spilled at the beginning of a phrase, there is no way to get more air to replace the wasted supply in that particular phrase. Students must learn to hold back air at the ribs and diaphragm, not at the throat, which, at all times while singing, must remain firmly open with no feeling of tension. The teacher must instruct his choir so that the members conserve and control their breath and energy and sing on breath pressure, not on spilled air. Let them imagine their bodies to be eggs that they dare not crush or squeeze (or blown glass, which will shatter if the slightest pressure is applied; the original expanded shape must be carefully maintained). Holding the ribs out builds a pressure *under* the larynx that assists greatly in firming vocal cords and bringing them together so that a clear tone may be sung (the Bernoulli Effect). The trick is to allow the expansion at the waist to relax slowly enough. Pressure must be held back at the beginning of the phrase and added a little at the very end, for accurate pitch depends upon uniform air pressure. Ordinarily, singers will obtain much finer results by expanding to breathe, instead of breathing to expand. The vacuum created when bodies are kept expanded will cause the lungs to naturally and automatically fill with air.[14] "Breathing to expand" usually causes local effort, and muscles tend to contract and stiffen. For these reasons, many of the exercises suggested previously are designed to induce breath to come into the lungs and intercostals and be controlled automatically *because bodies are expanded.* Isometrics (muscle against muscle) is the basis for many of the preceding exercises.

PRONUNCIATION

To some extent, the choral director is also a teacher of English. Not only must the students be helped to an understanding of the lyrics, but they must also be able to analyze each individual word and divide it into vowels and consonants. An important part of this skill is knowing which vowel sounds need to be elongated and which consonants or vowels must be released quickly. Indistinct diction is a fault so common as to be almost expected in amateur ensembles and soloists. This weakness makes the performance less pleasurable to the listeners because they are unable to understand what is sung. Listening to this kind of diction is like attempting to read a piece of music that was blurred when it was printed. Listeners will soon become so discouraged that they will not even attempt to understand the words. Even more serious, many vocal faults and bad sounds result from improperly formed vowels (and consonants) caused by lazy lips, jaws, and tongues.

Vowel Sound Analysis

The first step in the process of word dissection is the identification of vowel sounds. Let us start logically by analyzing the sounds that are commonly identified as "long" vowels: a,e,i.o, and u. (Sometimes $\overline{oo}$, is also considered to be one of the long vowels. For treatment of $\overline{oo}$, see the "Table of Single Phonetic Sounds.") Actually, all but one of these so-called

---

[14] Fill the *bellows*, not the balloon. Blowing up a balloon is more difficult than filling bellows, because the bellows expand and the vacuum created by the expansion causes them to be filled with air—while with the balloon, the *air* forces the expansion.

"long" vowels are *diphthongs*[15] (when sung in English); $\overline{E}$ is a pure, or primary, vowel. Following is a brief analysis of the other four.

A is actually ay and $\overline{ee}$ (the ay is held out and stressed; $\overline{ee}$ is the vanishing vowel). For example:

International Phonetic Alphabet symbol: eI, e (long a)

Dictionary diacritical marking: ā (long a)

Word examples: may, day, late, raid, play, pray, delay, great

There are some differences of opinion among authorities concerning the exact vowels produced in the diphthong. Ivan Trusler and Walter Ehret agree with the IPA symbol (e = ay, I = ih). Madeleine Marshall deviates only slightly (ε = eh, I = ih). Most other authorities (Westminister, Waring, Kortkamp) give the pronunciation of e(ay) i(ee) as in the illustration. Undoubtedly the *same* vowel sounds are being sought by each of these authorities.

When the untrained singer in junior high or high school is instructed to sing those vanishing sounds as $\overline{ee}$, he or she unconsciously resists the production of quite so bright a vowel, and so actually sings a "bright ih" placed toward $\overline{ee}$. Trusler's ih vowel is the bright ih described in the "Table of Single Phonetic Sounds" pp. 83–84. This should be the identical sound produced by emphasis upon $\overline{ee}$ with beginning students. If the student is carefully drilled upon the bright ih, he can learn to produce it well and consistently, but the average singer without experience will sing ih with a dead, improper sound. Consequently, it has been this author's experience that untrained singers are apt to respond with the proper sound immediately with no further explanation necessary when $\overline{ee}$ is suggested, while the proper "bright ih" requires additional work and explanation. The reader should feel free to experiment to see which method works most advantageously. There is actually more "intellectual honesty" in the bright ih concept.

$\overline{I}$ is actually ah and $\overline{ee}$ (let the $\overline{ee}$ sound only long enough to be heard clearly). For example:

International Phonetic Alphabet symbol: aI (long i)

Dictionary diacritical marking: $\overline{I}$ (long i)

Word examples: might, light, bright, aisle, white, eye

[15] According to Webster's dictionary, *diphthong* is derived from the Greek *diphthongos* (*di-, two* + *phthongos*, voice sound). PH has an "f" sound; thus, "diffthong" is the preferred pronunciation.

Even though the IPA lists a ("ask") as the first syllable, all authorities suggest the use of α (ah). The remarks given concerning ay and ih are also pertinent to the second part of this diphthong.

When $\bar{O}$ occurs on a *stressed* syllable, it is actually ō and $\overline{oo}$, $\overline{oo}$ sounding only briefly. For example:

International Phonetic Alphabet symbol: oU, O (long o)

Dictionary diacritical marking: $\bar{O}$ (long o)

Word examples: road, home, snow, sew, cold, flow, know, below, so

(The singer is likely to allow the lips to move to the $\overline{oo}$ shape almost immediately. Be sure to retain the feel of a long square shape, lips flared outward, until the vanishing sound occurs.)

Note: When $\bar{O}$ occurs on an *unstressed* syllable (polite, obey, memory, anatomy) the vowel is pure as it is in Italian and is *not* diphthongized.

Dr. Trusler, Walter Ehret, and Madeleine Marshall again agree with the IPA symbols o ("obey"), U ("look"). Most of the other authorities use O(o) + u ($\overline{oo}$). When inexperienced singers are told to release with $\overline{oo}$, their lips will not quite move to the $\overline{oo}$ shape and the vowel formed will be U ("look"). If these youngsters are admonished to use U for the vanishing sound, the vowel produced will probably be uh until much more training has been given. Either concept will work if the director knows the correct sound and insists on *that* vowel being sung. See "Tips on Correct Pronunciation of Vowels" for other information.

$\bar{U}$ is actually $\overline{ee}$ and $\overline{oo}$. This is the only diphthong where the vanishing sound is at the beginning and the sustained sound is at the end. Move quickly from $\overline{ee}$ to the sustained sound $\overline{oo}$. For example:

International Phonetic Alphabet symbol: Iu, ju

Dictionary diacritical marking: $\bar{U}$ (yoo)

Word examples: new, few, dew, you, beauty, view. (Be careful not to pronounce "new" and "dew" as "noo" and "doo." The word "do" *is* pronounced "doo.")

Trusler and Ehret seem to be the only authorities who insist on the IPA symbol I(ih), u($\overline{oo}$) or j(y = ih) u ($\overline{oo}$). Madeleine Marshall concurs with the other authorities on ($\overline{ee}$) u($\overline{oo}$). The $\overline{ee}$ concept seems to be an easier concept for the young beginner to grasp and sing as an acceptable vowel immediately. However, I agree with Trusler and Ehret that the sound actually produced should be bright ih (sing ih and think $\overline{ee}$).

Other diphthongs are:

$$\text{OU} = \text{AH} + \text{OO}$$

International Phonetic Alphabet symbol: aU

Dictionary diacritical marking: OU

Word examples: round, bound, hour, now, ground, pound

All authorities appear to agree that a ("ask") should be ɑ (ah). Marshall, Trusler, and Ehret are in accord with the IPA, U ("look"). See the previous discussion of u ($\overline{oo}$) versus U ("look").

$$\text{OI} = \text{O} + \text{EE}$$

International Phonetic Alphabet symbol: ɔI

Dictionary diacritical marking: oi

Word examples: joy, rejoice, boy, toy, boil, toil

The authorities are generally in harmony concerning the initial sound ɔ(aw), although Waring states that the sound is in reality somewhere between aw and short o. In the author's experience, the o of oi is between long o and aw (closer to aw, but the sound has a little bit of the o quality in it). Students, told to sing aw, tend to not round their lips forward enough and so usually sing ah for aw.

These same students will be more likely to round their lips properly if told to sing ō. However, they will resist going all the way to ō and will sing the aw sound with a little ō in it. If great power or extreme high or low pitches are needed, alter the ō to aw. See the discussion concerning the I(ih) versus i($\overline{ee}$) controversy.

Table of Single Phonetic Sounds

INTERNATIONAL PHONETIC ALPHABET SYMBOLS	EXAMPLES	HELPFUL HINTS ON PRONUNCIATION [16]
i (long e)	he, three, queen, sheen	Sing $\overline{ee}$, drop jaw open, especially on medium high to high pitches or when singing with power. The easiest way to sing ee softly is with round lips (especially if the pitch is high) or simply sing $\overline{ee}$ as an umlaut.

(cont.)

INTERNATIONAL PHONETIC ALPHABET SYMBOLS	EXAMPLES	HELPFUL HINTS ON PRONUNCIATION [16]
I (short i)	still, lift, his, ring, dear, hear	On accented syllables, sing ih and think ee, *or* sing e͞e and pucker the lips, o͞o. On unaccented syllables, sing without modification.
ɛ (short e)	fair, lair, where, there, sped, dead, get	On accented syllables, sing eh and think ay. The jaw must be dropped open. On unaccented syllables, sing without modification.
æ (short a)	hat, had, an, and, ran, sang, man	This can be an ugly sound. Sing the sound properly, but drop the jaw open to ah (ä).
a	dance, path, staff	Sing the proper sound, but be sure the jaw is dropped open to ah.
ɑ	ah, cart, arm, balm farm	When ä and o are sung, the resultant vowel sound produced is so similar as to make it practical to treat them as the same sound. Use a basic ah jaw position.
ɒ (short o)	lot, not, forest, odd	
ɔ	saw, lawn, yawn, wall, jaw	Sung with long, dropped jaw, lips somewhat belled open.
U	wool, pull, put	Sing uh and think o͞o.
u	noon, room, rude, food, June, cool,	Lips pursed and rounded.
ɝ	her, furl, heard word, sir	Occurs only on stressed syllables. Sing uh with the lips pursed.
ɚ	wav*er*, sing*er* lead*er*	Occurs only on unstressed syllables. Sing uh with the lips rounded to o͞o.
ə	*a*bound, di*a*dem, sof*a*, *u*pon, *a*lone	Occurs only on unstressed syllables. Sing uh and think ah. If elongated, sing it as ah.
(Short ʌ)	up, under, st*u*dy won, some, love	Occurs only on stressed syllables. Sing uh and think ah.

The brackets indicate an almost identical position of the articulating organs.

[16] See "Vowel Modification" on pp. 122–23 for further insights.

Mouth-Shaping Hints

A vowel must be sustained, unchanging in the slightest degree, for as long as the note is supposed to last. The mouth must be in the same shape when the singer finishes as when the vowel was begun, not having been gradually allowed to fall toward a closed position.[17] Consonants and vanishing vowels are sounded with great speed.

In essence, before a performer sings a word, it must be decided what vowel sound must be elongated and how the mouth must be shaped to produce that sound correctly. The vowel settled upon is held out with a rolling tone; the jaw is relaxed but remains in a fixed position until the diphthong, another consonant, or another vowel is clicked. The vowel must sound at the beginning of the beat.

For good style in ending a final tone or word that ends on a vowel, *do not* end with a sudden snap of the jaw or with a quick closure of the throat accompanied by a click or push. Do end clearly, elegantly, by regulating the breath and leaving throat, jaw and tongue free. End by leaving the mouth open and inhaling sharply but quickly.[18]

The Tongue's Importance in Vowel Production

The tip of the tongue must always touch the fleshy ridge at the base of the lower front teeth on all vowel sounds. This permits the tone to flow, or roll out. The tongue must remain relaxed; otherwise, it will interfere with the tone. If the singer is not used to this feeling, it may be difficult at first to keep the tip of the tongue in the vicinity of that lower fleshy ridge; but this must be done. Check in a mirror to be sure.

While the tip of the tongue stays down and forward on all vowel sounds, the front or back of the tongue moves into various positions according to the vowel sound produced. The front of the tongue is in its highest position for the sound e̅e̅. It is slightly lower for ay, still lower for eh, and relatively flat for ah. The back of the tongue is in its highest position for o̅o̅. The back of the tongue gradually moves toward the floor of the mouth through o, short a, and short o, to the lowest position for aw.

There is also the problem of vowels that must be "modified" in the upper range. For some suggested solutions see the section in this chapter on jaw position and in the next chapter on the vocal palette of colors.

---

[17] Ivan Kortkamp, *One Hundred Things a Choir Member Should Know* (rev. ed.; Tower, Minn.: Mohawk Publishing Company, 1969).

[18] The trumpeter, John Haynie, nationally-known performer and teacher, and also an authority on the action of the diaphragm and breathing, talks about this same "sense of inhalation" in a good tonal release on his instrument.

Rests and the Precise Ending of Phrases

If there is a rest following a note, normally the cut-off occurs *on the rest* and the end consonant and/or vanishing vowel is placed exactly on that rest by the singers as they end the phrase. For example:

If there is no rest following a note but the phrase suggests a release, cut off soon enough so that the singers can take an adequate breath and come back in on time. If the end note is longer than a beat, it is usually a good plan to cut off exactly one beat before the new attack. This will give the singers adequate time to make a good release and a full inhalation for the new attack. For example:

Other complications may arise; for example, the sustained part cannot be released until the coinciding moving part has sounded its final note in that phrase:

The possibilities are endless. The ones listed above are some of the most likely to occur. The director must realize that the voiced consonants will also be taken from the beat (see the section on consonants for more details.)

Therefore:

Italian vs. English

Many teachers of singing prefer to start their students with songs in Italian rather than in English, since all vowels in Italian are primary vowels, that is, the vanishing sounds that make the vowel diphthongs are not found in this language.

Since pure vowels promote good quality in the voice, these teachers feel that voices will develop and that students will feel a confidence in always attaining good quality on certain vowel sounds more quickly through the Italian. After the voice is established, the teacher will move to the more difficult English.

Other teachers choose to attack the English songs directly, feeling that the student must learn to sing sounds such as ih, eh, uh, and a with good quality in English throughout junior and senior high. Since these sounds are so troublesome, why not give assistance on them from the beginning?

A middle ground may be the best solution, but a really fine teacher can use almost any method and be successful.

Tips on Correct Pronunciation of Vowels, Particularly in Problem Words

Pronunciation typical of the various regions of the United States should be avoided, except in regional folksongs, popular songs, and various other songs that demand performance in a dialect. Whenever dialect is called for, the song will be much more effective with the Scottish burr, without the r in black dialect, and so on. In fact, a good dialect is part of a good and authentic interpretation.

In all other songs, the director must strive to obtain a pronunciation that is used universally by choral singers. This is a diction that transcends colloquialism and that is used by professional artists. The rule to follow is: sing a pure vowel sound, unless the word sounds "affected" with the change, in which case the singer will pronounce the word as it would be pronounced in correct speech, being sure the jaw is dropped out of the way.

If your section of the country has difficulty with extra vowel or double vowel sounds, analyze this problem and do not allow it to occur. Train your group to go directly to the correct vowel.

yes = yehs, *not* yeh-yus
round = rah-oond, *not* ra-ah-oond.

Notice in the phonetic table that ih is sung with the color of $\overline{ee}$, and eh with the sound of ay in mind. Not only will this help the placement of these sounds, but it will also prevent eh from sounding like ih and vice versa, for example, din for den, den for din.

"King," "sing," and other "ing" words should perhaps be tipped even more toward $\overline{ee}$ than are the other ih words previously mentioned in the phonetic table. Many directors suggest to their choirs that these "ing" words be sung with a pure $\overline{ee}$, knowing that the students will *not* get a pure $\overline{ee}$ sound, but an ih sound tipped strongly toward $\overline{ee}$. This kind of device is used often, particularly by clinic choir directors. (Another example is to leave the r off entirely, knowing that enough students will forget and put it in so that the r sound will be about right for the total choir.)

Sing "you're" as "yoo-r."

Sing "your" as "yuh (shape o͞o with lips)-r."

(People in many parts of the country sing "your" as "yoh-r.")

There may be some justification for using the unstressed ŏ vowel whenever possible, even on many stressed ō sounds, since one of the most troublesome problems posed by ō is that of retaining the square shape with flared lips and not moving too quickly to o͞o.

> *Try singing:* "flow," "go," etc., without allowing the lips to move to the o͞o shape
>
> *Try singing:* "note," "road," etc., and flip the "t" or "d" with the tongue without moving the lips. Listeners will still be able to easily understand the words, and the tonal line will be easier to keep uniform when o doesn't move to o͞o.

"In the definite article preceding words beginning with vowel sounds, e is long (thē apple); preceding consonants, e is pronounced like u in 'sung'; that is, 'the boy' is pronounced 'thuh boy'." [19]

The word "hallelujah" is derived from the Hebrew words "hallelu" and "yah." "Hallelu" is the plural form of the word "hallel," which may be interpreted "make a joyful noise" or "praise loudly." "Yah" is one of the several Hebrew terms for God. Russian pronunciation of the word "hallelujah" is "aliluya." According to A.A. Wihtol, the singing of "alliluia" or "alli-loo-ee-ah" as if these were Russian linguistic idioms is *not* correct.

To sound truly reverent, usually "God" should be sung as "Gawd." "Lord" is usually sung best as "lo-oord" unless extreme power or very low or high pitches are needed, when it should be altered to "law-oord." Both sounds have their dangers. "Lawrd" is apt to quickly degenerate to "lard" with youngsters; the o of "Lord" is liable to move too rapidly to the o͞o lip position.

Words containing "en" ("spok*en*," for example) must be sung as "ehn," not "uhn." Other examples: "ed ("lift*ed*") must be sung "ehd" and not "uhd"; ess ("holin*ess*") must be sung "ehs" not "uhs." Since all of these situations will arise on *unaccented* syllables, it is necessary to lighten and ease off on "ehn," "ehd," and "ehs" or the brightness of the vowel will pop the syllable out too loudly. Many directors take the easy way out and have their groups sing the dead uh sound in order to avoid the likelihood of accentuation of these unstressed syllables. Take the trouble and the pains to have your choir sing it right!

Be sure that ɛ(eh) is not sung in place of e (ay). This vowel replacement will result in "Hail, All Hail to the Queen" sounding like the junior high choir the author heard sing "Hell, All Hell to the Queen."

----

[19] Archie N. Jones, ed., *Music Education in Action* (Dubuque, Iowa: Wm. C. Brown Company, Publishers, 1960), p. 164.

Even though a word starts with a vowel sound, that word should be separated from the previous word *if* the word needs more power or feeling to bring out its meaning or if the previous word ends with the same vowel sound, for example, "the/evil."

Six Rehearsal Suggestions
to Use in Vowel Improvement

Sometimes it is effective to use only *one* vowel (to get smoothness, correct tone placement, and open jaw position, which results in the solving of range problems). Then put the correct vowels and consonants back into the tonal line, retaining the same sound and feel.

Sing a song using only the phonetic sounds found in the words to increase the ability to move smoothly from one vowel to the next and to select the correct phonetic sounds to sing. This will also remove the troublesome consonants so that proper tone placement and maintenance of the tonal line may be practiced with only vowels. When the consonants are added, snap them without any time allowance for them. Since this is a difficult procedure, the director may wish to confine the technique to a single phrase.

When vowels begin phrases, they must be attacked with as much rhythmic precision as if they were consonants. That precise attack must not be a glottis stroke (which is accomplished by closing the lips of the vocal folds and opening them with a click).[20] Attack vowel sounds *on the breath* (with an h) to help insure that the attack is "from the waist," not "from the throat." Work with the choir over a period of time so that the h disappears,[21] but the tone's power still starts at the abdomen.

Try adding the first vowel sound to assist pupils in discovering what vowel is formed when the breath is taken ("ah-LAH-EET" for "light," for example).

To learn elongation of vowels, sometimes put two vowels in each syllable ("cle-ear").

Consonants

Whereas the tip of the tongue remains anchored low in the front of the mouth on the gum line of the lower teeth on all vowels, consonants are usually formed: by the lips (p,b); by the lower lip and upper teeth (f,v); by the tip of the tongue and the back surface of the upper teeth (th); by the tip of the tongue and the juncture between the gum line and the upper teeth (t,d); by the hard palate and the front part of the tongue (sh, ch); by the back of the tongue and the velum or soft palate (k,g); and by the glottis (h).

[20] The vocal cords are literally "exploded open" by the pressure. Even though a glottal plosive is used in speech, it must not be used in singing.

[21] See the "imaginary h" and "Bernoulli Effect" discussed in connection with the section on breathing earlier in this chapter.

Consonant sounds are delivered as quickly as possible so that the tip of the tongue can return to its normal vowel position at the gum line.

There are three main kinds of consonants: *voiced* or *tuned* consonants, subvocals, and all others. Improper handling of the voiced consonants (consonants on which a pitch can actually be sung and the sound elongated) will cause many difficulties to arise such as a tendency to sing on the consonant rather than the vowel, scooping, and delayed vowel sounds. M, n, ng, l, and r are the chief offenders. Other voiced consonants are v, z, zh (as in, "azure"), s (pronounced as z), and th (as in the word "thee"). The sounds of l and r are especially ugly because the tongue is pulled into a position in which the tone is blocked. M, n and ng are the most pleasant consonant sounds, but beware of holding them too long. A good rule is to hold the m, n, and ng about one quarter as long as the vowel sound preceding it and with enough power to balance with the vowel sound. For example:

$$\text{\textonehalf} \quad = \quad \text{\textonehalf}. \quad \text{\texteighth}$$

$$\text{long} \qquad \text{law} + \text{ng}$$

Treat all other consonants, voiced or otherwise, as clicks at the *ends* and *middles* of words. B, d, j and g are subvocals, and they also have pitch. Sing these subvocals and voiced consonants in tune at the *beginnings* of words; treat all other consonants as "clicks" (but think the pitch of the first vowel *in tune* before clicking).

A singer can test for voiced or subvocal consonants by putting the index finger lightly on the larynx. If any vibration of the cords can be felt or heard, it is a *voiced* or *subvocal* consonant. (Check with z and s—z is *voiced*.)

Paired Consonants

It may sometimes be helpful to the conductor to know the paired consonants (in which the articulating organs react in an almost identical way). Occasionally it is even possible to substitute the voiced for the voiceless for example, z for s to eliminate the ugly hiss, if meaning is not sacrificed in the process. See the table on page 91.

Another useful way to classify the consonants is: explosives (plosives) and continuants.

The *explosives* cause an explosive sound (as is suggested by the title) when the articulating organs come in contact with each other in some manner, thus causing the flow of breath to be interrupted for a very brief span of time. The explosive consonants are: b,d,j,g (the subvocals) and p,t,ch,k (voiceless). (Note the paired consonants, page 91.)

The *continuants* continue, or remain in a relatively stable position. Continuants are: a) m,n,ng,l,r,v,z,zh,th (voiced consonants); b) f,th,s,sh,

VOICELESS	SUB-VOCAL	EXAMPLES		
T	D	tome	or	dome
		tote	or	toad
P	B	pole	or	bowl
		lope	or	lobe
K	G (hard)	Kate	or	gate
		Dick	or	dig
CH	J (DZH)	choke	or	joke
		pitch in	or	pigeon

VOICELESS	VOICED	EXAMPLES		
F	V	face	or	vase
		a life	or	alive
S	Z	seal	or	zeal
		ice (s)	or	eyes (z)
SH	ZH	shock	or	Jacque (zh)
		mesh her	or	measure (zh)
TH	TH	thigh	or	thy
		teeth	or	teethe

h,wh (voiceless); c) w,y (as was mentioned in the section on vowels, w is really the vowel $\overline{oo}$, y is usually the vowel $\overline{ee}$ as in "mighty," occasionally i as in my).

Consonants With and Without Duration

Consonants with duration (tuned or voiced) and the sibilants ss and sh must be *ahead* of the vowel sound, timed so that the vowel sound begins exactly on the beat. For example:

My   M+AH + EE

Consonants without duration are sung exactly on the beat and are attached to the following vowel (except when meaning is distorted by so doing).

Too   (T)oo

All consonants having pitch but no duration (sub-vocals) must arrive on the rhythmic unit, *but take the pitch of the following vowel.*

All consonants having both duration and pitch (tuned) take the pitch of the previous vowel except on an initial attack or in detached singing, in which case they take the pitch of the coming vowel. Use moderation in length of the tuned consonant.

In staccato passages, sing voiced consonants on the end of the syllable, sing sub-vocals and all other consonants on the new syllable. Examples: "Syn-co-pa-ted" and "On-ward Chri-stian Sol-diers."

Other Suggestions Concerning Consonants

By judicious treatment of consonants, much may be done to affect the style of delivery of a phrase or sentence. Sometimes the explosives may be sharpened or softened in such a way as to intensify the effect of word and music.

Initial consonants should be delivered swiftly, so that the vowel will be reached as quickly as possible. This rule is subject to an occasional exception, as when a special effect in delivery is desired and only to be gained through dwelling upon an initial consonant. Such words are *m*ighty and *d*eath.

In light, delicate passages, especially, the harsh sibilants s and z, sh and zh need modification to minimize, as far as is compatible with intelligibility, the unmusical hiss. It may be desirable to sing s as z or even ts. (In your imagination, touch a hot iron.)

In most cases, ease of emission is promoted by allotting the consonant to the vowel following; this is especially so when the second syllable is taken by a skip in pitch (with the exception noted at the top of this page).

Generally, the final consonant of a word will be allotted to the word following unless it is at the end of a phrase or natural break or affects the meaning.

set my	=	seh-tmah-ē
but bless you	=	blehss/eoo, *not* bleh-sshoe
and lead us not	=	lee-duh-s/nah-t, *not* lee-duh-snot
and let us pray	=	leh-tuh-s/preh-ee, *not* leh-tuh-spray

Many times consonants stop the tone for an instant. The singer's task is to make these tonal halts extremely brief and still click the consonants so they are heard with ease. This necessitates strong movement by the tongue and lips. Let the "tip of the tongue tell the tale." Keep the power turned on through vowels *and* consonants. Consonants must be sung about three times louder than most students think they must if an audience in a large auditorium is to hear all the words. Explode the consonants as hard as it would be necessary to hit them in whispering to the back of the auditorium. Let the consonants act as springboards for the vowels.

Be sure *all* consonants are sounded if they should be: for example, recognize, *not* reconize. Be sure consonants are not sounded if they shouldn't be: for example, "toward" = "tord," not "too-ward." Be sure "wh" is not pronounced as w ("when," not "wehn"). On words with "sts" hit the s, then the ts ("hoh—oo*s ts*"). "Ed" is pronounced as t when it is directly preceded by a voiceless consonant in any one-syllable word ("guessed is pronounced "guess*t*"). "Ed" is is pronounced as d when it occurs immediately after a voiced consonant in a one-syllable word ("praised" = "prayzed").

Remember that the eight explosives should snap with power when they begin or end words ("*tight*"). These sounds should all be softened when transposed to the beginning of a syllable ("light and"—soften the t).

A doubled explosive consonant inside a word will be sung in its softened form ("mi*dd*le").

Ch and j are *never stopped.* They are always sounded, even when doubled ("mu*ch ch*ange" or sage *j*ust").

The only consonants that require an extraneous sound are d, b, and g. All voiceless explosives and continuants should be sounded by the emission of a vigorous puff of air; no vocal sound should be heard.

All of the voiced continuants should be sounded on pitch and ended without an alien noise (like uh), keeping the tongue and jaw in position until the breath is ended.

The subvocal j (soft g) has two sounds, but the last sound should be treated as a voiced continuant to its completion.

The subvocals d, b and hard g will make *no sound* unless the consonant is released. There is no problem whenever one of the vowels follows immediately, because the consonant is released by the vowel. However, when d, b or hard g occurs before a consonant sound or a stop of any kind, most authorities suggest an uh sound of some duration, which could easily be misinterpreted to mean an actual uh after the consonant. What is actually wanted is only a neutral pitch that sounds simultaneously with the release of the consonant and is immediately released.

Whenever the word "you" comes after a word that ends with a consonant, handle the fusing of these words with care. For example:

help you = help/you, *not* hell-pew
can't you = can-tyou, *not* can-chew

Ng never has a hard g in one-syllable words. For example:

Long Island, *not* Long-Gisland

A problem discussed under *"Tips on Correct Pronunciation of Vowels"* is the singing of an extra neutral syllable before the consonant l. For example:

Well = Weh-l, *not* weh-uhl or weh-yuhl.
Sail = Say-l, *not* say-uhl

Sing a good vowel and move the tongue quickly to the l position at the exact end of the word.

When directing, use the fingers to indicate consonants. M, n, and ng must be elongated and sung with more power to be heard plainly and to balance the vowel sounds. T, d, p, k, and f are consonants that must be emphasized particularly. Click these off *with precision* on the ends of words.

Use the following information to train the choir. For example, establish correct habits by vocalizing the choir on various vowels while employing *only* the consonants on which the jaw does not move *or* those on which the tongue tip does not move *or* while using paired consonants, and so on.

The tongue should not move if the jaw does.   The tip of the tongue stays anchored at the fleshy ridge at the base of the lower front teeth:

1. Lips and jaw move on p and b (paired explosive consonants), and m (continuant). These are *bilabial* consonants (formed by the upper and lower lips).
2. Lower lip and jaw move on f and v (paired continuant consonants). These are *labio-dental* consonants (breath is driven at an audible level between the lower lip and the upper teeth).
3. Jaw may move slightly on "wh" (lips form the vowel oo and air is forced through the opening). This is a *glottal* consonant.
4. Lips and jaw move slightly on w and y. These are "consonants which are actually vowels." W is the vowel oo at the end of a word, a voiced continuant consonant at the beginning of a word. Y is the vowel ee as in "mighty," the diphthong i as in the word "thy," or a consonant at the beginning of a syllable as in "youth."

Remember: All *vowels* belong in this category (because of the placement of the tip of the tongue), although the jaw may or may not move.

The jaw should not move if the tongue does.   The jaw stays relatively motionless, and the tip of the tongue is involved on:

1. "th" as a voiceless or voiced continuant. These are *lingua-dental* consonants, which are heard when breath is forced between the tip of the tongue and the back surface of the upper front teeth where the tongue's tip touches.
2. t and d (paired explosive consonants), n and l (paired continuants). These are

lingua-alveolar consonants. The tip of the tongue stays approximately at the juncture between the gum line and the upper front teeth.

3. ch and j (soft g, occasionally a y sound) and r as a voiced continuant or trilled. These are *lingua-palatal* consonants, formed by the hard palate and the tongue. For ch or j allow the tongue to slip back from the t position to the first high ridge, and then remain. The back of the tongue comes up against the upper back teeth halting the flow of air; then the tongue is released explosively. To perform the voiced r, curl the tip of the tongue back over itself as though starting for the uvula (the pendent fleshy lobe in the middle of the posterior border of the soft palate). The trilled r may be performed as d-d-d-d or with a tongue flutter. It is used for Scotch and Irish brogue, foreign languages, and extremely high pitches. Otherwise, the voiced continuant r should be used.

Exceptions:

Neither tongue tip nor jaw movement is involved in:

1. k (hard c) and g (hard g), which are explosive paired consonants.
2. q (k, usually used in "qu" [koo]) and "ng" (voiced continuant). These are *velar* consonants, formed when the back portion of the tongue comes in contact with the velum.
3. h (a voiceless continuant). It is a *glottal* consonant, which is formed by air forced through the glottis (the opening between the vocal cords in the larynx).

Jaw and tip of tongue are involved in:

1. s (soft c) and z (paired continuant consonants). These lingua-alveolar consonants are formed when the sides of the tongue stay against the upper back teeth. The tip of the tongue does *not* quite touch the bottom front teeth.
2. "sh" and "zh" (as in "measure") are paired continuant consonants. These are lingua-palatal consonants. The tongue position is as on s and z, except the tip is withdrawn somewhat onto the hard palate.
3. x ("ks"), a double consonant that is velar *and* lingua-alveolar. The k involves only the back of the tongue; the s involves both tongue tip and jaw.

Jaw Position

When a singer opens his mouth in a normal manner, the jaw sweeps down and back as smoothly as though the synovial cavity and condyle were bathed in oil. The jaw is designed in a wonderfully balanced fashion, and as long as the vocalist allows the movement to be in only two directions (down and up), the action of the jaw will be free and without friction. On the other hand, if the jaw is jutted out or shoved to one side, the muscles involved in its operation will become tense and will not function properly. This will cause the enunciating and articulating mechanism to function

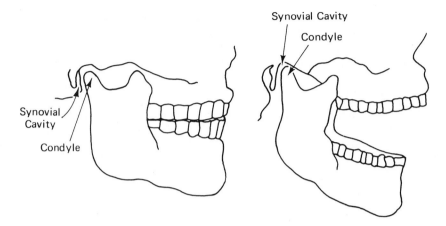

FIGURE 4-3   Jaw must swing *down* and *back* in opening the mouth.

improperly. It is essential, therefore, that the jaw be allowed to swing with the utmost facility (see Figure 4–3).

Jaw position must be relaxed on vowel *and* consonant sounds.[22] In the first stages of development most singers will have difficulty opening the jaw *enough.* Although no two singers will have exactly the same jaw depth, it is essential that the jaw be allowed to drop open loosely. The chin must move downward and back toward the chest. A good device for showing students the importance of opening the jaw is to have the students say or sing the word "olive" with the mouth almost closed, and then open naturally and say or sing it again. Other good words to relax the jaw are: yawn, clock, squaw, gong, claw, paw, or ding-dong. It is particularly important that on all vowels with medium high to high pitches the shape of the inside of the mouth be long and narrow with the soft palate lifted (but not tense).

It does very little good to keep telling students to open their mouths. Many of them will think they are complying with your wishes when their jaws are still tense, tight, and relatively closed. The director needs to have some teaching techniques available to dramatically and consistently demonstrate how jaws feel when they are opened the correct amount and how much more mature the tones then sound.[23] There are two particularly efficacious methods that may be used to keep the jaws open while the choir sings the words of a song.[24]

[22] See "Vowel Modification," Chapter 5, for more information on the need for the open jaw and ways to open it.

[23] It is very important to junior high students and even older singers to have relatively mature rather than childlike voice qualities.

[24] Check carefully and make sure that *all* students are doing each technique correctly. The director cannot prove the excellence of the method unless *everyone* complies.

Dropping the jaw open will cause an indentation to form where the condyle fits into the synovial cavity (see Figure 4–3). This indentation may be located next to and just in front of the ear, at about its vertical midpoint. Have the students put their fingers around this spot, and open and close the jaw until they locate this "hole," which is caused when the back of the jaw opens. Then have them open their jaws and keep their fingers inserted lightly, without pressure, in these indentations while they sing, keeping them open on all vowel sounds (of course there is *some* variance from aw to $\overline{ee}$). This procedure will help the students keep their jaws dropped open. The indentions will disappear, at least some, on all consonant sounds except the *velar* (k, g, ng) and *glottal* (h). Other consonants like t, d, n and l may be sounded without moving the jaw, but the tongue position is not quite normal. It is most important that the students endeavor to keep the indentations open at all times when they sing, even through the consonants like m that tend to close the indentations when the students speak. This technique works beautifully to induce correct humming as well as "open-jaw" singing, and students may test to see if their jaws are open by touching their synovial cavities (or absence of cavities) with their fingertips.

When the sopranos[25] are having trouble with a high phrase in a song (trouble that is usually accompanied by tight jaws, thin, pinched qualities, and inability to hit high notes), the time is ripe to introduce the second method: Direct the soprano section as they sing the passage exactly as they have been singing it. Ask the sopranos to listen to their quality, and also ask the entire choir to listen critically. Next, ask the sopranos to open their mouths; place their hands on each side of their faces with fingertips on their cheekbones; push their mouths into long, square shapes, leaving jaws loose; then sing the high passage on the vowel aw while holding the mouths and jaws in this position. (Direct the sopranos to help them sing more confidently.) Finally, direct the sopranos as they sing the words, while holding mouths and jaws in the long square shape. There is a slight tendency for the students to pull tongues back out of position; this must be counteracted by reminders to keep the tongues relaxed, down, and forward.

Everyone, including the sopranos, will be able to hear the vast improvement in sound, the increased fullness and maturity of the voices, and the much better quality, particularly on the high notes. Once the organization agrees that this is a more desirable sound, the director may point out that this is only one way[26] of insuring an open, relaxed jaw. Work this technique also with tenors, basses, and altos whenever jaws are tight or a

[25] It could be any section, but the sopranos make such a convincingly big improvement that they are the logical first choice.

[26] The first method can be just as convincingly demonstrated as the second, but it is harder for the director to *be sure* that all students are obeying instructions.

fuller, yet forward and resonant, sound is needed in the choir. Other ways to open the jaws may be introduced from time to time to promote a broader concept of the importance of the relaxed jaw.

The psychological approach to opening the jaw can work almost as well as the physical approach. There are several of these approaches (imagining a ping-pong ball, a hot iron, or a marble in the throat, etc.). Probably the *soundest* psychological idea is to place an imaginary egg in each singer's mouth, big end at the back (at the soft palate) and the smaller end touching the bottom front teeth. Close the mouth around the egg. Get the feeling of this arrangement of space inside the mouth and sing all vowels this way (particularly bright vowels such as $\overline{ee}$ and ay). Be sure the tip of the tongue is down, loose, and forward.

A helpful technique, used by many voice teachers but also effective when used with groups, is to have the singers sing ah. Tell them to keep their jaws as though they were continuing to sing ah while they sing ah-ay-$\overline{ee}$-o-$\overline{oo}$. Let the *tongues* form the vowels, but keep the tips of the tongues down, forward, and relaxed. This exercise helps train singers to keep their jaws open and relaxed, and to know the sensation of *open jaw* while singing the smaller vowel forms.

The most used technique, and perhaps the least helpful, is to check with two fingers (forefinger and middle finger) between the teeth, even on the $\overline{ee}$ vowel. Turning the underside of the arm "away from" the body (middle finger on top, and lifting the elbow) will improve the singing posture as well as the jaw position. This technique works fine for a quick check to show singers that their jaws still are not open and relaxed; but it is impossible to sing in a normal way since fingers in mouths will stop resonance and obstruct tongues (also is not very sanitary).

One of the least effective techniques, but still worth mentioning, is to open the jaws and push dimples into the cheeks with the index fingers, shoving flesh into the jaw openings at the molars. Keep the jaws opened to this position while singing. The disadvantage of this method is the inability to sing words, for the flesh shoved between the teeth would become chewed to bits by the jaw movement. Vowel sounds, however, may be sung efficiently by this method.

The director must watch to see that the singers keep their chins relatively level. If singers duck their chins on low notes and raise them on high notes, they are straining for pitches and tensing muscles. As a temporary expedient for these students who are experiencing difficulty in keeping their chins level, tell them (individually) to deliberately lift their chins a little for low notes and duck them for high notes until correct vocalises and habits take over to help them sing correctly. Lifting heads forward and up may accomplish the same result.

As singers become more expert, they learn not to "jaw" every tone. Excessive jaw movement will distort the tonal line. For example, practice moving from $\overline{oo}$ to $\overline{ee}$ without changing the jaw-line, also moving from oh to ay.

The saggy faced "hangdog" look is a necessary step with most beginning singers in order to build correct habits of loose, relaxed jaws. From the very beginning, however, the teacher must realize that all really good singing artists have life in the upper part of their faces when performing. These singers use their *zygomatic muscles* (surrounding the zygomatic bones that form the prominence of the cheek). These are the smiling muscles, one of whose functions is to elevate and tighten the upper part of the face. If any object is inserted between the teeth and gently bitten on just enough to keep it in place, then if the bite increased a little, the action of the zygomatics will be felt just under the cheekbones. They have nothing to do with the movement of the jaw, whose action is controlled by a different system of muscles. The higher the pitch, the greater support is required. Singers must allow the fully relaxed jaws to drop open while firmness is retained in the walls of the cheeks.

Be careful that the upper lip is not pulled down so that the teeth are covered, regardless of the vowel that is sung. Inspire your singers to "look like the music" with the upper part of their faces when they sing. Have them "talk" with their eyes and not permit their cheeks to droop. (Bringing the eyes into play will assist in the realization of this ideal singing condition.)

To summarize, the good teacher must not give up until his students sing with relaxed jaws and until he obtains "spark" and "sparkle" from the eyes and faces of his students. These ends may not be accomplished by telling students to tighten certain muscles. They *may* be realized through the inspiration of music and the enthusiasm of the teacher, the singers singing the music as though it were words and music that they had written and in which they believed.

HUMMING

To hum correctly, sing *any* vowel and close the lips lightly, still singing the vowel inside. Sing with more power when the lips are closed (otherwise the sound will fade out of proportion to the vowel sounds before and after it). Be sure the jaw hangs long and loose at the back. Try the 'synovial cavity' technique mentioned in the previous section. *Fill* the mouth with sound. The singer should hum so that much buzz and vibration is felt in the frontal masque (the front of the face, nasal passages, and even the sinuses and forehead). The hum and ng are shortcuts to singing softly with control, ease, and vibrancy. It is also one of the best ways to help the untuned singer to hear pitch. (Since the voice is heard principally through the bone and muscles in the head, not through the air, closing the lips intensifies the singer's pitch sensation. It has an added advantage to a director in that this untuned voice is softer while it is struggling with pitch.)

The usual method of humming is "closed-mouth humming" just described. If more power is needed (the section is too small, or some similar reason), use the open mouth with n. If still more power is required, have the section or sections sing oo. For various colors in humming, try having the choir sing, with lips closed, ee, ah, o, oo, or ay. Each of these hums will have a different basic sound that may be especially effective on a particular passage.

To obtain an easy, floating voice quality, base it upon the hum:

> Begin a long tone on "ng." It may be necessary to start with "hung" or "sing" for students to find the "ng" position with the tongue. Now let the back of the tongue come down the slightest amount possible so that an infinitesimal amount of tone can flow between the top of the mouth and the arch of the tongue, and sing "win-win-win-win" on a starting pitch of g′. The singers should attempt to sing a unison that sounds like one continuous hummed tone, even though words are being carefully pronounced.

> Try to become conscious of a feeling of pressure inside the front of the face (nose, forehead, sinuses, etc.). After this feeling is obtained, attempt to augment it. That sensation of pressure is very helpful in obtaining correct tone placement.

> Replace the vowel found in "win-win" by eh, ay, ah, oo, and oh, for example, "woon, woon," etc.

> As another exercise sing "linga-linga-linga-linga" or "zinga-zinga-zinga-zinga" or "vinga-vinga-vinga-vinga." All vowels (ay, ee, ah, o, oo) may be used to assist with this new humming exercise.

> Have the singers try out their new-found skill by singing the words of a number that *requires* this hummy, floaty quality for correct interpretation, for example, "The Island" by Rachmaninoff.

Moving Tone

Singers must always keep tones alive and traveling somewhere. Remember, air pressure is to vocal tone as a bow is to a violin's sound. If the bow stops, the violin will no longer speak. If the air pressure stops, vocal tone can no longer sound. As the air pressure fades away, the lack of support will cause the tone to go flat. Many singers have unconsciously absorbed the percussive quality of the piano, the initial "hit" and steady fading thereafter. Good singing is ordinarily *legato* singing, not staccato or percussive. To keep the tone from hitting and fading there normally must be a feeling of moving or swelling any tone of a dotted quarter or longer. (The speed of the music will naturally determine exactly how long that note will be.) Singers must not allow tones to become thin or uninteresting, which will happen if they simply hang onto notes and wait for them to end. The audience will be as bored as the singers must be to permit such tones to exist. *Make* the audience listen by keeping tones vital. Employment of rolling tones and vibrato will help keep life in the voices. *Never drive* the voice. Never sing louder than lovely. When singers sing very loudly voices are liable to straighten out and become harsh in quality. Vocalists must feel that they can still sing five to ten percent louder, even when singing *ff*. This will give added polish and control, will avoid strain, and will add a margin of safety and power if it is needed. As singers increase volume, they think bigger and deeper tones and automatically make more space for the tones to occur. Think small vowels (little space) when singing softly, big vowels (much space) when singing loudly. Singers must not forget to use extra support on soft passages.

Legato singing takes a smooth, continuous action of the abdomen and diaphragm. Runs require the same kind of action from the breath control organs as is necessary in staccato singing (use a panting or laughing type of action).

5

Vocal Fundamentals, Continued

INTONATION

Faulty intonation is one of the biggest problems in choral singing. Singing out of tune creates noise, not music. It is extremely important that groups and soloists sing beautifully in tune. There are so many pitfalls in reaching perfect pitch that it is amazing that anyone comes even close to attaining it.

Let us consider the limitations of the human voice. Considered as an instrument, it is smaller in power than some instruments, often less beautiful than the tones of the violin. It does not have the capacity for accuracy or nicety of tone that other instruments have; we tolerate a singer's being off key to a far greater degree than we would a violinist's deviation from true pitch. A voice covers only a limited range, compared with a piano, organ, or symphony orchestra. It is far from agile; rapid runs and skips, which any piano student can play with ease, are next to impossible for even the best singer, and when accomplished by a virtuoso coloratura soprano, arouse audiences to incredulous oh's and ah's. The cellist has an instrument that is perfectly adjusted, ready to play. The human instrument is apt to be affected adversely by poor posture, poorly placed tone, improper breathing, and many other physical factors. Voices are subject to catarrhal complaints and other indispositions to which inanimate objects are not subject. Vowels and consonants cause this instrument extra difficulties in sustaining a beautiful legato and in intonation.

The choral director must always be aware of any pitch inaccuracy. Immediately analyze the discord and decide where it happened (the chord and the voice part that was out of tune) and what caused the intonation difficulty, and prescribe the appropriate remedy quickly and efficiently.

If flatting or sharping is caused by acoustical mistakes made by the architect in the rehearsal room, the director can request the addition of Sound-tex or hard-surfaced materials to partially remedy those defects. Acoustical and atmospheric conditions are beyond the control of the performers when a program is being sung, but the director and singers can do certain things to partially counteract pitch problems.

The Effect of Acoustics on Pitch

Too much echo in the room, caused by hard surfaces (windows, hard walls, etc.) will result in sharping. In overly live rooms, avoid singing the music at too fast a tempo or sharping will result. Absorption of tones by the surroundings (drapes, rugs, large audience etc.) will tend to cause flatting. As a general rule, avoid singing the music slowly in this type of room, or pitch will suffer.

The Effect of Atmospheric Conditions upon Pitch

Humidity in the atmosphere has a depressive effect. Singers will flat because, instead of feeling perky and vital, they feel emotionally depressed and lacking in vitality. Lack of oxygen (poor ventilation) in the rehearsal or performance hall will cause flatting. Stale air causes a choral group to sag physically and vocally. Extreme heat will also sap a group's energy and will cause flatting.

To counteract these three problems, the director must direct with extra vitality; use quick moving, cheerful songs in major tonalities; and be sure the singers are breathing extra deeply and using excellent posture.

The Relationship of Correctly-Produced Tones to Intonation

Accurate intonation is basically dependent upon correctly produced tones properly supported by the breath. Incorrect tone quality and production may block the hearing of the singer so he or she will sing sharp or flat without being aware of it. If the tonal production is in any way out of balance, the resultant tone may suffer in pitch and quality. For this reason, the experienced voice teacher, hearing a musical student sing out of tune, will immediately suspect faulty tone production as the villain. Christy states:

> Some who rate high on native capacity in pitch tests, and are highly sensitive to off-pitch singing when listening to others, nevertheless sing out-of-tune atrociously and are apparently unaware of this error. As a rule in such cases, when production difficulty is corrected, intonation is greatly improved. Nevertheless, ability to hear their own voices varies greatly from student to student, and most pupils need assistance in learning how to think and hear the more difficult intervals accurately. Singers sometimes have only one area or 'island' of two or three tones that are sung off-pitch habitually. This occurrence is most frequent on the several notes just below where 'head registration' begins. It normally is corrected by more generous breath support and proper concepts of free and balanced resonation.[1]

This out-of-tune segment is most apt to occur in the soprano voice, and it happens often enough not to be unusual. The tones referred to are just below the top lift in the voice down to the next lift: c″ or d″ up to f″ or f″-sharp (see the vocal color chart).

Exercises at the beginning of the period, warming up the voice, and tuning up the ear will help intonation. The quality of tone will suffer if intonation is poor. Furthermore, tone must spin and must always be thought of as "on top" of the pitch, or the voice will sound out of tune to the listener. If the period is early in the day, warming up the voice (especially the male voice) is essential.

Pitches will be in tune when the vocalist mentally hears the correct pitch *before* singing it, when the sound has enough breath pressure to resonate properly, when all muscular interference is eliminated, and when good diction is used. Working for a focused tone, hummy, with a forward placement will enable singers to hear and sing pitch more accurately.

Problems in placement will be cased by rigidity of the base of the tongue, lips, jaws, chest, or pharynx; by not using enough breath pressure to make the vowel forms resonant; by failure to open the jaw enough (modify the vowel) in the high register; by using too large a vowel form in the low voice register; by failure to use pure phonetic sounds whenever possible and allowing the vowels to be "chewed"; by fear of high notes, or singing high with a heavy chest quality (to correct, have the student sing more like a tenor or soprano but with the jaw open at the back on high notes); by yawny tone production (have the student sing in the frontal masque); and by singing loudly with too heavy a tone quality. The last three errors will cause flatting. For further insight concerning the curing of poorly placed tones (excessive vibrato, straight tone, etc.), see the rest of this chapter and the entire section on "Causes, Cures, and Cautions." In

---

[1] Van A. Christy, *Expressive Singing*, vol. 2 (Dubuque, Iowa: Wm. C. Brown Company, Publishers, 1961), p. 88.

order to be completely safe concerning pitch accuracy, one must develop an accurate concept of the way one's voice sounds to others.

Physiological Factors in Weak Intonation

Physical fatigue is another cause of problems in placement. Fatigue is caused by physical labor, poor physical condition (basic lack of physical vitality, weak body not able to hold up under anything that demands endurance), poor posture (even in a good body), muscle tension, shallow breathing (causing the singer to run low on breath and go flat), poor tone placement (too yawny a tone, for example, will cause the throat to ache, and too small a vowel form on high pitches will cause a tight throat), unsuitable tessituras (see "Worn Musical Groove," page 112), or laziness. Wrong classification of voices will lead to many difficulties in pitch, quality, blend, balance, and so on, so classify voices frequently, especially in junior high. The problem of a musical phrase that is too sustained and demanding for a singer's technique at a particular stage of development may be alleviated by staggered breathing. Singing too powerfully or too long will cause problems, particularly with junior high or undeveloped senior high voices.

The teacher of students who are lazy, tired, or not breathing deeply enough must convince the choir of the necessity of assuming good posture and breathing deeply. Breath control exercises used regularly in class will help build bodies, breath, and posture. For correction of tense muscles and poor tone placement generally, see the section on "Catechism of Vocal Problems."

The Relationship of Dynamics to Pitch

Too much muscular tension in the abdomen or diaphragm, caused by singing too loudly, trying too hard, excitement, or anxiety (fear) will cause sharping. Young sopranos under tension are particularly apt to sharp because of this lack of poise. Have the singer sing on top of the tone, instead of pushing it, and deepen the tone so it will roll out. Using more breath pressure than the young singer is able to control at this stage of technical development will cause sharping. To correct this, reduce the volume by one dynamic.

Singing loudly with too heavy a tone quality (the so-called *chest voice*) will result in flatting. Have the singer lighten the tone quality and reduce the volume.

Pianissimo singing will tend to lack vitality and will be apt to go flat. Good soft singing, with a resonant sound, takes a more highly developed technique than is required for *forte* singing. A singer cannot sing a forte without supporting to some extent. To correct flat and breathy soft singing *use extra support*. Work for increased resonance and vitality in the tone.

Be sure the ribs are kept expanded (use the exercises suggested to obtain better breath control).

It is always more essential to obtain accurate pitch and good tone quality than it is to obtain overpowering louds and softs. However, do make as much contrast as is possible. If the valleys are deep enough, the hills will seem like mountains.

Within choir sections, varying dynamic levels of individual voices may be a problem. A good singer, who is aware of a section's deficiencies may sing louder in order to help intonation. If the singing is powerful enough that a voice "sticks out," intonation will actually suffer because pitch and color will not be uniform. This same result can happen with a soloist who sings with a full solo quality in a section that is lying down on the job. Inspire and work with the entire section until the other singers carry their share of the load, at which time the good singer can feel free to ease up a little and blend into the part.

Don't rehearse loud passages continually at their full dynamic—it may tire the voices (but beware of *sotto voce* to save voices, it is much better to use *mf* to avoid voice strain).

When drilling notes, rhythms, etc. on long and high passages, rehearse them an octave lower to prevent strain on the voices.

The Relationship of Lack of Mental Alertness to Intonation

A student's attention will wander to other parts, usually the melody part, when the singer is attempting to negotiate a harmony part; when the other parts are moving higher than the line he is supposed to sing; for example:

the f ' may tend to move higher in sympathy with the moving note and will slide sharp; and when other parts are moving in a downward direction, for example:

f ' will tend to slide flat.

Lack of mental alertness will also cause flatness, carelessness, or inattentiveness to pitch; vowels and consonants will be sung indistinctly, without vitality; and precision and breath support will be lacking.

The director must rouse singers to wakefulness. Do such things as: move the key of the number up or down or change activities or songs; sing a quick-moving bouncy number; be erratic with the beat pattern; call for crescendos where there aren't any, etc.; sing the number staccato style with words, or sing the number with "Pah" for precision; have the group stand and stretch, or sit down if it is standing; move the group (if a top outfit) from a regular seating position to mixed seating to challenge it; work with deep breathing exercises, posture exercises, vowel and consonant exercises; tell a funny, appropriate joke; or do any of many other activities that will startle or wake the group into alert participation.

The Effect Inability to Hear Mentally Has upon Intonation

To sing in tune, every singer must hear mentally every pitch *before* singing it. Failure to do so causes careless singing, poor intonation, and inaccurate attacks. There is no true sight-reading of music without this skill, for otherwise the singer is simply copying the piano pitch (after it is heard) or someone else's pitch (after it is heard), and the singer only needs to remember *one tone* at a time.

As an exercise have the choir members engage in silent practice: Have them stop singing at a given signal, sing silently, then sing on the pitch that follows what they have been singing silently (use a song they are sure to know, such as "America" or "Home on the Range").

A singer can be a leader in a section only if he or she can mentally hear the pitch ahead of its utterance. Singing mentally is one of the most important skills to cultivate for accomplished musicianship.

Continuous use of the piano will hide intonation problems. Neither singers nor director can hear mistakes as clearly when the piano is sounding, and students become aurally dependent upon the piano. Therefore, rehearse without accompaniment whenever possible. This forces the group to use some degree of mental hearing. A cappella singing will reveal mistakes that the piano covered; will create better blend and balance in the group, because the singers will be listening to the chord instead of the piano; and will force the choir to watch the director more carefully, since the conductor, instead of the piano, is the creator of rhythms.

Even when the number being rehearsed requires accompaniment, the number will not be truly learned until the group can sing it well without the assistance of the piano. The group *must hear mentally* instead of depending upon the piano to give the pitches. When a number is this thoroughly rehearsed, the accompanist may even make an occasional mistake and the group will stay in tune.

The singer must sing slurred notes smoothly and connectedly, but without sliding. Tell the vocalist to imagine the tone going neither up nor down on the note following, and to progress to the next note without anticipation of pitch. If the singer does anticipate, the resultant tone will be out of tune *while* the pitch is *sliding*. For a singer to sing as a real professional chorister might sing, have the choralist visualize putting pegs in a peg-board or walking all the way over to the other corner of the room (with the pitch remaining exactly in tune) before sitting down in the chair (on the next pitch). In order to accomplish this result, the singer must *mentally think the new pitch while staying exactly in tune on the old pitch*.

See Chapter 6 for many additional suggestions on ways to improve students' mental hearing.

The Scale

The evolution of the scale should be considered briefly in order to understand intonation.

The three scale systems of particular interest are the Pythagorean scale, the just or natural scale, and the equal-tempered scale.

Good orchestra and a cappella choral groups still use slight pitch deviations that bear a remarkable resemblance to the Pythagorean scale (developed by Pythagoras around 600 B.C.). Characteristics of this scale pattern are the highest leading tone of the three scales, the highest major third of the three scales, small semi-tones, and flats lower than enharmonic sharps (B♭ lower than A♯), resulting in the greater contrast of dark and bright tone colors.

Didymus (30 B.C.), and later Ptolemy (A.D. 150), were instrumental in developing the just scale. Distinctive features that mark this pattern are the lowest leading tone (causing the tones to be lusterless), low major thirds and sixths, and a dulling of contrasts by making flats higher than enharmonic sharps (B♭ higher than A♯).

The modern piano keyboard illustrates the equal-tempered scale. The octave is composed of twelve equal semi-tones (of great advantage in free modulation). This scale pattern assumes about a middle position between the other two scales. It is a common thing to hear choirs who "sing like pianos." Not only do they hit and fade on notes, emulating the percussive quality of the keyboard instrument, but they also fail to hear and sing the purer harmony of the Pythagorean scale. This results in drab, dull tone color and lack of contrast between major and minor.[2]

The purist might insist that the scale used in a particular period should be used when music of that historical era is sung. This is not practicable when working with junior high and high school youngsters. It is doubtful that even a professional organization could sing a program moving from one scale to the other.

A comparison of the logarithm values for diatonic intervals is very interesting.[3] Following is an interesting side-by-side look at the Pythagorean

---

[2]Lawrence A. Hanley, "Some Factors of Scale Usage and Interval Adjustment Affecting Ensemble Intonation Practices in Music Education" (unpublished Doctoral dissertation, University of Colorado, Boulder, Colorado, 1951).

[3]*Ibid.* Hanley's comparison involves all three scales, but only two are used here.

scale (whose basic characteristics are being advocated in this book) and the equal-tempered scale.[4]

Dr. Hanley states that auditory discrimination has been found to measure, on the average, about one-tenth of a half-tone in the middle of the hearing range. He goes on to say that it is safe to state that aural perception is such as to take in the spread involved in the differences noted above.[5] The ability to *match* pitches lags considerably behind aural perception. This discrepancy is of serious concern to the choral director.

The director must cultivate an awareness of slight pitch deviations

Table Comparing the Logarithm Values for Diatonic
Intervals in the Pythagorean and Equal-Tempered Scales[6]

INTERVALS	PYTHAGOREAN	EQUAL-TEMPERED	WHAT THIS MEANS TO THE SINGER
Major 2nd	.05115	.05018	The Major 2nd must be sung higher than the piano sounds.
Major 3rd	.10230	.10036	Raised even more above the piano. *Note:* This is the third of the I chord and the major scale. (Also the leading tone in the lower tetrachord.)
Perfect 4th	.12493	.12545	The 4th is sung flatter than the piano sounds. The raised 3rd and flatted 4th makes these pitches very close together.
Perfect 5th	.17608	.17553	Sung only slightly above the keyboard pitch.
Major 6th	.22723	.22571	Raised much above the piano sound. *Note:* This is the 3rd of the IV chord.
Major 7th	.27838	.27554	Lifted so it is very close to 8. Remember, *8* is at the same pitch point in both scales. *Note:* This is the 3rd of the V chord, and the leading tone of the major scale.

[4]For an interesting discussion of *temperament*, and the Pythagorean ratios used by Dr. Hanley to figure the logarithm values, see J.A. Westrup and L.I. Harrison, *The New College Encyclopedia of Music* (New York: W.W. Norton & Company, Inc., 1960), pp. 650, 651.

[5]Hanley, *op cit.*

[6]*Ibid.* The comments are mine.

that resemble those in the Pythagorean scale whenever they occur in the music, and anticipate and correct any pitch vagrancy.

Keeping in mind the Pythagorean scale pattern, the conductor will know that sharping will occur if the perfect fourth of the scale is not flatted; if the octave is not sung exactly in tune (if the singer is not careful, too great a space will be allowed to exist between the leading tone and the octave, with resultant sharping); and if the minor seventh of the scale is not lowered. Remember the flats are lower than enharmonic sharps in the scale advocated.

Any special ♯, ♭, or ♮ signs in a song call for even more treatment than the same signs in the signature would. Such signs, called *accidentals*, throw the song temporarily out of the key and into a new key. This calls for more change of pitch than the sharps or flats represented in the key signature, so the voice must sing higher for the ♯ sign and lower for the ♭ sign than would seem natural for the original key. (The ♮ sign may be flatter *or* sharper, depending upon the key.) Carry out this pitch change courageously, for without the higher or lower pitch, the key change will not come through to the listeners, and the audience may think a mistake was made. So, singers will sharp if they do not deliberately sing lower whenever a flatted accidental occurs. Particular places to watch are the third of a minor chord and the diminished seventh of any chord.

Flatting will be caused if the third of a major scale is not sung very high (the third is the leading tone for its part of the tetrachord); if the third of any major chord is not sharped; if the leading tone of a scale is not sung very high (the leading tone is also the third of the V chord); if the sixth note of a scale is not somewhat raised (the sixth is also the third of the IV chord); and if the major second is not sung as a big step. Also remember that singers will flat anytime they do not deliberately sing extra high whenever a sharped accidental occurs.

The top note of an ascending melody will flat unless there is continued support and a feeling of "singing on top" of the note. Any interval leaping from the medium part of the voice into the top must be sung meticulously in tune on the top note. A melody that descends and then turns upward will flat on the upturned note unless the note is sung "high."

Condition the singers to always take big steps on top of notes on ascending passages. Suggest to the singers that singing is like a person walking up stairsteps; the mental "pitch-picture" is over and on top of the note, just as the foot must swing over and on top of the step or the walker will stub a toe and fall down (flat the pitch). For even more vivid imagery, suggest walking upstairs "in the dark."

Singers habitually make descending intervals too large. To correct this tendency, which is a natural result of laziness, tell the students to step (sing) as carefully and lightly as if they were walking on ice. Imagine the carefulness that must be exercised when walking downstairs "in the dark."

All jumps downward, especially the drop of the fifth in the basses, will be flat on the lower note, unless that note is thought "high" and is supported. (Singers will just "let go" because they feel no effort is necessary.) The bottom note of a descending minor third is also very troublesome.

Recurring intervals in sequence will tend to flat through singers' carelessness on repetitions of those notes. Whenever possible avoid monotony by making dynamic variations to sustain interest, and, if necessary, also warn the students to be careful that succeeding pitches must stay exactly in tune.

Dipping on repeated notes will cause flatting. Each time the singer starts to sing a new note and has to tune it up, the pitch will be a little flatter. To correct this flaw and that of scooping of attacks, be sure tuned and subvocal consonants are sung in tune and that other consonants and all vowels are sung with precision. Staccato singing helps to cure scooping. (Even better use "Tah," "Pah," or "Too.") The singer is forced to begin in the middle of the pitch because there is no time to adjust, and the pitch must be mentally heard ahead of its utterance. There is no place to hide. (See pages 89–95 for more precise information concerning the handling of consonants.)

Sustained tones tend to flat. The director must sense the correct tempo of the number being performed so that the *flow* of the music may always be felt by the singers; otherwise, pitch will "sag" as the music "drags." Keep the tone supported, vibrant, and alive throughout its duration and the pitch is more likely to remain in tune. The process of keeping a pure phonetic sound for the duration of the tone and ending with precision is always important, but it is *essential* with sustained phrases. Even if all of the above suggestions are observed, many other items (to be discussed in the next few pages) could cause flatting or sharping.

A singer, after a period of practicing the scale, will ultimately build a sensory perception for each scale step. The sensory perception can eventually be trusted to be quite accurate, at which time we may say the singer has good relative sense of pitch. The violinist who always tunes to a′ may eventually establish "perfect pitch" on a′. A few students acquire "perfect" or "absolute" pitch on all notes. The student cannot make scale jumps with accuracy unless they are heard accurately, and this also involves sensory perception. The sensory perception needed for singing the minor mode accurately cannot be established without practice and experience in it.

Director's Quick-Reminder List:

1. Remind singers to take small steps on all half steps (which are usually leading tones or thirds of scales). This is a major cause of flatting.
2. Train your group to habitually take big steps when going up the scale and small, light steps when coming down the scale.

3. Take care on all downward leaps. Think them high and supported.

4. Sing all out-of-the-key accidentals extra high or low.

5. When a note sequence descends and then turns upward, the upturned note must be thought high.

6. Recurring intervals in sequence must be sung carefully in tune.

7. Repeated notes and sustained notes or phrases must be sung with vitality through the consonants and vowels. Don't allow scooping.

8. Unaccented syllables, consonants, and the last note of a phrase need special care (see the section on moving tone).

The Worn Musical Groove

Raising the pitch of a selection by a half step will usually snap the choir out of the "worn musical groove" and will result in better intonation. Occasionally, lowering the pitch will accomplish the same result, particularly if the song is moved from a flat key to a sharp key. One result of the practice is to almost always cancel the effect of "key-monotony" induced through long practicing in one key, and to bring about a fresh mood. Slow music, particularly, may be vitalized by this procedure.

If the tessitura of one or more of the voice parts lies consistently at the "lift," moving a half step up or down will ease the strain on that part and probably stabilize the pitch of the entire choir. However, raising a song a half step may result in too much brilliance or strain on some voices, and lowering it a half step may produce dullness and deadness. Only experimentation by the director will determine the best method. However, it may also happen that the original key of the song is wrong (too high or too low) for the most favorable tessitura. If this is the case, moving to another key may solve the problem. One choral director who has perfect pitch has solved the problem by singing songs out of key the day of the performance and then in the key at the performance. This causes only temporary discomfort.

If it disturbs you as a conductor to move into a key other than the original, remember that the vibrations per second of a' have fluctuated throughout the centuries. Pitch gradually rose from Bach's time, until in 1859 the Congress of Vienna set A above middle C at 435 vibrations per second. It wasn't until the twentieth century that 440 became the standard. Many orchestras, requiring a high third and seventh, request pianos to be tuned to 442 or higher. Knowing about these pitch changes should set your conscience at ease.

The conductor must be careful that two numbers are not programmed in the same or related keys immediately together in a concert. When no key relief is afforded the singers for some length of time, some degree of tonal deafness may occur. The director may cause the same problem to occur in rehearsal by staying in the same keys (or on the same number) too long, with resultant flatting.

Defective Hearing

According to Seashore, a poor ear can be insensitive to pitch differences as large or larger than a semitone. On the other hand, the average person can hear pitch deviations as small as one seventeenth of a tone, and those of superior acuteness may be able to detect one-one hundredth of a tone or less. With the exception of very few persons, everyone has the native capacity to sing fairly well on pitch.[7]

According to some authorities, only one percent of all people are actually tone deaf.

A student can have something physically wrong (for example, a severe hearing loss in a particular frequency range) and still sing well in tune, *if* trained to match any audible pitches, and sing the remainder of time on the pitches heard mentally. This process is similar to the strong vocalist singing a solo with the church organ as an accompaniment. The organ will blend with the voice whenever the vocalist is singing, and the singer will only be able to hear and check on accuracy of intonation when the singing stops. The rest of the time the singer must rely completely upon mental hearing. It has been this author's pleasure to have trained a number of singers with serious pitch losses who have won the highest honors in district competition. (One even won the distinction of "Outstanding Vocalist" in district competition.)

Poor Musicianship and its Effects upon Intonation

The singer who is not a good enough musician to realize the demands of the whole phrase will not have enough foresight to inhale the proper amount of air, so will probably take too much breath and waste it, or take too little breath and run out.

Lack of musicianship will usually cause a singer to be afraid to sing out and to be afraid of high notes, and there will be tight throat, tense tongue, not enough breath, and other similar problems caused by this fear.

To remedy the difficulty of adjusting for high or low notes tell the singers to look ahead and see the whole phrase at a glance and adjust their voices for the note hardest to manage before beginning the phrase.

Endeavor to teach the students to watch all parts while reading music. The really valuable member of this big team called a "choir" is the person who keeps one eye on what is supposed to happen in the other staves of the music as well as what is supposed to happen in the singer's own part. By doing this, the vocalist can fit into the harmony better. If there is a piano part, the chorister catches the beginning pitch from the piano, etc. The student who is not a good enough musician to do these things will have many intonation problems that would be absent if this musicianship were present.

[7] Christy, *Expressive Singing*, p. 87.

It is a good technique to expect your singers to call attention to mistakes they hear in their parts. Often, individuals within a section still have trouble with their part after enough of the other choristers have learned it so that it sounds all right to the director at the front of the room. Also, if students know they will be asked to ferret out pitch deviations, they will listen much more critically, and better student musicianship will result over a period of time.

It is important for all singers to learn their parts as quickly as possible, for a memorized song will be sung with more freedom and, consequently, better in tune. If is even more important that the poor musician memorize quickly.

The inadequate musician will articulate carelessly. This will cause poor diction and faulty intonation (see the sections on vowels and consonants for reasons and solutions).

The weak musician will not be alert enough to hear each pitch mentally before its utterance. (See the section on mental hearing for other insights on this problem. See also Chapter 6.)

The Effect of Lack of Confidence on Intonation

Even in a good musician, lack of confidence will cause nervous or tense inhalation; rigidity of tongue base, lips, pharynx, jaw, or chest; failure to use enough breath support to free the tone and resonate the vowels properly; self-consciousness; fear of high notes; failure to inhale enough breath for the demands of a phrase; careless articulation; the habit of dependence on the piano; inertia; or lack of familiarity with music.

The Problem of the "Untuned" or "Inaccurate" Singer

This problem is caused by lack of coordination of the vocal muscles; by an insufficient musical background; by inattention to pitch; by lack of interest; by a psychological block (resulting from a teacher or parent telling the child he or she can't sing); or physical disabilities (particularly defective hearing).

The teacher will strive to stimulate the student's desire to improve and to want to listen to others and try to imitate their pitches, and will make music activities interesting enough that there is eagerness to participate in them. Unless a student is completely tone deaf physically, which is very rare, a teacher can greatly improve *anyone* who is willing to work to become skillful in the ability to hear accurately.

Place the inaccurate vocalist in the midst of good singers, but occasionally move either the untuned vocalist or the good singers, since it may become extremely annoying to the good singers to have to "fight" the inaccurate pitches. The humming tone is one of the best ways to hear pitch.

The buzz (z or v) is almost as helpful. Be sure the key and rhythm of the song are established and in the student's mind before singing commences. Insist on correct posture and breathing (use the exercises mentioned earlier to obtain it), for the human body is the vocal instrument and it must be treated properly so that it will produce accurate tones. Tensions will make it inaccurate. Physical exercises, such as the breathing exercises discussed earlier, will not only keep the body expanded but will also assist the student to go high with the voice as hands go high. An excellent exercise is to have the student speak "1234561," starting low and speaking as high as possible at 4, then going back down on 1. Follow this by singing "1234561," using the tonic arpeggio up and down and singing as easily as when talking. (This is also one of the best exercises to attain range with any singers.)

Use the various suggestions for improving pitch that are mentioned earlier in this section on intonation.

Inability to hear pitch mentally is the most obvious fault of the inaccurate singer. Refer to Chapter 6 for many suggestions on ways to improve student's abilities to hear mentally.

The young man whose voice changes quite rapidly will nearly always have a real pitch problem for a while, because his vocal muscles do not coordinate. The teacher must help him make that adjustment and must keep him from feeling too "different" or too "self-conscious" because of his lack of coordination. When the instructor works individually with this boy, or with any other "untuned singer," it may be necessary to go to the pitch of the student if he is unable to come to the indicated pitch, then move him up or down from "his" tone, perhaps even sing the melody in "his" key. If a vowel is used, use o͞o on the ascending scale (not ah). The vowel o͞o will almost force the voice to go into the head. Ah becomes louder and louder and will almost always stay in the heavy, chest voice. Work the "head voice" with o͞o down through to the lower voice. Add "weight" as the tone descends.

Some other suggestions that may help these students with pitch follow.

Sing and sustain the beginning pitch of a song until everyone has it. Use many songs with a limited number of tones, like "Jingle Bells," and parts that only move to I, IV, and V, with repeated words and tones. It might be necessary to rewrite some parts.

Don't allow students to drone away below pitch; it becomes more and more difficult to teach these youngsters voice flexibility. Provide assistance on a daily basis, if possible. It doesn't take long for every student to sing the first two notes of the bass line (or any line) accurately.

Punching a young man's diaphragm, or pretending that you are going to punch it, may help him to feel enough strength to support his tone.

This device appeals to his feeling of masculinity and strength. Use his pride in his manliness to help him to get strength into his body and into his singing. (Remember to use the breath control exercises, mentioned earlier, to keep bodies expanded and strong.)

A teacher may move a book up and down the student's spine to help the student move the voice up and down.

Let the student imagine lifting heavy weights from a squatting position (low tone) to a standing position (high tone). This imaginary weight-lifting will make breath-support muscles strong enough to support the tone.

Have the student stand behind the piano and put hands on the sound board to feel the pitch vibration, then match these sound vibrations with the voice.

Have the student put an index finger just inside the mouth, pointing at and touching the roof of the mouth. This may psychologically assist the student to *focus* tones. Have the singer imagine the tone is focused at the point where the finger touches.

The director moves a hand up and down in conformance with the melody line and has the singer also draw the melody line in the air while singing.

Have the student play the piano and try to match the tones with the voice. Have the student tune a violin, guitar, or whatever instrument is available and try to match the instrument's pitches.

Have the student match pitch by whistling.

Have the student simulate a siren. The siren moves up or down until it crosses the pitchpath of the note the student is tuning to, then signal the siren to stop.

Ask the student to "tune in" the pitch beam you are sending. Let the ear tune it in, then the voice, and then with the voice come in for a safe landing (radio, T.V., supersonic beams, etc. may be used for this kind of analogy).

Ask the student to try to hit the pitch target with his voice as accurately as he would try to pass a football to the receiver down field. (Other analogies: arch the voice into the pitch as you would arch a basketball into the basket; hit the center of the pitch with your voice as you would try to hit the center of the target in any marksmanship contest.)

Set up a record of the untuned voices in each class and see how many voices can be improved each week until all voices are "tuned." The class will cooperate wholeheartedly in such an undertaking. This can be made a real challenge to a student to learn to control voice muscles as well as arm and leg muscles. It is easy to point out that being a "vocal cripple" is as real a disadvantage in life as being a physical weakling or needing to use a cane. Students will feel great satisfaction in gaining control of their voices.

CATECHISM OF VOCAL PROBLEMS

Causes, Cures, and Cautions

Too Hollow, Throaty, Yawny, or Dark

Some choral directors teach their choirs to use the "overly dark" tone quality. This placement will give a false maturity to the voices that may sound great to the public, but will result in voice damage to the youngsters over a period of time. Dark quality has the added dangerous advantage of causing all voices to sound alike, and thus blend is achieved effortlessly. (The director *should* stimulate the minds and imaginations of the singers to sing individual words, phrases, or even songs with dark color when the words or music are best expressed by that vocal color. However, the basic tone must be kept a bright, full, forward placement.) "Ring" or "resonance" must be developed. Make frequent use of $\overline{ee}$ and ay to bring the tone placement forward. Sing all the vowels with the tongue as much in the position for $\overline{ee}$ as is possible (perhaps the thought of the back of the tongue almost touching the back teeth will help keep it there). The voice instructor who investigates the cause of the dark sound will find that the tip of the tongue is very likely to be pulled back. Allow the tongue to relax and come forward into its normal vowel position. Start the $\overline{ee}$ with "ng," k, or hard g, and let the back of the tongue come down the smallest amount possible. Work the "ng" and the "hhm," keeping the hum in the voice during vowels also (feel the pressure in the frontal masque of the face). Use "um-huh" like you really mean it. Vocalize with "ve," "ze," or "mah" to pull out dark tones.

Too Covered

Teeth, lips, and jaws are too closed. Drop the jaw open. Put at least two fingers between the teeth. Everyone has a different jaw depth, but the jaw must be relaxed and open enough so the tone is not muted. The tip of the tongue pulled back will sometimes cause the tone to sound covered.

Hooty Tone

Caused by too much yawn in the tone with no vibrato. Avoid dark vowel sounds, particularly $\overline{oo}$, sing lots of $\overline{ee}$, ay, and bright ah. Smile.

Straight Tone

One school of thought in choral directing teaches the repression of natural vibrato and attempts to eliminate it (for an "instrumental" blend). This is most unwise. Well-produced voices will blend beautifully (however, any voices with the "too-large" vibrato need to *be corrected*). It is very difficult to produce a tone with *no* vibrato without tensing or restricting in some manner, and the tension in the vocal membranes and ligaments will interfere with normal vocal production. A well-placed tone *must* have vibrato (which is the very basis of "warmth" and "life" in a voice). To treat this problem, simply work for a free, well-placed voice. For treatment of other problems that may cause or be caused by straight tone, see "Hooty Tone," "Inability to Sing Softly," "Hard Tone," "Pinched Tone," "Shrill Tone," "Tight Jaw," and "Cold, Uninteresting Tone" discussed in this section.

Inability to Sing Softly

The singer's voice is almost bound to be strained if the vocalist can't sing softly. Don't try to sing bigger and bigger as the pitch goes higher; instead, "lighten up" and open the jaw at the back. Work from "ng" and hum. Use $\overline{oo}$ in the upper part of the voice (this almost forces the voice to lighten and go into the head). Think down as the voice moves up. Use high, downward-sliding whines on n to feel the high, light tones. Use staccato exercises.

Hard Tone

Caused by too much effort. To cure, support harder (that is, keep the ribs out), but sing more easily. Work with "ng" to get the feel of the tone spinning. "Hung" or "sing" helps singers get to the "ng." Be sure the jaw is loose. Use staccato exercises to keep muscles from becoming set. Have the singer bend over and sing easily. If the neck feels tense and set, move the head from side-to-side to relax the neck.

Pinched Tone

Arch the back of the mouth at the soft palate, as though holding an egg inside the mouth, big end at the back of the mouth.

Shrill Tone

Use the jaw position of $\overline{oo}$ or o for the vowels, especially bright sounds and high pitches. Shape the lips somewhat like a megaphone on $\overline{oo}$ and o. Singing the darker vowels will help the tones to round out.

Tremolo

This is a very common fault among singers, which seems to retrogress until its extreme in taste is found among older sopranos in church choirs. It is an uncontrolled sound caused by uncoordination and muscular tension and may be unaesthetic in timbre, intensity, pitch, or any combination of the three elements. The vibrato of a good singer has a regular and smooth variation of about six or seven times a second in the above three variables; and the further a singer's voice deviates from this norm, the worse the tremolo sounds to an audience. Any singer with a tremolo is the bane of a director's existence, for his or her voice *will not blend* with other voices.

Improper breath support will cause a voice to tremble and shake, so work for proper breath support and the power will come smoothly and evenly.

Insist upon good posture. The body being out of balance (especially the head and chin) will *cause* tremolo to occur.

The bleating sound of a tremolo that is too fast is caused by high larynx.

A tremolo that is too slow is caused by pressure on the larynx *or* the tongue, making these organs move slowly. Use "ng," m, or n to drop the velum and relax the swallowing muscles. Work for correct placement of tone. The more nearly correct the tone, breath, and posture, the more pressure is taken off the tongue and larynx and the more normal the singing becomes.

Insist that the singer concentrate upon the center of the pitch and not allow the tone to have a wide pitch variance.

Tight Jaw

Beware of tight, closed jaws, clenched teeth, and exaggerated grin (especially on e̅e̅). All the mellowness will be cut out of the tone. Have teeth at least one finger apart, usually more. It is impossible to have a properly placed tone if the jaw is tense. Students with this trouble are likely to also lift the chin and stretch and tighten the neck. Work with posture until these individuals get their chins level and the heads back over the bodies so that a string dropped from the ear would bisect the shoulder. Sing ya-ya-ya, dropping the jaw open and back. Just let the jaw flop, like it is made of jelly. Have the student pretend to chew gum while vocalizing to loosen the jaw. Never open the mouth with the jaw. Let the vowel open the mouth (keep the jaw relaxed). (See the section on "Jaw Position" for other suggestions.)

Tension in the Genio-Hyoid Muscles

These muscles (just back of the chin bone and underneath the chin), which connect the top of the larynx with the chin, must always remain in a relaxed state during the act of singing. Although the genio-hyoids are not involved in the process of articulation, the whole articulation system will be affected adversely and thrown out of adjustment by any rigidity of those muscles. Furthermore, the front of the throat will become taut, and the singer will very quickly experience throat fatigue. "Tight jaw" and "high larynx" are the constant companions of any tension of the genio-hyoids. Proper jaw action will probably permit the muscles to remain dormant.

High Larynx

When the elevator muscles overcome the depressor muscles and pull the larynx into too high a position in the throat during the singing act, many problems ensue. The high larynx disability is usually found in tenors, sometimes in baritones, and only occasionally in women's voices.

The larynx *should* remain in a mid-position in the throat whether the pitches sung are high or low. When the instructor notices a high position of the student's Adam's apple, know that the rising larynx is pushing up the tongue, which then results in an equal pulling down of the soft palate. The consequence of this action is the narrowing of the space between the palate and the surface of the tongue and a more open (white) tone. As the larynx ascends even higher (as pitches become higher) the tone may "bleat" and even become nasal as the tongue and palate approach each other. The tone will be completely cut off if the organs meet. If the high larynx is vibrating against the chin muscles, those muscles and the genio-hyoids will resist and will harden. The teacher should be suspicious if a student's chin is observed to be wobbling.

To observe this phenomenon, touch the larynx (Adam's apple) and swallow. It will be observed that the larynx moves upward as the elevator (swallowing) muscles are employed. Now yawn, and the depressor muscles will move the larynx to a lowered position. The bright vowels $\overline{ee}$, eh, and even ah must be avoided in the early remedial stages, because they will tend to lift the larynx. The only way to correct the problem is to strengthen the depressor muscles until they are as strong as the elevator muscles. Exercising almost totally on the dark vowel sounds oh, $\overline{oo}$, aw, and perhaps the rounded ah will eventually correct the disability. The larynx has to go downward, pulling the tongue with it and arching the soft palate whenever the dark vowels are sung. Do *not* attempt to lower the larynx through direct muscular effort or physical manipulation. *Do* lower it through employment of the dark vowels.

Breathy Tone

A tone is breathy when air slips through the vocal folds (see suggestions in the section on breath control for singing with breath pressure). True contraltos in junior high and high school are apt to have unusually breathy voices. Do everything you can to get these singers to hold ribs out, etc., but don't worry unduly if their voices still remain somewhat breathy, for maturation will bring resonance if other things are done correctly. A singer must sing on breath pressure, not on breath.

Nasality

The sound is pinched and forced *into* the nose. It will also be nasal if the sound is kept *out* of the nose. To remedy, open the throat. The feeling of a beginning of a yawn, getting ready to drink a glass of water, feeling gentle surprise, listening for a distant sound, and so on will help cure the nasality. Sing aw,o,$\overline{oo}$ to assist in pulling down the larynx (Adam's apple) and strengthening the depressor muscles. Sing "ng-ah" to get the feel of an open throat.

Inability to Sing Low

The singer must have resonance in the head voice in order to sing low. Chest resonance is not enough. The feeling of a snarl or "extra nasality" may bring the ring and focus into the lower tones. Many singers have trouble producing resonant lower tones.

Rattly Tone

This problem is caused by mucus in the edges of the throat touching and striking together in the throat. Keep the throat firmly open (but not taut) so the edges can't touch.

Cold, Uninteresting Tone

The student must learn to interpret the song. Make literal word paintings ("cold," "bright," "strong," "love," etc.). Listen to and sing with singers who have warmth in their voices. Sing songs you understand and make the words your own; you must sing the words as though you were the author of the words (that is, get inside the song). Vibrato must be present if there is to be warmth in the voice.

Hoarseness

Yelling or screaming, such as is done by cheerleaders, may cause nodes to form on the vocal cords. Singers with this condition cannot produce soft tones (particularly soft high tones). They must either sing loudly with great effort, or not at all. They can be cured by correct vocalization and avoidance of strain, unless they are in too advanced a stage. These nodes may have to be removed by surgery, particularly if they start to hemorrhage.

The most common symptoms of nodes are hoarseness, a break in the voice, and tiredness of voice. Causes of singers' nodes or polyps are improper vocal habits or body tensions (forcing the cords together too hard). A node is a swelling from the size of the head of a pin to the head of a match stick. A polyp is an advanced stage of a node. A node is usually on the anterior portion of the cords and affects the higher notes. When it is on the posterior area, contact ulcers occur. Smoking and alcohol are the commonest causes of chronic laryngitis, according to John Russell, M.D. They cause thickening of tissue and increased blood flow.

Vowel Modification

Voice teachers give lip service to an *ideal* of smooth and even voice quality from the bottom to the top of a singer's range. It is possible (but not likely) that a singer may instinctively modify vowels and voice quality so that perfect vocal adjustment in the tonal line is maintained at all pitches. If these proper adjustments are made, don't disturb them; just leave well enough alone.

On the basis of having given voice lessons to a good many singers, it is this writer's observation that ten out of ten are apt to need at least minor adjustments and that there will be one or two out of the ten with obvious "voice break" problems.

Try singing a bright $\overline{ee}$ from the bottom to the top of the voice range; hear the shrieking sound and feel the tonal stranglehold that results at the larynx. Now drop the jaw open, long and narrow as you ascend, singing the scale $\overline{ee}$. This "vowel modification" *must* occur somehow, and if it doesn't occur instinctively, the director must teach the student how to do it.

The young woman who is assigned permanently to an alto (or tenor) part and sings only with her "lower mechanism" or "chest voice" is almost sure to develop a voice break between her chest voice and her head voice. Much vocalization of the total range will keep this catastrophe from occurring. Even at the bottom of the range *some* head voice should be mixed with the chest voice (perhaps felt as nasality or "snarl") and *some* chest voice should be mixed with the head voice in the upper range (felt as depth and a long, narrow, loose jaw). Stated differently, the bottom of the range employs bright vowel placement and a smiling, but relaxed jaw; this tapers up to a dark vowel placement (with forward focus of tone) and long, narrow, loose jaw at the top of the range.

General suggestions may take care of minor "voice lift" problems. Suggest to singers that it will help them to sing high pitches, to cover a voice break or "lift" so it doesn't occur, and to maintain enough air pressure to complete a phrase, *if they*: feel gently surprised or "amazed," have a feeling of "lift" or "ecstasy," or sing with an "inner smile."

The director may need to take more drastic measures than those just discussed if the voice break is severe. Much "downward vocalization" is essential. The downward glissando is very good medicine to smooth out the voice. Vocalize from light to heavy as the tones move downward, and add any of the minor voice lift suggestions as the "lift" is approached. Low tones can be heavy, but only if the singer is not moving on into the upper register on that phrase, *and* the quality remains *easy*. From the third space bass clef (for a man) or the first line treble clef (for a woman) downward is the safe area to sing relatively heavily, but tone must never be *driven*. It should also be sung more brightly for forward focus of the tone. Forward sensation makes the swallowing muscles relax.

Try the following *Vocal Palette of Colors*,[8] changing to the suggested vowels when voice lifts occur (the lifts may vary ½ step to 1½ steps, especially if the voice has been "trained").

When these vowels are sung properly, with a resonant forward placement, the voice is automatically freed so that an even scale will be produced from the top to the bottom of the singer's range. The change of vowel (vowel modification) will bridge and cover the break so it is no longer present. This device has a tremendous advantage in remedial work, for a singer may *help himself or herself* in between voice lessons. Whenever there is vocal difficulty, sing the proper vowel for that part of the voice, and then sing the word's regular vowel while carefully retaining the previous tonal placement. The rolling hand—up and over—may assist the singer in keeping the same placement while moving from the vowel to the word. (The singer with a voicebreak problem should certainly also have a voice teacher to help conquer bad habits.)

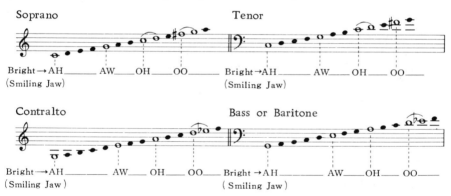

In this chapter and throughout the remainder of this book, it will be helpful to refer to the following chart for an accepted way to identify pitch:

[8]The author has been using this chart since it was given to him at the University of Southern California in 1940 by George Hultgren. The chart works beautifully for vowel modification and also to classify voices.

SUGGESTED CLASS ACTIVITIES

Assign class members to teach and demonstrate for the rest of the class:

1. The suggestions on interpretaion
2. The tips for correct posture
3. The suggestions for obtaining deep breath breathing
4. The suggestions to improve breath control
5. The way all kinds of vowel sounds are sung
6. The handling of consonants with and without duration
7. Jaw position tips
8. Humming correctly
9. Moving tone (crescendo and diminuendo)
10. How to stay in tune (intonation)
11. Causes and cures for vocal problems

STUDY AND REVIEW QUESTIONS

Students in Methods classes may find it profitable to answer the following questions and place them in a notebook, along with class notes, ready to be handed in at the conclusion of the discussion of this chapter.

1. Describe in your own words how you would remedy:
   a. breathy tone quality
   b. voices driving too hard
   c. sopranos that cannot sing g″ or higher
2. How can you get students to:
   a. open their mouths?
   b. sing loudly enough?
   c. support?
   d. continue phrases with vitality to the end?
   e. sing out, when they have no confidence in themselves?
   f. sing low with free and resonant quality?
   g. realize the correct sensation for good singing posture?
   h. hold their books correctly?
   i. hum correctly?
3. A private student:
   a. can't sing softly in the upper register. What procedure will help her?
   b. has a yawny, dark voice. What procedure will help him?
   c. has a high larynx. What can be done to assist him?
4. How do you convince a class with sloppy posture that they must sit or stand tall? If a student asked you why it wasn't all right to cross legs when sitting and singing, what would your answer be?

5. Can you demonstrate correct and incorrect breathing for the students so they'll want to breathe correctly? Describe what you would do.

6. Do you know how to show students how to start a beginning tone, using the word "home" and g′ as pitch? Describe this procedure.

7. Why would you want students to obtain the firm, open throat with relaxed neck muscles? What suggestions to the students would help them obtain it?

8. If some students in your choir have wide, out-of-tune vibratos, how can they be corrected?

9. Can you tell a class about diphthongs in English, and demonstrate correct and incorrect singing for them? What would you say and do?

10. Can you demonstrate and help the class sing $\overline{ee}$, ih, eh, a, and er correctly? (Use the words "leave," "sing," "far," "man," and "master," respectively, and tell what could be said and done.)

11. Can you show a class how to sing voiced consonants? What are the voiced (tuned) consonants and what would be your procedure?

12. The choir is not mentally alert. What things can you do to wake them?

13. The day is humid! What difference would this make in song selection, the conductor's actions, etc.?

14. Should most vocalizing be done in extreme highs and lows of the voice or in the middle? Why?

15. What can be done with "solo" voices to induce them to blend in a choir?

16. Discuss the importance of posture to breath support.

17. What will you do about an out-of-tune singer in a performing group?

18. Outline some procedures you will use to develop the tone quality of your choir as a whole.

19. How old should a child be before he or she starts formal voice training?

BIBLIOGRAPHY ON VOCAL PEDAGOGY

APPELMAN, D. RALPH, *The Science of Vocal Pedagogy.* Bloomington, Ind.: Indiana University Press, 1967.

BARTHOLOMEW, W.T., "The Role of Imagery in Voice Teaching" and "The Paradox in Voice Teaching," *Research Committee Release No. 1.* Chicago, Ill.: National Association of Teachers of Singing, 1951.

CHRISTY, VAN A., *Expressive Singing,* 2 vols. Dubuque, Iowa: Wm. C. Brown Co., Publishers, 1961. Two companion song anthologies are available.

DEYOUNG, RICHARD, *The Singer's Art.* Waukegan, Ill.: North Shore Press, 1958.

FIELDS, V.A., *Training the Singing Voice.* Morningside Heights, N.Y: King's Crown Press, 1947.

GARRETSON, ROBERT L., *Conducting Choral Music* (5th ed.). Boston: Allyn and Bacon, Inc., 1980.

HAYWOOD, F.H., *Universal Song,* 3 vols. New York: G. Schirmer, Inc., 1942.

HOFFER, CHARLES R., *Teaching Music in the Secondary Schools* (2nd ed.). Belmont, Calif.: Wadsworth Publishing Co., Inc., 1973.

JONES, ARCHIE N., ed., *Music Education in Action.* Boston: Allyn and Bacon, Inc., 1960.

KLEIN, JOSEPH J., *Singing Technique: How to Avoid Vocal Trouble*. Princeton, N.J.: D. Van Nostrand, 1967.

KORTKAMP, IVAN, *Advanced Choir* (rev. ed.). Tower, Minn.: Mohawk Publishing Co., 1969.

——, *One Hundred Things a Choir Member Should Know* (rev. ed.). Tower, Minn.: Mohawk Publishing Co., 1969.

MARSHALL, MADELEINE, *The Singer's Manual of English Diction*. New York: G. Schirmer, Inc., 1953.

MYER, E.J., *Position and Action in Singing*. Boston: The Boston Music Co., 1897.

——, *The Vocal Instructor*. Bryn Mawr, Penn.: Theodore Presser Co., 1918.

PFAUTSCH, LLOYD, *English Diction for the Singer*. New York: Lawson-Gould/G. Schirmer, Inc., 1971.

TRUSLER, IVAN, and WALTER EHRET, *Functional Lessons in Singing*. Englewood Cliffs, N.J.: Prentice-Hall, Inc., 1960.

WILSON, H.R., *Artistic Choral Singing*. New York: G. Schirmer, Inc., 1959.

VENNARD, WILLIAM, *Singing: The Mechanism and the Technic* (rev. ed.). New York: Carl Fischer, 1967.

6

Sight-reading

The teaching of music by rote is an extremely slow and laborious process. Too many directors resort to pounding notes into the basses, then the tenors, then the altos, then the sopranos. Students cannot accumulate the necessary knowledge of music from such a teaching method, for it does not provide for learning with increasing perception in the future. The choral director must teach the basic skills and knowledges of musicianship, which will result in student interest and in the development of musical taste. One of the most important skills is sight-reading, since its development will enable the students to read each number with increasing speed and knowledge.

The ability to look at the music, hear it mentally, and sing it immediately is called sight-reading. Skilled sight-reading, according to this definition, is the ability to read pitches and rhythms accurately. The highest degree of sight-reading skill, however, which most singers do not attain, goes far beyond mere pitches and rhythms to an *artistic* first performance of the music. This is the development of all the student's musical experiences to the point that the total musical score is skillfully and quickly interpreted.

No one can really sight-read who cannot recognize immediately and perform rhythmic patterns, melodic patterns, scale patterns, and word phrases. The students must also see beyond the small patterns, for example, (♪. ♪) to recognize the shape of the whole rhythmic or melodic phrase. It is essential to hear all pitches mentally *before* singing them and obtain a basic awareness of the chordal structure of the music. All modern methods of teaching reading emphasize speed as well as comprehension, and the two elements obviously complement each other. The person who sees only one letter at a time has trouble putting even one word together. The student who plods along reading word by laborious word cannot meld words into bigger meanings and phrases, so cannot comprehend the purport of the words. This student will always be a poor reader until the skill of recognizing *word phrases* is acquired. The sight-reader of choral music will be badly hampered unless possessing the ability to intelligently read the lyrics and musical elements at a glance. Whatever approach is used, it is necessary to drill regularly on the various rhythms and tonal problems common to all songs, or the student will not acquire the skill to perform those problems on sight. There must be a certain amount of rote teaching in order to acquire this desirable skill; however, the students must understand *in what way* this drilling will help them read music with more facility.

The teacher can check to see whether students are able to follow the notes by directing and having the singers sing mentally, then stop directing and have the singers designate the word they are on; or by directing and having the singers snap their fingers on rests only. Other methods would include directing and having the singers sing the consonant or vowel that should sound on each beat; directing or counting the beats aloud for one measure and having the singers mentally count the beats of the next measure and clap when they think beat 3 (4 or 2) has arrived; or having the singers sing the rhythm using "tah" and snap fingers on the rests. Another teaching method involves playing the song on the piano or on a recording, stopping the piano or record, and having the students show the pitch, chord, or word where the stoppage occurred. Any of these creative evaluative procedures will challenge the students and will simultaneously provide a starting place for remedial procedures.[1] Students of junior or senior high school age who cannot read notes need to experience the same steps and processes that are used to teach the elementary child to read, *but* the steps and processes must be adjusted through the vocabulary and song materials to the proper maturation level. Aural concepts of tone and rhythm grow with each encounter with singing, with every performance

---

[1]The students will not be able to avoid speeding up in their counting, so spend some time on teaching them to keep a steady beat.

on instruments, with each taste of listening to music, and with each thrill the student feels when there is a creative experience in music.

TWO CONCEPTS OF TEACHING SIGHT-READING AND MUSICIANSHIP[2]

Hand Signals

Zoltan Kodaly has had great success in reviving an approach to solmization through a system of hand signals. This approach, not a new one historically, is based upon the reinforcement of the singing sensation by a physical act. There is some evidence of its helpfulness. The instrumentalist, for example the cornet player, who pushes down certain fingers and associates certain pitches with those physiological sensations seems to learn to read more surely and accurately through this reinforcement. The average singer does not have such reassurance and stabs blindly at a pitch. Needed reinforcement may be provided by band and orchestral instruments, Orff instruments, resonator bells, the piano, the Chambliss system (discussed later), movable or fixed *do*, or numbers.

The hand signal approach linked to movable *do* also provides some measure of reinforcement. The English clergyman, John Curwen, devised these hand signals in the nineteenth century and Tonic Sol-fa (a system, used particularly in English music to assist sight-reading and eartraining, of placing the first letter of the correct tone syllable in movable *do* in the notation, for example: d = doh, r = ray, and so forth). The old English hand signal system is advocated by I. Cooper and K.O. Kuersteiner (in their book *Teaching Junior High School Music*, Boston: Allyn & Bacon, 1965), and by Kodaly and his interpreters in the United States.

The hand signal system makes sense because the movements are graphically descriptive of the sizes of the intervals and relationships contained within the scale. Students sing *do* as they make a fist, palm facing downward. *Re* physically depicts upward motion through opening the fist and lifting the fingers upward while the arm remains horizontal. They sing *mi* with the hand flat, palm downward. *Fa* is sung with the thumb pointing downward, indicating the closeness of the pitch to *mi*. (Thumb is up for *fi*.) The arm is horizontal, the palm vertical and the thumb pressed against the hand on *sol*. (The thumb is raised for *si*.) The hand points downward on *la*. For *ti*, the forefinger points upward to *do*. (The forefinger is bent downward for *ta*.) You will note that all of the scale and some of the frequently used accidentals are used. These movements involve the students actively in the music, combining the ears, eyes, hands, and arm.

[2]These concepts are usually used only in elementary school, but they may be effectively adapted to general music classes in middle school and junior or senior high school.

Much of the basic work in the Kodaly method is rhythmic (chanting, clapping, walking, and hand signals) with a constant emphasis upon the relationship between muscle, eye, and ear as notes, rests, and rhythmic combinations are read. The first melodic approach is through the pentatonic scale and the interval *sol-mi*, the falling minor third of childhood.

$$\begin{array}{ccccc} & & 6 & & \\ 5 & 5 & & 5- & \\ & & 3 & & 3- \end{array}$$

Students enjoy using and following signals in rhythmic and tonal dictation. The teacher will find it useful to remind students of interval relationships through hand signals and to conduct two-part singing when both hands are used. Students like to direct voice sections or songs silently while fellow students sing or identify the songs. The technique also may be used in a choir for vocalizing.

Resonator Bells

Almost everything that can be accomplished with the Orff instruments (plus a few additional things) can be done by means of one or two sets of resonator bells, and the price is negligible in comparison. Dr. Patricia Bond, while a music supervisor in the Dallas public schools, used the following procedure in junior high general music classes with great success: Start with a new song, with chord symbols over the appropriate places in the music. Place the staff, key signature, and chord numbers, on the chalkboard. Ask the students to identify the pitch that is the base of the I chord in that key. The first student who raises his or her hand and correctly names the pitch will be permitted to get the appropriate tone bar and mallet from the resonator bell keyboard and take them back to his or her seat. The teacher will place that pitch on the staff over the I on the chalkboard (or will require the student to do it). The third and fifth (seventh, if there is a seventh in the chord) are identified, notes placed on the board and the tone bars picked up. The IV, V⁷, II, and VI chords are identified, and resonator bars picked up in a similar manner. Student must notice when a chord tone is not new, and the student already in possession of the resonator bar will play in both chords; for example, the fifth of the I chord and the tonic of the V chord are the same note.[3]

Direct the students to play the tonic, the third and the fifth of the I chord; then to roll the full chord continuously as if playing a drum roll. Follow the same procedure with each of the other chords. Then start from the beginning. Direct the rhythm and have everyone sing the melody while continuously rolling the chords. Students will soon learn to observe the

[3]A student deliberately playing on the tone bar at the wrong time will immediately lose the bar to another student.

changing of the chord symbols and will change chords without the teacher's help. This enables the director to move about the room and still have a harmonic background furnished by the continuously rolling bell chords. The singing will proceed until everyone can sing the melody, which is harmonically oriented through this teaching procedure. Then have everyone sing alto until it is learned with the bell chordal accompaniment. Next, have the altos and sopranos sing with the harmonic background (the men are not left out since some or all of them are occupied playing the tone bars). Have everyone sing tenor, then bass. Put the four parts together, using the same procedures. As a final step, have the students sing the song a cappella. A skillful teacher can help a general music class sight-read one to three songs in a forty-five minute period from raw beginnings to a very acceptable performance of a cappella singing. Complex harmonies and rhythms may be accomplished that would be very difficult without the help of instruments. The twelve-tone row (original, retrograde, inversion, retrograde-inversion, octave displacement, and spreading out the notes—see Chapter 10) may be brought to the attention of the students and demonstrated by random selection of the twelve chromatic notes. Tone clusters, bitonality, polytonality, and atonality also may be demonstrated with ease. Rhythmic patterns may be experienced by striking the bells with any single rhythm or polyrhythm instead of with continuously rolled chords. Illustrate syncopation, familiar meter, free meter, polymeter, and so forth. (See Chapter 10 for some illustrations.)

RHYTHMS

There is much controversy among authorities concerning whether rhythm or pitch is the proper area to emphasize first. Whichever one is emphasized, the other will be involved either simultaneously or immediately. The teacher must be careful that pupils are not confused by a multiplicity of facts or concepts presented in one lesson. Usually one concept at a time will be enough for the students to assimilate; however, the teacher should watch the students' reaction and not go so slowly and methodically that they are bored. When working on sight-reading, the elimination of even one element (e.g., words) will allow more intense concentration upon the other musical elements (if the number is complex enough to defy successful sight-singing with all the elements present). Errors in pitch, phrasing, and pronunciation must be corrected immediately before they become habitual (of course, *don't* correct the mistake if it is obvious that students have enough experience to make corrections on a second reading). According to psychology, the more times the error is repeated, the stronger will be the memory connection. The error will not be forgotten, so it must be abandoned and replaced by a more desirable response (in this case, right rhythm, note, or word).

One- and Two-Beat Rhythmic Patterns

The o note in 4/4 and the o· in 12/8 are conducted and sung exactly alike. Conduct and have the singers sing the note(s) in the left column and then the corresponding note(s) directly across in the right column. The two notes or patterns will be be found to be identical.

Left	Description (4/4)	Right	Description (12/8)
o	4 beats ($\frac{4}{4}$)	o·	4 beats ($\frac{12}{8}$)
𝅗𝅥.	3 beats ($\frac{3}{4}$)	𝅗𝅥.⌣𝅗𝅥.	3 beats ($\frac{9}{8}$)
𝅗𝅥	2 beats ($\frac{2}{4}$)	𝅗𝅥.	2 beats ($\frac{6}{8}$)
♩	1 beat ($\frac{1}{4}$)	♩.	1 beat ($\frac{3}{8}$) in $\frac{12}{8}$
♩♩♩ (triplet, 3)	1 beat ($\frac{4}{4}$)	♩♩♩	1 beat ($\frac{3}{8}$) in $\frac{12}{8}$
♩♪ (triplet, 3)	1 beat ($\frac{4}{4}$)	♩ ♪	1 beat ($\frac{3}{8}$) in $\frac{12}{8}$
♪♩ (triplet, 3)	1 beat ($\frac{4}{4}$)	♪♩	1 beat ($\frac{3}{8}$) in $\frac{12}{8}$
♩𝄾♩ (triplet, 3)	1 beat ($\frac{4}{4}$)	♩𝄾♩	1 beat ($\frac{3}{8}$) in $\frac{12}{8}$

It may be easier for the students to think in $\overline{4}$ than in $\overline{8}$. Have them try erasing the dots (in their imaginations) from

$\frac{12}{8}$ o(·) , 𝅗𝅥(·)⌣𝅗𝅥(·) , 𝅗𝅥(·) , and ♩(·) ,

so they sing the notes as

$\frac{4}{4}$ o , 𝅗𝅥⌣𝅗𝅥 , 𝅗𝅥 , and ♩ .

Students tend to sing ♩♩♩ (triplet) in $\overline{4}$ time as ♩♩♩ . It may be easier for the student to perform the triplet accurately if it is thought as ♩♩♩ in $\overline{8}$ time. Have the student sing a full | ♩♩♩ ♩♩♩ ♩♩♩ ♩♩♩ | 12/8 measure, then sing the 4/4 measure

| ♩♩♩ ♩ ♩ ♩ | as

$\frac{12}{8}$| ♩♩♩ |$\frac{4}{4}$| ♩ ♩ ♩ | or even as

$\frac{12}{8}$| ♩♩♩ 𝅗𝅥. 𝅗𝅥. 𝅗𝅥. |

Treat the dotted eighth and sixteenth as if the sixteenth is a pick-up note for the note following, in any medium to fast tempos. Be careful that ♪. ♪ (3 to 1) is not sung as ⌐³⌐ ♩ ♪ (2 to 1) in slower speeds.

Additional common one-beat patterns in 4/4 times are: ♩♩ ,

♩♫ , ♫♩ , ♬ , ♪. ♪ , ♪♪. ("scotch snap"), and ♪ ♪ ♪.

Common one-beat patterns in compound time may be seen in the columns on page 132.

Common two-beat patterns in 4/4 are: ⌐³⌐ ♩♩♩ , ♩. ♪ ,

♪♩ ♪. ♩ , and variations such as ♪ ♩. , ⌐³⌐ ♩ ♩ and ⌐³⌐ ♩ ♩ . The last two patterns are actually compound rhythms. To solve difficulties with the

triplet figure ⌐³⌐ ♩ ♩ ♩ , have the students think of each of the three notes falling slowly into the next note or of a circle with resistance on each

note ₃◯₂ . When the difficulty cannot be solved so simply, count 6 and accent 1, 3, and 5:

$$
\frac{6}{8}\ \overset{>}{\sqcap}\ \overset{>}{\sqcap}\ \overset{>}{\sqcap}\ =\ \frac{2}{4}\ \underset{3}{\underbrace{\ \ }}\ \ \ \ \ \
$$

Beats→ 1 2

Underbeat→ 1̲ 2 3̲ 4 5̲ 6

while beating two (the two will hit exactly on beat 4 as though beating four times in 12/8 time). Difficulty will also be experienced with the other two-beat patterns. To clear up rhythmic problems with a choir, beat the

following: (♩. ♪). Notice that the dot is *on* beat 2 by showing the following comparison of note values:

$$
\begin{array}{c|ccc|}
\ & \quad ♩ & \quad ♪ = \\
& 1 & \overset{\uparrow}{2} \\ \hline
& ♩ & ♪\ ♪
\end{array}
$$

Then beat 2 beats and have students tap, keep their hands on their desks, and press beat 2 (also sing "tah" and use extra weight in their voices on the second beat). The physical action and voice accent will help students feel the proper note length and the maintenance of the rhythmical unit.

In the two-beat pattern ♪ ♩ ♪ , show the following comparison of note values:

$$
\begin{array}{c|ccc|}
\ & ♪\ ♩ & ♪ = \\
& 1 & \overset{\uparrow}{2} \\ \hline
& ♪\ \sqcap\ & ♪
\end{array}
$$

Notice that the *middle* of the ♩ is on beat 2. While the director beats two beats, the students will tap the eighth and second eighth and without lifting their hands from their desks will press the third eighth, which is on beat 2, then tap the fourth eighth note. The students must also sing the notes on "tah" while tapping and pressing. As a rule, have students feel a pressure accent with their voices "on the beat" any time *syncopation* is sung (and, if necessary, use their hands also so they can feel the beat). For example:

A way to teach one-beat and two-beat rhythmic patterns effectively in any class that requires help with rhythms is to construct a measure of

any basic rhythm pattern, for example, ♩ ♩ ,on the chalkboard:

Have the class repeat it by tapping and singing "pom" until it can do the measure. Construct

and practice until the class can perform it easily and accurately. Proceed by practicing a measure of each pattern, but keep switching back and forth. For example:

Then mix patterns by pointing on the board, disregarding measure bar lines, until the class can react precisely. For example:

Go to the next rhythmic pattern:

Rehearse the measure; do consecutive measures of the three patterns, then continue until the class can perform all three patterns in any combination. Continue this procedure, day after day, adding more rhythmic units. Pay special attention to rhythms that will be present in the first song[4] to be rehearsed seriously. Be sure to repeat the rhythms learned the previous days, so they are reinforced and not forgotten. Spend no more than three to five minutes in drilling and challenge the students with the swiftness with which the patterns are jumbled. After working over a period of time, the hypothetical mixing-up can be as complicated as:

Miss Flagg, former music supervisor of the Dallas Public School System, had her teachers use the following drill[5] for the establishment of a few elementary rhythms and pitches (placed on the chalkboard or overhead projector in the key of the first song to be taught.[6]

(Adapted from Abby Whiteside's *Indispensables of Piano Playing*)

This drill may quickly be placed in the bass clef for the entire class to read, or in both clefs of the great staff. The sol-fas, numbers, or pitch names may be drilled with the above tonal and rhythmic patterns (and swiftly mixed) until done with facility. It will be amazing how well a class will then read a song in the key used for the drill, and how accurately the pitch identification symbols will be used. Other "one-beat" patterns such as:

can easily be adapted into a basic exercise:

---

[4]The time signature must correspond to the one in the song. This will involve the teaching of compound rhythms and longer rhythmic phrases, involving rests as integral parts of rhythmic patterns.

[5]Marion Flagg, *Music Reading as Tonal Thinking* (Dallas Independent School District, 1962), p. 3.

[6]In Miss Flagg's drill, measures 3 and 4 are reversed, also 5 and 6 and 7 and 8. The above arrangement will be easier for the vocalist.

or drilled without pitches being involved.

Two-beat patterns:

$|\frac{2}{4}| \quad \quad |\frac{6}{8}| \quad |$

may be drilled either way. Rests may be practiced by simple substitution in any pattern.

If a simple procedure is desired for a quick reminder of note values, use single pitches *or* chords with all the class singing. For example:

Teacher:	Quarters				Eighths				Sixteenths				Quarters			
Students:	1	2	3	4	1 &	2 &	3 &	4 &	1 e & e	2 e&e	3 e & e	4 e & e	1	2	3	4
or	mo	mo	mo	mo	momomomomomomomo				etc.							

In the general music class, tap rhythms or have class members do the rhythm tapping, while the class guesses the tunes. Pick songs that are suitable to whatever instruments are available (Latin American songs, calypso, etc.) and teach the students to use the instruments as an accompaniment to their singing. Use the body as an instrument (cupping hands, clapping hands, clapping knee, tapping feet, snapping fingers, clicking tongues, SSSS, SHHH) and if the body is to imitate an instrument that has pitch, a nasal "panning" thrown into the nose makes a wonderful banjo, "thmm" makes a fine string bass. Adapt familiar songs to any of the "boogie basses" suggested on p. 152 and use "thmm" or "pmm" to imitate a string bass (boogie-woogie has as much interest rhythmically as it does chordally). For a novelty use some of the following rhythms and make the melodies conform to the rhythms.[7]

Bolero   Polonaise

Beguine   Cha-Cha-Cha   Samba-Polka   Baia

Conga   Claves   Mambo

[7]Unless the teacher is quite clever, it will be wise to have experimented with and mastered some usable combinations before class. Use rhythm instruments, vocal chording, chanting, or any combination thereof, and give the students some experience in polyrhythms.

Calypso   Tico-Tico   Spanish (Habanero)   Rhumba

[musical notation]

Shuffle Rhythm Jazz Beat   Rock 'n' Roll   Another
                                                      Jazz Rhythm

[musical notation]

Bodily Movements Help Students Feel Rhythms

The director must help the students feel a metronome pulsating inside them, with the beat pounding rhythmically and perpetually. Passing music in and out rhythmically while singing a song that swings, like "He's Got the Whole World in His Hands," will help students feel rhythm in their bodies. One of the best ways to teach students to feel and beat rhythms is to teach a unit on conducting and having the students use the correct beat patterns while they sing the notes. If the beat pattern will distract the students or interfere with the learning process, some good noiseless activities are to have the students move their hands on each beat as though bouncing basket balls; have the students move their hands down and forward in a pushing motion, then allow the hands to roll upward in a circular motion back to the original position of the hands (somewhat like rowing a boat); or make a circle on each beat as though an automobile or old-fashioned ice cream freezer is being cranked. Have the students tap the left hand with two fingers of the right hand, then hold the fingers and shake them on each beat *or* slide the fingers over the palm when a half note or longer must be indicated; tap the fingers together *or* tap the wrist *or* heel of the hand. If it is desirable for some reason (such as staging) to rock the entire body in a modified fashion on each beat, be careful, for this activity is likely to result in overly boisterous behavior unless it is carefully controlled by the teacher. Tap the heels on the beat, clap the rhythm with the hands (the student shakes hands with himself once per beat on a half beat or longer), hands *out* on a rest; hit the palm of the hand against the knees *on* the beat (slide up or down on sustained notes), for example,

tap the foot on the beat (slide left or right on sustained notes); click the tongue or snap the fingers on the beat.

Rests

Many students learn to count and perform *notes* quite well, but ignore the *rests*. An important part of learning to perform rhythms is learning to remain silent for the proper amount of time whenever a rest occurs. Vandre (Scott) points out that the student who *reacts* in some way during the rest is more likely to learn and sense the proper length of waiting time needed. Suggested ways for students to react are to "say 'tah' on the notes and whisper 'too' on the rests; clap the hands on the notes and pat the knees on the rests; clap the hands on the notes and click the tongue on the rests; clap the hands on the notes and tap the feet on the rests; say 'ssss' on the notes and whisper 'shhh' on the rests; say 'cha' on the notes and whisper 'chi' on the rests."[8] Vandre suggests that students "clap the hands on the notes and say the word 'rest' on each rest; clap the hands on the notes and whisper the word 'rest' on each rest; clap the hands on the notes and be silent on the rests; clap the hands on the rests and be silent on the notes; tap the foot on the notes and clap the hands on the rests."[9] This procedure may be varied in many ways not mentioned, such as snapping the fingers, whispering "shhh," hitting the knee, and so forth. One word of caution; don't allow the clapping or tapping to become boisterous or rowdy. If the teacher cannot control the activity, it should not be used (however, some of these activities are very much quieter than others)! Undoubtedly, the most "transfer" will occur if notes are sung or chanted and one of the other devices is used for the rests.

Verbal Devices Help Students Learn and Remember Rhythms

Speaking the words of the song in rhythm or using neutral syllables (singing "tah," "too," or "pah," because the use of t or p as the initial consonant forces immediacy and mental thinking ahead by the singers) performs the very useful function of directing the singers' attention to only one or two of the musical elements and thus making success more plausible. In the remainder of the verbal devices described here, students associate the rhythm of the word, symbol, or phrase with the rhythm of the pattern, which helps them remember and perform the rhythms correctly upon repetition. One of the oldest devices is still one of the best ones, that is, counting the rhythm by one--ee-and-uh *or* one-tah-tah-tah. Elementary school teachers have long taught the action words "walk, walk" for two quarter notes, "run, run" for two eighth notes. These are useful words for elementary school students (so long as the teacher also teaches students the correct words for the notes), but the concept is too simple to use in secondary school. Other *mnemonic* words and chants may be useful.

[8]Richard Scott, *Two Part Choral Method* (New York: Mills Music, Inc., 1959), p. 34.
[9]Vandre, *Two-Part Sight Reading Fun* (New York: Mills Music, Inc., 1940), pp. 9–10.

Examples:

$$\text{♩♩♩♩}\quad = \quad\text{Mississippi or Minnesota}$$

$$\text{♩♩♩}\quad = \quad\text{tri-ple-it or mer-ri-ly}$$

The words used may be the names of states, names of students in the room, names of animals, names of vegetables, names of political figures, or anything the class or teacher may wish to invent. The use of *chants* helps students remember more complicated rhythmic patterns and long rhythmic phrases.

A more sophisticated type of verbal device is the system of *speech patterns*. For the teacher who wishes to try any of these, it would be best to go to a source book and learn all the details. Some of the best known are the French time names (taa-tai for two eighth notes, etc.),[10] Vandre's[11]

lah - da   lah-mah-dah-mah   and[12]   down - up   down - up

and Scott's[13] ♩ ♩ ♩♩ . If the instructor wishes to add pitch to the

too - too   too - tuh

difficulties of reading, any of the verbal devices may be used; however, pitch identification symbols, *do-re-mi*, numbers, or pitch names (omitting the word "sharp" and "flat"), may sometimes be preferable.

Techniques for Isolating and Recognizing Rhythmic Patterns

Students who are taught to isolate and recognize rhythmic patterns will probably be able to handle them when they occur in song material and recognize and correct at least part of their errors. The more of the common rhythmic problems they learn and relate to songs, the more independently they will be able to use *transfer of training* in new song materials.

In either a general music class or a performance-oriented organization, the teacher may start by isolating all of the rhythmic patterns in the song to be rehearsed. Place them on the chalkboard, mimeograph them, or prepare a transparency for the overhead projector. Drill the students on these patterns until they can do them correctly (challenge the group by quickly reversing and mixing until they can perform the rhythmic patterns

---

[10]Described by Eugene Reichenthal in *Music Education in Action*, Archie N. Jones, ed. (Dubuque, Iowa: Wm. C. Brown, Publishers, 1960), pp. 319–24.

[11]Vandre, *Rhythmic Sight-Singing* (New York: Mills Music, Inc., 1958), p. 2.

[12]Vandre, *Three-Part Sight Reading Fun* (New York: Mills Music, Inc., 1940), p. 17.

[13]Scott, *Clap, Tap, and Sing* (New York: Mills Music, Inc., 1960), p. 42.

in any order). Conclude the learning process by guiding the students into discovering where the patterns fit in the song context. Then sing the song.

The teacher may prefer to start with the song as a whole and guide the students' discoveries of the various rhythmic patterns inherent in the number. After patterns are isolated and placed on the board, rehearse and mix the patterns until the students can tap and sing the rhythms accurately; then return the patterns back to the song.

With either approach, the teacher will solve rhythmical problems quickly and efficiently by referring the problem in the song back to the rhythm drill pattern on the board *or* starting with the rhythm drill and referring it to the problem rhythms in the song.

A related type of rhythmic activity that may be used effectively to keep any class busy and interested while the music is being passed out (or until the final bell after music has been passed in) is to set a rhythm and start all of the students tapping their heels steadily. While the pupils continue to tap quietly, the director sings or taps a melodic or rhythmic pattern a measure or two long. Choose some troublesome patterns out of songs being rehearsed currently, and then relate these melodies or rhythms to their sources. This procedure is excellent for ear training and rhythms, and the students enjoy doing it.

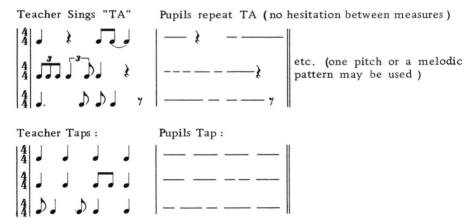

After students have responded by tapping or singing the rhythm correctly, the teacher may wish to challenge them to name the symbols and pattern used and reproduce the appropriate symbols on the chalkboard or at their seats.

ESTABLISHING MELODIC PATTERNS

Even the simplest melody involves at least two musical elements, pitch and rhythm. It is difficult to divorce melody from some consideration of harmony since melody is usually composed from broken chords, arpeggios, interval leaps, and scales which are major, minor, or modal. In advanced sight-reading, the best technique is to read a great deal of increasingly difficult chorales and octavos in varying styles. Weak sight-reading groups must learn some basic musical skills before they may be exposed to quantities of music and derive any benefit from it in terms of increased sight-reading skills. Two of the essentials that students must learn are the construction of scales (especially major) and enough fundamental knowledge of the keyboard that steps, half steps, and chords may be visualized and related to a music staff.

Teaching Keys and Scales
Through Keyboard Experiences

Have the students in a general music or general chorus class draw their own keyboards, noticing particularly the relative positions of the two black keys and the three black keys. Start with the key of C to show the normal major scale pattern with its intervals of 1-1-½-1-1-1-½. Demonstrate to be sure the class knows that the nearest note, whether black or white, is a half step and that two half steps constitute a whole step. After working with C until there is some familiarity with the building of a scale and key in its simplest form, let the students discover that all keys except the key of C must be altered before they will fit the major scale pattern. For example:

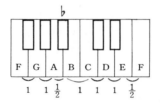

What must be done to B? The scale step must be named B♭ not A♯ because every note in the scale must be named and must be in alphabetically correct order. If the scale step were named A-sharp, B would be missing. The key of F has one flat because the scale of F has one flat.

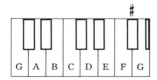

In the key of G, what must be done to F to make a whole step?
The key of G has one sharp because the *scale* of G has one sharp—F♯.

After working for several days with scales and keyboards, arrange some chairs as a keyboard when the students come into the room; eight in front and five in back according to the white and black note pattern of the keyboard.

Chair Arrangement for the Key of C:

```
        Db Eb   Gb Ab Bb
        C# D#   F# G# A#
        X  X    X  X  X
        X  X  XX  X  X  XX
        C  D  EF  G  A  BC
```

What Scale Is This?

```
        X X X  X X
        X X X XX X XX  =  ?
```

Let the students guess why the chairs are arranged this way, and then tell what the key is. Then pass out the resonator bells for the scale and have students sit in the chairs that correspond to the bells they hold. Ask the students who are in a particular scale to stand (call C, or G, or F, and so on). Don't look at the ones who should stand. Make them think. Have them play the scales with the bells (those in the C scale stand and play the C scale; those in the G scale stand and play the G scale, etc.). This technique was used successfully by Dr. Patricia Bond in the Dallas Public Schools.

Use the chording technique mentioned earlier in this chapter while singing. When building chords, use the guitar to play examples, because of the students' familiarity with it. Give the students some actual experience at the piano keyboard. Start with the close harmony triads used in vocal chording (described on p. 153), arpeggios, and scales. The teacher may point to the keys on a large imitation keyboard (visible to the entire class) and have the class sing the pitches simultaneously; play a simple four- or five-tone tune on the mock keyboard and have the class or one student repeat the melody that was played (an exercise in tonal memory); or play a short melody on the piano, within the five-finger range, and challenge a student to come to the keyboard and correctly play the notes (while students play their silent keyboards at their seats to test their own skill). The reward for the student who plays correctly is the opportunity to make up and play a tune for the other students to try to guess.

Be sure the class is thoroughly familiar with the Grand (Great) Staff. They must learn the names of the notes and relate them to the keyboard so they may see and experience steps, half steps, and intervals in music *and* on the keyboard. Point out and drill on the obvious facts that from a line to a space is one step, from a space to a line is one step, from a line to the next line up or down is two steps (the uninitiated student tends to ignore the spaces). Explain how leger lines are used on the staff. Use of the following superimposed staves[14] will facilitate this learning and will also work

[14] Used by permission of Alan Richardson, School of Music, North Texas State University.

beautifully for singing modulations and showing the relationships of flats to sharps and to naturals.

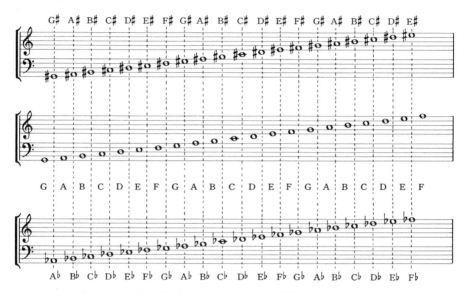

Teach the circle of fifths, but also give the students the simple rules for determining the key from the key signature; that is, call the last *sharp* to the right *ti* or 7, and move up a half step to *do* or 8; call the last *flat* to the right *fa* or 4, and move up or down to *do*, 1 or 8 (with more than one flat in the key signature, the next to the last flat *is* the key); show the minor scale as based on *la* or 6 of the major scale if movable *do* is being taught as a basic technique. Teach all other scales and modes as they occur in the music the class is learning.

Teaching Inner Hearing

The teacher must make a decision concerning the technique to be used for teaching intervals. The path of least resistance is to discover what the local elementary schools are using (movable *do*, numbers, etc.) and capitalize and expand upon any skill in the technique the students still possess. Changing techniques can confuse the students, but often there will be so little vestige of the technique left by the time students arrive in secondary school that a new technique will do just as well. The choice lies between movable *do*, fixed *do*, numbers, neutral syllables, and pitch names (the instrumental approach). Whatever system is chosen, the students must be taught pitch names; and they must be taught numbers so they will understand chordal relationships (neutral syllables are often very useful). A short consideration of the other techniques may be helpful to the reader.

Chapter 5, in its consideration of intonation problems, briefly reviews the evolution of the scale through three systems: the Pythagorean scale, the just scale, and the equal-tempered scale (represented by the modern piano keyboard). It is pointed out that good melodic singing emulates most closely the Pythagorean scale, which has the highest leading tones of the three scales, the highest major thirds of the three scales, and small semi-tones. The table comparing logarithm values for diatonic intervals in the Pythagorean and equal-tempered scales treats each scale step in careful detail. First, notice the two tetrachords, with E being the leading tone for its segment of the scale and B for its part of the scale.

	C	D	E	F	G	A	B	C
	Do	Re	Mi	Fa	Sol	La	Ti	Do
	1	2	3	4	5	6	7	8

The table shows that E is also the third of the I chord in the major scale and B is the third of the V chord, and therefore these notes must be sung high. Notice that F and the upper C must be sung low. The teacher should have the students do some singing of numbers and pitch names, but these symbols do not lend themselves to singing very well because of the complex muscle patterns involved in their pronunciation and some lack of vowel purity. Specifically, C, F, and G will cause problems, and additional difficulty may arise in the proper handling of the glottal stroke on E. One, three, four, five, six, and seven will be awkward numbers to sing. Another inherent difficulty is the singing of the added word "sharp" or "flat," and without the addition students may ignore or be unaware of the accidentals.

The Guidonian syllables (*do, re, mi*, etc.), although devoid of meaning, contain consonants and pure vowel sounds that are easy to sing. When the scale steps are considered, it becomes clear why they seem to promote in-tune singing. *Do* has a good, full vowel; *re* contains a brighter vowel, and a big step will result; *mi* employs the brightest vowel possible to produce, and the bright, forward placement will encourage high pitch; *fa* has a darker vowel and a smaller interval tends to be the result; the vowel in *sol* is still darker, and the interval remains small; the brighter sound in *la* stretches the interval slightly; the vowel in *ti* elevates the interval with its brightness; and the darker sound of *do* favors the singing of a small interval.

Most American schools favor the movable *do* system over the European fixed *do*. As long as major and minor tonalities are sung, movable *do*[15] performs efficiently. Frequent accidentals and modulations into other keys will create great difficulty because the name of each designated pitch changes each time the key of a song is changed (thus G can be *do* in the key

[15]The number system is a form of the movable *do* system.

of G, *sol* in the key of C, and so on). The student becomes understandably
confused by the constantly changing names of pitches, even when no
modulations and accidentals are involved. Furthermore, the tonally
centered system tends to make students unaware of the existence of flats
and sharps. Movable *do* becomes totally useless in contemporary songs
built on a twelve-tone scale or with atonal, bitonal, polytonal, or aleatory
(chance) structure. Unless students have been thoroughly indoctrinated in
movable *do*, do not teach it in secondary school. Students will be more
receptive to numbers and will progress faster into concepts of chordal relationships.

The fixed *do* system always has the same symbol for the same pitch,
so C is always *do*. Advocates of this system point out that seventeen different names are all a singer needs to learn in the entire scale, contrasting
with a possibility of seventeen names *for each pitch* in movable *do*. Orchestra directors trained in Europe attain such facility in fixed *do* that they
can use this method to sing violin parts in rehearsal with great speed and
read new orchestral scores by singing all instrument parts. Although this
system is an excellent tool for reading, it is doubtful that enough skill will
be attained to justify teaching it in secondary school.

An excellent technique to use in teaching movable *do* is the one
developed by Jack Chambliss, professor at New Mexico State University.
His visual device permits the students to perceive the basic triad of any key
with more clarity, and consequently to grasp the fundamental arpeggio
and related notes with greater quickness and surety. It is also very helpful
in teaching chord relationships. Notice that it may be taught in an abstract
form, then placed in the key and on the very lines and spaces to be sung in
the song about to be taught. Thus, students will have experienced the
distance from the second to the third line in the key of the song. If the
group is steeped in the tradition of *do*, *re*, *mi*, those symbols may be
substituted for 1, 2, 3, (even neutral syllables may be used).

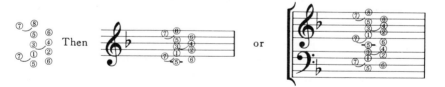

One suggested procedure is to have the class sing some patterns, such
as 1-3-5-8-5-3-1, 1-3-5-3-1, 1-4-6-4-1, 7-4-5-4-7, 1-3-5-3-1-5-1, as they are
pointed to on the board. (The line below a number means the lower octave.) This will establish the tonality, which must always be one of the first
and most basic steps in reading all but contemporary music. Then point to
some of the melody the class will be singing next (or any voice line) until
these intervals have been learned (all of this might be done with the book

closed, if the teacher prefers). Have the class open its music and ask the students to tell what the denominator and numerator means in the time signature (teach or *re*teach the time signature if it is needed). Check, and drill if necessary, on note and rest values and rhythmic patterns. Establish the rhythm of the song. Finally, sight-read the song (although the class will already have the feel of the basic rhythm, the way the intervals look in the music, and the sounds of the intervals in its ears). If the class has problems reading an interval, reverse the procedure and have the group read the correct intervals from the blackboard or overhead projector and then relate back to the troublesome problem in the music. See Professor Herbert Teat's technique, described in Chapter 7, for another way to employ the Chambliss technique and patch to teach reading through *Composition*.

The teacher may find it desirable to use the procedure of the previous paragraph with a scale written on the chalkboard in the key of the song to be sung next. The key of C is used as an example.

The teacher will probably want to add these 3 notes to the bottom of the scale.

Excellent teaching can be done with this device, but the music cannot be visualized chordally, which is the way students see the music when they actually read it.

After using any of the three techniques for teaching movable *do* (especially when it is taught by numbers,) the teacher may wish to work on interval jumps. A good procedure, especially with a musically weak group, is to have the singers sing 1, the director calls 6, the singers (mentally and silently) go up through 2, 3, 4, 5, and land on 6. If the students cannot hear these steps mentally, the director can have the students sing these tones audibly, and then try mentally again. (While introducing this *mental singing*, the conductor may need to have the choir sing a simple tune, e.g., "America," to prove to the group that it *can hear* mentally. At a given signal, the singers will sing mentally, then audibly again at a prearranged signal. This may be done several times in the same tune.) The director will then call another number, 4, for example and the group will mentally sing 5 and land on 4. This may go on and on, with the group working for more and more speed. This exercise gives the group definite pitches to sing instead of just wild guesses. Be sure to encourage the singers to remember 6 once it has been sung. The *do-re-mi* system may be used instead of numbers.

When the class is singing from songbooks, stimulate interest in pitches by playing the pitches of a new page number on the piano instead of announcing it. Page 154 is announced by playing the tonic, dominant, and subdominant in the key of the new song. Students who misjudge the pitch intervals are frustrated by being the last ones to find the page, and a real motivation for learning pitch is created. This procedure serves to orient students to the key of the new song and to develop their pitch perception. Performing telephone numbers also will be fun.

A temporary device to assist with interval recognition that may be of service in the general music class or even the advanced choir rehearsal at times is to have the students think the opening-notes of a well-known song:

Ascending

Minor second:
  "Star-dust"
  "Reaching for the Moon"
  "White Christmas"

Major second:
  "Are You Sleeping?"

Minor third:
  Brahms' "Lullaby" ("Wiegenlied")
  "Five Foot Two, Eyes of Blue"

Major third:
  "Christ the Lord Is Risen Today"
  "The Marine Hymn"

Perfect fourth:
  "Here Comes the Bride"
  "The Eyes of Texas"
  "Auld Lang Syne"
  "The Farmer in the Dell"

Augmented fourth:
  "Maria" (from *West Side Story*)

Perfect fifth:
  "Twinkle, Twinkle Little Star"

Augmented fifth:
  "Go Down, Moses"

Major sixth:
  "My Bonnie"
  "The Old Oaken Bucket"
  NBC identification

Minor seventh:
  Introduction to Act II of
    "Lohengrin" (see example)

Descending

Minor second:
  "Joy to the World"

Major second:
  "Three Blind Mice"

Minor third:
  "The Caisson Song" ("Over Hill,
    Over Dale")

Major third:
  "Swing Low, Sweet Chariot"
  "Sentimental Journey"

Perfect fourth:
  "Dona Nobis Pacem"

Perfect fifth:
  "The Star-Spangled Banner"
  "For Unto Us a Child Is Born"

Major sixth:
  "Nobody Knows de Trouble
    I've Seen"

"Emperor Waltz" (Strauss)

Major seventh:
  "Bali Hai" (first and third notes)

Octave:
  "Over the Rainbow"
  "The More We Get Together"

The teacher may wish to give musical dictation. In this procedure, the teacher plays and the students listen, the students sing what the teacher has played, the students write what they have sung, then selected students read aloud what they have written. If the students cannot write intervals and rhythms at the same time, begin by working on the two aspects separately. When working with *pitch only*, use an X instead of a note for clarity and speed; for example:

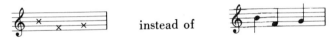

Even in an advanced choir the teacher may wish to place "mystery melodies" on the board to see if the students can hear mentally well enough to identify songs. These melodies may be placed in regular notation; for example:

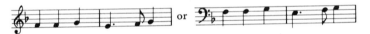

Do not use words. Place numbers, *do-re-mi*, or key names under the notes to help the slow ones, but not until the quicker students have guessed the tune. Then sing the melody with pitch symbols. The mystery melody may be shown in many ways; for example:

```
                2        2
         1  1      7-  1


                 G        G
           F  F      E-  F


                 re        re
         do  do      ti-  do


                 __       __
         __  __      __
```

The conductor may use excerpts from songs being currently rehearsed, including particularly some problem areas from bass, alto, or tenor parts. Consult Chapter 9 for more advanced ideas on ear training that are suitable for the choir. In the general music class, have students bring tunes and challenge the class to guess them. Advertisement themes make excellent mystery melodies, for TV and radio have made these melodies well-known to the students, and young people receive great satisfaction from identifying these tunes. (See Chapter 10 for an interesting way to present a whole-tone scale.)

Another technique to use in the general music or chorus class is to place on the board a tune the group does not know. Have a student come to the board and then have the class tell the pupil what numbers or syllables to place under the notes. After the melody has been numbered, have the class sing 1-3-5-3-1-5-1 in the proper key and then sing the melody by numbers without the aid of the piano.

ESTABLISHING HARMONIC FAMILIARITY

This section applies only to the general music class or non-selective chorus class. Many of the students in these classes will be unable to hold a harmonic part because of musical inexperience. The few students who are able to sing harmony must be involved in leadership roles, assisting in the development of harmonic independence in those who are within their voice sections. The teacher must realize that development of rhythmic and melodic independence does not insure any degree of harmonic independence. The seating arrangements discussed in Chapter 2 will assist but will not solve the problem. Students become confused and cannot hold their vocal line, especially if voices are sounding above and below them. A very simple way to give a beginning group some idea of how it sounds and feels to sing harmony is to start all of the choir on 8; have the sopranos hold on 8 while all of the other voices move to 7, then to 6, then to 5; have tenors hold on 5 and continue singing the pitch while all remaining voices sing 4 and 3; have the altos hold on 3 while the basses sing 2 and hold the pitch after they sing 1.

One of the first experiences the teacher will want to give the harmonically unoriented group is the singing of songs that may be adapted rhythmically and harmonically so they may be sung at the same time. Students who can hold their parts on a song or round while another melody is being sung are obtaining experience in holding their parts in a harmonic structure. Some songs and rounds that may be adapted to be sung together are "Solomon Levi" and "Spanish Cavalier," "Ten Little Indians" and "Skip to My Lou," choruses of "Shoo Fly" and "Jimmy Crack Corn," "Are You Sleeping?" and "Row, Row, Row Your Boat," "Are You Sleeping?"

and "Three Blind Mice," "Are You Sleeping?" and "The Farmer in the Dell," "The Farmer in the Dell" and "Row, Row, Row Your Boat," "The Farmer in the Dell," and "Three Blind Mice," "Row, Row, Row Your Boat" and "Three Blind Mice," "Keep the Home Fires Burning" and "There's a Long, Long Trail," and "When You and I Were Young, Maggie" and "Darling Nellie Gray."

Another introductory experiencing of harmony may be provided through the singing of rounds or canons where the student must learn to hold a part against three or four others parts. Since most of the rounds are built on the I chord, the harmonic intervals are extremely consonant and easy to hear. After the group attains some skill, rhythmic interest may be added by simultaneously singing the round at varying speeds, that is, the speed of the second and third parts may be doubled or quadrupled, or slowed to one half or one-fourth speed. For example:

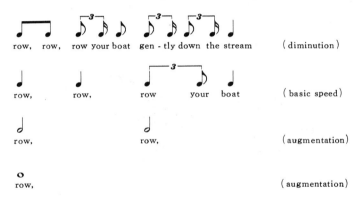

Following are a few rounds and their keys:

"Row, Row, Row Your Boat"
 (Key of C)

"Little Tom Tinker" (Key of C)

"Are You Sleeping? (Key of F)

"Scotland's Burning"
 (Key of A♭—*sol*)

"Three Blind Mice"
 (Key of D—*mi*)

"The Farmer in the Dell"
 (Key of F—*sol*)

"Oh How Lovely is the Evening"
 (Key of G)

"Sweetly Sings the Donkey"
 (Key of F)

"Hello" (Key of E♭)

"Merrily, Merrily Greet the Morn"
 (Key of E♭)

There are a number of fine descant books (Krone, Foltz, Kjelson, and others) that may be used as other sources for harmonic enrichment. A canon or a round may have an independent melody above or below it, and any song may be made more enjoyable by the addition of a descant. Even when a group can sing harmony, the descant adds variety and interest.

The use of ostinato and chanting techniques is one of the most creative and interesting ways to teach beginning harmonies. A teacher may quite easily have four- or five-part harmony going at the same time as the melody, even with third or fourth graders. Chants and ostinatos may be used on one-, two-, or three-chord melodies, but they work the most easily with one-chord songs. One-chord songs are usually rounds or they are songs based on the pentatonic scale, for example, "Little David, Play On Your Harp" (key of F, beginning tone on 3). If a round is used, it may be sung in parts when it is added above the ostinato.

Some chant or ostinato patterns for I chord songs are 1, 3, 5, or 8 singly or in any combination, for example, 1-1-1; 3-3-3; 5-5-5; 8-8-8; 1-8-1; 1-3-5; 3-5-8; 1-3-1; 5-3-5; 3-5-3; 5-3-1; and so forth. Other combinations are 1-5-1; 1-7-6-5; 1-5-6-5; 5-6-5; and so on. The words used for the chant must fit into the song's meaning. The rhythms may be simple or sophisticated, so long as they fit into the rhythmic structure of the song. The teacher may call upon the students to make up the chants or may have some ready to use. Some examples of chanting on "Row, Row, Row Your Boat" follow:

Merrily,   merrily,   merrily,   merrily

Then start the melody on C. Other voices continue on these pitches through one verse of the song, then taper off.

Then start the melody and go through the verse. The sixth or seventh of the chord (in this case A or B♭) may be added if modern-sounding harmony is desired. Remember also the possibility of using the three-part round above the chant or a round with rhythmic variations.

Ostinato patterns may also be used with two- and three-chord songs, and although the process is a little more difficult, the experience is rewarding to the students. The scale tone 5 is the only pitch common to both the I and the V⁷ chords, which are the chords used in two chord songs. The scale tone 6 can also be added and the sound will not be offensive to the ears. The I chord patterns have already been discussed. Some patterns for V⁷ are 5-5-5; 5-6-5; 5-2-5; 5-4-5; 7-7-6-5; 7-6-5-5; 7-5-6-7; 7-5-7; 7-5-6-5; 2-5-6-7; 2-5-2; and 4-5-4. When ostinato or chant patterns are used on three-chord songs, use the I, IV, V chords suggested under the following paragraphs on "vocal chording" and change pitches on the chant whenever the chords suggest. The teacher who wishes to appeal to young people may want to use boogie bass patterns and change to various chords; for example:

Or use a I chord round like "Frere Jacques" and use only the I chord above. One of the following boogie-woogie patterns might be used:

Another way to teach elementary harmony is through vocal chording. If students have not already learned how chords are constructed, show them, using the number system (1-3-5).

The most elementary step, though not the easiest to perform, is to have the entire group sing the root of the chord. Here is an example in the key of C:

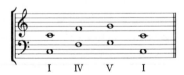

Have part of the group sing melody while the rest of the class sings the chord roots (then reverse sections). Use any of the three-chord songs listed later in this chapter.

The following table is the easiest one to use when teaching the three chords for use by the student at the keyboard or in vocal chording. The reader will notice that the chord is placed in close position.

Notice that the bottom part moves only on V⁷ and then a half step down; the middle part goes a half step up on IV and V⁷; and the top part lifts one step on IV only. Any singer, no matter how inexperienced, can make these simple changes and get the experience of singing harmony. Assign one section to the low part, one to the middle, another to the low part, and the remaining students to the melody. Teach the bottom part, using finger signals; teach the middle part; then do these two parts together. Teach the top part; then have the three parts sing together, mixing finger signals until the chords are thoroughly learned. Add the melody above the chord, and indicate chord changes by finger signals whenever the melody requires the changes (or have the students indicate when the chord sounds wrong and needs to be altered). Variety may be provided by having the melody sung by a section, sung by one person, played on the piano by the teacher or by a student, or played on any instrument by a student, while sections of the class sing the chords. Variety may be provided by reversing roles and having the class sing the melody while chords are played on the piano, one pupil at a time playing the chord changes in close position; on the piano, three pupils at a time, each student playing his note in a different octave, for example, C, e, ǵ; on the resonator bells (see the procedure earlier in the chapter); or have students take turns playing the chords on the Autoharp, ukuleles, guitars, or string bass.

Comparison of vocal chording in minor and major keys:

Note:
1. The lower line is the same in major and minor
2. The middle line is one whole step up in minor
   The middle line is one half step up in major
3. The upper line is one half step up in minor
   The upper line is one whole step up in major

On songs having only two chords (I and V⁷) use the above chord progressions, simply leaving out IV.

Some two-chord songs (I, V^7):

"The Big Corral" (G-D^7)
"Buffalo Gals" (F-C^7)
"The Deaf Woman's Courtship"
    (C-G^7)
"Ezekiel Saw de Wheel" (C-G^7)
"Goin' to Leave Old Texas"
    (F-C^7)
"It's Me" (G-D^7)

"The More We Get Together"
    (F-C^7)
"Old Ark's A'Moverin'" (F-C^7)
"Orchestra Song" (C-G^7)
"Polly Wolly Doodle"
    (G-D^7 or F-C^7)
"Sandy Land" (G-D^7)
"Ten Little Indians" (C-G)
"Three Blind Mice" (C-G^7)

"Blow the Man Down" (F-C^7)
"Come, Thou Almighty King" (G-D^7)
"Down in the Valley"
    (G-D^7 or F-C^7)
"Happy Birthday" (C-G)
"Long, Long Ago" (F-C^7)

"Oh, My Darling Clementine"
    (G-D^7)
"Old MacDonald" (G-D^7)

"A Paper of Pins" (G-D^7)
"Rocka-My Soul" (F-C^7)
"Skip to My Lou" (F-C or G-D)

"This Old Man" (F-C^7)
"White Coral Bells" (C-G^7)

Some three-chord songs (I, IV, V^7):

"All Through the Night"
    (G-C-D^7)
"Auld Lang Syne" (F-B♭-C^7)
"Battle Hymn of the Republic"
    (B♭-E♭-F^7)
"Blow the Man Down" (F-B♭-C^7)
"The Caisson Song" (C-F-G^7)
"Dinah" (G-C-D)
"Dixie" (C-F-G)
"For He's a Jolly Good Fellow"
    (F-B♭-C^7)
"Go Down, Moses" (g minor or
    f minor)
"The Happy Wanderer" (C-F-G)
"Jacob's Ladder" (C-F-G)

"Jimmy Crack Corn" (F-B♭-C^7)
"Johnny Schmoker" (E-A-B^7)
"Little Mohee" (C-F-G^7)
"Loch Lomond" (F-B♭-C^7)
"The Marine Hymn" (C-F-G^7)
"Nelly Bly" (B♭-E♭-F)
"O Christmas Tree" (F-B♭-C^7)
"Old Dan Tucker" (G-C-D^7)
"Old MacDonald" (G-C-D^7)
"O No, John" (G-C-D^7)

"O Worship the King" (G-C-D^7)
"Silent Night" (C-F-G^7)
"Soldier, Will You Marry Me"
    (F-B♭-C^7)
"We Three Kings" (g minor)

"America" (F-B♭ -C^7) (G-C-D^7)

"Away in a Manger" (G-C-D^7)
"Sweet Betsy from Pike" (C-F-G^7)

"Bound for the Rio Grande" (F-B♭-C^7)
"Come, Thou Almighty King" (G-C-D^7)
"Dinah Won't You Blow" (G-C-D^7)
"Faith of Our Fathers" (G-C-D^7)
"Get on Board" (G-C-D)

"Go Tell it on the Mountain"
    (F-B♭-C^7)
"Home on the Range" (G-C-D^7)
"Jesus Walked this Lonesome
    Valley" (F-B♭-D^7)—begins on D)
"Jingle Bells" (G-C-D^7)
"Joy to the World" (C-F-G^7)
"Li'l Liza Jane" (C-F-G^7)
Brahms' "Lullaby" ("Wiegenlied") (C-F-G^7)
"My Lord, What a Mornin'" (D-G-A^7)
"Night Herding Song" (G-C-D^7)
"Oh! Susanna" (F-B♭-C^7)
"Old Folks at Home" (C-F-G^7)
"Old Smoky" (C-F-G^7)
"Our Boys Will Shine Tonight"
    (G-C-D^7)
"Red River Valley" (G-C-D^7)
"Smoky Mountain" (G-C-D^7)
"Stodola Pumpa" (B♭-E♭-F^7)

All of these harmonic adventures appear to lead toward a goal of harmonic performance. Although the ability of students to sing harmonically is the obvious target, a development of an appreciation of the role of harmony in the music of the Western world is also an important goal. Thus, the student should be led to discover that harmony may be vertical or horizontal, serves in the capacity of supporting or accompanying the melody, may be rhythmic, and may have varying textures. Harmonic experiences should include the singing of two songs simultaneously, rounds, canons, descants, ostinatos, chants, vocal chording and instrumental experiences including keyboard. Although homophonic forms of music will be performed much of the time, students must be exposed to all the ways polyphonic music is organized and to contemporary harmonic practices. The teacher must make students cognizant of the expressive qualities of consonance and dissonance, the way chords resolve into other chords at cadence points, and the role of chords in modulation. Students should be able to at least see and hear a chord progression, and should be aware of the location of their pitches in relationship to other notes in the chord. Further experiences in harmony may be supplied by the singing of chorales, hymns, and authentic folksongs. Students will be interested in a unit that shows the historical development of harmony. Some sensitivity to the beauty of harmony in music must be cultivated. Chapter 9 contains additional information that will assist the more advanced group. Note Chapter 10 for an interesting technique to demonstrate polytonality.

There are many common musical names and symbols that a teacher must know and teach to the students. It is necessary for students to learn the music vocabulary in order to understand music, for students negotiating the highway of music will soon lose their way when they cannot read the music road signs. However, the teacher must teach these music signs in the context of music being rehearsed, not as so many abstractions. It will be a total waste of time for students to memorize lists of terms that are not correlated in some meaningful way with music being studied.

SIGHT-READING FOR CONTESTS

The conductor must realize that no one can sight-read who cannot read rhythmic patterns and melodic and scale patterns at a glance and hear all pitches mentally *before* singing them. When the director prepares for sight-reading contests, chord and scale construction must be taught as part of the daily procedures. The teaching of basic rhythmic problems and the use of regular drill on ear training must be related to a sight-reading song. Do some sight-reading every day. Talk through the problems and sing the song as though in a real contest. Use progressively difficult numbers as the choir learns to read more fluently. Use the tape recorder frequently so students can criticize themselves objectively. Hold 'mock' sight-reading contests in class and grade the efforts. Try sight-reading on a concert after the choir has developed some ability. (Be sure the audience *knows* you are sight-reading.)

Materials

If the level of sight-reading ability is low, start by using one of the books written specifically to teach sight-reading skills. These include numerous books by Carl W. Vandre (Richard Scott), published by Mills Music, Inc. Additional books are *The Key to Sight-Reading* by Theron Kirk, and *See and Sing*, Volumes I, II, III, by Walter Ehret, both published by Pro Art Publications, Inc., the five-part *Read and Sing Series* arranged by H. M. Shellans, published by Staff Music Pub. Co., *Melodia* by Cole and Lewis, published by Oliver Ditson Co., *Teaching Choral Sight Reading* by Jack Boyd, published by Parker Publishing Co., Inc., and *The Choral Singer's Handbook* by Roy C. Bennett, published by Belwin Mills Publishing Company. For a different approach try investigating *The Warmer Upper* by Ivan Kortkamp, published by Mohawk Publishing Company.

Hymns, chorales, and authentic folksongs are the next logical materials to use. Do not neglect the use of regular octavo numbers chosen from the concert repertoire, which provide varying problems (include contemporary music also). Work especially on modulations in some of the songs.

At the Contest

The director can *conduct* the dynamics, so don't waste time talking about them. Do call attention to the time signature. Establish the basic rhythms and beat patterns in the song (one of the most efficient ways to do this is to beat the pattern and chant the words in rhythm). Direct the choir's attention to any irregularities in rhythmic figures and parts that move when other voice lines do not. Show the group any phrases that are alike or almost alike, and, if they differ, *how* they differ. Particularly identify any unisons that occur between bass and treble clef voices. Point out scalewise passages and melodic skips along chord lines. Find the key modulations and brief the students on what each part must do, for example, go up one half step or one whole step, etc. Teach the choir through daily exercises to always be able to negotiate half and whole steps. Sometimes the most efficient way to orient a choir to difficult skips in a modulation is by means of the opening notes of a well-known song. Point out common tones often held by certain parts through modulating sections. Point out the accidentals, and remind the students that these notes throw the song temporarily into a new key and so must be sung slightly *sharper* or *flatter* than if they were flats or sharps in the key signature. Remind the group of any notation meanings that will help them read the number better, but don't waste time giving any unnecessary reminders. If the group has sung a song in this style, remind them of the similarity. Show the choir how and where each voice part enters; and if there are any troublesome releases, tell what to do with them. Direct the choir from beginning to end without allowing a break in rhythm. Anyone losing their place must catch on and come back in. The accompanist (if it is legal to use one) should bring out the base of the chord, which ordinarily is in the bass line.

CONCLUSION

Everyone blames someone else for the poor sight-reading ability of students. The professional organization blames the college, the college blames the high school, the high school maligns the junior high, and the elementary program is chastised by the junior high teachers. The elementary school actually does the best job of teaching sight-reading, wherever capable music specialists are in charge of the program; but the shortage of qualified teachers remains an unsolved problem. However, even when a good music program is functioning in the elementary school and musical concepts and sight-reading are being taught well, the program breaks down in junior high because of changing voice problems and overly ambitious musical programs. In order to learn too-advanced literature, the director resorts in desperation to rote processes in order to learn the program in time for performance, in the meantime neglecting the basic musical concepts that should accompany the learning. Notation unlike that seen in elementary school, and the addition of bass clef, add to the students' confusion. Junior high teachers fail to use the base that has been provided by the elementary school, review any knowledge the students have acquired thus far, and build new ear training and sight-reading attainments to the spiral of learning. Even more excellent musical attainments will result from this process than from desperately pounding the piano into students' ears through rote note drill, but the progress will seem much slower to the teacher at first. As the sight-reading skills and better musical information begin to bear fruit, students will be able to read faster and more knowledgeably.

Lack of sight-reading ability becomes an even more serious problem in high school where more sophisticated music will be performed. In the school system where sight-reading skills have been neglected or ignored in the junior high, students will have lost any skills they might have possessed in elementary school. Many students do no singing in junior high and thus lose musical ability. Very few students will be totally lacking in information, but it may seem to the teacher that nothing has been taught. Instrumentalists and students with some background in piano become the leaders by default. Where a great variety of differences in reading skills exist, which is the situation in most classes, the teacher must make an effort to discover what actual skills and knowledges are possessed and build as soundly and rapidly as possible. Bear in mind that written and oral knowledge will *not* help the students sight-read. Music is a nonverbal language, and living musical experiences with pitch and rhythm and harmony are the only means by which sight-reading skills may be built. Investigate the students' sight-reading ability by some of the aural devices described at the beginning of this chapter. Deepen and build upon these abilities through rhythmic, melodic, harmonic, and ear training drills that grow from problems presented by interesting literature. Although the weak sight-reader must be taught habit patterns in rhythmic and melodic phrases, constant effort must be made to have the students gain the capacity to deal with several elements simultaneously. None of the musical elements must be an entity unto iself. Although *rhythm* is the element most easily isolated, it must grow out of the music and be related quickly back into the music. *Melodic patterns* cannot be isolated from some aspects of rhythm and harmony and the essential need for inner hearing of a note before it is sung; and unless students can be shown how these patterns are used in a song they are learning, they will not be motivated to work on the abstraction. *Harmonies* may begin with very simple concepts, but all the musical elements are involved, including form analysis. Since harmony functions as a foundation and accompaniment for live music, it cannot be intelligibly divorced from it. And so the teacher must work *with* and *from* live music at all times, drilling on first one concept then another, but always coming back to the making of music.

7

The General Music Class and Some Junior High Problems

Knowledge of this chapter's contents is as vital to the high school instructor as it is to the teacher of middle school or junior high classes. High school music classes can be taught intelligently only when the teacher has obtained thorough understanding of junior high music and musicians. Since the teaching of general music or general chorus classes is part of the high school teacher's responsibilities, this chapter presents essential instructional information. The reading of this chapter will provide insight into the characteristics of the junior high age group, some logical ways to give instruction to the new arrival in junior high (usually a seventh grader), ways to interest the student who is not successful in music and to involve the extremely bright student who may be bored, and a discussion of the changing voice and some recognized plans for its development.

TABLE OF JUNIOR HIGH CHARACTERISTICS

Young Women   *Young Men*

Voice Changes

The young women's voices may be very much like the voices of senior high women. Sopranos will have about the same range: firsts will be able to sing g" or a" easily; seconds, e" or f". Alto parts shouldn't extend below b or a, and should not stay for any extended time in that tessitura, for these young women are not really altos (there is an occasional rare alto).

In childhood, up into late adolescence, there is less resistance by the vocal bands to the outward-flowing air pressure than in adults, because the cartilaginous structure of the larynx is in a soft and pliable state. Thus it is to be assumed that usually children and young adolescents will sing with a somewhat breathy quality since they do not usually press or force too much energy into the vocal instrument. In adolescence the cartilage and vocal cords grow and develop rapidly and become better adjusted, tending to settle themselves into the correct sounds of adulthood. The teacher will be able to help the maturation process by insistence on proper breath support, posture, and vocal placement.

The voices of the young men at this age are beset by innumerable problems of change and range. These unsettled voices and some ways of dealing with them will be discussed elsewhere in this chapter. Before the change, the boy soprano voice is clearer, purer, more brilliant than the feminine voice, particularly in the "high" range. Low tones of both sexes will be thin and breathy.

Musical Background

Many young women have had piano lessons since many parents still subscribe to the early American concept that every cultured female must know how to play the piano. This exposure, plus quite a bit of contact with music in early life, makes them generally quite amenable to any music activities.

The male musical background is much more varied than the female. It is not unusual to find young men who have excellent instrumental or pianistic training, but there are many who have had little or no training in music. Some of these young men will be quite verbal about the fact that they don't like music.

Interests

Young women are likely to enjoy music, if it is presented in a way they can accept. They are willing to come for out-of-school rehearsals, etc., in order to be a member of a music group.

Most males of this age are more interested in athletics than in any other activity. Since most of the bodies are clumsy, it is difficult to determine yet which one is going to be the fine athlete, so even the nonathlete still feels he has a chance.

Young Women	*Young Men*

Emotional Natures

Expect these young women to be extremely emotional. Their emotions are very unstable, varying from happiness to moodiness within a short span of time.

The young man's emotional nature is likewise very changeable. However, he will try to make everyone think that he is unaffected.

Willingness to Participate

If the young women like the teacher, they will immediately be willing to do anything within reason that the teacher asks them to do in the music period.

Usually the young men will need to be won into active participation in a music class. They tend to react negatively toward any complete inclusion into all the activities of a class.

Importance of Peer Approval

The young woman is very conscious of what her peers like and do, and will usually conform. However, she is willing to be individualistic if she becomes really interested in something.

The young man must be completely positive that the other fellows approve and are doing the same things he does. He is not usually willing to be different. The teacher must attempt to convince *all* the young men in order to influence their behavior.

Maturity

The young woman is not mature, but she seems almost sophisticated and "grown up" in contrast with the junior high male. She is liable to talk constantly unless she is dealt with firmly.

The young man is not a mature being psychologically, sociologically, or physiologically. He tends to resist class discipline and to do things just to attract attention. He also tends to talk too much.

Song Selection

The young women will tend to go along with any music that the men like.

For the most part, the instructor should deliberately pick music that the young men will enjoy. The teacher must be able to convince them that it is a music a grown male would enjoy singing.

Some Special Problems of Grades 6–9

Educators recognize that youngsters in grades 6–9 are going through some very difficult stages in the process of growing up. Not only may one pupil be twenty inches taller than another, but these same inequalities of maturity will exist in emotional makeup, mental capacity, and personality traits. It is the specific aim of the school to help students make proper adjustments during this awkward transition period. Classes are taught by several teachers rather than by just one, and most students profit from this variation in teacher personalities. There is a tendency toward assignment of classes to one teacher for two or three periods, especially in the seventh grade, and gradual development toward a different teacher each period in the eighth and ninth grade.

The junior high school and middle school attempt to provide wide exploratory experiences, to surround the student with helpful situations, and to offer guidance so that the student may develop the ability to choose and better evaluate the courses that will be taken in high school and in college. General music is the key music class.

Teachers have not been adequately prepared to teach in the middle school or in the junior high school, and consequently there has been much "fumbling." Required are special skills, knowledges, and understandings such as how to handle changing voices, how to teach general music classes, and how to cope patiently and knowledgeably with adolescent attitudes. It has been common practice to "promote" the most skillful teachers to senior high (where they will usually be less effective, at least for a while). It is to be hoped that successful junior high teachers will choose to stay at that level and that they will eventually obtain as much prestige and salary as senior high instructors.

The junior-senior high school combination is likely to result in domination by the senior high school. Even when the junior high is separate, a new building erected near the high school so it can be shared by both schools usually results in the junior high building yielding to the senior high program. Many times the junior high inherits the old senior high building and equipment, and ways must be discovered to adapt and improve the existing situation. Frequently, junior high programs are essentially miniature senior high programs with little or no adaptations to the needs of that age.

Important differences may be noted between the seventh grade that is an extension of the elementary school and the seventh grade that is the lowest grade in junior high. The elementary seventh grader is "king of the walk"—cocky and sure of self. The seventh grader in junior high is low person on the totem pole. This student is made to realize by environment, teachers, and eighth and ninth graders that he or she knows next to nothing about life and school. These young people expect to be treated as young men and women, but don't be surprised when they act like children.

There is real danger in a music program that does not require general music through the eighth grade. One danger lies in the changing voices of the boys. Unless Johnny sings while he has his worst problems in the control of his vocal muscles, he is almost certain to stop singing permanently because of this embarrassing lack of control. He is likely to hide behind such statements as, "Music is sissy," to keep from revealing the fact that he does not have skill. A young man who is kept in the music program until after the eighth grade will ordinarily have been through the worst of the voice-changing problems and miseries and will have started back on the road toward enjoyment. The young man may be able then to see vocal music in its proper perspective.

A student should not be forced to choose between instrumental and vocal music. There is a need to learn to control vocal muscles as well as arm and leg muscles, and vocal control will not be learned when the instrumental program is chosen.

There is some controversy concerning specialized groups in middle school and junior high, especially if these organizations use the same kinds of uniforms, robes, music, etc., that are used in senior high. This kind of program can "take the edge off" the senior high programs. However, properly handled, there can be a tremendously successful program that grows as naturally into the more mature senior high organizations as a small tree grows into a large one.

GENERAL MUSIC

The core of the music curriculum in middle school and junior high is the general music class. High schools are beginning to realize that it may be a desirable course in their curricula, also. There will always be, and *should* always be, fine performing organizations. However, performance pressures will not permit members of a choir to learn all they need to learn to be generally educated in music. The nonperforming general music class has the potential to fill this knowledge gap by allowing students the opportunity and time to experience all the facets of music and to experiment with them until some answers are gained.

The MENC Committee on Music in General Education has published a list of eleven outcomes that may help to define the task of music as a part of general education.[1]

Skills

    I. The student . . . will have skill in listening to music. *The generally educated person listens with a purpose.* He recognizes the broad melodic and rhythmic contours of musical compositions. He is familiar with the sounds of the instruments of the orchestra and the types of human voices. He can hear and identify more than one melody at a time. He can recognize patterns of melody and rhythm when repeated in identical or in altered form. He can concentrate on sounds and the relationships between sounds.

    II. He will be able to sing. *The generally educated person is articulate.* He uses his voice confidently in speech and song. He sings in a way that is satisfying to himself. He can carry a part in group singing. His singing is expressive.

[1] *Music in General Education* (Washington, D.C.: MENC, 1965), pp. 4–8.

III. He will be able to express himself on a musical instrument. *A generally educated person is curious.* He is interested in how instrumental music is produced and willing to try his hand at making music, if only at an elementary level with a percussion instrument, a recorder, or a "social-type" instrument. He experiments with providing accompaniments for singing and rhythmic activities. He is familiar with the piano keyboard.

IV. He will be able to interpret musical notation. *The generally educated person is literate.* He understands arithmetical and musical symbols. He is able to respond to the musical notation of unison and simple part songs. He can follow the scores of instrumental compositions.

Understandings

V. He will understand the importance of design in music. *The generally educated person understands the structure of the various disciplines.* He knows the component parts of music and the interrelationships that exist between melody, rhythm, harmony, and form. He is able to recognize design elements aurally, and he uses musical notation to confirm and reinforce this recognition. He realizes that the active listener can, in a sense, share in the composer's act of creation. By understanding how music communicates, he has come to gain insight into what it communicates.

VI. He will relate music to man's historical development. *The generally educated person has historical perspective.* He recognizes that music has long been an important part of man's life. He understands that its development in Western civilization is one of the unique elements of his own heritage. He is familiar with the major historical periods in that development and the styles of music which they produced. He has acquaintance with some of the musical masterpieces of the past and with the men who composed them. He relates this knowledge to his understanding of man's social and political development.

VII. He will understand the relationships existing between music and other areas of human endeavor. *The generally educated person integrates his knowledge.* He has been helped to see that the arts have in common such concepts as design resulting from repetition and variation. Sociology and politics are recognized as pertinent to the development of art as well as to economics. He understands how literature and music enhance one another and together illuminate history. The mathematical and physical aspects of music are known to him through aural experiences as well as through intellectual inquiry.

VIII. He will understand the place of music in contemporary society. *The generally educated person is aware of his environment.* He understands the function of music in the life of his community and he accepts some responsibility for exercising his critical judgment in order to improve the quality of music heard in church and on radio and television. He is aware of the position of the musician in today's social structure and understands the opportunities open to him to engage in musical endeavor both as a vocation and as an avocation.

Attitudes

IX. He will value music as a means of self-expression. *A generally educated person has developed outlets for his emotions.* He recognizes music not only as a source of satisfaction because of its filling his desire for beauty, but also because of the unique way in which it expresses man's feelings. If he is not prepared to gain release by actually performing music, he has learned to experience this vicariously. He looks to music as a source of renewal of mind and body, as an evidence of beneficence in his life. He recognizes the importance of performers and composers and is grateful for the pleasure and inspiration which they give him.

X. He will desire to continue his musical experiences. *The generally educated person continues to grow.* He seeks additional experiences in areas in which he has found satisfaction. He looks for community musical activities in which he can participate. He attends concerts and listens to music on radio, television, and recordings. He keeps informed concerning happenings in the world of music by reading newspapers and magazines.

XI. He will discriminate with respect to music. *The generally educated person has good taste.* He has learned to make sensitive choices based upon musical knowledge and skill in listening. He evaluates performances and exercises mature judgments in this area. He is not naive with respect to the functional use of music for commercial purposes nor to the commercial pressures which will be exerted to obtain what money he can spend for music.

The realization of these outcomes presents a challenge of considerable magnitude to the music educators of America. As a set of even minimum goals they may appear remote from the current situation in many communities today. Remoteness of an objective is not an unfamiliar situation for the profession, however. Consider the progress made towards the establishment of a truly musical nation since the days of music education in a frontier society. Let us assure ourselves that nothing less than these outcomes, or a comparable set of objectives, is acceptable as a goal for music in general education.

Although this statement is intended to express minimum specific goals for the twelve or thirteen years of school, it may be used as an idealistic goal in planning general music classes. The quoted book is a source of many fine ideas and suggested activities, but is not much concerned with teaching techniques.

The general music class is liable to be a dry, uninteresting subject unless students are taught creatively and are encouraged to actively participate in the music by experimenting with it.

The most important word in creative learning is *discovery*. The excitement of a new revelation will cause students to work at developing skills and techniques that will assist them in learning and doing more with the issues in which there is such great interest. The teacher must share in their excitement and enthusiasm, even when the new learning has been "discovered" with several previous classes. "In music, the teacher knows a child understands a concept, not when he can tell it, but when he can show it, perform it, or apply his knowledge to a new situation."[2] Reading about singing until the principles can be verbalized will never enable a choir or soloist to sing well. The only way singers can learn to sing properly is through practice and experience. "In learning by discovery the name (statement of the law or rule) is not presented first, then the meaning, but the conception is first discovered, and later the name for it is assigned."[3] Both art and music are essentially nonverbal. Music teachers must understand music nonverbally, or they are *not* musicians and certainly cannot explain to students that which they themselves do not comprehend. The method of discovery is one of the few methods by which music can be approached and understood on a nonverbal level.

Creativity in Listening

Both the student and the teacher are inclined to consider musical composition as the only true form of creativity. It is, indeed, the most outstanding example of individuality and originality, but there are other aspects of creativity that may be even more important for those in music education to explore. One of the most important is listening.

The teaching of listening skills is a vital part of teaching a general music class, a privilege that is usually delegated to the choral music educator. Creativity in listening consists of discovering and obtaining insight into the music's basic elements. Listeners must be able to identify with the music and express their individuality. Since there are many kinds of music, many levels of understanding and musical maturity, and almost as many ways of listening as there are listeners (from the one who simply soaks music up in a passive way without really understanding it, described by Ellison as a "tone-bather,"[4] to the sophisticate who perceives all or most of the musical elements when he or she listens), the approach needs to be varied to fit the music and situation.

Ellison[5] advocates the use of the developmental approach to listening, which comprises a sequence of cycles. Each cycle includes a preface by the teacher, class listening to the record, followed by class discussion. Each new record is played to see if the students like it. Each cycle then explores the following questions with greater and greater depth. How many liked the music? How many didn't? Who can't decide until the music is heard again? (The main thing is that the students *respond*; it is not important at

---

[2] Charles B. Fowler, "Discovery Method and Music Education," *Journal of Research in Music Education*, XIV, No. 2 (Summer, 1966), p. 134.

[3] *Ibid*, p. 129.

[4] Alfred Ellison, *Music With Children* (New York: McGraw-Hill Book Company, 1959), p. 199.

[5] Ibid., pp. 216–24.

this point whether the response is positive or negative.) Who can give some reasons why the music is liked or not liked? When students listen, what things do they listen for? (Students may listen for a story, for kinds of instruments, for tone color, for rhythms, for melodies, for harmonies, for structure, or even for *nothing*.) Ask if the class can perceive what one member of the group notices in the music. (Replay the record to see if they can.) Such types of questions are excellent, regardless of the basic approach to listening. Ideal as Ellison's creative approach seems, in an actual classroom situation many discipline problems are apt to arise from a "just listen" atmosphere. Young people are so accustomed to hearing music as a background accompaniment to doing homework or chatting with their friends that the habit of not being intellectually aware of the music tends to continue. Teachers have found it usually more practical to raise a question the students must answer by listening.

Reimer's approach[6] to listening stresses the necessity of teaching music for aesthetic education. If music is to give students an aesthetic experience, the music must have great variety and be expressive and worthwhile (see Chapter 3 on music selection). Furthermore, the general music class will not have a high enough degree of performance skill to be able to *perform* a great deal of the music that needs to be experienced, so the only way additional learnings and insights may be experienced is through listening and analyzing. Reimer suggests that the *sequence of learning* (way to study and learn about music) should usually follow an a-b-a pattern of (a) musical experience, (b) musical study, (a) musical re-experience. Study, through which deeper musical sensitivity and perception may be accomplished, is carried out by exploring the music in a creative manner. The process of exploration may be carried out through locating and inspecting the musical elements, then identifying, classifying, and comparing them by finding characteristic traits and similar or contrasting elements. Additional understanding about the music and the musical elements will be gained when modification of the music takes place through rearranging, reconstructing, combining, or developing. Perception may also be gained through discussion. Explain and clarify music by defining; by demonstrating and manipulating instruments, rhythms, melodic themes, styles, etc,; and by recalling what has been learned. Music analysis can be an exciting and rewarding study experience that should result in heightened musical perception and sensitivity.

Following are a few concrete ways to implement these two approaches. Reimer would probably agree almost entirely with the techniques discussed on pp. 170–71. He would *not* agree with some of the other techniques proposed, on the grounds that they do not lead directly to aesthetic learning. Nevertheless, all of these teaching techniques may be ways to obtain student interest and involvement. Student interest may

----

[6] Reimer, *A Philosophy of Music Education*, Chapter 8.

then be directed by the teacher into the deeper and more valid musical understandings.

One technique is to utilize the titles of compositions or names of movements. A composition may be introduced by writing the title or names of movements on the board and asking the students questions about them. Thus, a discussion of Dvorak's Symphony No. 9 ("From the New World") should bring out questions about the circumstances under which it was written, why it contains melodies that remind us of the Negro spiritual, and so on. The movements, Adagio, Allegro Molto, Largo, Scherzo, and Finale, have tempo characteristics and general meanings that will contribute to the students' understandings if they are discussed.

Another technique the teacher may wish to use is that of having the students listen in order to determine the title of the composition, possible names of movements, or the story without previously giving them this information.

Before the music is introduced, the teacher or one of the students may tell an interesting or unusual story. The story may be about the composer, as in Deems Taylor's fascinating story of "Wagner the Monster." The story of the music may be told; for example, that of "Dans Macabre." A story about people associated with a historical period will many times make the period more meaningful; for example, George Washington's time was the time of William Billings' fuging tunes in this country and the time when Mozart was composing in Europe. Relating the customs of the period represented by the music may be interesting, for example, Beethoven and the customs and mores that were prevalent during the French Revolution. Motion pictures of great composers or people associated with the period will introduce music well when timing is good in obtaining the film.

Imaginatively introduce music through the use of various audio-visual means. If the composer based his music upon a painting, a story, or a poem, use the appropriate medium and the background information concerning it to introduce the record. For a number like Ferde Grofe's *Grand Canyon Suite*, use still photographs, slide-films, motion pictures, rocks collected from the site, and personal experiences the class has had in the Grand Canyon. Even when the music is not inspired by any visual or auditory materials, painting or poetry of a similar mood may be used as correlative material.

Tell the students to listen carefully and see if any particular *colors* are visualized in their minds. If so, have the class try to analyze the music to determine why those particular colors might have been suggested by the tone-colors, rhythms, melodies, harmonies, or other of the musical elements.

Themes written on charts or on the chalkboard may be played or sung by the instructor so they will be recognized and can be readily identified by the students when they hear them in the music. It is even better to have the students *sing* the theme, then follow the notation of the themes on the chalkboard or on the chart while they are being played.

Local musicians may be invited to perform the music and to demonstrate instruments or voice. Most communities contain a reservoir of untapped talent.

An interesting technique may be used when familiar songs or folk tunes are included in the work. Nationalist composers, particularly, use songs of their countries. Have the students discover these melodies on the first hearing; for example, they should try to discover "The Old Chisholm Trail," "The Dying Cowboy," and "Git Along Little Dogies" in Copland's *Billy the Kid* Ballet. The same technique can be employed to have students find a melody that has been *stolen* by a popular song writer. Tchaikovsky's Symphony No. 6 ("Pathetique"), for example, has been plagiarized frequently.

Students may temporarily assume the role of composers when a number like Honegger's *Pacific 231*, Debussy's *La Mer*, Smetana's *Moldau*, or Haydn's Symphony No. 101 ("Clock") is to be studied. Have the students make intelligent guesses about the way the music will sound when it is played. Determine what instruments will be used, the kinds of tempo, the type of harmony, the basic style that might be expected from the composer, whether staccato or legato will be used, etc. Then let them hear the record and make comparisons between what they thought would happen and what actually transpired.

The teacher must try not to dominate or control the student's personal response to the music, but must attempt to make each student's musical perception keener through an examination of the musical elements, so that the student has the knowledge and skills to *independently* experience the music with greater understanding and deeper appreciation.

Descriptive words and phrases should not be used to the exclusion of, or in place of, legitimate musical terms. Be careful to call things by their right names; for example, use *fermata* instead of *bird's-eye*. However, creativity may be greatly stimulated through the use of imagination-stirring words. When students use various descriptive words, it is not a matter of one word being right and another one wrong. Each student has a right to his own descriptions. Much more creativity may be expressed by the students when they are encouraged to say that music *gallops* or *scampers* or *dances* or *bounces* or *swings* along than when the teacher simply states that the music is *fast*. One teaching procedure is to choose a few appropriate and inappropriate words from a thesaurus or a dictionary of synonyms and either have the students think of new appropriate words of their own or choose from the list.

Students may be challenged to use descriptive words to describe *any* of the musical elements: varying moods, tonal characteristics, rhythms, melodies, harmonies, and structure.

Discovering Musical Elements Through Listening

The teacher needs to help the students investigate and "discover" answers to the following questions about the musical elements:

What kinds of contrasting *moods* are present in the music? Can the listeners tell when mood change occurs? (Have the students draw or paint a picture inspired by the music. A song like Debussy's "Clair de Lune" would be an excellent mood study.)

What are the *tonal characteristics of each instrument?* Can the students recognize this sound when they hear it? Can the class recognize each instrument when they see it, even the more unusual instruments? Is the basic function of each instrument in the orchestra clear (to provide the base of the chord, the melody, color, etc.)? There are many examples that may be used, including such standards as *Peter and the Wolf* of Prokofiev, "Tubby the Tuba," and others.

If the music has a story, how did the composer manipulate the instruments and music to create the narration? (Students may prefer to make up their own story.) This comes under the category of "program music." You might wish to have the students dramatize the music or write a story inspired by the music. Such numbers as Dukas' *The Sorcerer's Apprentice* and Strauss's *Til Eulenspiegel* may be used for example and study.

What occurs in the *rhythm?* (Investigate many of the kinds of rhythmic patterns that are available. See Chapter 6 for some assistance.) Rhythm may be responded to by experimentation with body movements (hand-clapping, etc.), and with percussion instruments. An outstanding example is Ravel's *Bolero.*

What happens in the *melody* (major, minor, steps, skips, phrasing)? The study of melodic themes is fascinating. Students can learn to follow the main melodic line and eventually may also hear counter-melodies, melodic fragments, and so on. There are many beautiful melodies in music literature. Two of the symphonies most famous for their melodies are Tchaikovksy's "Pathetique" Symphony and Schubert's "Unfinished" Symphony.

What takes place in the *harmony?* (What style harmony was present in Pre-Renaissance, Renaissance, Baroque, etc.? What are distinguishing characteristics—polyphonic, etc. See the analysis sheets in Chapter 3 of this text for characteristics.) Use, for example, the Introduction to Brahms' Third Symphony.

What kind of style and *structure* does the music have? Learn to recognize music of the various nationalities and historical periods. Study sonata form, strophic, through-composed, etc. Use the simple folksong (strophic), the art song (through-composed), the sonata form in the first movement of the "Unfinished" Symphony, etc.

The preceding seven elements tend to become progressively more complicated. The sixth and seventh require real musicianship to negotiate with any skill. Familiarity with these seven elements will help to attain an ultimate goal of the ability to discriminate between good and bad music.

OTHER GENERAL MUSIC CLASS ACTIVITIES

Many times the person who is not successful in singing will be a discipline problem in the general music class. It is natural and normal to dislike whatever one cannot do. Somehow, the teacher must help this student to obtain some feeling of progress and at least a little success, in something. The student must be given the opportunity, in each class period, to do *some things* in which he or she has as much chance of success as other members of the class. While it is true that part of the general music class is spent singing, the teacher must realize that the student will be deprived of a complete musical experience unless given a chance to be creative (in *all* musical activities), learns to read music with more facility, has rhythmical experiences, has further experience with instruments, has additional insights through correlations with humanities and arts, does some composing, and is exposed to more music listening. It is highly possible for the unsuccessful singer to be completely successful in one or all of these other musical facets. The feeling of satisfaction accompanying any success may flow over into more rapport with music class. At the same time, the musical experiences of the entire class will be enriched.

Use the problem student to do routine tasks such as checking the class roll and passing out and putting away music. This tends to make the student feel more important and will usually result in a cooperative attitude.

There must always be the first splash somewhere in the pool of student musical interest. It doesn't matter too much *where* that contact occurs, so long as it happens. From that initial impact an ever-enlarging spiral of knowledge will move out into other facets of music. Thus, investigation of the more common rhythmic patterns used by electric guitars or in "soul rock" will eventually lead to the exploration of the distinctive rhythmical characteristics of the tango, waltz, march, tarantella, and so forth. The discussion of American folk music may be guided into a consideration of folk music of the various countries, and the influences of nationalism in Romantic and contemporary music. Folk music may logically be related to Baroque style with its extensive use of ostinato and figured bass. The thrill of harmonization that students feel even while singing a simple chant or vocal chording with a song will lead naturally to more elaborate experimentations with harmony. Most students like to manipulate instruments, even simple instruments, and it will be difficult for them to resist an opportunity to experiment with them. This can be a wedge to enriched musical realizations. The possibilities for causing that first splash are unending.

The student who cannot make his or her voice move up or down can ordinarily do rhythmic activities successfully such as square dancing, playing any kind of rhythm instrument (bongos or castanets), or tapping or patting rhythms (see Chapter 6 for supplementary ideas).

The plucked open strings of the cello (CGDA) or string bass (GDAE) make a fine base (bass) for the chord. Don't allow students to bow the instruments or the sound will not be so pleasing to the ear. Guitar and ukulele are excellent for chording with all songs except the most formal. If there are a number of instruments available, teach part of the class to finger the I chord, another class segment to finger the V chord, and so on, then point to sections as the song is performed. The piano will adapt to melodic *or* chordal treatment. Chapter 6 gives procedures for teaching the piano keyboard and resonator bells. Although the autoharp and omnichord are usually associated with elementary school, they may be used in middle school profitably. Any of these instruments also may be used rhythmically.

The problem with doing certain phases of theory such as building scales or learning what musical terms mean is that the unmusical student may not be interested enough in the music class to want to learn this type of information. Chapter 6 gives many interesting ways to teach theory and help students read music. Have the students do some composing to build their musical understandings and interest in theory.

Ask the students to contribute to the class unit, project, or program through some activities at which they excel, such as building musical instruments, props, and scenery; making posters; painting scenery; dancing; dramatics; helping write the script for the unit; helping with the costumes, with lighting and curtains, or with publicity if it is a public show (see Chapter 11 for full particulars concerning various kinds of programs).

Strangely enough, the students who are very bright in music are apt to be real discipline problems, especially if they are extroverts. These students will give a teacher trouble because they are bored and not challenged. The teacher needs to provide for individual differences by giving these good students extra responsibilities and supplementary, enriching opportunities. Challenge the bright students to use their abilities constructively to improve the class. In a private conference, tell them that you expect great things from them because of their superior abilities. Remind them that they can lead and inspire the class through their attention, posture, etc.; theirs is a great responsibility, since they also have the power to lead the class in the wrong direction. These students would usually make good class officers (president, section leader, student director, section pianist, etc.). The teacher may want to put them in charge of the bulletin board, have them make extra reports on various musical subjects, have them help with demonstrations, or ask them to sing solos. Be careful, however, that the extroverted students do not monopolize the class to the exclusion of offering enough opportunities for the quiet students.

COMPOSITION

Creating original melodies, harmonies, and rhythms is nearly always associated with the use of traditional musical notation. A more logical place to start with composition, when working with students who are relatively musically illiterate, is through a technique popularized by R. Murray Shafer (see Bibliography). This technique involves the building of sound-pictures or sound-scapes using various kinds of materials. Room sounds (chalk squeaking, venetion blind sounds, door sounds, desk sounds, etc.) may be employed by several groups of students to create compositions. Body sounds (patchen, fingers snapping, tapping, etc.) may be used to create other compositions. Musical instruments (resonator bells, guitars, recorders, piano, rhythm instruments, etc.) are another possibility for composition. Things brought from home (brake drums, oatmeal boxes, water glasses, etc.) will present interesting variations. Each of these ideas, which may be used as separate genre or in combination (perhaps adding voices or whistling), will give the students opportunity to create their own compositions and perform them for the class.

Some form of notation must be devised by the class members, but it is likely not to be traditional notation. Their contrived score must indicate certain lengths of time for the various kinds of sounds to last, and symbols for each kind of sound. If the composition is built around a central idea (portraying a tornado, describing a car going through a city and the sounds that might be heard, representing a skyscraper, depicting a rain storm with thunder and lightning, etc.) the composition will have a great deal more unity, continuity, and interest.

This whole process is a CMP approach, that of introducing students to music by having them compose it. Students tend to become highly motivated through this method of learning. Obviously, the greatest purpose of this kind of technique is to rouse students' interest in music and to pique their curiosity about musical notation. It then becomes easier for teachers to teach traditional notation and how it relates to the unconventional. Many of the suggestions in Chapter 6 may be used as starting points for rhythmic, melodic, and harmonic learning. As an example, ostinatos, chants, descants, and so forth may be created by the students.

A method created by Herbert Teat has merit at this stage in the student's development. Briefly, the system begins with very elementary pitches and rhythms. Moveable *do* or fixed *do* may be used instead of numbers if the teacher desires.

1. The starting pitches are 1, 3, and 5 used with a patch:

1	5	3	or with blips;	⑤
1	5	1		③
5	3	1		①

   The students sing the pitches in the patch or blips as the teacher points to the numbers. As the singers grow familiar with the procedure and pitches, move more rapidly with the baton and mix the order of the pitches. Make it exciting by trying to outguess the class members. (The blips used throughout this technique, are an adaptation of the Chambliss technique, explained in Chapter 6.)
2. The rhythm patterns are the ♩ note and 𝄽 rest in $\frac{4}{4}$ meter. Use no staff at the beginning. Students clap, count, and/or sing "tah."
3. Students may immediately start to invent melodies using these tools; and every student's melody is sung in class.
4. The learning sequence for pitches is: 1, 3, 5 up and down; then 1, 2, 3 up and down; then 1, 2, 3 up and down; 7; 4; and finally 6.
5. The meter sequence is: $\frac{4}{4}$, $\frac{3}{4}$, $\frac{2}{4}$, $\frac{3}{8}$, and $\frac{6}{8}$.
6. The notation sequence is: ♩. 𝄽. 𝅝. 𝄻. 𝅗𝅥. 𝄼. ♪. 𝄾. and the dot.
7. The key sequence is: C, F, G, B♭, D, E♭, A, A♭, and E.
8. Use 5–10 minutes per day for these exercises. Students fashion increasingly complicated original melodies and perform them.

This system has been tested in school systems and works very well. Don't hesitate to be flexible and adapt it to your own situation. If you wish more detailed information, contact Professor Herbert Teat, Music and Art Department, Tarleton State University, Stephenville, Texas 76401 for an inexpensive publication that will give a complete description of this innovative system.

THE SEVENTH GRADE SINGER

The teacher should use favorite songs carried over from elementary school to give the new seventh graders a feeling of security. It is important that there be a quick review of the musical principles learned the previous year. Instead of blaming the sixth-grade teacher for what the students do not appear to know, it is important to realize that students seem to lose about 90 to 95 percent of what they have learned the previous year. Try to find out exactly what was taught and then spend a few days reviewing these principles with the students, thereby refreshing their memories and driving the facts deeper so that they may be recalled in the future.

After establishing the basic principles, the instructor will move ahead into new music and more advanced work with part-singing. Since the students are used to reading from a *closed score*, the teacher must help them to feel comfortable and secure while reading from a score that looks entirely different, the *open score*. This may seem to be a small point, but seventh graders may feel that this different-looking music does not have the common properties of the score they are used to seeing. In most cases, the notes will be much smaller in junior high school books than they were in elementary school books, and the seventh grader will probably not be able to tell the voice parts from the piano score. Until the teacher orients the students to the correct vocal line, they will be justifiably confused.

Approach singing through the use of descants (a descant choir is an excellent group to use in the seventh grade), through short phrases or cadences that may be sung in *parts* in conjunction with a unison song, through the learning of uncomplicated antiphonal response songs like "Swing Low, Sweet Chariot," and through the reading of simple four-part songs (hymns, Stephen Foster songs, or folksongs). Junior high youngsters should build up a permanent repertory of memory songs (folksongs, art songs, hymns, school songs, patriotic songs, and fun songs). Have seventh graders do a tremendous amount of singing. Keep them busy singing, but teach harmony, theory, and other musical elements as an integral part of the learning. Don't neglect composing, listening, and instrumental activities.

In most localities real problems with the male changing voice problems will usually become more marked or troublesome in the seventh grade. Seventh-grade voices generally will be breathy and immature. A great deal can be done with these young men and women in the development of proper concepts and habits of breath support, posture, vowel formations, good consonants, and ability to sing mentally. It is especially important that young women as well as young men become acquainted with, and practice reading, the bass clef.

CREATING MALE INTEREST IN SINGING

As a point of departure for discovering how students may be interested in singing, here is a comparison of some factors that will cause a boy to lose interest or to gain it.

The Young Man's Lack of Interest in Music May Be Caused By:	The Young Man's Interest in Music May Be Aroused By:
Continuous use of smooth, soft singing —head tones only.	Allowing the young man to sing out but not shout.
Assignment to harmony parts that are likely to be difficult. The one who cannot read bass clef, cannot make his voice behave, and is asked to sing a music part that isn't interesting will undoubtedly dislike music.	Singing melody a proportionate amount of the time. Part singing should be added to unison singing to take care of the limited ranges.

The Young Man's Lack of Interest in Music May Be Caused By:	The Young Man's Interest in Music May Be Aroused By:
Absence of male teachers. Music that is taught does not seem grown-up or manly.	Male teachers. Emphasizing the manliness of singing.
Uninteresting rhythms or melodies.	Strong rhythms, good melodies.
Uninteresting music texts. *Don't* sing songs about the birds, daisies, and butterflies.	Using music texts that will thrill the redblooded male (see Chapter 3).
Lack of opportunity to express himself.	Giving the young male an opportunity to express himself in music.
The disturbance of mutation, causing the young man to think he cannot sing.	The skilled teacher who explains the physical problems as a natural occurrence and keeps him singing. The problems will be minimized in the adolescent who is kept singing with proper posture, breathing, and quality while the voice changes.

A young man's interest may also be aroused by inviting outstanding men in any walk of life to tell about the important part music has played in their lives; by visiting male soloists or groups (male quartets are excellent; use the local chapter of the Society for the Preservation and Encouragement of Barbershop Quartet Singing in America [SPEBSQUA] if there is one); by attending concerts given by college choirs on tour (or local high school choirs or male choruses); and by social gatherings and parties for music groups, particularly if there is *food* available (undoubtedly one of the real interests of a boy this age).

Be sure that the student learns at least *one* new thing about music every time he comes to music class and that he is aware of this learning. Keep him (and the class) aware of every improvement, no matter how slight (beginning to match pitches, beginning to be able to move his voice up and down, etc.). Use some of the suggestions listed in Chapters 4 and 5 for assisting the untuned voice.

Stress the values and importance of good posture. Point out to the class that first impressions and lasting impressions are dependent upon the student's *looks*, which are certainly enhanced by the good singing posture the music teacher advocates.

Discuss the importance of training the voice. Even the student who does not go on into music derives many positive values from voice training. Many of the finest public speakers have deliberately developed the use of their voices through vocal study (knowing how to sing will usually result in the improvement of the speaking voice). Whatever the student's ultimate vocation, a pleasant, resonant voice will be an asset, and a weak, monotonous, unpleasant voice will be a detriment.

It is very important to the teacher of junior or senior high students that the choral groups include athletes. Get the coach to back the choral program if you can. You will, of course, back the athletic program in the school (and dramatics and all other activities). The best male singers in these two age groups are almost invariably athletes. The reason for this is obvious; the athletes have the most mature bodies and are the strongest, most vital people. This maturity evens out a little when the students arrive in the college community, and the difference is not so great. The other reason for the importance of the athlete in the program is the prestige it gives to the music department. Other students are attracted because these athletes are in the choir. If music is required through the seventh or eighth grade, use some of the athletes in "small ensembles" to stimulate their involvement and interest in choral music. These young men will then be much more likely to remain in vocal music when it becomes an elective.

It takes strength and virility to produce a good singing tone. Remember that when anyone becomes sick, weakness is immediately apparent to everyone through a weak, shaky voice. Challenge them to hold their ribs out and hiss smoothly for 45 seconds or more and hold phrases out to their full duration. This kind of approach counteracts any feelings the young men may have that singing is sissy.

Male chorus and quartet or octet will interest young men, especially if manly music such as "Stouthearted Men" is used. A mixed choir may not interest them, especially if there are many women and just a handful of men. It will probably be necessary to start these male organizations outside school hours. After they become a success, as they are almost certain to be, they may be used as a springboard to promote men into choir. The school principal may usually be convinced that the male chorus belongs in school time. Ultimately, however, the male chorus will serve as a feeder for the more flexible concert group, the choir.

Many times a young man won't want to sing *tenor* because he feels it is less manly than it is to sing bass or baritone. The teacher can effectively remove this idea by citing the names of tenors the class knows. These tenors need to have been extremely good at some sport or have a manliness that everyone respects.

The young male desires nothing so much as to sound and look like a man; and unless he can be convinced that he is not detracting from his manly status, he will strongly resist any attempts to have him sing falsetto (which sounds, to him, like a girl singing). Pointing out the effective use of falsetto by barber shop quartet tenors (usually baritones) or by singers or singing groups that are current favorites of the adolescent (there will always be some who use falsetto) helps take away the stigma of sounding like women. The manly teacher singing for them in falsetto will also help. It is easier for the young singer to float into falsetto when he uses the $\overline{oo}$ vowel. Speaking numbers (1–2–3–4–5–6–1) floating high and low and then singing the arpeggio as lightly as if speaking it, will enable the teacher to fool the singers into using falsetto without realizing what is happening (see also page 115.) Yodeling is another possibility.

The Changing Voice

Physiological signs that foretell a young man's voice change are the widening of the features, especially the widening of the nose, enlargement of the nostrils, and more fullness of the lips; some awkwardness caused by muscles not keeping pace with other physical development; hair on the face and the darkening and coarsening of hair on arms and legs; development of the Adam's apple; and usually the appearance of facial blemishes. The first warning of a voice change will probably come in the deepening of the *speaking* voice, followed very quickly by a deepening in the singing voice. Besides the heavier quality that may occur in the speaking voice, there is likely to be a loss of control and the voice may even break at the most unexpected times, huskiness is a usual condition, the cambiata voice will have a "scratchy" speaking quality, additional brilliance occurs just before and as the voice shifts downward, and more power may be expected (males like to yell with this new vocal strength they feel).

The teacher must discuss the physiology of the voice with each class, giving both sexes some knowledge of the approximately one-sixth of an inch lengthening of a boy's vocal cords (along with their thickening), which causes the voice to drop approximately an octave lower than the soprano register. Studies have shown the average length of a boy or woman soprano's vocal cords to be about 5/12 of an inch and the average length of the boy's cords after changing to be about 7/12 of an inch. Muscles, cartilage, and membranes all tend to be bigger and stronger in the man than in the boy and the woman.

The voices of American boys will probably start changing when the boy is around twelve years old. Boys' voices may change as early as the fourth grade (around ten years of age), and better diet and nutrition appears to be causing maturation to take place earlier.[7] Students of some nationalities seem to mature more quickly. Latin-American students, for example, are usually through most of their voice-break problems by the eighth grade, whereas the peak of vocal problems is usually reached in the eighth grade with most American males. However, the language barrier and cultural mores of the Latin-American students may cause the student to *be* older when he reaches the eighth grade. Rare instances may be found where nineteen- and twenty-year-old boys of any nationality still have unchanged voices. The change may take place in two or three months, or it may take a year or more in the process. (It is apt to be *several years* before

---

[7] Dr. Irvin Cooper stated at the 1968 Texas Music Educators Association convention that 45 percent of 2500 fourth-, fifth-, and sixth-grade boys tested in a Florida research project were found to have voices in the cambiata range (first change). He also stated that practically all of the sixth-grade boys' voices had already entered the first change.

the voice is completely settled.) Sometimes the change is so gradual that the young man is not bothered by it and goes through it singing lightly and avoiding notes that might prove troublesome, finally developing a stable compass. This youngster will probably have an Adam's apple (protuberance of the thyroid cartilage) that is so small that it must be located by feeling rather than by sight. The noticeable Adam's apple and undependable voice are so often present in the changing voice that they are the norm.

Adolescence is an unsettled period. It is essential that the teacher have some knowledge of the changes that are taking place in these young bodies and minds. It is most important that the teacher be able to lead the young people to realize that voice changes are as normal occurrences in maturing young people as the growth that occurs in arms or legs. Every male singer in the eighth or ninth grade needs special attention whether his voice is unchanged, or at the beginning, middle, or final stages of transition; the teacher must handle emotional adjustments as well as the physical. The one whose voice is still unchanged in the ninth grade has an even bigger problem (because the changed voice is a symbol of manliness) than the person does whose voice is changing but won't behave (squeaking when least expected). Young people tend to be somewhat cruel and unkind by nature. Those whose voices do not sound manly, or are unmanageable, are likely to be ribbed unmercifully by both sexes.

The voice teacher should remember that the adolescent voice is not organically different from the adult voice although the vocal instrument and physique are immature and may be in an unbalanced condition. The difference is of degree, not of kind. The four kinds of voices to be considered are the young womens' voice, the boy's unchanged voice, the young man's changing voice, and the male changed voice.

For specific suggestions concerning the handling of the young woman's voice, see Chapter 4.[8] The main thing to remember with this undeveloped voice is to *protect it* from too much heavy singing. There is no reason why this voice cannot sing *fortissimo* or in extreme ranges, but it should not do so for long periods of time (and the tone must roll and be free). Switch them from part to part to promote reading ability and to develop range. Without switching parts, these voices are likely to settle into chest register *or* head register only. Occasionally there may be an exceptional alto or soprano who should be treated individually. For a more mature sound, to protect against strain, and to give ensemble experience to more singers, use double sextets or triple trios instead of sextets or trios (madrigals of 18–30 instead 9). There is real danger that the junior high teacher, coming straight from the mature sounds of college age voices, may try to obtain this sound. The too dark tone will cause untold damage to these voices. As a basic placement, work for fullness in these voices with a *forward, ringing* quality.

[8] Also see Chapter 2 for additional information on ranges, tessitura, and other advice.

The boy's unchanged voice will ordinarily be soprano, occasionally alto. These words must *not* be used, for the young man does not want a feminine name attached to his voice. One plan would assign a *number* to the young man's voice, that is, soprano–4, alto–3, cambiata or alto-tenor–2, and baritone or bass–1. The instructor who has the 4's sing with the sopranos or the 3's with the altos must see to it that the 4's and 3's are seated on the edge of the sections and are next to the tenors and basses. Young men of this age will accept SA music graciously, if the music is virile and interesting. If there are not too many 2's and 1's, it may be best to put male voices of all categories on the alto part, and all women except the few natural altos on the soprano part. The changed and changing voices will sing the alto part down an octave *or* up, whichever is in the most comfortable range for them. The unchanged boys' voices will sing alto where it is, omitting any notes that go too low. Allow the changed and changing voices to sing bass and tenor on the responses and on an occasional four-part number. This plan also works quite well with a junior high church choir. These fellows are so anxious to become men that it is common for some of them with unchanged voices to sing baritone until the instructor tests voices and puts them into the proper section. With an all-male class, assign 4's and 3's to Tenor I, the 2's to Tenor II, the changed voices to Bass I and II. The 4's may need to omit or transpose some of the lower notes (with the teacher's assistance).

Except in the United States, it has been traditional that when the boy's voice starts to change it is no longer used in a musical sense until control has been achieved in the lower register. It will usually take two to four years to gain this control, then the sixteen- or seventeen-year-old man may be able to start singing again. There are still boy choirs in the United States who follow the traditional concept (inherited particularly from the English school of thought) of having the boys sing soprano until their voices break. This process frequently smashes a voice into tiny bits for life. The junior high schools of the United States have been the proving grounds for the Alto-Tenor Plan, the Cambiata Plan, the Baritone Plan, and other plans that recommend the use of the young male voice during its period of mutation. Much of the writing, research, and arranging for changing voices has been done by Irvin Cooper, Duncan McKenzie, and Frederick Swanson.

All of the American plans agree that the young man may sing throughout the interval of time it takes for his voice to change, provided he is trained to use his voice correctly. A student should sing in his comfortable range and *avoid strain*. Correct use of the voice will improve the quality and responsiveness of the vocal instrument, and the voice will emerge from its period of transition with a wider range and a better quality than if it had not been used. Voices must be tested frequently and moved, if necessary, to the correct voice part.

During the process of change, in which the larynx, muscles, and cartilage all grow in size, the vocal cords and the cartilage to which they are attached often do not grow in exact proportion to one another. The tension is sometimes unsteady and the voice uncertain. Some male voices change suddenly and erratically, while other male voices mutate more slowly and regularly. It is on this point that the various authorities clash. The Cambiata and the Alto-Tenor Plans work best for slowly-changing voices. The Baritone Plan is designed for fast-changing voices. Other plans are variations of the slow or fast-changing voice plans. As a practical procedure, analyze the voices in each class and decide which plan will work best for that one class; combine concepts and use any plans that work most effectively when the class contains both slow- *and* fast-changing voices.

There is a tendency to use the terms "Alto-Tenor Plan" and "Cambiata Plan" synonymously. Both refer to the same stage of development in the male voice, but they disagree concerning range and how the voice should be handled in its changing state. Following is a quick review of the various plans, showing some similarities and contrasts.

Alto-Tenor Plan.   The Alto-Tenor is older than the Cambiata Plan; therefore, many arrangements were made for this plan. This voice works well as a tenor with soprano, alto, and baritone in four-part SATB music. It combines with these voices to make a warm, mellow sound. It will not have a great deal of volume, but it will sing with color and resonance when properly trained (see Chapter 2 for additional information on vocal color and range). All young male voices change slowly through the following stages: Sop. I, Sop. II, Alto, Alto-Tenor, and Tenor or Baritone (Bass). The voice that is in the Alto-Tenor stage is a voice of limited range with the upper tones gone and the lower notes not developed and with an accepted maximum range of G below middle C to the G above it, often only able to sing four or five of these notes. The changed voice is encouraged to develop.

Cambiata Plan.   Irvin Cooper, the originator of the Cambiata Plan, made many arrangements for this voice. The voice timbre is the same as that mentioned under Alto-Tenor Plan (see also Chapter 2 for information about range, tessitura, and quality). This concept anticipates the voice change and by allowing the voice to lower gradually avoids an actual voice break. The accepted range is about F below middle C to C one octave above middle C (keep vocalizing the upper range). This plan seems to be especially suitable to those who become *tenors.*

The plan that is the most suitable for quickly changing voices is the *Baritone Plan.* The boy soprano is transferred to alto as soon as any signs of adolescence appear in either voice or physique. When a young man's voice has lowered until he can sing a good quality E below middle C, he is transferred to baritone, regardless of what alto notes he can still sing. He sings any bass notes he can, and is warned against reaching for either high or low notes. If tenor quality is noticed in the baritone and there is good control over e', the voice is transferred to tenor. Occasionally, an alto is transferred directly to tenor when he retains his unchanged voice for a longer time than usual on the basis of age or physique, if another note or two is added to his low register. The *Compromise Alto* voice can sing with equal ease in his changed (baritone) and unchanged (alto) voice. There tends to be little provision for the tenor part.

Range will probably be one of the biggest problems of the changed voice. Individual attention should be given to help the student become adjusted to this new location of notes. A voice may move temporarily to a range that will not fit *any* of the accepted plans. Many students retain a portion of their high range and can also sing in a low range, but have a middle range that is hard to handle or completely tacet. The teacher must not succumb to the temptation of overworking the voice in the upper register, at the expense of the development of the lower voice. Many vocal instructors allow the students to use only the *lower* voice (boys will naturally want to sing with their lower voices *only*), but this procedure will cause almost as many problems as the high-voice procedure. The proper pedagogical procedure encourages development of the lower range, retention of the upper range, and development of the middle range until the two segments join together in one smooth, continuous range. A complete and balanced development of the voice may be attained by singing in as big range and dynamic spread as is possible, within the boundaries of unforced, free-sounding quality. Be sure that the voice is allowed to lower gradually, but keep the upper tones and experiment and work with them. Usually the treble tones of the immature voice remain controllable for some time after the vocal change begins. When vocalizing, it is important to prefix a labial or lingual consonant to the vowel sounds in order to keep uppermost in the young singer's mind the necessity of forward focus. Without this precaution, the unsettled condition of the larynx is liable to cause swallowing of tones.

It is almost impossible to sing unison melodies with newly changed and changing voices. The junior high teacher will be unable to locate a melody in a common range that all voice parts can negotiate simultaneously (see Chapter 2). It may be necessary to write easy parts for problem voices. Have only *one* voice part at a time sing a melody in its range. Eight-part harmony lends itself to eighth grade, permitting young men to sing tones that are comfortable for them. The baritone part should emphasize tonic and dominant pedal points and patterns that are stepwise and scalewise, along with some chances to sing a melody in the proper range. These kinds of experiences will help the male find the pitches in his new voice.

Tradition has handed down *soft singing* as the safe method for handling voices. Teachers now know that *mf* is the safest and best dynamic. Wilcox states:

> One of the significant things that the scientist has proved is that the voice mechanism functions at its maximum efficiency with the minimum expenditure of energy when producing tones of considerable intensity (mezzo forte power). This indicates that vocal practice designed to develop the muscular strength of the vocal organism and coordinate a correct vocal habit should be carried forward with tones of mezzo-forte intensity. The mechanical devices which revealed indisputable evidence to the scientists in the research laboratories established the reasonable fact that the extensor muscles which must resist the interfering pull of the constrictor muscles in order to keep the throat open during phonation are put under much greater stress with a "soft tone" beginning.[9]

Some teachers believe strongly in separate male and female classes in junior high. Others just as firmly believe in the mixed-class approach. Advocates of boys alone–girls alone say the young man is willing to sing soprano or alto, but *not* with young women. It is less embarrassing to the one with the unmanageable voice to have only men in the class. They understand his problem and singing seems more manly, somehow, in a male chorus. Although young women are usually willing to sing what the young men wish to sing, if the classes are separate each sex can sing what it wishes. The young women can progress at a more rapid rate and the young men can receive the extra individual attention they need. In the mixed class, the men will usually receive insufficient help, and the women will not progress as far as they should. Mixed classes have the advantages of having many more excellent materials available and needing fewer teachers. With good teaching the other disadvantages of this plan may be effectively overcome.

CHOOSING MUSIC TEXTBOOKS

The teacher may have little control over the type of class arrangement. Textbooks may have been requisitioned or purchased for mixed classes *or* segregated classes by his predecessor or by the administration. If this is the case, and it probably is, the school will ordinarily be unable to conform to the new teacher's preferences if they do not coincide with the situation that exists. Nevertheless, occasionally the instructor *can* determine the organization of the classes (particularly after he has been in a school for a few years), and he needs to present some sound facts to the administration to validate his beliefs.

All of the textbook-songbooks published by major publishers are relatively well done compared with the older books. The material is more

[9] J.C. Wilcox, *The Living Voice* (New York: Carl Fischer, Inc., 1935), p. 11.

vital and interesting, ranges are handled better, teachers have many more imaginative hints and helps in the text. The instructor must decide which book or books conform most closely to the ideal. Even in senior high, buying a collection of songs in a book may be much better economy than buying octavo music, especially when building a new library. A number of states have state-approved books that are available. If this is the case in your state, you need to find out how to acquire these books and all other available information in order to make wise choices.

Many times a teacher will have the opportunity to pick songbooks or textbooks for the classes, especially when the state has selected state-approved texts. The following will provide some basis for making correct choices.

RATING SHEET FOR THE EVALUATION
OF JUNIOR HIGH VOCAL MUSIC TEXTBOOKS
(To evaluate senior high texts, leave out items that are not applicable)

Textbook Series_____ Copyright Date_____

Title of Book_____Suitable to Grade_____

_____

1–Excellent; 2–Good; 3–Fair; 4–Unsatisfactory
In comparison with other junior high textbooks of_____grade level, I would rate this   1   2   3   4   5   6   7   (circle your rating).

Presentation of material

	1	2	3	4
Proper tessitura _____				
Range suitability _____				
Student appeal _____				
Desired difficulty _____				
Some part songs that will challenge your group's best efforts _____				
Several interesting part songs that can be learned easily and quickly, that students may sing spontaneously _____				
Compatibility of music and text _____				
Variety of book content				
Structure				
Note-reading songs _____				
Part songs. Some of the arrangements permit other than soprano to sing the melody_____				
Rhythmic variety _____				
Variety of mood _____				
Diversity of form _____				
Period representation _____				

Type	1	2	3	4
Enough seasonal songs of all holidays				
Fun songs				
Patriotic songs				
Folksongs				
Spirituals				
Sacred songs				
Art songs				
Some familiar or traditional songs				
Sufficient songs of lasting value				
Many rounds, canons, descants, and songs with optional harmonic parts				
Some a cappella numbers				
Teaching aids				
The index is so well-arranged that any types of songs or materials may be located quickly and easily				
Glossary of terms				
Well-organized teacher's guide, complete and convenient to use				
Piano accompaniments that enhance the beauty of the songs				
Provisions for keyboard experiences				
Chord markings				
Provisions for the use of orchestral instruments				
Parallel listening. Good quality listening materials				
Listening selections include themes for score-reading				
Recorded material of good quality to accompany books				
Suggestions for creative experiences				
Background information for music selections and biographical sketches of composers				
Suggestions are made for books, films, and filmstrips for student and teacher reference				
Physical aspects of book				
Size and spacing of notes and words. Words and music easy to read				
Attractiveness of book (illustrations appropriate and attractive)				
Durability (binding, grade of paper, ability to open flat)				

THE IMPORTANCE OF STUDENT ORGANIZATION

Because every sense is acute at this age, junior high students need organized emotional activity. They want *experience* more than anything else in the world. They want to express themselves. They aren't happy unless they get somewhere. The music director should give them the opportunity to share activities, to do better in music, and to feel grown-up by setting up the class as an organization.

Music directors often feel that they must do everything themselves. But junior high students value organization and leadership and like a good deal of business and ceremony. They expect, and should receive, stability from the director, but if they are allowed to elect officers for various duties, they will feel that they have a voice in the management of the organization. When youthful responsibilities are wisely directed, they powerfully affect the group.

Each person should have some responsibility in the organization, if possible. Since each individual is different from his or her neighbor and cannot do the same things, each one should have the opportunity to do something at which he or she excels. Having a particular responsibility in a group will give a student greater personal interest and pride in that group (see Chapter 2).

Treat these young people as adults, but remember that they aren't mature enough to be left completely alone.

LESSON PLANS

The basic lesson plan for *general music* class is described in some detail on pp. 49–53. Chapter 9 details an 'Order of Rehearsal' for any *performance organization.*

The *performance organization* in middle-school or junior high will use procedures almost identical to those used by the senior high. A good ninth grade or eighth and ninth grade choir will use music that may even duplicate some of the literature used in high school. The critical variable is range and tessitura, for care must be exerted to make certain that voices do not remain in extreme ranges or tessituras for too long a time. The conductor must exercise judgement in not using music that is so ambitious that young voices are jeopardized. Sixth and seventh grade organizations will use very different voicing and music. The teacher will probably have to rearrange some of the voice parts in the music, and change songs and activities more frequently.

See Chapter 2 for ways to test voices, junior high ranges and tessituras, selection of performance groups, student officers, and seating arrangements. Music selection is described in Chapters 3 and 7. Class control, vocalizing procedures, presenting a new score, selecting a rehearsal procedure, etc., are enumerated in Chapter 9. Sight-reading is described in Chapter 6. Besides the 'Order of Rehearsal', use the lesson plan suggestions in Chapter 3 to make your lesson plan.

The *general music* course is basically a survey course. The voice and folk instruments are used to achieve a familiarity with and an understanding of music by performing it. Experiment with musical materials and with their organization and manipulation. Use describing activities by refining the ability to use music notation, refining the ability to listen to music with understanding, and developing a familiarity with the sound of and with the vocabulary for discussing music of various styles and periods. Some performance skills will be developed on folk instruments (guitar, ukulele, Swiss hand bells, African instruments, strikers, etc.) and piano through the study of idiomatic literature. Compose original works and improvise musical examples in various styles. Perform or present electronic music, create music using electronic media, and study a variety of examples of electronic music. Create and perform works or examples in the various performing arts while studying the relationships, role, and function of the arts or the humanities in civilization.

There will be *some* singing in the class. When there is, use the performance information and procedures. However, many other musical facets must be incorporated into each class.

This chapter has enumerated ways to obtain creativity in listening, some exciting techniques for composition, and various other general music activities. Another description of skills, attitudes, and understandings is related. The sight-reading chapter describes the Kodaly method (handsignals, etc.), how to use resonator bells and keyboard experiences, and elementary to more advanced techniques in the development of rhythm, melody, and harmony.

Many of the learning possibilities are not adequately described in this text. That does not make them less valid for the general music class. Little is said about the use of movement, or of guitars, ukuleles, hand bells, African instruments, and various rhythm instruments to achieve musical learning. Electronic music should be performed or presented. Don't neglect to study the relationships, role, and function of the arts and/or the humanities in civilization.[10] After planning general and specific objectives for each class, use the lesson plan form in Chapter 3 and use the various ways suggested for achieving your musical goals. Do include group instruction, individualized instruction, and music laboratory experiences in the planning.

CONCLUSION

The junior high teacher who seems to be the most successful with these young adults is the teacher who is able to find out how junior high students think. Being up-to-date is very important to junior high

---

[10] *Learning to Look* by Joshua Taylor has a chronological table that enumerates the visual arts, literature, and music from antiquity to the present.

youngsters. The teacher must know what is happening in popular songs, current Broadway musicals, movies, TV shows, and junior high fads.

Next week is a long way off to junior high students. Each experience in education is an end in itself. Who knows what these youngsters will be doing next year? Most young men terminate their musical experiences with the seventh or eighth grade! The teacher must strive for the most enrichment possible each day for these young men and women. Let much of the experience in music be of immediate interest and value. Get students to express feelings, form, and texture, and keep them alive to the beauty around them. See that music lessons are so planned that the outcome will leave students with a definite consciousness of gain in musical ability and insight. Success is the greatest motivator.

Start with music the students know and love, and *deepen* their musical understandings and experiences with music. Every song says something if it's worth teaching. Be careful about telling youngsters that their love for a song (no matter how poor the qualities of the song may be) is tawdry and cheap. If there is a necessity to tear down, be sure to put something in its place. Touch the heart and *then* develop the mind. It is true that students must have technique to get the utmost from music, but they must start with *interest,* not with technique. It may be necessary to start with a "Jazz Unit" and go ahead from there. Remember, however, it is not valid to merely entertain youngsters; they must be made to work.

Help the students develop a tolerance for all kinds of musical literature. The critical ability of students needs to grow. The teacher can assist with this growth by *doing* it (performing the music or skill), then *naming* it. The instructor can pick out some simple things of any area and from them build a bridge to more complicated forms. The young adults will soon recognize that people have different tastes and various likes and dislikes. After a tolerance for the enthusiasms of others has been developed, they will take pleasure in learning that there is a great breadth of musical literature sufficient to meet the needs of other members of the group as well as their own.

GENERAL MUSIC BIBLIOGRAPHY

ADES, HAWLEY,   *Choral Arranging.* Delaware Water Gap, Pa.: Shawnee Press, 1968.

ANDREWS, F.M.,   *Junior High School General Music.* Englewood Cliffs, N.J.: Prentice-Hall, Inc., 1971.

BAIRD, JO ANN,   *Using Media in the Music Program.* West Nyack, N.Y.: Center for Applied Research in Education, 1975.

BALDWIN, L.,   *Listener's Anthology of Music,* 2 vols. Morristown, N.J.: Silver Burdett Co., 1948.

COOPER, IRVIN, and KARL O. KUERSTEINER,   *Teaching Junior High Music* (2nd ed.). Boston: Allyn and Bacon, Inc., 1970.

DWYER, TERENCE, *Composing with Tape Recorders.* London: Oxford University Press, 1971.

ERNST, K. D., and CHARLES L. GARY, eds., *Music in General Education.* Reston, Va.: Music Educators National Conference, 1965.

GLENN, N.E., WM. B. McBRIDE, and G.H. WILSON, *Secondary School Music,* Englewood Cliffs, N.J.: Prentice-Hall, Inc., 1970.

HUGHES, WILLIAM O., *Planning for Junior High General Music.* Belmont, Calif.: Wadsworth Publishing Co., Inc., 1967.

HUGHES, WILLIAM, and LEE KJELSON, *General Music: A Comprehensive Approach, Zone 4.* Menlo Park, Calif.: Addison-Wesley Pub. Co., 1975.

LANDON, JOSEPH W., *How to Write Learning Activities Packages for Music Education.* Costa Mesa, Calif.: Educational Technology Publications, 1973.

LEACH, ROBERT, and ROY PALMER, eds., *Folk Music in School.* Cambridge: Cambridge University Press, 1978.

McKENZIE, DUNCAN, *Training the Boy's Changing Voice.* New Brunswick, N.J.: Rutgers University Press, 1956.

MARK, MICHAEL L., *Contemporary Music Education.* New York: Schirmer Books, 1978.

MARPLE, HUGO D., *Backgrounds and Approaches to Junior High Music.* Dubuque, Iowa: Wm. C. Brown Company, 1975.

METZ, DONALD, *Teaching General Music in Grades 6–9.* Columbus, Ohio: Charles E. Merrill Publishing Co., 1980.

MODUGNO, ANNE D., *Creating Music Through the Use of the Tape Recorder.* New Haven, Conn.: Keyboard Publications, 1975.

MONSOUR, SALLY, and MARGARET PERRY, *A Junior High School Music Handbook* (2nd ed.). Englewood Cliffs, N.J.: Prentice-Hall, Inc., 1970.

MUSIC EDUCATORS NATIONAL CONFERENCE, *The Eclectic Curriculum in American Music Education,* Landis, Beth, and Polly Carder, eds., 1972.

NATIONAL COMMISSION ON INSTRUCTION, *Individualized Instruction in Music,* compiled by Boardman, Eunice, and Carroll Rinehart. Reston, Va.: Music Educators National Conference, 1975.

REGELSKI, THOMAS A., *Teaching General Music: Action Learning for Middle and Secondary Schools.* New York: Schirmer Books, 1981.

SCHAFER, R. MURRAY, *Creative Music Education.* New York: Schirmer Books.

SUR, WILLIAM, and CHARLES F. SCHULLER, *Music Education for Teen-Agers* (2nd ed.). New York: Harper and Row, Publishers, 1966.

SWANSON, FREDERICK J., *Music Teaching in the Junior High and Middle School.* New York: Appleton-Century-Crofts, 1973.

WESTERMAN, KENNETH, *Emergent Voice* (2nd ed.). Ann Arbor, Mich.: Carol F. Westerman, 1955.

PART THREE

8

Conducting

The conductor who is a fine musician and who has a thorough knowledge of vocal pedagogy may train a choir to perform excellently, even with inadequate conducting techniques. However, the director with good musicianship and vocal knowledge who also has acquired conducting skills will obtain finer results than is possible without the possession of those skills. It is possible to move more quickly and efficiently in rehearsal and control and inspire singers to new heights in performances. Superior conducting techniques will be especially rewarding in sight-reading contests and times when a group stumbles during a concert and the director must skillfully extricate it from its difficulties in full view of the audience. The director with good hand skills will benefit in confidence and authority. The weak choral conductor will be confused and embarrassed conducting operas or instrumental-choral music when he doesn't possess clean techniques that the instrumental students may immediately interpret. Students will benefit from the training of a good conductor who employs traditional techniques, because they will feel at home in an all-state group or under the guidance of any other good conductors.

Conducting is a systematic body of knowledge that must be learned and applied with thoroughness. Directors must acquire a style and method of their own. Mastery of conducting skills takes hours of individual practice and consistent and critical self-analysis that must result in the elimination of faulty techniques.

QUALITIES AND RESPONSIBILITIES OF A CONDUCTOR

1. A conductor must possess the somewhat intangible quality of *leadership*, the ability to inspire and control the group through a conducting personality. Relationships with the choir depend upon the morale, the esprit de corps, the teamwork of the choir as a whole. The director will have the ability to take command of a choir and make it an exciting experience.

2. Obviously, the conductor must be able to demonstrate a *good conducting technique*. A choir, accompanist or accompanying organization must be able to follow with no difficulty. Ambidexterity is imperative, for without it the director cannot be free to interpret the words and music. Furthermore, the face and body must be always employed as well as the arms to convey styles and subtle musical pulses and impulses to the performers.

3. The choral conductor must know *vocal pedagogy*, so that good tone quality is attained in the choir. Teaching students to sing correctly is at least as important as knowledge of interpretation, for groups will be judged in concerts and contests on their quality and the director will be condemned if the quality isn't there. The director is responsible for the tonal production of voices, including posture, breath support, relaxed jaw and tongue, intonation, vowels, consonants, range, flexibility, voice classification, and expert management of changing and immature voices as well as mature voices. In the choral group, knowledge of vocal pedagogy must extend to the manner in which balance and blend is attained.

4. The conductor must have *musicianship* that the organization can respect. The choir will quickly lose faith in the director it catches repeatedly in mistakes in musicianship. Regular work with ear training and theory will greatly improve the quality of the choir, and a most important responsibility of the leader is to challenge and stimulate the group toward finer musicianship.

5. The director must know the *traditional interpretations* and the

rules of interpretation involving unmarked notes as well as the markings in the music. This knowledge should be combined with a creative imagination. This creative imagination enables the choral director to mentally hear how a song should sound in its ideal state and strive to attain this ideal with the choir. Corrections in the rehearsal are made on the basis of attempting to make intonation, balance, blend, tonal production, diction, phrasing and interpretation conform to the conductor's mental concept of the song. This mental concept cannot occur until the score is mastered.

6. To be truly successful the conductor must be *well organized*. The ability to plan, select and evaluate material and music, efficiently handle the physical aspects of the department, etc. is essential.

7. There are several other significant qualities that are essential to success:

A sense of humor.

Clearness of speech. Speak distinctly, pleasantly, with correct grammar, and without hesitation. Spoken directions must be concise and clear.

Eye contact with the choir. Only with the score in the head, not the head in the score, can this happen. The director's eyes must be expressive and helpful. The conductor must insist that the choir *watch*; and the conductor who does not watch the choir cannot know if the singers are watching.

Facial expression. The choir will be helped and inspired more by the facial expressions of the director than by any other factor. Facial expressions should reflect the mood or character of the music and communicate feelings so the chorus knows much of what is wanted from it. If the music is felt intensely enough the face will respond almost automatically and come alive. The conductor whose expression is deadpan or inappropriate will not inspire a choir to the heights.

A cheerful, businesslike manner. Be sharp, alert, and poised whenever a class is being conducted. The instructor who is too cocky or too timid, too tense or too relaxed, too lazy, too uncertain, or too unconcerned is in for a lot of trouble.

A commanding posture. A singing posture by the conductor (with expanded ribs, relaxed shoulders, chin level, weight poised on the balls of the feet, etc.) will psychologically induce a choir to assume the same kind of posture and alertness of manner. The alive body and expanded chest are essential to phrasing, vital singing, and interpretation. Avoid excessive movement of the head, torso, knees, or feet.

Sincerity. Directing is *not* a performance; it is the directing *of* a performance or expression of music. The director should reflect the music by truly experiencing it, not by making an 'artificial show' of involvement. Sincerity of feeling is a major quality in the work of a director. An exception is the student conductor who feels insecure. Put up a "front" of confidence until more assurance is begun to be felt.

THE PREPARATORY BEAT

Preparatory and starting positions must be commanding and authoritative. Extend the arms at shoulder height with elbows slightly bent, palms of the hands downward, fingers slightly curved. This initial position must be visible to every member of the performing group, and it must be held long enough to obtain everyone's undivided attention.

The preparatory beat is the preliminary upbeat that "prepares" the singers for an initial response. This preparatory beat serves to intensify the choir's concentration just before the singing begins, to induce spontaneous synchronized inhalation by the singers, to indicate the volume of the first note, and to give the exact tempo of the first beat.

Prior to beginning a selection, the conductor must thoughtfully consider the desired tempo and the appropriate preparatory movement. All preparatory beats start with the hands up in the position of "attention." The preparatory beat for beat 1 will be a higher, smaller version of the beat that precedes 1 (usually 4 in $\frac{4}{4}$, or the third beat in $\frac{3}{4}$ time).

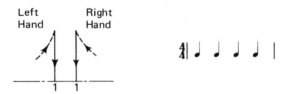

Other than for the first beat, the direction of the preparatory motion is made in the *opposite* direction (the hand *backs up* from the direction it will travel on the beat). For example, when a conductor beats a $\frac{4}{4}$ pattern, the preparatory motion and second beat is:

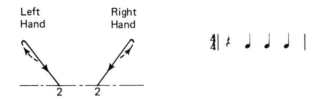

The third beat is:

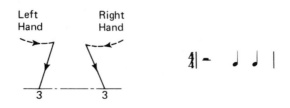

Second beat in $\frac{3}{4}$:

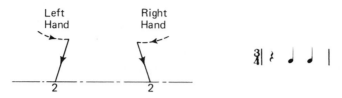

Final beat:

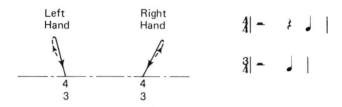

(The dotted line represents the preparatory beat.)

Eighth note entrances take a special technique. Practice the following entrances:

The above entrances may be accomplished most simply by inconspicuously beating the rests, breathing on the eighth rest just before the entrance, and attacking the entrance upbeat note with vitality (see 'Floor-Ceiling' beat described on page 218).

When any of the above entrances are beginnings, the conductor can begin an eighth note before the attack and use either of two methods:

1. Breathe on the downstroke eighth note and attack the entrance on the upbeat. This will result in a relatively percussive attack.
2. Employ the preparatory beat shown in the diagrams. Start with the eighth rest just before the entrance note and breathe on the preparatory upstroke. The downstroke is *on* the eighth note entrance. The attack has more style and dynamic flexibility than does the upbeat attack.

When entrances are even quicker, the starting note will usually be most competently performed like a grace note. The choir must *sense* that the beginning note is sung just before the downstroke.

Poor attack may often be caused by a weak preparatory beat. Unless the conductor makes a motion of the proper length and appropriate speed, and breathes while the preparatory gesture is being made (to induce the singers to do likewise), a precise beginning by the singers will be unlikely.

Some conductors form such a habit of one or two measures "for free" ("one, two, three, ready, sing") that students don't ever bother to watch. There are occasional times (for example, when playing the piano while students read a new number) when the verbal beginning is not only acceptable, it is the *best* way to prepare the singers for their entrance.[1] However, most of the time the way the preparatory beat is executed should show the conductor's intention regarding the tempo, dynamics, and style of the music. Rhythm *begins* with the preparatory beat. The conductor should also shape the first vowel sound with his or her mouth (while the vocalists shape it with their mouths) and breathe with the singers to give the organization a sense of timing. When the conductor sees that mouths are still closed, it becomes obvious that the singers have *not taken a breath*; therefore they will not be able to come in on time for a good attack. This procedure will also afford the director an opportunity to check whether the singers *know* what the first vowel *is*, and whether the vowel is properly framed with their lips and jaws. If o is sung as ow, have the students silently shape their lips and jaws correctly to produce a good o and caution them against moving anything when they practice singing it. Have them sing the correct o several times until certain they can perform it correctly, and work for good choral attack and precise following of the beat even while emphasizing the correct vowel sound. (The teacher Mary Taylor gives the following word of remonstrance to her class, "Remember, you can't chew anything in here, even the warm-up pitch.")

Form the habit of taking a good look around at the apex of the preparatory "motion and breath" before swinging into the downstroke. If there are any singers not paying attention or having improper singing position, stop! Then try again. A couple of times, even without words, will make the choir attentive to the director.

TIME-BEATING PATTERNS

Conducting gestures are usually initiated by the forearm, with the wrist and fingers following closely (not in an exaggerated manner). The graceful and natural-appearing conducting movement is dependent upon a wrist joint that flexes with the beat. A rigid wrist, resulting in a stiff immobility, or a too-limp wrist, resulting in a flapping hand, are singularly unattractive. Curve the hand as though the fingers are around a soft ball, ordinarily palm down, fingers together but relaxed enough that they flex with the beat. Do not turn the palm to face each beat. Direct with energy, but be

---

[1]If the verbal beginning is used, avoid two traps: "One, two, three," must be spoken in rhythm or the whole purpose of the oral command will be dissipated; the *timing* of the "Ready, sing," as the final two orders before singing is tricky and unless the command is practiced carefully the statement may come out as, "One, two, ready, sing, *one*," and the students will be thoroughly confused.

sure that every gesture has meaning. Use economy! Make every motion count!

Ordinarily, the beat size should go no lower than the waist and no higher than the top of the head (the rebound of beats will usually not be as high as the chin) and should flow no more than six to twelve inches horizontally outside the body. The conductor who reaches too far forward or stretches too far to the left or right will appear uncoordinated and awkward. The director must avoid a position where elbows are too close to the body or too prominent.[2] Keep the left hand in an easy, natural position near the waistline when it is not being used.

Many choral directors have found that directing occasionally with a baton refines their beat pattern techniques. If a baton is used, it must not be held stiffly. There is little reason for anything other than the wrist, hand, and fingers in the control of the baton. As a rule, the palm of the hand should be held downward, and the ball of the baton will be in the palm. The baton is essentially controlled by the thumb and first two fingers. Remember, the main purpose of the baton is greater visibility for the group and so is actually an extension of the arm or forefinger. Most choral directors feel that the hands are more expressive, but all choral conductors should have skill with the baton for the times when they may need to direct instrumental organizations or large choral groups of two or three hundred.

A director cannot obtain the utmost from the choir unless conducting is crystal-clear. In order to attain this precision, it is essential that every beat have an exact starting point. This clearness may be secured with a beat that rebounds against a fixed plane, at least *most* of the time. This imaginary fixed plane should usually be located level with the elbows. The director operates against this plane with a bouncing ball technique.

If a ball is thrown straight down, it bounces straight up:

For clarity, the rebound must never be more than half the height of the initial downbeat, except in one to a bar or in syncopations. The downbeat is *straight*, no curls or curves.

---

[2] Keep the elbow as close to the body as is possible and still have it relaxed and free. The elbow of the arm employed in the beat pattern will extend in front of the body and beat one should come down the center of the body. When two hands are occasionally employed at the same time on the beat pattern, beat one comes straight down from the shoulders to avoid crossing the hands. Use the arms, not the body, to beat time. Any excessive body motions, such as leg bobbing and head nodding, are distracting. Usually stay erect with body expanded and stand with your feet only as far apart as is necessary to maintain good balance.

Thrown to the left toward that plane, when the downbeat hits, it bounces upward in the logical direction:

to the right:

and back again on beat 4:

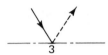

With this technique there is an exact point where the beat starts, exactly when the hand or baton hits the imaginary plane, and every beat is a form of *downmotion*.

Beat 1 is nearly always longer and stronger than the other beats, and in *all* patterns the hand moves straight down. This straight-down beat with its extra length makes it easier for the singers to find the beat if they become lost while reading music. Occasionally, beat 1 will be *unaccented*, as when a rest occurs on it or when an accent occurs on the second half of the beat.

Beat Patterns for the Right Hand

The *one*-beat pattern is usually the basic beat pattern for $\frac{3}{4}$, $\frac{3}{8}$, and the fast $\frac{2}{2}$ and $\frac{2}{4}$. This is the only beat pattern where the rebound always bounces all the way up to the initial point of the downbeat. The conductor may wish to "suggest" beat 3 in the upbeat when directing $\frac{3}{4}$, or $\frac{3}{8}$.[3]

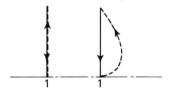

[3]In "Tempo di Valse" most conductors allow the downbeat to swing ⌣ ⌣ to emphasize the lilt of the music. In quite rapid passages, $\frac{4}{4}$ and other meters *may* be conducted in one.

The *two*-beat pattern is one of the most useful. Usually $\frac{2}{4}$, ¢ , $\frac{2}{2}$, $\frac{6}{8}$, and occasionally $\frac{4}{8}$, are conducted using this pattern. An exception is when $\frac{2}{2}$ is used in *andante* and *adagio* movements in music of the early Classic period; here four beats should be used. In modern works, $\frac{5}{8}$ and $\frac{7}{8}$ are sometimes conducted using a lopsided two-beat pattern ($\frac{5}{8}$ = 2, 3 or 3, 2; $\frac{7}{8}$ = 4, 3 or 3, 4). *Note*: The two-beat pattern is the only one that violates the bouncing ball principle by bouncing to the right instead of straight up.

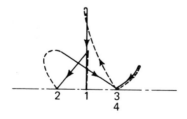

The *three*-beat pattern is used for $\frac{3}{4}$, $\frac{9}{8}$, and *adagio* $\frac{3}{8}$ meters. "Tempo di Valse" normally calls for one beat to the measure; "Tempo di Valse Lento," three beats to the measure.[4]

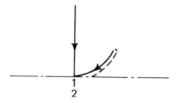

The *four*-beat pattern is used so commonly that one way to designate it is **C** for *common time*. Other meters usually conducted in four are: $\frac{4}{4}$, $\frac{12}{8}$, and occasionally $\frac{2}{2}$ (in slow movements), $\frac{4}{8}$ or $\frac{8}{8}$. The agogic accent may dictate that other meters be done in 4, e.g. $\frac{9}{8}$ in 2, 2, 2, 3; $\frac{11}{8}$ in 3, 3, 3, 2; etc.

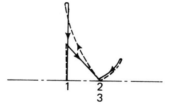

The preceding patterns are the ones usually needed in choral conducting. However, other directional patterns will occasionally be needed.

---

[4]Fast contemporary works may follow the agogic accent, e.g. Britten's "Rejoice in the Lamb" ($\frac{7}{8}$ divided into 2, 2, 3 or $\frac{8}{8}$ into 3, 3, 2).

The *five*-beat pattern customarily will be conducted as a three-plus-two pattern, or its reverse, depending upon the general structure of the music (where the accents and strong words are located in the measure). If beat 5 is very light and unaccented, it might be placed higher (but should still move downward).

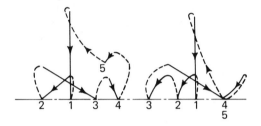

The *six*-beat pattern usually is the traditional German pattern, shown in the first diagram below. If the fifth and sixth beats need to be lightened, they may be placed higher, but downward (see second diagram below).

There is some justification to feel that a subdivided basic two-beat, using three downmotions moving right and three downs moving back, would move very easily to the two beat pattern when the tempo speeds up (see third diagram below).

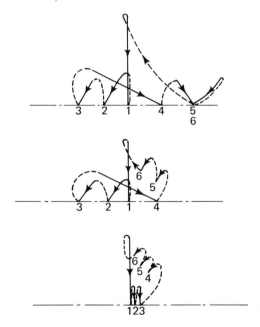

Many instrumental directors use the Italian six. It may be used, since it is a more aesthetic pattern, whenever 4 or 5 or 6 need not be controlled by an ictus.

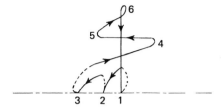

Melisma will cause the beat to revert to a subdivided three-beat.

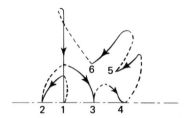

The *seven*-beat pattern commonly will be conducted as a four-plus-three pattern, or its reverse, depending upon the music structure.

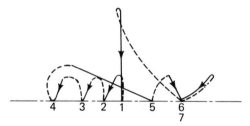

With beats 6 and 7 light and unaccented, these beats might be placed higher (but should still move downward). Agogic accents *may* dictate using five-plus-two or some other combination. Direction is changed on the strongest words or notes.

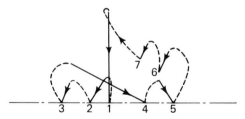

The *eight*-beat pattern is really a subdivided four-beat. This is: two downmotions, two lefts, two rights and two rights moving back, with beat 8 sweeping up the start of beat 1. (Be careful that the second beat in each case is much shorter.)[5] With this pattern, if the director needs to speed up, he may easily shift to the basic four-beat.

[5]For clearness, the director may wish to conduct beats 1 and 2 in exactly the same spot, 3 and 4 in the same place, etc.

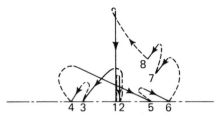

The *nine*-beat pattern reverts to a three-beat pattern, with three downs, three rights and three rights moving back.

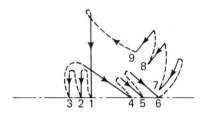

The *ten*-beat pattern is usually a six-plus-four pattern, or its reverse. In contemporary music and quicker speeds, the ten- and eleven-beat patterns often swing in *four*.

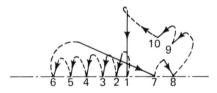

The *eleven*-beat pattern is ordinarily a six-plus-five pattern, or its reverse. The slow ten- and eleven-beat patterns change direction *only on* the strong beats (agogic accents).

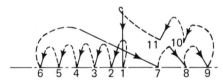

The *twelve*-beat pattern is a four-beat pattern, with three downs, three lefts, three rights and three rights moving back. For extra clearness, consider placing 1, 2, and 3 on the same spot, etc. Twelve will easily change to four when the beat accelerates.

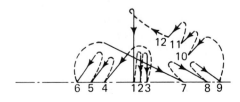

The beat will usually flow and curve, rather than appear as angular as the patterns shown in the diagrams. The beat pattern must reflect both strong and unaccented words and parts of words, phrasing, style, and even half and whole step pitch changes. Consequently, the lopsided beat pattern is the norm in good conducting. The conductor may go out of the beat patterns for a special interpretative effect, but must not stay out for more than a measure or two. Almost any effect may be obtained *within* the basic pattern. The conductor should never get lost; but realistically it will happen, so use a figure eight pattern until the beat is rediscovered (which must be as soon as possible). The final beat in all patterns often needs to hit a higher plane when the tempo is faster, e.g. beat three in $\frac{3}{4}$:

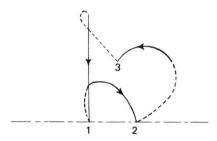

The legato style of conducting will work efficiently and clearly in *all* beat patterns. The "bounce" should be used for staccatos, quick-moving madrigals, ballets with fa-la choruses, swiftly moving syncopations (requiring the floor-ceiling divided beat, which is described later), *and all music whose tempo is fast*. Always think of *pulling a phrase* from the choir. As the speed of a piece increases, the 'pull' is gradually lost until it finally disappears and only the *beat points* remain.

How to Control Vowels, Consonants, and Pitches

When the style is legato (characteristic in singing) or when the tempo is slower, an adaptation of the "bouncing-ball" technique is used. A hand motion that is particularly well-adapted to choral conducting is a quick downward motion to the ictus (beat point) and a pulling or lifting motion to the apex of the beat (usually keeping the palm downward unless more volume is desired), then a quick downward motion to the ictus of the next beat and a pulling motion from it, and so on. (See illustration on following page.) This style, with slight adaptations, will operate efficiently for *legato, powerful, light* (elevated), *marcato* (more sideways motion with a stop before the quick motion), *crescendo*, etc. The *unreleased fermata* also employs this technique.

This motion accomplishes several things for the choral conductor. There is a precise ictus. The vowel sounds begins exactly *on* the beat point. As long as the hand moves upward (as though moving through molasses),

Pulling on all four beats:

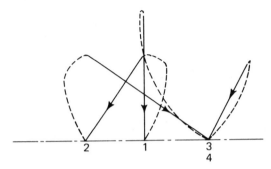

_____ = Quick downward motion to the ictus.
- - - - - = Slow pull (pull keeps moving upward until the quick downward motion to the ictus of the next beat).

the conductor psychologically pulls sound from the choir. Instrumentalists sustain sound adequately *without* this pull, but vocalists hit and fade in imitation of the piano. With the pulling motion the choral conductor can almost force singers to sing words in an organlike style and keep phrases moving and tone rolling out to the end. Only *one* phonetic sound is sustained as long as the hand moves upward. The director must insist that the singers' jaws remain open, relaxed, and motionless, and that the tips of their tongues remain down, forward, and relaxed until the second the hand plunges swiftly downward, even if the upward pull continues for a long period of time. When the hand starts its quick downward motion to the ictus, vanishing vowels, ending consonants, and new beginning consonants are clicked so that the new vowel may begin precisely on the new beat point (ictus). For example:

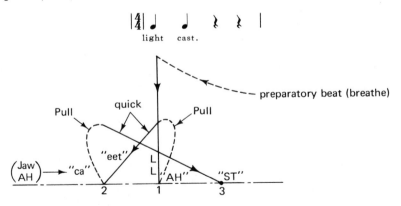

Just as important is the control this hand style exerts over *pitch*. As long as the hand pulls upward, a pitch or set of pitches in a chord may be sustained exactly in tune. When the quick downward stroke to the ictus occurs, the *new pitch* will sound without time allowance for out-of-tuneness. For example:

As long as the hand moves upward with vitality, F may be kept exactly *in tune*.

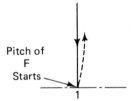

If the singers start to slide toward G, remind them that they are out-of-tune, and continue to pull upward. They will be forced to return to the original F pitch. Have the group think the next pitch (G) mentally while they are still singing F and staying perfectly in tune. The slur above is connected as on the organ or piano (demonstrate to the students how the slur sounds on the piano), *not* as it sounds on a slide trombone or Hawaiian guitar portamento.

The quick down-stroke gives the singers only time to move to the G they had heard mentally while they were still holding the F pitch.

Be sure the new pitch is attacked on top, like walking up stairs in the dark (see Chapter 5).

The pull on beat 2 continues as long as the conductor wishes G sustained in perfect tune, and the singers must think an in-tune A while singing G.

If the singers deviate in pitch, keep pulling and have the students go back to the G.

On the quick down-stroke to beat 3, the singers will move to the A they were mentally singing while sustaining G.

As long as only one beat is involved, this choral hand style will operate beautifully and efficiently for pitch, vowels, and consonants, or all three controlled at the same time. However, there are numerous times when the phonetic sound or the pitch (or both) needs to be sustained over *several* beats instead of over just one. There is an excellent technique for controlling the choir on these variables of pitch and phonetics that involves the addition of the *left hand*.

Conduct the regular beat pattern with the right hand (in whatever style is called for by the piece) while the left hand is used to beat and hold the exact time value of any note it is desirable to control or any phonetic sounds that should be precisely handled. The left hand will hit its ictus at the same point that would be used in a normal beat pattern and will pull upward and outward *with tension* for the duration of the pitches and sounds that are to be controlled. The pitch or phonetic sound should be clicked off with the left hand on phrase endings, while the right is beating 1 2 3, 1 2 release:

The left hand would hit on 1 and would sustain and move upward with tension through "Ho----," would hit again at a higher level on "--ly," would pull upward and outward through beat 2, and would release on beat 3.

When a single phonetic sound is to be sustained and controlled, pitches may move around. For example:

Conduct the regular pattern with the right hand and sustain the "lah" with the vital lifting left hand for the three beats, clicking off with "eet" on beat 1 of the next measure. If the *pitch changes* take place on the beat pattern (as in the example), the right hand can control pitches perfectly while the left hand controls the phonetic sounds.

One very practical use of this technique is the supporting of one or more voice parts while conducting other parts in voice(s), orchestra, or piano that are moving on the beat pattern. It is almost impossible to be *clear* without the employment of this type of technique in a situation like the ending of "Ye Watchers and Ye Holy Ones" arranged by W. A. Fisher (see p. 209). Following is *one* of the ways measures 34, 35, 36, and 37 might be directed so the moving voices are indicated plainly:

Measure 34 involves the left hand hitting and pulling through the entire measure while the right hand will beat 1, 2, 3 (cueing the bass and alto on beat 3).

Measure 35 will use the left hand hitting on beat 1 and pulling until the release exactly on beat 3. The right hand has an option, either doing the same as the left hand or beating 1 and 2 and releasing on 3.

Measure 36 will find the right hand subdividing beats 2 and 3, the left hand hitting only on beat 1, 2, and 3. Both hands will release after the fermata, which is on the "and" of the third beat.

Measure 37 will find the right hand making six subdivisions. The left hand may subdivide beat 1 (but it isn't essential). Beats 2 and 3 are handled in traditional style, *but* the eighth note will also be indicated.

"Ye Watchers and Ye Holy Ones," *Master Choruses* (complete edition), selected by Hugh Ross, John Smallman, and H. Alexander Matthews, 1939. Used by permission of Oliver Ditson Company, Bryn Mawr, Penna.

THE USE OF THE LEFT HAND

Usually the motions of the left hand require as much coordination as the motions of the right hand, so it is generally the best policy (even with a left-handed person) to use the right hand most of the time for the basic beat patterns. However, a good choral conductor needs to be ambidextrous so that, for example, the right-handed conductor can use the left hand proficiently in a beat pattern and the right hand for dynamics and other shadings, if necessary.

Conductors are very apt to overuse the left hand in the reiteration of the beat pattern. Besides making the conductor ineffective, the constant use of the left hand to repeat the patterns of the right will remind the audience of twin winshield wipers.

The left hand pattern goes in the *opposite* direction from the right hand. For example:

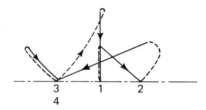

When it is advisable to use both hands, don't allow the hands to cross each other, because it will look and feel awkward. Move each hand out two to four inches (right hand to the right, left hand to the left), so beat one comes straight down from each shoulder.[6]

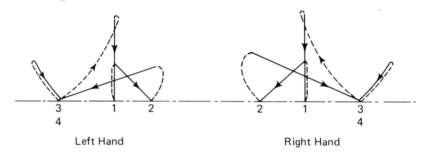

Left Hand   Right Hand

The left hand is used to call the singers' attention to anything in the music that is out-of-the-ordinary. It is used to assist in securing clear, precise attacks, entrances, and releases. The left hand adds force to the gestures of the right hand. Anytime special emphasis is needed (accents, abrupt changes in tempo, cueing entrances of certain sections, crescendos, decrescendos, ritards, or fermatas) the left hand should be employed. The left hand may also be employed effectively to indicate individual notes or rhythms, syncopations, and other irregularities, while the right hand beats the regular pattern. Preventative motions and various teaching movements (to assist in good pitch, vowels, etc.) are efficiently accomplished as a function of the left hand. See the previous section on "How to Control Vowels," etc.

THE RELEASE

Even seasoned conductors sometimes experience difficulty in attaining a precise release because they have slipped into habits of double motions,

[6]For a very broad, powerful effect, use *both hands* in a sweeping parallel motion.

flourishes, or hesitations. Many choral conductors employ an *upward* release, which has the advantage of having a sense of lift and expectation at the end of the phrase. It is highly improbable, however, that the cut-off that moves in an upward direction can be made as clear as the precise *downward* motion, and the lift can be accomplished through the conductor's expanded body and expressive face.

THE FERMATA

The fermata only signifies the ending of a phrase in the chorales of the early church (in the works of Bach and others). The conductor will be correct from the standpoint of style when the phrase is adhered to and the punctuation is obeyed. Except for the early chorales, the fermata must be longer than the written note. The fermata may have an exact predetermined length. For example, the fermata is held precisely twice as long as the written note in certain numbers of Mozart and Haydn. Fermatas are used to heighten the emotional qualities of the music and add suspense, among other things. It takes some musical maturity and experience to know exactly how long to hold the fermata. Most beginning conductors are afraid to hold it *long* enough and tend to almost disregard this sign. A slight ritard usually precedes the fermata. When this occurs, use both hands and conduct with a larger beat pattern to obtain the group's attention and prepare them for the fermata. The director must keep his hands moving constantly in order to keep breath support within the choir. The steady, slow, pulling movement of the hands along the directional beat pattern assists the singers in maintaining the even, steady flow of power needed for adequate tonal support. The conductor must guess approximately how long to hold the fermata, so that the hands will be able to move steadily until the cut-off without running out of "graceful" space. (If the conductor moves too fast with the pulling motion, it will result in overextension, and hands will be too high.)

The cut-offs that should be used much of the time for *released fermatas* are described in the following diagrams. Also described are the preparatory motion and breath that follows immediately after the release. The hand must continue in an upward direction until the motion is made for the release. The release must be a relatively quick downward motion (the size of the movement will depend on the style, velocity, and mood of the music). If the hands make a definite *stop* at the bottom point of the cut-off motion, the director can demand silence as long as the hands are stopped in the post-cut-off position.

For cut-offs at the end of the one-beat, pull relatively straight up and use a straight downward motion to cut-off. Make the preparatory motion for beat 2 in either $\frac{3}{4}$ or $\frac{4}{4}$ (see the patterns on the next page for the correct direction).

Another way of describing the fermata release is that the release and

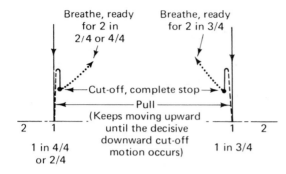

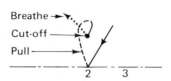

2 in 4/4 time
From the end of the dotted
line, move to the ictus
of beat 3 as a quick downward motion (See next Figure.)

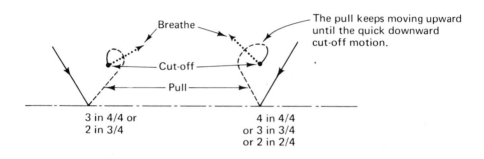

The pull keeps moving upward
until the quick downward
cut-off motion.

3 in 4/4 or   4 in 4/4
2 in 3/4   or 3 in 3/4
                     or 2 in 2/4

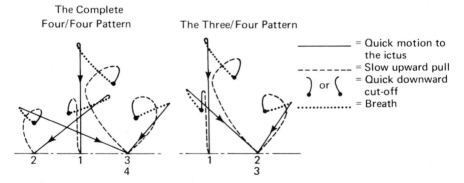

preparatory motion after it are basically a repetition of the previous beat,
only much higher and smaller—with a stop after the release. See the
previous diagrams (note the third beat and release, for example).

If the releases are made in the opposite direction of what is suggested,
singers will be unable to tell if the fermata is going to be released or unre-

leased. Also, awkward double motions must be made for preparatory beats.

Kinds of Fermata

The *unreleased fermata* is treated as a kind of ritardando on that particular tone or chord. The directional pattern is kept intact, although slowed so space will not run out, and then the conductor simply proceeds with the beat pattern in the original tempo, e.g., or .

The basic motion of directing a regular legato beat and an unreleased fermata is the same with exception of the longer, slower pull (follow the diagram under "How to Control Vowels," etc.).

The sign (') after a fermata should always be treated as an unreleased fermata in choral music. The sign means "breathe only if you have to"; and since the choir can always use the staggered breathing technique, the phrase should be continued without a break.

Ordinarily, when the fermata is followed by a rest and the notes resume immediately, the cut-off for the fermata will come exactly *on* the *rest*, in this case the ictus of 1, and the rhythm for the next notes will commence with the cut-off even without the a tempo sign. This is another type of unreleased fermata. For example:

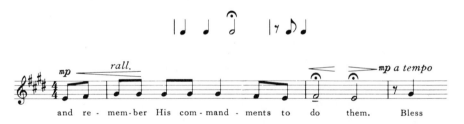

and re - mem-ber His com - mand - ments to   do   them.   Bless

"Bless the Lord," soprano line, Ippolitoff-Ivanoff. Arranged by Clough-Leighter, *Master Choruses* (complete edition). Used by permission of Oliver Ditson Company, Bryn Mawr, Penna.

For the *released fermata* that requires only a very short pause such as would be needed for a breath mark above the score', or a comma or a semicolon in the text or both, keep the hands moving on the beat pattern, cut off in a downward direction and in the same motion do the preparatory movement leading to the next beat (the conductor and choir should breathe with that preparatory motion). The hands will hold momentarily at the top just as they are ready for the down-stroke on the regular beat. Then the hands will simply move rhythmically, on the downstroke of the directional pattern of the next beat (follow the detailed diagrams drawn in this section).

For the released fermata that is a complete cut-off, as on a period in the text, a ⌢ over a barline or over a rest, or a grand pause (//), use the same patterns shown in the diagrams; the only difference is the length of the complete stop. (See the note in the "Suggested Exercises" for a difference in the treatment of the ⌢ over the rest.)

The fermata that is held for two or more beats (where there are no moving parts) will generally be conducted without beating out the pattern, but the director must count silently and hold at least a little *more* than the note's regular time value.[7] The heart-shaped motion with both hands is the most common pattern for this hold (the cut-off is *down*):

Sometimes it is necessary to hold a fermata for one or more voices, while one or more other voices (or the piano or orchestra) continue to move. To indicate this hold, the director extends the left hand (or the index finger of the left hand) in the air while the right hand continues with the beat (this may sometimes be reversed). For example:

OTHER TYPES OF RELEASES

One type of release is accomplished by simply stopping the hand. There are many times in choral conducting when phrasing or word meanings must be indicated in some way, and there may or may not be a "breath" before the new phrase starts. The motion called for in phrasing is much gentler in character than the one used for the fermata. It is much like placing the last note of the phrase on a shelf (usually the hands *stop on* the beat point).

When this temporary stop is required for meaning but no inhalation is desired, the hands must move from the temporary stop to the new phrase so quickly that singers have no chance to take a breath. In the unpretentious example, "O beautiful for spacious skies, For amber waves of grain," this temporary stop is required on the comma at the half-cadence and a continuance must be made with no breath. Later, in the same song, "America! America! God shed His grace on thee," requires a stop (but not

---

[7]The beginning conductor is highly likely to not hold the fermata long enough. To be safe, consider using the technique described in the following paragraph.

an inhalation) after each "America." Songs are full of these temporary stops, usually indicated by some kind of punctuation mark.

Many times on cadence points and the ends of phrases, a complete stop and a breath are required, but anything more than the hand stop would be awkward and unnecessary. When this is the case, the conductor's raising of the elbows slightly and opening the hands while breathing expansively but silently will tend to induce the choir to inhale; the new phrase will be picked up off the shelf (at the same dynamic level at which it left off). It may be necessary to rob the last note of the phrase of some time value in order to come in on time with the new phrase.

Cut-off on the ictus of the beat (when there is no fermata marking). If there is a rest following a note, normally the cut-off occurs *on the rest*, and ending consonants, vanishing vowels, or both are placed exactly *on* the rest by the singers as they end the phrase. If there is no rest following a note but the phrase suggests a release, cut soon enough that the singers may have time to take an adequate breath and come back in on time. If the ending note is longer than a beat, it is usually best to cut out exactly one beat before the new attack. This will give the singers adequate time to make a good release and a full inhalation for the new attack. Make the cut-off occur on the ictus of the beat pattern whenever possible.

Only when the tempo becomes quite slow as in an *adagio* will the ♩ be sustained for extra length; then the number would probably be conducted in eight (subdivided four) and the release would then occur on the ictus of beat 8 (this is explained in more detail in Chapter 4).

On a release such as the one in either of the two previous examples, simply "hit" the fourth beat *harder* than normal, remaining fairly close to the basic beat pattern. Breathe as the hands move into position for the quick downstroke to the ictus of beat 1, then go ahead with beat 1 *in rhythm*. For example:

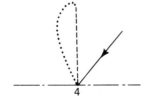

1. Hit beat 4 harder.
2. Breathe in rhythm.
3. Quick downstroke on beat 1 in rhythm.

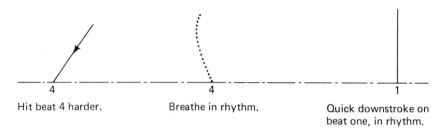

Hit beat 4 harder.   Breathe in rhythm.   Quick downstroke on
                                            beat one, in rhythm.

Presented with the following phrases, on what beat will these singers release the word?

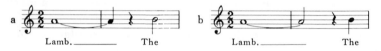

If this number moves slowly enough that it needs to be conducted in $\frac{4}{4}$ or in a subdivided two, it is obvious that the release on example a. will then be:

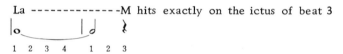

b. will be sung:

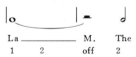

However, when the number's tempo is fast enough to require conducting in two to be clear, the clicking off on the ictus of the main beat probably should always be observed. Thus, a. will be:

b. will be:

When there is no time for a full arm movement, there must be another type of release. Sometimes, as in the following example, there is only time for a quick closing of the hand or fingers:

REST;   FOR

REST;

The music above, written for women's chorus, can be handled by hitting beat 1 and beat 2 so *all* voices will be sustained until F-sharp sounds distinctly; then the fingers will click together for the "st." The attack on "for" can be started either at the top of the "and" as a click, or with a quick, small downward motion. In either case, a sense of inhalation must be given by the director before "for" so that a firm, breath-supported attack will result. (Other uses of the fingers are discussed in this chapter under "Getting Singers to Watch.") *Warning*: When both fingers and an arm motion are used for a release, *don't* put the fingers together before the release. (There is an occasional exception such as an "n" to be sustained for 1 beat and then an arm movement to cut *all* sound.)

DIVIDED-BEAT PATTERNS

There are two basic ways to subdivide beats, and the good conductor must use both methods if maximum effectiveness is to be attained. An extra motion, slightly smaller than the principal beat but placed almost exactly on the same point, allows improved precision in *slow* passages, thus:

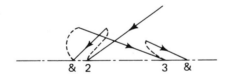

& 2   3   &

Whenever the beat is subdivided, it is extremely important that perfect regularity in beating the *main* counts is maintained. Do not subdivide the beat unless the conducting is clearer by this device; otherwise, the extra beats will simply confuse the choir. Use the smallest number of beats possible to make the direction precise. Subdivision is needed for emphasis (accenting, cueing entrances, indicating syncopation, etc.) or to clarify music that moves so slowly that the precision of the beat is lost. A speed of M.M. 60 or slower for the beat note usually requires subdivision. Subdivision will enable the director to bring out the rhythmic movement of a particular passage or to stabilize and coordinate the rhythmic precision of the group during a ritard (likely to happen at the ends of phrases or at the end of a composition). A piece like "Behold, the Lamb of God" from *Messiah* must be subdivided.

The conductor may wish to *eliminate* certain beats within the pattern. The director may in this way emphasize certain words and notes and de-emphasize others. He must be careful in doing so, however, that the basic rhythm is preserved and that he silently counts the omitted beats. Generally the director will indicate rests or unaccented words or parts of words by beating the directional pattern in an inconspicuous fashion. When this kind of divided beat is used to indicate *syncopation*, be sure that the motions before the syncopation are small or even omitted and that the hand moves suddenly and sharply on the syncopated note.

When a divided-beat pattern is necessary in a quick tempo, the "floor-ceiling" beat is the only efficient one. In addition to the imaginary floor of the beat, add an imaginary ceiling. Then when the beat hits the ceiling it clicks as it does when it hit the floor, thusly:

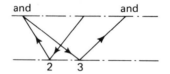

Subdividing as in the first method (by placing an extra motion on a beat point) will make the hand travel about twice as far as is required with either the "regular" beat pattern or the "floor-ceiling" divided beat, and this will cause awkwardness in a fast number.

Elizabeth Green calls this the "Gesture of Syncopation." This is truly the only practical use for this technique, as the pattern should continue normally, with *no ceiling*, until a syncopation is encountered. At that point, the downbeat should be small and unaccented and the upbeat vigorous.

Whenever rhythm becomes difficult or complicated, particularly if it is necessary or desirable to shift to or from a subdivided beat, think in terms of the "underbeat" (subdivisions) of the rhythm. The simplest motion which will efficiently accomplish the desired result is usually the best.

Many times it is necessary or desirable to shift to a subdivided beat, particularly at the conclusion of a song:

$\frac{2}{2}$ may be a subdivided $\frac{2}{2}$, or go to $\frac{4}{4}$; $\frac{4}{4}$ will probably go to $\frac{8}{8}$. Think the subdivisions even before the beat is slow enough to demand the subdivision. This will enable the conductor to move smoothly from 2 to 4 to 8 on a ritardando, to gradually put on the brakes. Lean backward slightly and use both hands in a gradually larger beat pattern as the arm movements slow down. It becomes even more imperative when the conductor beats $\frac{12}{8}$ in 4; $\frac{9}{8}$ in 3; $\frac{6}{8}$ in 2; $\frac{3}{8}$ in 1 (or $\frac{3}{4}$, in 1) that the 1 2 3, 4 5 6 be counted carefully (mentally) so the change to 12, 9, 6, or 3 will be smooth.

In accelerating, if the speed becomes great enough, it may be desirable to shift to the next mathematically divisable speed: $\frac{12}{8}$ to 4; $\frac{9}{8}$ to 3; $\frac{6}{8}$ to 2; $\frac{3}{8}$ to 1; $\frac{8}{4}$ to 4; $\frac{4}{4}$ to $\frac{2}{2}$; $\frac{2}{2}$ to $\frac{1}{1}$. For smoothness and safety, be sure to keep counting in twelve subdivided beats while shifting to four beats to a measure. Lean forward slightly and use both hands in a smaller and smaller motion, with tension, as the beat pattern gradually picks up speed.

This rule is related to another important one: keep the eighth and quarter note speed constant when changing from one time signature to another within a number, *unless* there is a marking that clearly indicates a change of tempo, for example, in "The Lamb" from *Songs of Innocence* by Earl George. Measures 13 and 15 are particularly tricky. Start thinking in eighth notes in measure 12. Measure 13 should be conducted in two as though the measure were in $\frac{6}{8}$, but the eighth note should be preserved. Keep thinking in eighth notes in measure 14, and measure 15 should be negotiated with no difficulty (it will also be safer to think measure 16 in six eighth notes until reoriented).

Another good example is Tchaikovsky's "Forever Worthy Is Thy Lamb" in the change from $\frac{3}{2}$ to $\frac{4}{4}$. It is necessary to start thinking in quarter notes (instead of half notes) not later than measure 16, two measures before the tempo change, to safely transfer to $\frac{4}{4}$.

CONDUCTING TECHNIQUES THAT HELP
IN SECURING GOOD PHRASING

The conductor must feel the surge of the correct musical phrase from within and must do everything possible to impart his feeling of phrasing to the choral group. This "pulling of a phrase" is the basis of musicianship. The director must always feel compelled to interpret the music. *Never* just beat time. Following a beat pattern most of the time is necessary for clarity, but what the conductor's attitude, body, and face say are always more important than the beat pattern.

The conductor's body should gradually expand until the peak of a phrase is reached, then *stay* expanded. The expanded body of the director and pull and vitality will help the singers keep their ribs expanded and breath under control. The conductor will benefit the choir when some of the techniques for obtaining good breath control described in Chapters 4 and 5 are used on a regular basis. To prevent the choir from breathing in the center of the phrase, *anticipate* the place at which students will normally breathe and start a feeling of ◄——— *before* the danger point is reached. The conductor should lean forward slightly, using good singing posture, with a face that is alive and expressive of the music and with eyes that are expressive and sparkling. Use the left hand in some manner to create added momentum. Even more vitality is essential when the dynamic is soft, but the motions must remain small.[8]

Women, particularly, usually need more *strength* in their conducting. Their directing should be as strong and vital as it is possible for it to be and still be unquestionably feminine.

Following are some specific techniques for carrying phrases successfully:

A circular motion toward the group indicates that the musical phrase is to be extended and a breath must not be taken. This circular movement must commence at least one beat (and in faster tempi, two beats) prior to the end of the phrase to be carried over.

The lifting up of the left hand with intensity (usually moving out toward the choir) will help the choir continue a phrase without breathing, *if* the vital lifting action anticipates the collapse of the phrase and starts before the sound starts to fade.

Make *"one roll per beat,"* starting before the phrase begins to sag and moving past the danger point. This circular motion should start in front of the body and pull *toward* the body, then roll over the top out *toward* the choir. The bottom of the circular motion should hit *on* the beat each time.

A pulling motion with the open hand asks for continuance of the

---

[8] A well-known example of an octavo number that requires extra vitality to keep its soft, sustained phrases alive is Bortniansky's "Cherubim Song, No. 7" arranged by Tchaikovsky.

phrase. This pulling motion (or lifting left hand) may indicate the sustaining of a phrase while the right hand beats time.

Use the fingers only to show clearly that the consonants are to be ended but the phrase is to continue. This procedure will give the director complete control of consonant precision and timing.

Phrase endings must be treated with particular care. The usual treatment is to cut the phrase short, let it dwindle out too soon, or punch the last note too hard (especially when a breath must be taken quickly). The director must keep the body expanded and lifted to support phrase endings, especially those that have a tendency to die out. Do have an expectant, alert attitude, an alive, vital facial expression and lift hands higher, palms up. Keep the dynamic intensity of the last note until the cut-off. If the note is loud and dramatic, the singers may even make a slight crescendo until the cut-off to increase the effect of excitement. Nothing is a worse letdown than a phrase that ends by dwindling half-heartedly into a muffled deadness. In diminishing (*dim.*), a choir should be able to achieve the absolute "vanishing point" where sound melts into soundlessness. Blend sound into stillness. This is one of the thrills of singing.

GESTURES TO ASSIST PITCH RETENTION

Cup the hand or hands and come down on top of the beat (to psychologically suggest the rolling tone lighting on top of the pitch). Be sure the singers are thinking and singing up and over the pitch, not driving to get it from underneath. The choir must have a feeling of *lifting* the tone rather than of *pushing* the tone. The right or left palm up on half steps or interval jumps downward will assist the group in singing smaller steps or jumps. (It helps the singers to support the tone and not just allow it to fall, without support.) A finger pointing upward, directed toward a section, will signify to them that they are going flat. Train the group to slide the pitch gradually upward until they are signalled to stop (when the choir is tuned-up). A finger pointing downward, directed toward a section, will inform the section that it is sharp. Train the choir so that sections can slide gradually up or down until the chord is in tune. In case everything else fails, the director may touch an ear, telling the group to listen to the total chord and tune up its part.

GAINING SINGERS' ATTENTION

The beat must be kept small when the conductor works for precision. Small motions force singers to watch. Also, be deliberately erratic with the beat to force the singers' attention. It does no good to *tell* a choir to watch. Cut off suddenly, speed up, slow down, or hold a note to force them to look. A good singer, who is singing strongly, will be afraid to sing without watching the director. The "bouncing ball" technique advocated throughout this chapter gives the conductor a precise beat point (ictus) that is especially helpful when extra precision is needed. Vowels, consonants, and pitches are controlled by means of the pulling motion off the beat point. Snapping fingers (or tapping a baton on the music stand) may be useful for precision in attacks.

The fingers will assist the conductor greatly in obtaining precision on consonants. Sometimes they are needed for better vowel precision, also. One big difference between instrumental and vocal conducting techniques lies in the use of the fingers. In vocal conducting, use the fingers of either hand to indicate vowels and consonants. Use space between the fingers for vowel sounds, the fingers touching for consonants. The fingers may click together for delicate releases on consonant sounds. Fingers *exploding open* will give power to an initial consonant. The beginning conductor may wish (or *need*) to start with the same motion for *all* consonants at first. He must be particularly careful to emphasize or click the explosive consonants (voiceless: p,t,ch, and k) (subvocals: b,d,j, and g) wherever they occur on the ends of words (also snap f). The consonants (m, n, and ng) must be indicated with the fingers and must be elongated and sung with more power to be heard plainly. The fingers (or the mouth and jaw) are the only way to give effective *tension attacks* of tuned or voiced consonants or sibilants (see Chapter 4). However, the budding conductor must not lose sight of the basic rhythmic structure of the number and the beat pattern. If it happens, stop trying to use the fingers until becoming more skilled with the beat pattern and other conducting techniques. Use the fingers only on difficult consonant articulations where the group requires assistance (or on a release that must be accomplished too quickly for a full hand or arm motion).

CUEING

Give cues to give the singers a sense of safety and to assure them that all is well and that they may have faith in the reliability of the director. Cueing enables the director to be sure that a section will enter precisely at the designated spot in the music and enables the conductor to direct the attention of the listeners to the particular section or soloist in prominence at that exact time.

Cues are given when a section makes its initial entrance in the song, when a voice-line enters after being mute for a long period of time, or when a section or soloist begins a melody line or solo of consequence. When the prominent theme is sung by an entire section, the director many times will turn toward that section and conduct its melody line. When a melody moves from section to section, cueing will keep the singers aware of the section that has the melody so that their part may be maintained in its proper dynamic perspective. Cue different melodic themes or a recurring theme that occurs in different voice parts. Clear cueing is required for basic figures of rhythmic interest that move from one part to another or for entrances that follow each other in quick succession in tricky rhythms that are hard for singers to negotiate. When one or two voice parts move and the others do not the conductor must indicate the moving parts. If the director wants, or needs, to handle word beginnings or tonal qualities in an exact way or if any voice part has a number of measures of *tacet* and then enters with a loud dynamic, it is advisable to cue the part. Sometimes a conductor will find it necessary to cue a part that would not ordinarily require assistance in order to help a weak section.

There are a number of effective ways for a director to give a clear cue to the singers. These melodies vary somewhat since the music is sung in various styles and tempi, and the frequency of cueing in a song also affects the kind of cue that may be performed. Always look toward a section *before* cueing it, as advance warning that something is about to occur. The director must anticipate everything, or gestures will be too late to do any good. Usually accents, entrances, etc., should be indicated one or more beats in advance in slow tempi, two beats or more ahead in fast tempi. If only one section, or a few people, are to be cued, make the motion to or look pointedly at that group. If more than one section is to be cued, use an all-inclusive motion with the hand(s) and eyes. Cueing must be done *by level*, high or low, when some sections are seated to the rear of other sections. The conductor *may* cue with the hand engaged in the beat pattern by keeping the direction of the pattern intact but pointing the hand in the direction of the section being cued, but usually the other hand will be employed. If the left hand is always used for cueing, take care to pivot the body to the right when cueing right so the hands do not *cross* when the cueing occurs. Cueing may be accomplished with the hands or finger(s); usually the hand closest to the section being cued will be used. At the proper time, a *look* toward a section is another effective way to cue; or the *head* may be used, usually with a *nod* toward the voice part (some directors use the chin effectively to indicate syncopations). There are unlimited ways to cue, such as the use of eyebrows, a smile, a wink, or the use of the shoulders, the only guide being that of good taste. There are times when combinations of any of these ways will be used advantageously.

INFLUENCING STYLE THROUGH FLEXIBLE BEAT PATTERNS

Many conductors do not change the size of their beat patterns noticeably, even when dynamic variations occur. They choose to keep the beat constant and show the dynamics with the other hand. Although there are some real advantages to this method, conducting a medium to large beat pattern with one hand while indicating soft singing with the other hand, or asking for loud dynamics while employing a small beat pattern, has an element of the ludicrous. The conductor loses the opportunity to immediately influence singers when hand style does not reflect the style and dynamics of the music. Also forfeited is the nuance and fluidity of phrasing that may be brought about through smaller motions on weak beats and larger motions on strong beats.

The director's beat pattern should reflect weak and strong beats, the rise and fall of each phrase, and pitch changes (whenever needed). In addition, style and dynamics may be indicated by height of beat, weight of beat, length of beat, the distance of the beat from the body, and muscular tension. The torso, face, eyes, and other hand will assist in the style indications. Customarily, the heaviest beat originates with the shoulders, the next heaviest starts with upper arm, a still lighter beat begins with the forearms, and the lightest beats are from the wrist and fingers. In general, use fingers only (or fingers and wrist) for *pp*; fingers and wrist for *p*; fingers, wrist, and a little forearm for *mp*; hand, wrist, and forearm for *mf*, whole arm for *f*; and arm and shoulders for *ff*. Rapidity also affects beat size. A fast tempo calls for a small beat pattern and the use of just wrist and fingers, slow tempo calls for a larger pattern and the use of more arm movement. Following are a few generalities concerning the motions that should accompany the various dynamics.

Softness may be indicated by small motions, head up and relaxed, the palm of the left hand *down* (especially when it moves downward) or facing the choir, moving downward. Softness is enhanced by the beat being away from the body except when a hushed, whispering, or dying-away effect is desired; then the hands should be brought back close to the body, the elbows hugging the torso tightly (or the hands brought back to the lips). The more the beat is elevated, the more it tends to indicate lightness or delicacy. Dainty passages must be conducted with flexibility of arm and with flowing beats. Lightness of beat is a characteristic of conducting soft passages, but it is necessary for the conductor to use even more vitality when the dynamic is soft and motions must be kept small.

Loudness may be indicated by large motions, the chin down, and the palm of the left hand *up* (especially when it moves up). If muscular tension accompanies the motion, even more intensity and loudness should result. Arms close to the body and conducting with strength or tension encourages loud singing. It is quite possible to use too much strength and vitality in conducting, especially when they are combined with the use of the doubled fist. Used constantly, this gesture will cause the group to drive too hard vocally. If a group is straining to sing loudly, critically analyze conducting techniques being used; it is likely that too much strength is being used. If a shout is desired, *do* double the fist(s). Otherwise, for a show of strength, tense the fingers, hands half-clenched.

Heaviness may be indicated by a greater length of beat, muscular tension, and use of the shoulders. Intensity is expressed by muscular tension in the body. Muscular tension always demands movement, vitality, and aliveness in the tone. Long, sweeping beats indicate moods of confidence, expansiveness, and fearlessness. The conductor may demand intensity and volume by employing *stringendo* (trembling caused by muscular tension). It is usually the left hand that is employed in this way, but sometimes the right hand or both hands are used. For great power, combine heaviness, length, and tension of beat. Starting the beat low and raising it higher and higher along with increasing power and weight and intensity will create tremendous power for a climax. Be sure the music demands this much strength.

A sudden change in volume from loud to soft can best be expressed by abruptly bringing the elbows tight against the body or rapidly moving the hands to the vicinity of the lips. A sudden change from soft to loud would be expressed by a quick, big motion, executed with tension.

A crescendo will ordinarily not grow more than two dynamics louder and may be indicated by cupped hands pulling apart as though playing an accordion (either horizontally or vertically), with muscular tension in the hands and body. This movement psychologically calls for enlargement and deepening of the sound by the singers. Don't ever ask a choir to sing *louder*, for ordinarily they will drive harder with their voices. Tell them to sing *bigger* or *fuller* or use a larger vowel form. If the choir starts to strain, use the accordion motions to suggest expanding the ribs and allowing the deepened tone to flow. It is usually necessary to use the palm of the left hand moving upward with vitality whenever the beat pattern must be maintained. A small beat pattern growing to a larger beat pattern, especially when both hands are employed, is another way to indicate a crescendo. The *diminuendo* or *decrescendo* may be indicated by using the reverse of the suggestions given for the crescendo. Take care that the loudness does not decrease too rapidly. The vibrant hand moving upward with the palm down asks for continuing vitality in the singing, but no increase in volume.

ACCENTS

The conductor needs a good understanding of the various kinds of accents in order to project styles adequately. These accents will be treated very briefly in this section and more fully in Chapter 10 (with the exception of the dynamic accents, which will be treated at greater length in this chapter).

An important type of accent is the *tonic accent*, in which the highest note will always naturally have the greatest weight. For example, in this phrase

the F will be sung more strongly than the other notes. The *agogic accent,* in its simplest form, occurs whenever a note has greater length than the surrounding notes. For example:

The half note above receives the greatest emphasis. Many authorities list *all* changes of tempo under the term agogic (*agogik*), so fermatas, rests, breathing signs, rubato, ritardandos, accelerandos, and all other tempo modifications are agogic accents. These two kinds of accents were more important in pre-metric music, which had no dynamic markings to guide the performers, than they are today. Properly written vocal music will have the most important words and parts of words *on* the tonic or agogic accents, making the bar line unnecessary, perhaps even causing accents to occur in the wrong places when editors insert bar lines in music that was written without them. An exception occurs in some contemporary music where the meaning of the word is unimportant. A most important kind of agogic accent in music of the Renaissance is the *word accent.* This must be used even when the important word does *not* correspond to the accent.

    Metric accent became a reality soon after bar lines were added.[9] Metric accent involves the well-known primary and secondary accent; for example, in $\frac{4}{4}$ time, beat 1 gets the primary accent and beat 3 the secondary accent. A very important type of metric accent occurs when the conductor insists that the first note of a triplet be emphasized, so the triplet pattern is felt (but the amount of emphasis would vary according to the beat on which the triplet falls within the metric pattern). For example:

Beat 1, first note, will be heavy. The first notes of beats 2 and 3 will have a feeling of pressure, but will be much lighter than the first beat.

    In a running passage, like in "For Unto Us a Child Is Born" from *Messiah,*

the first note of each pattern must be pushed in order to maintain clearness and precision of execution by a chorus. The larger the group, the more im-

---

[9]The first bar lines were added during the Renaissance so that singers could keep their place in the music.

perative it becomes for this "pattern accent" to occur. Be sure to maintain proper balance within the *metric* system (primary accent on 1, secondary accent on 3, etc.). It is also extremely important to feel and conduct the pull of the *entire* phrase, from the time the general direction of the "patterns" changes until the direction changes again (upward or downward) and a new phrase begins. (See Chapter 10 for more information).

A *dynamic accent* results from sounding one tone with more power than other notes around it. It is usually indicated by some type of marking (> *sf*, etc.). Following are conducting suggestions that may help.

1. Lengthen the beat for accented notes; shorten it for unaccented beats. When the hand is *advanced* in front of the body, the effect is that of more force.
2. > Stylistically "hits" and then "fades," just as this symbol does. The beat should reflect this percussive attack and dying-away characteristic. Sometimes the wedge-shaped accent ∧ indicates unusual emphasis.
3. *Sforzato (sfz)* should be executed one to two dynamics louder than the remainder of the passage in which it occurs. It is, in effect, an even more powerful accent.
4. Be sure the motions before the syncopation are small or even omitted, and that the hand and arm move suddenly and sharply *on the syncopated note*, e.g., ♪ ♩ ♪ . Keep the wrist relatively stiff, and make the quick motion with the forearm or the entire arm.

ARTICULATION

The *non-legato* mark (P̄) requires that the note be sustained for its entire length, but performed so as to detach it from other notes. Composers have used this horizontal marking to indicate so many different things that it is necessary to study the score and words carefully before it can be properly executed. Ordinarily, it should be sung with a feeling of pressure. The non-legato sometimes indicates marcato. *Marcato* is a different kind of accent. It is usually used only in *mf* to *ff* and is used a great deal in marches. The word means "strongly accented, marked." The word *marcato* may be written in the music, but sometimes the non-legato marking (P̄) is used when the marcato style is indicated. A heavy movement with the force of an accent but in "block" style (▭▬▭) is called for. The entire arm is used in a pushing type of motion to signify pressure on the note, and stops moving to signify the block style with space between notes. Beat 1 should come straight down as always, but then should press forward *toward* the choir. On all other beats, the hand should stay close to the beat pattern, but should move in a more horizontal gesture with a feeling of weight or pressure. *Tenuto (ten.)* may be indicated by the word or word abbreviation over the note, but is sometimes indicated by –. Tenuto (from *tenere*, "to hold"), held out and sustained for full time value, *sometimes* means that the note, rest, or chord is held even longer than the note value indicates. Ordinarily, the volume will be *mf* or less, and the non-legato style should be observed with what might be called a "pressure accent." *Sostenuto (sostenendo, sostenente)* usually means holding notes out for their full value, well-sustained with a singing, legato quality. Sostenuto, when the–mark is used for it, should not be non-legato. *Portato* or *mezzo-staccato* is indicated as ♩ ♩ ♩ . This marking is performed long but detached, the notes being more distinctly separated than in non-legato, but not as much as in *staccato*. Conduct all of these markings except *sostenuto* in the hand style discussed under *marcato*, except with a "smooth pressure" in the horizontal "brush stroke" motion, instead of with so much force.

A good example of the non-legato occurs in "Bless the Lord" by Ippolitoff-Ivanoff, arranged by Clough-Leighter. In the beginning phrase, the word "Bless" must *not* be conducted with a syncopated note accent with strong upbeat. This will cause the tone to be accented instead of *caressed*. Instead, indicate the breath and preparatory beat for the singers on the *rest* while giving the organ pitch to the organist with a small gesture. Then make a sweeping (gentle pressure) motion straight in front of the body toward the singers to include the second half of beat 1 and the first half of beat 2. Give sweeping (gentle pressure) motion straight in front of the body toward the singers to include the second half of beat 1 and the first half of beat 2. Give a beat to the left for the second half of beat 2, and then go along in regular ⁴⁄₄ style. "Soul" will have the movement described for beat 1 in marcato style, except with a *gentle* pressure.

"Bless the Lord," Ippolitoff-Ivanoff. Arranged by Clough-Leighter, *Master Choruses* (complete edition). Used by permission of Oliver Ditson Company, Bryn Mawr, Penna.
Special note: Bring out any suspension or clashing note. The tenuto motion can be used to advantage whenever more feeling or weight is desired for *any* word.

Staccato defined, literally, means "separated." Ordinarily the round dot staccato (sometimes called the half-staccato) takes away approximately half the length of the note it is over or under, depending upon the speed. For example, ♩ is sung like ♪ 𝄾, and *in the same style* as the notes surrounding it. In the French eighteenth-century style, the dot meant something else (see Chapter 10). Usually staccato will be conducted by small and quick gestures, in which the hand stops moving at the peak of the rebound (psychologically signifying the rest following the short note) and then moves rapidly to the next beat. The staccato is usually executed with the fingers and wrist, somewhat like shaking drops of water from the tips of the fingers. Do not *accent* the staccato unless it is written in the music or unless the words suggest this kind of attack; for example, singing about "hail" coming down should be conducted with a percussive attack on each note, while the words "snowflakes" or "rain" should be conducted with a soft, floating motion suggestive of the snow drifting down or of rain drops falling.

♪ *staccatissimo* in its modern meaning is very short and detached, sung approximately one quarter of the note's length or ♪ 𝄾˙ and is likely to be sung somewhat percussively because of its shortness. The wedge-shaped staccato was the exact equivalent of the modern staccato from Couperin to Beethoven.

Legato is used a great deal in singing. The words or basic style of the number may indicate the use of legato. The slur or phrase mark is also indicative: ⌒ . Employ a very smooth, flowing beat and move the hand as though it were being pulled through water. Think of pulling out a long string of chewing gum or of pulling taffy with your hands (only stay on the beat pattern). Another suggestion is to think of the legato bow movement of a string player. If the group begins to lose precision, *snap the beat points*. (Use the technique described under "How to Control Vowels," etc.)

Unaccented or unimportant words, parts of words, or rests are indicated by small gestures or the movement even "omitted," the hand not vital or alive, and the hand withdrawing toward the body. The hand must move as inconspicuously as possible, so the singers will not sing during the rest and will not accent the unimportant word or syllable.

MEMORIZE THE SCORE!

The conductor must be so familiar with the music that it is not necessary to glance at it except as an occasional aid to memory. Any absorption in the music on the stand will cause the director to be somewhat unobservant of class behavior and participation and will prevent the use of one of the finest choral helps, that of facial expression. Also, keep the conductor's stand out from in front of the body. There is much more feeling of contact and empathy with the choir if the stand does not come between you and the choir. Set the stand off to one side, to be used for reference only, so you will feel free to move over *into* the bass section, alto section, etc., to pull more sound or better pitch from them. (*Exceptions:* Keep the music stand low and in front of you, with the score open, when rehearsing and directing final performances of operas, cantatas, oratorios, or any extended choral work.)

THE CONDUCTOR AND THE PIANO

Be sure the piano is in a position where the accompanist will be able to see the conductor's motions. Also be sure the piano is where the choral group can hear it adequately. When conducting the piano *alone*, use a small inconspicuous beat. If there are cues for the pianist, make them directly to her. This will avoid confusion for the choir or the accompanist. Enlarge the beat and look at everyone in the choir just before they are to start singing. As a director, *don't follow the piano!* The conductor is the one who establishes rhythms. Be aware if the pianist plays wrong pitches. Make the corrections immediately in as quiet and inconspicuous a manner as possible. Have the accompanist give pitches from the bottom up. The bottom is usually the base of the chord and will give the group a stronger feeling of tonality. (Tips for the accompanist will be found in Chapter 9.)

Before conducting a choral group the conductor must choose a tempo. To decide upon the correct tempo, do the following:

1. Look at the composer's or the arranger's broad tempo marking (*presto, andante,* etc.).
2. Look at the metronome marking, if there is one (there was no metronome before Beethoven, so any markings on pre-Beethoven music are placed there by an editor).
3. Sing the melody line (mentally) in at least two speeds and quickly decide which speed sounds most convincing.
4. Look quickly through the number and check the selected speed against the fastest notes in the song, then accept or reject the tempo choice.
5. Think this tempo and then confidently call the group to attention and start conducting.

REHEARSAL AND PERFORMANCE GESTURES DIFFER

The motions a conductor uses in rehearsal will ordinarily be larger than those used in a performance. In a rehearsal "teaching gestures" are employed that psychologically induce good tone quality, musical interpretation, and so on. These motions become progressively more refined as the number becomes polished. Small gestures (but with much vitality) demand the close attention of singers who have music memorized. Large gestures will tend to make the singers inattentive.

Good rehearsals make good performances. The gestures you see the conductor make in concert are those that were made at the rehearsals. They serve as a reminder to the singers of what they were taught. Without the conductor, the choir would fail to give you a thousand subtleties that the director can evoke with these reminders. A really fine conductor can actually *inspire* a choir to a greater height than they have ever attained previous to that performance.

The choir (except on large works such as *Messiah*) must have the number perfectly memorized so it can give one hundred percent of its attention to the interpretation asked for by the director. Of course, the director must also have the score perfectly memorized so that if any tiny mistake occurs it can immediately be recognized, analyzed, and remedied so quickly that the audience will not be conscious of the miscue.

Prearranged Signals

One or two fingers may be used to signal first and second endings. Other TV signals may come in handy, such as "cutting the throat" meaning to stop, etc. Other prearranged signals may be worked out ahead of performances; for example, if chords start to go sour, at a signal a core of the best singers sing alone until things are straightened out; then, at a signal, everyone sings again.

A Check-list of Things to Watch for and Correct when Conducting:

Intonation
> Note *accuracy*
> Tones attacked *on top of the pitch*
> If the group is flatting or sharping—*why* are they?

Diction
> *Vowels* pure—*phonetic sounds* correct, not chewed
> Are the *consonants clicked?*
> Are the *voiced* and *sub-vocal consonants in-tune* at the beginnings of words?
> Can the *text* be *understood* clearly—without having to *strain* to *hear* it?

Interpretation
> *Dynamics* (enough contrast, or too much to be in good taste?). The dynamic range of a particular group depends upon the age level, physical maturity, and vocal development of the singers. Conductor must not attempt to have junior high voices sound like adult voices. Effectiveness is attained by dynamic contrast. *There must not be vocal strain!* *Adherence* to the *Score* (notational signs observed). Use the correct style of music, mood, and animation.
> Accurate *Rhythms*
> *Phrasing must be Correct.* Is *feeling* for the music evident?
> Do tones always *move*—or do they hit and fade?
> Correct *tempi* for the style and mood of the music being sung.

Tone Quality
　　　Resonant, *well-placed* basic *sound*.
　　　Evidence of good *breath-support* and *breathing habits*
　　　Extremes of Range (easy or strained?)
　　　Flowing Tone

Chord Balance
　　　Do any *voice qualities* 'stick out' in a voice part or in the total chord?
　　　Do the *number of singers on a part* cause the chord to be out-of-balance?
　　　Does the *range* that some parts need to sing on this number cause a lack of balance?
　　　Is the *important vocal line brought out* (melody, moving parts, etc.?)

Blend
　　　Is there a *unified tone* (same kind of quality)?
　　　Good Intonation
　　　The same style of diction (vowels, particularly, must be produced the same way).

Precision on Attacks and Releases

Posture
　　　No evidence of lifted, *thrust-out* jaws?
　　　Bodies alert and straight, but not stiff

Sensitivity to Conductor Evident?

The Accompaniment and the Accompanist

Appearance when Singing in Public
　　　Excellent conduct on stage—good stage presence (poise).
　　　Neat and uniform appearance. Group's heights taper in a reasonably uniform manner.

SOME METHODS YOUNG CONDUCTORS MAY USE FOR IMPROVING THEIR SKILL

1. Observe the techniques of other conductors at clinics, concerts, contests, etc.
2. Observe the successes and failures of the students and the teacher in the conducting class.
3. If possible, secure a group to direct (fraternity chorus, church choir, etc.).
4. Practice often in front of a mirror. Be self-critical and self-analytical.
5. Have a friend in the conducting class (or your spouse, if you have one) watch your conducting and criticize it.
6. Direct the score just as though a choir were in front of you. Give cues, attacks, releases, dynamic shadings, and everything needed.
7. Every little while, check in the mirror to see whether your facial expression and gestures look convincing to you.
8. Secure a recording of the number if one is available. Conduct while playing the record and watching the score. This is one of the best ways to learn correct interpretations of music, since the recordings are usually made by great choirs. Study the suggestions given for lesson plans in Chapters 3 and 7 and the rehearsal procedures in Chapter 9. Plan your rehearsal accordingly.

SUGGESTED EXERCISES FOR DEVELOPING CONDUCTING SKILL

Study the information and techniques, pp. 131–35. The technique of isolating and practicing one- and two-beat rhythmic patterns described should be followed, except that you should beat metric patterns with the right hand while tapping with the left. This will help you become more ambidextrous while your rhythmic perception becomes more accurate. The TAP System should be used, with the same directing and tapping method, if it is available to you in your school.

Student conductors should find the following Hand-Skills Exam a challenging way to develop some directing competencies. Teachers of conducting should feel free to use or reconstruct these exercises as a practical conducting examination.

1. Construct a hypothetical exercise like the following, then change it after you can master it. Rests may be substituted for any note or notes. Think the underbeat always until the patterns become automatic. Conduct the $\frac{12}{8}$ in 4:

2. Lift and lower the left hand steadily, using more intensity as the tone becomes louder. The body should expand and the eyes open as you crescendo. With the right hand, beat a larger pattern on louder sounds, a smaller pattern on softer sounds. Keep the intensity on the diminuendo. Do meter changes and keep the eighth note constant. Change beat direction on agogic accents only in the $\frac{11}{4}$ and $\frac{5}{4}$ measures. Remember that the first of a sequence also receives more weight $(\frac{5}{4})$. (Use all kinds of beat patterns in practice drills.)

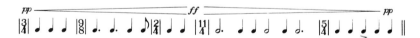

3. Practice conducting one measure of $\frac{4}{4}$ with the right hand, while conducting one measure of $\frac{2}{2}$ with the left hand. Then reverse hands, e.g.

4. Practice conducting one measure of $\frac{4}{4}$ with the right hand, while conducting two measures of $\frac{2}{4}$ with the left hand. Reverse hands, e.g.

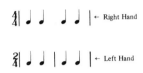

5. Practice the following kinds of fermatas:

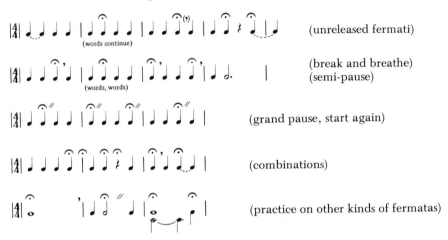

(unreleased fermati)

(break and breathe)
(semi-pause)

(grand pause, start again)

(combinations)

(practice on other kinds of fermatas)

Note: When the students come to a grand pause (///), they should stop and wait until the conductor proceeds. A similar break and wait occurs when the fermata is placed above a rest or a bar line. The beat is omitted when the fermata is over the rest.

    ' above the staff means to "breathe."

    (') means "optional breath." Don't breathe unless you have to breathe.

    ‿‿ indicates "no breath."

6. Beat a regular pattern with the right hand while the left hand is used to beat and hold the exact time value of each note by tapping and lifting in the air. Carrying the phrase and releasing endings must also be done:

Conduct the measures in a different order or use different time patterns. One practical use of this technique is the supporting of one or more voice parts while the other hand moves on a beat pattern, conducting other moving parts in voice or piano or orchestra. Other utilitarian uses are to dictate word rhythms in sight-reading, hit syncopations, and control phonetics and consonants.

7. Practice starting and stopping. Always breathe with the singers on the preparatory beat and form with your lips the first vowel the group will sing. With the following exercise, use the words "home," "name," "whom," "I," and "be," and interchange them on entrances.

8. Practice the two kinds of divided-beat patterns, at various speeds on the following exercise:

9. Practice cueing in at least the following ways: by "nodding"; by using only the left hand; only the right hand; and by using the hand or hands closest to the section.

The Seating Arrangement:

Soprano	Bass	Tenor	Alto

Director

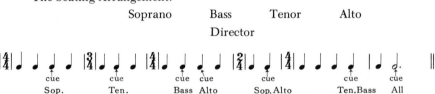

10. Practice the following exercises *legato, staccato, tenuto* or *marcato, accented, delicately, hushed, heavily, powerfully* (conduct smoothly and continuously from beginning to end).

a.
2 4 5 1 7 3 6 9 10 12 8 11
4, 4, 4, 4, 4, 4, 4, 4, 4, 4, 4, 4.

b.
4 1 12 8 9 3 2 6 5 7 11 10
4 4, 4, 4, 4, 4, 4, 4, 4, 4, 4, 4.

c. Assign *tenuto* etc. to the various measures and conduct them that way. Use correct beat pattern, style, and dynamic markings. Try to look ahead, then go completely through without a pause.

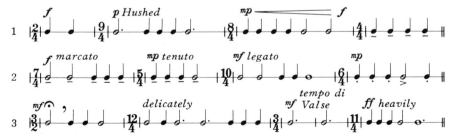

Practice until it is easy, then reassign the markings.

11. Practice:
    a. *Accelerando*. Starting in 12, go to 4; 9-3; 6-2; 3-1; 8-4; 4-2; 2-1.
    b. *Ritardando*. Starting in 1, go to 3; 2-6; 3-9; 4-12; 1-2;2-4; 4-8.
    c. *Accelerando*, then *ritardando*. 12-4-12; 9-3-9; 6-2-6; 3-1-3; 8-4-8; 4-2-4, 2-1-2
    d. *Ritardando*, then *accelerando*. 4-12-4; 3-9-3; 2-6-2; 1-3-1; 4-8-4; 2-4-2; 1-2-1.

12. Analyze ten or more good numbers for each of the following groups: sixth grade, seventh grade, eighth grade, and tenth grade general music class; junior high woman's chorus, male chorus, and mixed choir; high school woman's chorus, male chorus, and mixed choir. Use the analysis sheet and information in Chapter 3.

13. As a minimum, all songs assigned must be completely memorized. Leadership must be in evidence. It will be expected that the conductor show a facial expression that will tend to inspire the choir and that all notes will be conducted in the proper style. (This means that not only the basic period and style of the number will be preserved, but that marcatos, staccatos, fermatas, *pp*, etc., will be observed; that the gestures will be small and the hand dead when notes, words, or parts of words are unimportant, or when rests occur; and that the fingers will be used on consonants that need help for precision.) The difference between being average and being great is the extra effort!

BIBLIOGRAPHY

ANDERSON, IRA C., and SIMON V. SINGLETON, *Music in the Secondary Schools* (2nd ed.). Boston: Allyn and Bacon, Inc., 1969.

DECKER, HAROLD, and JULIUS HERFORD, eds., *Choral Conducting: A Symposium*. New York: Appleton-Century-Crofts, 1973.

EHMANN, WILHELM, *Choral Directing*. Minneapolis, Minn.: Augsburg Publishing House, 1968.

FINN, WILLIAM T., *Art of the Choral Conductor*. Evanston, Ill., Summy-Birchard Company, 1960.

GARRETSON, ROBERT L., *Conducting Choral Music* (5th ed.). Boston: Allyn and Bacon, Inc., 1980.

GREEN, ELIZABETH A.H., *The Modern Conductor* (3rd ed.). Englewood Cliffs, N.J.: Prentice-Hall, Inc., 1981.

HABERLEN, JOHN, *Mastering Conducting Techniques*. Champaign, Ill.: Mark Foster Music Co., 1977.

LAMB, GORDON H., *Choral Techniques* (2nd ed.). Dubuque, Iowa: Wm. C. Brown Co. Publishers, 1979.

LAMB, GORDON H., ed., *Guide for the Beginning Choral Director*. American Choral Directors Association, 1972.

McELHERAN, BROCK, *Conducting Techniques: For Beginners and Professionals*. New York: Oxford University Press, 1966.

MARPLE, HUGO D., *The Beginning Conductor*. New York: McGraw-Hill Book Co., 1972.

MOE, DANIEL, *Basic Choral Concepts*. Minneapolis, Minn.: Augsburg Publishing House, 1972.

——, *Problems in Conducting*. Minneapolis, Minn.: Augsburg Publishing House, 1968.

ROBINSON, RAY, and ALLEN WINOLD, *The Choral Experience*. New York: Harper's College Press, 1976.

RUDOLF, MAX, *The Grammar of Conducting*. New York: G. Schirmer, Inc., 1950.

THOMAS, KURT, *The Choral Conductor*. New York: Associated Music Publishers, 1971.

ANTHOLOGIES

ADLER, SAMUEL, *Choral Conducting*. New York: Holt, Rinehart and Winston, Inc., 1971.

KJELSON, LEE, and JAMES McCRAY, *The Conductor's Manual of Choral Music Literature*. Melville, N.Y.: Belwin Mills Publishing Corp., 1973.

McKELVY, JAMES, *Music for Conducting Class*. Champaign, Ill.: Mark Foster Music Co., 1977.

ROBINSON, RAY, ed., *Choral Music*. New York: W.W. Norton and Co., Inc., 1978.

9

Class Control and
Rehearsal Techniques

Choral music in America has experienced several developmental stages. There was much interest in authentic repertoire from 1910 to 1935; proper rehearsal techniques were the center of interest from 1935 to 1945; vocal pedagogy occupied the center stage from 1945 to 1955; performances in the correct style with good performance techniques were emphasized from 1955 to 1965; and since 1965 the music instructor has been expected to be a music educator as well as to teach performance aspects of music. It is important that the music educator impart to students more than sight-reading and performance skills, the ability to follow directions, and some familiarity with literature. In order for students to be musically knowledgeable and to develop musical taste, they need to understand the theoretical and historical considerations of the authentic music they perform. When students creatively investigate and evaluate vocal techniques, discover the reasons a particular song was written in a particular manner, sing it in various historical styles, and find out why the key seems appropriate by singing the song in major, in minor, in a mode, and bitonally, they are beginning to develop their own musical standards. Many experiences of this kind may be incorporated into the music rehearsal. Students may investigate the word meanings, study the rise and fall of phrases as they perform them, note the active and rest tones, see how the interpretation must be varied when a pattern is repeated, and observe the tonal groupings and sequences. A great deal of fun and understanding may be obtained through singing a song at varying speeds or employing different basic rhythmic patterns, and music sung with contrasting dynamics will be interesting and informative to the students. Ear training and sight-reading do not have to be dull, and a number of interesting class activities are suggested in this chapter and in Chapter 6. Efficient use of the rehearsal period is the key that unlocks student musicianship and makes fine choral organizations. This chapter will provide some suggestions for obtaining good class control and will discuss several rehearsal techniques.

CLASS CONTROL

Discipline is of great concern to the teacher of vocal music. The director instinctively knows that music, the language of the emotions, will not thrive in an atmosphere of rigid military discipline. Good discipline will not bring fine choral music to the school. And yet, unless the instructor has the respect and attention of the student, it will not be possible to teach effectively.

All beginning teachers are likely to have trouble keeping control over their students, but there seem to be even more disciplinary problems for the choral director. The regular teacher quiets the classroom at the beginning of a class period and maintains that quiet the entire time with relatively little effort, simply because the class content deals mostly with intellectual matters. The music teacher, on the other hand, energetically strives to arouse in the students the emotions that are inherent in music. After the students' emotions have been stimulated each time, the director must bring the class back to respectful attention.

The three levels of discipline are: (1) self-control (most desirable), (2) social control by the teacher of the student's peers (desirable), and (3) the authoritative "No" (less desirable, but sometimes essential). True discipline is self-discipline. This is the subordination of immediate wishes, impulses, desires, or interests for the sake of an ideal, this ideal being a fine choir, a better voice, or musicianship. Teachers should work toward having the class take care of itself even when they are out of the room (self-control).

Some basic causes of misconduct are unsatisfactory home conditions (particularly poor discipline in the home); dislike of music (perhaps caused by a lack of training or by a feeling that music is useless); the growing boy-girl relationship (causing the student to show off); lax discipline on the part of the school; and poor teaching, poor class organization, or negative attitude on the part of the teacher.

Enthusiasm, creativity, musicianship, and good student-teacher rapport are primary ingredients in successful music teaching and may allow a teacher to be very successful even though possessing many personal faults. Enthusiasm is contagious, and it is the most important element in the teaching process. The teacher enthusiastically shares his love and knowledge of music with the students in order to persuade them to understand and enjoy music as much as he or she does. This approach will ensure a positive, optimistic attitude toward teaching and working with the students. It will also result in the teacher becoming so absorbed and busy trying to improve the students that there is no time to think of oneself and mistakes being made or that might be made in the process of teaching. The instructor who anticipates problems while planning will be able to make the correct quick decisions that will contribute to confidence and leadership. A teacher's vitality in the classroom will help pull more participation from the students.

A creative imagination will stimulate students, arouse their interest, and function in the handling of emergencies. Lack of creativity in a teacher should not be used as an excuse for uncreative teaching. It is easy to be eclectic and "borrow" other people's good ideas, whether they are seen in a demonstration or read in a book.

Student-teacher rapport begins with a teacher's belief in the inherent worth of every student, regardless of native intelligence, social position, race, color, or physical ability or disabiity. Each person is entitled to an opportunity to develop any inherent musical talents. Be cordial, friendly, and eager to help the students, and display a personal interest in their affairs. Take the trouble to learn the names of students as soon as possible. Nothing will so thoroughly convince a person of a teacher's lack of interest as not knowing ones name after a suitable length of time. When the teacher says, "You in the yellow sweater," or mispronounces or misspells the student's name, the student will feel rejected and will tend to resent the teacher. Commend students whenever they do anything to merit praise. Compliment a section or the class on improvements made in the music, for example, better dynamics or vowel sounds, but don't insult the intelligence of the class by telling it how wonderfully it sang when the singing was mediocre or poor. Remember that learning proceeds most effectively under guidance that stimulates and encourages the students in their musical efforts and provides for successes rather than discourages and has too many failures, so don't use the equally bad psychology of always telling the class how poor it is. They'll begin to believe it after awhile. Laughter breaks tension and acts as an antidote to a driving rehearsal. The teacher with a sense of humor will make friends. "Tongue-in-cheek" sarcasm is a kind of humor secondary school students appreciate, but sarcasm that makes fun of a student in front of peers is always bad. Good teacher-student rapport is promoted when the students feel the teacher is fair and does not play favorites. It is very difficult for a teacher to like the troublemaker as much as the student who tries to please; but if it is impossible to resist liking some students more than others, conceal that fact from the class if possible. The teacher must be loyal to the students and to the music department, or no loyalty can be expected from them. If a teacher must choose between a student's approval or respect, respect must always be the more important goal. Respect is likely to be lost when students are allowed to call the teacher by a nickname or first name. Insist that *all* teachers be addressed as Ms., Miss, Mrs., or Mr. by students. Being well-groomed and wearing attractive clothes that are in good taste in the locale helps to maintain the line of distinction between teacher and student and makes it easier for the student to feel respect for the instructor (especially when the instructor is young).

Beginning the Class Period

Arrive at the room ahead of time, for if you consistently get there after the students, you may expect to see them misbehaving when you arrive. Unless a learning situation involving the use of the piano is deliberately set up and carefully controlled, students must not be allowed to play the piano when entering or leaving the music room. Be at the door when students arrive, or they are likely to run in the hall and into the music classroom. The actions of all students in the hall are your responsibility, whether the students are yours or not. Students should be *in* their assigned seats when the bell rings, and something should happen immediately and keep happening until the bell rings at the end of the period. A seating chart is very desirable because it enables roll to be checked very quickly and efficiently by the simple process of noting which seats are vacant; it enables the teacher to learn students' names more quickly (and call them by name, from the chart, even *before* their names are known); it enables voices to be placed exactly where they fit into the ensemble; and it makes it possible for problem students to be effectively isolated from other problem students (close friends are likely to cause trouble because they like to talk to each other instead of listening to the teacher's instruction). It is important to not wait too long to change a student's seat when a trouble spot is located after permanent seats have been delegated. When the seating chart is made in pencil or with slots, changes may be made immediately and easily. Even when an informal seating arrangement or "scrambled" seating is desired, it is usually more efficient to check roll in the formal seating arrangement and *then* move to the other activity. When a student cannot take part in class activities for some legitimate reason such as a cold, have the student report any inability to participate *before* class or at the earliest opportunity. This student must remain in the usual seat, participating in any activities that will not be harmful and observing and learning whatever can be learned under these circumstances. It is no fun to sit and not participate, so if the student is faking, it probably won't happen again. The student who is allowed to move out of a regular seat and do homework for another class may become ill surprisingly often—in fact, every time a lesson is not fully prepared for some other class.

Citizenship

The teacher must not allow students to go out of the room frequently on various pretexts. Don't permit students to go to the rest room at all the first period in the morning or afternoon (unless there is a doctor's permit or an obvious emergency). Encourage students to come prepared to spend the period working. The instructor should not allow more than one member of each sex to be out of the room at a time. Set a maximum time of five minutes for a student to be absent or privileges will be denied the next time. Have the students sign out the exact time they left the room and sign back in. If students need to report to the office or to another teacher, ask the other teacher to send a slip back with the student with the exact departure time and the teacher's signature. This prevents students from wandering around the halls, congregating in rest rooms to smoke, or even leaving the building.

Have the students deposit gum in the wastebasket as they come into the room, if the activity is singing. The teacher must insist that everything be off the student's desk and lap except the music (this keeps the learner from fooling around with books and pencils, studying, and accidentally knocking books on the floor). Have books and pencils put away, unless the books or pencils are to be used during the class period. Students must not be allowed to write on music unless they are instructed to do so in a specific way. If any paper is thrown on the floor, have the student responsible pick it up and place it in the wastebasket. Any mess on the floor encourages more students to contribute without any twinges of conscience, just as writing on music or desks encourages other students to do likewise. Do not permit students to lean back in chairs. Not only is it hard on chairs, but students will occasionally *fall*, with consequent class disorder, and there is the danger of injury. Choir members should mount and leave risers only from the front. Mounting or leaving over the back of the risers may result in chairs being knocked over. If the rehearsal is on the stage, students must use the stairs instead of jumping off the front of the stage. Music to be used and other pertinent information will be on the chalkboard at the front of the room. The class member should check the chalkboard immediately upon entering the room. Be sure the music and materials are issued and gathered in a routine manner, all items being handled quietly, carefully, and quickly.

Teaching citizenship is as important as teaching music. Offer some opportunities for student government. Do realize that an excellent job of teaching is not being done when the choir sings well but behaves like a group of juvenile delinquents. Talk with the students at the beginning of the school year about the purposes of the class, and together set up guides for behavior and goals for achievement. This is one of the most effective ways to establish good rapport with the group and to use the various other principles of cooperative learning. Students must be offered some opportunities for learning cooperatively. *Cooperative learning* allows students to set up their own goals, to study ways to reach the goals, to make and assume responsibility for choices made by the class, and to evaluate cooperatively the advancement toward the goals. When standards are set up together, the teacher is then enforcing discipline and reaching toward definite standards with the approval of the class. Then a student is not punished on a personal basis. The student, and the entire class, will realize that the *act* is being punished, not the person, and that *anyone* committing this act must be punished, since detrimental actions endanger the success of the entire class. This type of discipline derives its authority *from the class* rather than from the teacher. With good group morale there will be student pressure against any student who steps out of line so often that a fine organization's performance is jeopardized. The teacher must not expect, however, to be able to build esprit de corps in a *general music* class. Good conduct must ordinarily be built through interest in subject matter and activities.

Whether the class is begun through a cooperative learning approach or in some other way, the group must understand the purpose of the course and some ground rules under which the class will operate. Be sure to give information about how grades will be determined, about home study, about how a student may receive additional help, and about general rules of room conduct.

General Classroom Activities

Teachers must always be aware of student response to them, to teaching ideas, and the music. Eye contact with the class is an essential factor in good teaching. When teachers direct with their eyes glued to the music or talk with their backs to the class while writing on the chalkboard, they cannot watch the class and anticipate and prevent any misbehavior. Trouble must be anticipated and stopped *before* it starts. Discipline problems are much more difficult to correct than they are to prevent, for when disciplinary problems are allowed to occur and students are "caught" in their misdeeds, some fitting punishment must be administered. Eye contact also enables instructors to use their facial expression and personality to pull participation from a class. Teachers must firmly but pleasantly and persistently insist that students stop talking and listen whenever they talk and must check to be certain that the attention of every student is obtained before instructions are given. Make the directions concise and at the students' level of understanding, and give the directions only *once* (of course, directions will need to be repeated if the students have been unable to understand them). Don't repeat directions several times because some of the students weren't listening. Make each student feel responsible for responding ("Mary, can you tell the class what was just said?"). A few students must not be permitted to monopolize the class discussion, for all students must be given an opportunity to recite, including the ones who do not volunteer. Make it necessary for the student to lift a hand and wait for recognition by the instructor before talking, and then insist that the class listen courteously to the student's comments. Orderly behavior during class should be common courtesy, yet it is surprising how often students can forget or ignore good manners.

The teacher must sing occasionally to help out a part or to demonstrate, but it is impossible to hear or see what is going on in the class as well while engaged in singing constantly. Avoid asking students if they like the music or want to do a certain activity, for they will almost always feel compelled to react negatively, even when they *like* the music or activity. Be careful to use vocabulary that is suitable to the age and maturity of a group. If a mistake is made in judging a group's maturity, let it be in the direction of being *too* mature. Students of secondary school will resent any suggestions that they are not mature. Emphasize the point that students must conduct themselves like men or women if they wish to be treated like adults. Emphatically bring attention to the fact that students' ability, or lack of ability, to keep their attention focused on the music or discussion for a period of time is a better way to judge their *true* maturity than is their age.

When an individual requires correction in singing or behavior, talk to the entire section to make the correction. It is very effective to move over to the section and talk quietly and personally. Habitual shouting at a class, pounding a desk, or breaking a baton will soon lose control of a class, although many successful teachers use a "blow-up" under control (once in a great while) to settle a class down. Habitually interrupting a class to lecture on behavior is also a poor procedure. The conductor should avoid leaving the arms in an "at attention" position for a lengthy period of time while lecturing the class. Be careful that a threat or warning should not be given to the group or individual when there is no intention to keep or enforce the threat (or perhaps the threat *cannot* be enforced).

Occasionally there is a type of individual who will respond *only* when embarrassed in front of the class. Ordinarily it is better to take the student out of the class into the hall so that any talking or disciplining may be done privately. Have an individual conference with the troublemaker to analyze the difficulty. Give the student a chance to offer a remedy for the misbehavior. If punishment must be resorted to, devise a punishment that "fits the crime" (requiring the student to stay after school and mend music when some music has been torn through careless handling in class is a fitting punishment). The punishment should be one that is likely to result in desirable changes in the attitude of the problem student.

Ignore the unintentional and accidental disturbance and go on with the lesson. The teacher who becomes involved in the trap of pouncing on every tiny thing anyone in the class does, either purposely or accidentally, will be so busy jumping on the offenders that there will not be time to do good teaching. The growing bodies of youngsters *will move around* some, so the teacher must become aware of what is intentional and what is accidental. The teacher will ignore the minor *intentional* disturbances if it is almost certain they will disappear if ignored. If a disturbance continues, give the student some simple reminder to cease the disruptive action; for example, *look* at the offender until the problem stops, or stop conducting and look; the conductor may point to a cheek or make a chewing motion if the student is chewing gum; or the director can simply say, "George," then go on with the lesson assuming the off-limits act will cease. *If it still does not*, then quietly and firmly insist that the action be complied with. (It should have been established already that a particular action is detrimental to the progress of the individuals and class as a whole. If it has not, this is a good time to sell the group on the fact that this is unacceptable behavior for their own ultimate good, or to motivate the class to analyze the end result of such actions being permitted.) The instructor should realize that youngsters are at a disadvantage when they can't sit down. This psychological fact may be used to advantage in insisting that good singing posture be maintained ("or we'll stand all the time") or in enforcing discipline (all students in the class stand when one student continues to misbehave).

Send students to the office only as a last resort. If there is no other way to handle the situation satisfactorily, get the help of the administration. In the cooperative situation that is required in a good choral class, one person's poor behavior may infect others of the class with the same disease ("He got away with it, why can't I!"). Important as the individual is, the welfare of the group must come first, and a problem student may be kept in a class only as long as his or her contribution to the organization exceeds any detrimental effects on the group. Each person has individuality (ways in which that person is different from every other person) and commonality (possession with another of a certain attribute). Each person should be different enough to be useful and should be enough like others to be happy. The *socialized person* is one who has a balance of individuality and commonality, who considers the actions of others to give meaning to his or her own actions. Music organizations have both an integrating function and a differentiating function. The student may find that individual rights must at times be subordinated in order to protect common rights. The student who is unwilling to do this is the one who becomes expendable because he or she *must* be an "individual," come what may. Students will tend to feel they can take advantage of a teacher who has begged them to sing in the group (because more tenors or altos are needed). A student is *always expendable*, no matter how much his or her voice is needed.

A teacher can never permit open defiance of authority. Such behavior must be immediately halted by a trip to the principal's office and the dropping of the student from class (if the administration permits it). Even if the administration will not allow a student to be dropped on a permanent basis, it will probably permit a teacher to send the student to a study hall on a temporary basis until such a time as the student decides to conform and reform. Sometimes the student is required to report to the principal's office every day at class time for a study period. Such an occurrence can happen in the best-taught class, when a student is maladjusted and a poor citizen; but if it happens repeatedly, the teacher needs to examine the facts and see if the problem lies in the teacher-pupil relationship.

Teach the students to remain in their seats until dismissed, and then walk in an orderly, quiet, mannerly fashion to the door, out the door, and down the hall. Many teachers dismiss students row by row, changing rows each day in order to be fair to the students. Stand at the door when students are dismissed, or there will be some who will walk to the door but will break and run as soon as they get just outside the door.

Before the teacher can expect the students to accept a new idea (or even *consider* it), proof must be given that the idea is logical, valid, and true. A teacher must be able to prove to the students, without a doubt, that they should breathe the way the teacher says it is correct to breathe. The instructor must be able to show them the logic, validity, and truth of the "singing posture" that they have been instructed to use. It is essential to make the students understand that the phrasing insisted upon is more logical and makes better sense than the way they were doing it. If this cannot be done, the teacher should not expect the students to accept the idea being advocated. Even after a method has been factually proved, the student may not emotionally be able to accept the change and so will not modify behavior. Seeing something firsthand *should* change concepts, but even this experience is no guarantee. Children will eagerly accept new ideas with very little verification. The older the student, the more painful it becomes to accept a new idea, and the more resistance there is to change of any kind. There may be antagonism to any change because of a feeling of loyalty (of which the student may not even be aware) to methods or materials used by some former teacher, especially if there is a high regard for that teacher. The teacher who tries to move too rapidly in the undercutting of concepts firmly established in an older learner may even disturb the learner's feeling of well-being and confidence. It is necessary for the learner to willingly approve and adopt the new set of values if reorientation is to be accomplished effectively.

Even with all these problems, there are some procedures that are likely to result in re-education. Begin with the known or familiar and proceed to the unknown. Don't progress so rapidly that the student is submerged and frustrated. Give the student time to acquire understandings and to develop new techniques. Start at a point that is almost certainly successful. *Use* whatever variance there is within the group in skills, inherited abilities, and natural interests. Wise use of mental imagery and similes bring concepts into a frame of reference that will be meaningful to the students. If the *organization* believes in the "new values," it is much easier for the individuals within that organization to accept these values (a majority vote will suffice).

The beginning point of good teaching, then, is the realization of the level of experience, understanding, and appreciation the students have in that particular class. The teacher must start with their interests and progress to higher levels. The material used must give self-satisfaction, must hold the attention and interest of the students, must be well-balanced, must move logically, and must provide for a variety of experiences. Techniques are important, but only as a means, not as an end in themselves. Interest must come first, the right motivation, a rich enjoyment, a deep experience emotionally felt. Teach the students where to go to get facts. Performance should be an important goal and accomplishment, but it must always open the way to other things, even more broad, yet to be experienced.

REHEARSAL TECHNIQUES[1]

Order of Rehearsal

One of the main concerns of the music teacher in planning the class lessons is the order in which activities and songs are done. This order must vary according to the day of the week and the mood of the students. It is usually imperative to start with something lively on Monday to wake them up. Do not start a Monday rehearsal with "Come Soothing Death" or the like. On Friday (the day of the big dance, football game, etc.) students are likely to be overstimulated. Use music that is calm. Try to sense the moods of the students. Don't hesitate to change lesson plans if a group is overtired or vice versa. No matter how you feel physically or emotionally, do project vitality with the eyes, face, and body (the very act of standing up straight and breathing deeply makes an instructor more dynamic and will influence the students to be more alive).

The teacher must plan the rehearsal so there are contrasts in mood, style, key, and difficulty. These contrasts will help keep the students in-

[1] See "Lesson Planning" and "Music Selection," Chapters 3 and 7.

terested. If you sense that the students are becoming restless, do move on to another song or activity even though the song isn't finished. If the rehearsal has gone on for a long time in one style and the group is obviously becoming fatigued, have the students stand and stretch or use a staccato exercise or vitality-producing exercise of some kind to wake them up, then "drive on" into a contrasting song. Usually, changing keys or going from a slow song to a fast one (or soft to loud or sweet to vigorous) will motivate and interest the students enough that the "stand and stretch" will not be necessary.

1. Open the rehearsal with a number that will go well and that students like. Use it at the beginning of the period or immediately following the exercises.
2. Use vocal exercises at the beginning of the period, or at least early in the period, to warm up the voices and sharpen the ears of the singers.
3. The most difficult number being rehearsed should be placed toward the beginning of the hour before the group is overtired. Detailed work on contest or concert material would be appropriate here.
4. Select from one to four additional numbers (depending upon the length of the period and how much is to be done with them). These should be in varying styles, difficulties, etc. Do some sight-reading in each period. Slow songs with simple chord structure and uncomplicated rhythms (chorales, for example) are best for developing a cappella singing.
5. The instructor must develop a sense of timing so that the period may be closed in an appropriate fashion. Usually close the hour with a song the students enjoy singing, or some pleasurable musical activity. Occasionally, even the best teacher will get "caught short" by the bell. Do not get carried away with rehearsal and forget that the students have another class to attend. Be punctual in letting them go at the end of the period. Allow enough time to put music away carefully and to dismiss the students in an orderly fashion.

The teacher must ask himself or herself at the end of each class period: What did I do to help the students love music? What did I teach that was new to the students? Was my class just a "community sing?" What did I do to help the students become independent readers of music? What did I do to improve the musical taste of the singers? What would I do differently if I were to do this lesson again? Jot down some problems that need to be solved in the next rehearsal. Plan some logical solutions before the next class period.

Vocalizing

There is some controversy concerning the importance of vocalization in a rehearsal. Most authorities believe that rehearsals should begin with exercises that warm up the voices gradually. This concept makes good sense to the students when it is pointed out that voice production involves muscular control, and that athletes always need to engage in calisthenics so their muscles will be safely warmed up. The process of vocalization should ordinarily not go beyond five or ten minutes. The exercises should include work on breath control, vowel production, the treatment of consonants, attack and release of tone, legato, staccato, agility, range, shading, tone color, phrasing, the blending of voices, and ear training. Various exercises may be used to achieve these goals, and students must be kept informed as to what certain exercises are accomplishing. Scales, arpeggios, and broken chords will develop range and agility (always work in the middle register for awhile and then gradually extend both ways). The singing of intervals will develop accuracy. Chord exercises and unisons, either sung or hummed in legato or staccato rhythm patterns, may be used for ear training, with emphasis on acquisition of the ability to hear pitch mentally before its utterance. They may also be used to train the choir to attack and release tones with precision and accuracy, and they will assist work on blending, shading, tone color, legato, staccato, vowels and the problems of handling phonetics, consonants, and breath control. Several of these elements may be handled at once, or each musical element may be drilled specifically (with the other elements present but in the background).

If students are not accustomed to drills and vocalizing, they may resist their introduction to the point of actual rebellion. If this is the case, don't force the issue. Instead, immediately begin by singing songs. When any section is unable to sing a high part, select a vocalization technique from Chapters 4 and 5 to help them sing the high notes more easily. Introduce breath support and select and drill on some ways to obtain it when the choir is unable to sustain a phrase. Drill on vowel purity and consonant precision as it is needed. At the beginning of the next class, remind the choir of the helpful exercises, use them again, and correlate them with the problem areas in the music. The class will then be able to see the need for these kinds of helps, and the conductor will continue to add to a repertoire of drills. Whenever possible, relate drills to the music or relate the music back to the drills. Usually avoid abstract drilling even after the students will accept it without protest. However, some drills may be justified on the grounds that breath control, range, and several other areas cannot be fully exercised in the music used during a choir rehearsal and so more than adequate capacity cannot develop as it should without additional exercising.

An important reason for vocalizing is the necessity of building certain mechanical habits into the singers. When learning is *mechanical* (automatic, habitual behavior), there is *no* "transfer." But it is possible to make an intelligent decision to learn certain types of behavior automatically so they will function efficiently. For example, until breathing is controlled automatically, the singer cannot be free to concentrate upon interpretation and other vital matters pertaining to musicianship, and the need to concentrate continuously on obtaining and keeping an expanded torso, correct jaw position, and tongue position will cause lack of concentration upon more important aspects. Vocalizing procedures will also build correctly functioning automatic habits of singing good phonetics, consonant closures, vowel modifications in the upper voice register, pitch relationships, rhythmic relationships, and so on.

Ways to accomplish "transfer" must be constantly sought by the teacher. Knowledge of a topic is obtained indirectly by transfer much less economically than by the direct study of the topic in question; for example, studying about phonetic sounds in a speech class will not be as efficient as studying and singing the exact sounds that need to be used in a particular song, although wherever the phonetics are *identical*, the transfer can be accomplished easily. Speaking a phrase in a song is an excellent way to arrive at both correct phrasing in singing *and* true word meanings; however, it is *not* a good way to practice vowel and consonant sounds, which students need to learn to elongate and click properly in singing. A group may learn to speak properly and excellently and still be unable to *sing* these sounds correctly. Practice vowel and consonant sounds in isolation *and* in the words and songs while singing, and the choir will learn with efficiency how to do these skills. Transfer will be accomplished most easily when the drill is in exactly the same form as the material or song in which it is to be used. The Identical Elements Theory of Transfer originated by Thorndike also points out that transfer may be accomplished through identical methods of procedure or ways of acting as well as through elements common to both areas. Bode states that transfer depends upon *meanings*, and students need to know all the meanings of an idea or word (the word "head," for example, may apply to person, class, ship, table, or start, depending upon its context) in order to accomplish transfer. According to Bagley, another way to teach transfer is to develop correct *attitudes* toward things. When a student emotionally wants to be a good citizen or wants to sing better, attitudes will transfer into favorable actions. Ultimately, transfer is the most valuable when the student can generalize[2] from specific experiences to broader concepts. The only way a child can understand that all mothers are not young is by observing other mothers who are not as young as it's own mother is. The only way a student can understand what breath support in singing is all about is through experiencing various drills that give a generalized picture of how to attain breath support; only then may an individual method be intelligently chosen. The teacher who employs only one method runs the additional risk that the concept will not be meaningful to some of the learners or will be only partially meaningful.

With no intention of limiting the ingenuity of the director, a few representative exercises are presented in this section.

For *range, agility,* and *vowel sounds,* in addition to the various

---

[2]Judd's Theory of Generalization.

vowels being sung in scales, arpeggios and broken chord have the students try:

(Pitch steps):

```
                        8
        5       5
        4
        3   3
        2
        1
```

Sing:
Yo_____oo_____ee_____
        Have them try:

```
        ho ho ho ho ho
        5  5  5  5  5
                            ho
                            4
                            ho
                            3
                            ho
                            2
                            ho
                            1
```

Be careful to retain the O shape, not moving the mouth and jaw, the impulse coming from the diaphragm.

        To loosen the tongue, have the students try:

```
                        rrrah
                        5
                rrrah       rrrah
                3           3
        rrrah                   rrrah
        1                       1
```

Try:

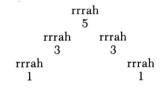

```
        no      no      no
       / \     / \     / \
    nee    nee    nee    nee
    1234543212345432123454321
```

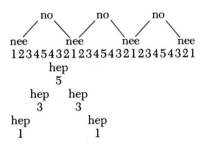

```
            hep
            5
        hep     hep
        3       3
    hep             hep
    1               1
```

To concentrate upon *intonation* and pure *phonetic sounds*, use any song and change to different vowels at will.

For *ear training exercises* that employ the keyboard, play any triad on the piano and have the class sing 3 or 5 or 1 without knowing in advance the note to which it must listen. Move around on various chords, changing the number called for. Play fifths and ask the singers to sing the major or minor third of the chord (both of these exercises will force the students to listen to the whole chord). Play up and down the scale rapidly, then omit various pitches and have the students identify the missed pitch, for example, 1234578754321 (6 was omitted). Play note patterns on the piano and have the group sing them back as exercises in tonal memory, for example, C E G E C, C E-flat G C, C D F G A.

For *interval drill*, work with the whole-tone and chromatic scales until the choir can sing whole and half steps even when they are out of the key and may sound wrong to the group. Start with unisons and progress to chords. Use finger signals and mix them rapidly enough to challenge the choir. It is tremendously important that singers learn to sing a tone perfectly in tune while mentally hearing the next pitch they will sing. The pitch must not be played on the piano until *after* the singers have sung the new pitch, and then only if it is necessary to check. Other interval drills will be found in Chapter 6. A very helpful chordal exercise is to assign chord tones to the various voice sections:

Move up and down by half steps and whole steps, having sections attacking *on the breath* (throat open with support). Do not let the section know *which* section will be pointed at for the attack. Have them attack strongly, without assistance from the piano:

Move faster and faster to sharpen the choir's alertness.

For *breath control exercises*, refer to Chapter 4. Some good *chordal and unison exercises* are described next, and a large variety of skills may be gained (see the list on page 249).

Use whole chords or unisons and move up or down by half steps or whole steps, or by changing to the 1, 4, and 5 chords. *Choir sings*

♪♪♪ ♪♪♪ ♩ , then changes pitch. Work on the staccato movement of
HA,HA,HA, HA, HA

the "breath support organs." Varying the beat and holding up on some staccato notes will force the group to watch. *Choir sings legato:* Meymeemimomoo. Intensive work may be done on producing the vowel sounds (vowels not chewed, pure sounds). Change rapidly to various consonant sounds (tayteetitotoo, kaykeekikokoo, etc.) and have the group really *snap* the consonants for clearness and precision. *Start with a basic major chord*, and move one, two, or three parts at a time to make other chords. For example, try the following exercise (this range is especially suitable for eighth grade):

The following exercise (also excellent for junior high) will permit the top and bottom lines to remain stationary, while the two inner parts change chords instead of also remaining the same.

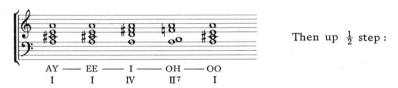

Then up ½ step:

AY —— EE —— I —— OH —— OO
 I   I   IV   II⁷   I

Then have the students sing the exercise up a half step.

A modern-sounding exercise will provide variety, and may even assist in interesting junior high students in music class. Use Italian vowel sounds.

SHO-DO - BN-SHO-BE -DO   SHO-DO- BN-SHO- BE- DO

SHO - DO_____   SHO - DO_____   SHO

When doing chordal exercises, if *two-part chord progressions* are desired, try the following chord positions (a line below a number means the lower octave):

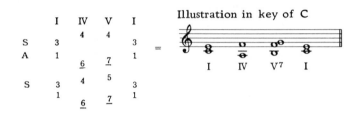

Basic chord position changes that may be made for *three-part chords:*

Any of the three-part progressions listed for SSA may also be used for SAB. The best sounding chord progression is probably:

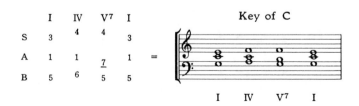

If the bass follows the root of the chord, here are some suggestions:

	I	IV	V⁷	I
S	5	6	7	8 / 5
A	3	4	4	3
B	1	4	5	1
S	5	6	7	8 / 5
A	3	1	4	3
B	1	4	5	1

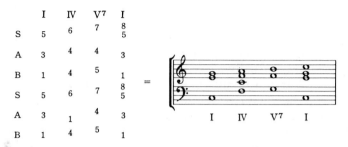

I   IV   V⁷   I

Some of the better positions for chords in SATB:

	I	IV	V⁷	I
S	8	8	9	8
A	3	4	4	3
T	5	6	5	5
B	1	1	<u>7</u>	1

I   IV   V⁷   I

	I	IV	V⁷	I
S	5	6	5	5
A	3	4	4	3
T	8	8	9	8
B	1	1	<u>7</u>	1

I   IV   V⁷   I

	I	IV	V⁷	I
S	3	4	4	3
A	1	1	2	1
T	5	6	5	5
B	1	1	<u>7</u>	1

I   IV   V⁷   I

Basses in root position

In the key of C

	I	IV	V⁷	I
S	5	6	5	5
A	3	4	2	3
T	8	8	7	8
B	1	4	5	1

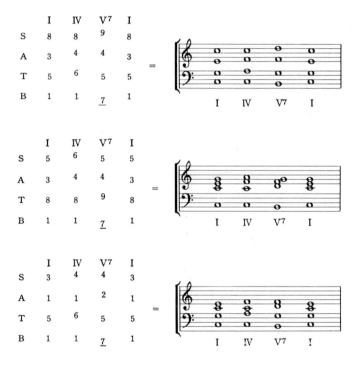

I   IV   V7   I

A great deal may be accomplished in a class period that begins with quick reminders, in the form of vocalizing, of how to do correctly the various facets of vocal pedagogy and musicianship. When the teacher starts by having the class sing songs, it may take half a period before the class is really alert and has been reminded of how to do things, and the first part of the hour is virtually wasted. When drills are executed at the first of a period in a swift, businesslike manner, the teacher can wake the students up and make them alert, ready to really *work* for the remainder of the period. Do drills in a way that challenges the students and really makes them think and stay with the beat. Experienced conductors may be able to select phrases from songs being worked on currently by the choir and use these phrases in vocalizing, then fitting them back into the songs. This is probably the most effective way to vocalize a choir, but it also takes the most skill and preparation on the part of the conductor. Attention must be given to ear training, sight-reading, and musicianship at each rehearsal, especially when driving for a contest or a concert.

Presenting a New Score

When a conductor presents a new score for the first time to the choir, it is essential to know the accepted traditional style including interesting information about the composer, correct tempi, dynamic variations, etc. The director must be familiar with the sound of the chordal structure and learn all the parts well enough to sing all voice lines correctly without assistance from the piano. Do analyze the music and words and mark the score with indications of anticipated difficulties, particularly in rhythm and intonation. Have some reasonable solutions for these problems. (To save rehearsal time, have measures 1, 2, 3, 4, etc., penciled into the choir's music so quick and precise directions can be given by simply stating the page, score, measure, beat, and word.) The conductor must know all word pronunciations and meanings and be able to read the lyrics expressively. The director should have checked to see that the music is mended and in good condition and that there are enough copies for everyone to see comfortably. Also check to be sure the accompanist can play the music correctly (piano part *and* open score).

Ways to Obtain a "Whole" Concept of the Score

It is usually best to give the class a "whole" concept of the score, unless the number is being used for the development of sight-reading skills. After the singers know what the song is all about, then the conductor may work on particular problems. Any of the following suggestions will help a choir obtain a concept of the whole song.

Have the accompanist play the vocal score, while the students hum their parts. Be sure the singers have their beginning pitches.

Have the choir struggle through the number, if it is not so technically difficult that it will be discouraging to them.

Eliminate the *words* so the reading may be simplified enough that the group may be able to sing the harmony and rhythms the first time through. Use "tah," "too," or "pah" to help with precision.

Have the lyrics of the song read by the class, teacher, or individual student. This reading may also be done rhythmically (see the suggestions later in the chapter).

Have the style of the song, something about the composer, a classification of the type of song, the mood of the music, and the period in history presented in some way to the students to give them a better total concept of the music.

Have a small ensemble prepare (or partially prepare) the song and sing it for the choir.

Have one or all of the rhythmical patterns (or problems) investigated, studied, and drilled previous to doing the song (see Chapter 6 for the procedure).

Play or sing a section or phrase of the song that will interest the class in the total song or that will be repeated one or more times, thus immediately and economically acquainting the class with a substantial piece of the song.

Have the students find the melody lines and which sections sings them when a melody is passed from part to part *or* when several melodies are present in the song. Sing the song, leaving out all parts except the one with the melody line. (When starting to rehearse with all parts, help the students keep in mind that the melody must always be just a little stronger so it may be clearly heard.)

Play a good recording of the song to give the singers a complete impression of the song to be rehearsed. Some phonographs have a calibration that permits the record's pitch to be tuned to the piano, if the director wishes to have the group sing along with the recording.

Select a Rehearsal Procedure

Rehearsal procedures may strive for perfection in one area only or in all areas. *Method one:* work only for the attainment of absolutely accurate *notes* in a song, and ignore incorrect vowels, consonants, dynamics, and all other musical elements. *Method two:* strive for perfection in all areas by stopping and correcting every error in vowel sounds, rhythms, expression, pitches, etc. *Method three:* use both kinds of procedures in various stages of the rehearsal.

Ways to Hold Students' Attention While Drilling

If there is any intention to continue work on the score for some time after the first reading, the conductor needs to know some procedures for occupying the attention of the entire choir while notes are being learned. Drilling needs to be held to a minimum, but there is always a necessity to do some of it.

Have the entire choir sing bass (tenor, alto, or soprano). Have them sing by numbers, letters, or some other melodic or harmonic device (see Chapter 6 for techniques to follow).

Have the entire choir hum its parts, except for one voice-line that will sing words.

Have all sections sing or hum while one voice-line is played on the piano to reinforce its pitches.

Have the choir sing or hum a cappella while the director sings one of the parts to support a weak section.

Have all parts played on the piano while the director supports a weak voice-line by singing it.

Have a short rehearsal with a single section, but ask all of the other singers to study their parts and listen to them in relationship to the other part (this takes a firmness on the part of the conductor, or choir members will start to talk). Rehearsing *sopranos only* for half a period, *basses only* half a period will result in real discipline problems over a period of time even if the director is fortunate enough to get by without a mishap the first day. If you work with the *altos only*, do be demonstrating and having the altos demonstrate the use of proper phrasing, correct tone quality, good vowel sounds, and other things that will make the rehearsal a musical experience, not just a rote note drill session. The conductor may profitably use the altos *as an example* (for not more than five or six minutes) with all the other sections watching and listening, and then doing the things demonstrated immediately. Even while working for that short time with the altos, the teacher may wish to throw a leading question at the other choir members, especially if it is suspected that they are not paying attention.

Test the excellence of a section by playing all the parts on the piano except one. The omitted part will be sung with no help from the piano.

Having the chords rolled on the piano (lowest to highest note) occasionally helps students hear their part.

Have any two or three parts sing together in one of the preceding styles.

Have some ways to teach rhythms, melody notes, and harmonic sounds to the group "as a whole" in order to make it an interesting learning experience for all (see Chapter 6 for suggestions).

Have any lengthy problems involving unlearned notes in sections referred to the sectional rehearsal. This is the efficient way to solve problems. Small problems should be solved in the main choir rehearsal, possibly with one of the preceding suggestions. *Note:* An interval missed, or two or three notes missed, will be cleared up much more quickly if only the missed notes are sung, then go back one note and tie it into the phrase, then add the next note forward, and finally tie it all into the longer phrase when the notes or intervals are correct without any doubt. The use of numbers or *do-re-mi* can assist in making the pitch relationships more solid and meaningful. Also, relate to previously sung pitches that are the same, or almost the same. Don't ever have the group merely "sing it again" without motivational instructions. Before the repetition of a song or phrase, always make suggestions of new things for the choir to do or watch out for (have them make the climaxes more effective, the diction clearer, etc.).

Memorization

When a song or part of a song must be memorized, use the whole method of memorizing whenever possible. The musical maturity level (usually dependent upon previous experience) and the age of the learners will make a difference in the method of learning employed. A score of more than 32 measures in length will ordinarily be learned more economically by the "part" method. Mursell says,

> The superiority of the whole method is far greater with sense material than with nonsense material. With relatively meaningless material the 'part method' or some variant of it was often found better. The superiority of the 'whole' method is greater with bright than with dull children. It is greater with easy than with difficult material. And one may get practically the full benefit of the 'whole method' by beginning with a good preview or synopsis and then learning partwise. The great necessity must be, not to organize learning in large units or to work always from beginning to end, but to organize it so that the learner will see interrelationships or the pattern or the plan in what he is trying to learn.[3]

The learner must obtain a "sense of direction" in the task to be done.

Read the lyrics of the song until the ideas and meanings of every word of the poem are known. Identify the key words in the text; each first word, subject, predicate, and rhyming word. The most important word to remember is the *first* word, and the next most important word is the *rhyming* word. Use "associations." Even far-out associations will help memory. Help the singers analyze the basic structure of the song and identify similar or identical phrases. One of the best ways to memorize is to mentally visualize the whole score and actually turn pages in the mind. Many students, however, are unable to accomplish this kind of memorization.

Proceed with some method of *particularization*, for example, singing a phrase while looking at the music, then singing the phrase *without* the music. The choir looks briefly at any missed notes and repeats the phrase without using music. Another phrase is added by the same procedure, and the two phrases are tied together, and so forth, until the song is learned.

Overlearning seems to be the only effective means to prevent forgetting. It is unlikely that overlearning is effective past 150 percent (representing 100 percent as the *first* accurate performance). Volumes 1 and 2 of

---

[3]J.R. Mursell, *Successful Teaching* (New York: McGraw-Hill Book Company, 1946), p. 125.

Christy's *Expressive Singing* give excellent and exhaustive statements on "how to memorize."

A Few Rehearsal Suggestions

Deviation from the ideals of note accuracy, pure phonetics, unified tones, and the like while rehearsing the choir calls either for attack upon the mistake to correct or partially correct it immediately or for a mental note (or written note to yourself) of a deficiency to be corrected in the next rehearsal. The conductor owes the musicians efficiency in rehearsal. When a problem that you are not prepared to solve arises during a rehearsal, do not waste time working out the problem. Do make a note of the problem and go ahead with the rehearsal, then solve the problem in detail before the next rehearsal. Don't stop for obviously accidental wrong notes. Never stop an organization to say what can be shown with a gesture. Don't talk too much at rehearsals; a chorus attends class because it wants to sing. When the conductor *does* stop the choir, he or she should compliment them upon anything they have done well (reading, dynamics, etc.) and challenge them to sing it better the next time in some designated way (accuracy, pronunciation, etc.).

"Beta Hypothesis," sometimes called "Negative Practice," is practicing the *wrong* way while realizing it is the incorrect way and hoping that the *right* way will result. For example:

is the pattern to be learned, and the singers sang it incorrectly the first time *with* F♮. Instead of correcting the error and singing F♯, the singers will sing F♮ every time but will remind themselves that they should be singing a half step higher. This has not been proved to be successful in music. What *is* successful is having the learners deliberately do the activity incorrectly, then having them do the activity the *right* way, and note the differences between the two (sound, sensations, etc.) so that it may be done correctly in the future. Many of the singers are singing with small mouth openings on the vowels, so have *all* the singers sing the word or phrase with mouths almost closed, then sing the same word(s) with jaws well-opened (or even have the singers *hold* their jaws open in some manner). Point out the difference in sound, and challenge them to continue singing with the better sound. Another way to use the "Beta Hypothesis" is to exaggerate the singers' mistakes in order to dramatize the need for correction. The director may overemphasize the incorrect vowel or pitch the choir sang and then sing it correctly.

The principles of "pacing" or "spacing" must be followed in a rehearsal. "Vertical" learning follows the vertical spiral of learning. Present the basic principles in simple form. As students mature, more and more complex work is taught, but be careful to match the level of maturity with the music and skills demanded. "Horizontal" learning continues while the learners rest. The difficulty of the material, the maturity of the learners, and how thoroughly engrossed they become in what they are learning determine how many minutes the activity may be continued profitably. Church choir directors use this principle effectively by working on four to eight numbers at each rehearsal and gradually polishing these numbers. Directors have discovered that much better literature and higher polish may be obtained by this "spacing" than if an entire practice each week is devoted to the perfection of only one number. Sometimes some maturation occurs even within one practice period, and what was learned at the beginning of a period may be reinforced and strengthened by its repetition at the close of the hour. (Church choir directors will use this technique with special effectiveness on the number to be sung the following Sunday.) Write troublesome phonetics immediately *under* the word to be corrected in the music. Write the vanishing phonetics and consonants under the point where the chorus is to "click" them. In contrapuntal passages, new entrances must be accented. The choir will require practice on these entrances. (Pick out and mark the entrances in the music.)

The human response to gesture is a psychological one. Choral conductors can obtain even more involuntary emotional responses to their gestures than instrumental directors can. This greater control is due to the fact that choral directors manipulate the instruments directly (human bodies, voices, and minds), whereas instrumental conductors must first influence the minds of the players and then the players must play upon the inanimate instrument.[4]

It is a good technique to expect the singers to call attention to mistakes they hear in their parts. Often, some individuals within a section have trouble with their part after enough of the others have learned it that it sounds all right to the director at the front of the room.

Intonation Rehearsal Techniques

Don't pick something that is technically too difficult for your choir. Don't hesitate to choose something difficult if the choir can handle it without physiological strain.

Insist that the singers learn their parts as quickly as possible, because a memorized song will be sung with more freedom and consequently will be sung better in tune. It follows that the choir will usually sing flat on a song they have not thoroughly learned and with which they are not thoroughly familiar. In fact, pitch will be aided when the song is so much a part of the singers that thoughts, not notes, may be sung.

---

[4]But a good performer will acquire an "empathy" with the instrument, in which he or she will feel that it is an extension of the body.

The seating of sections so the octaves and extreme ranges are together tends to make the chord hang together. Seating a choir in a modified quartet arrangement will enable all singers to hear all parts of the chord instead of just the section in which they are singing. It is much easier to maintain pitch in this arrangement. It cannot be used successfully, however, with insecure singers or with weak, beginning organizations until they have learned their music solidly while seated in sections (see Chapter 2).

In a concert, consider switching to a "prearranged core of good singers" until tonality is re-established (see Chapter 2). This procedure must be carefully rehearsed.

When the chords in the music do not seem to jell, listen for the outer parts (which are the ones most clearly heard) to find out if they are sung firmly and in tune. Then rehearse the inner parts together until they are sung accurately. Finally, sing the full chord again to check on the progress that has been made.

If two or more parts have the same rhythm, they may be rehearsed in isolation from the other part(s). For example, in "He's Got the Whole World in His Hands," discussed later in this chapter, the altos, tenors, and basses have the rhythm, and the most logical way to clear up any rhythmic problems (and pitches) would be to rehearse those three parts together. If necessary, it could be reduced to two or even one voice part. One part could be used as an example (the other two parts being told to listen carefully); then all three parts would sing or they would speak the rhythm until it is correct, then sing it.

Precision in consonants and good vowel sounds will help intonation. Poor consonants or vowels will cause problems in pitch. Be sure tuned consonants and sub-vocals are sung in tune.

Playing the piano an octave high or an octave low will many times cause the group to listen more carefully. Also, try a staccato accompaniment.

Cultivate the ability to retain pitch mentally without constantly referring to the piano. If you are unable to attain this skill quickly enough, carry a pitch pipe to avoid wasting rehearsal time by walking to and from the piano.

Chapters 4 and 5 have many additional suggestions that will help to attain good intonation in rehearsals.

Interpretation

If the singers can become thoroughly imbued with the spirit of the song, they can create living and exciting images of their innermost thoughts concerning the song, and part of this will communicate to the audience. Many of the other vocal principles will be established to a very satisfactory extent.

The musician must, of necessity, regard the score as the barest reference pattern. Each composition should be studied carefully in order that the thought of the composer may be truly expressed. Musicians must take the indications on the score and combine them with their imaginations to recreate or interpret the music. This is an exciting challenge to the singers and director to use their skill and imagination to turn printed notes into living music.

The musician's mental processes contribute as much to the performance as the score markings, and interpretation is therefore always essentially individual, for probably no song affects two people precisely the same way.

However, there are certain basic musical laws that pertain to all songs and should be observed by all performers. Many of these laws could not be reduced to written directions on the printed page without cramping the space allotted to the notes and standard markings so much that the music's readability would be seriously affected. An *unmarked note* is not always performed the same. Style, or lack of style, soon becomes evident in the way the unmarked note is treated. Its length and the character of attack and content depend upon many factors, such as tempo indications, traditional interpretations, general dynamic markings, the character of the passage or chord of which the note is a part, and emotional suggestions. Other factors are such things as the influence of associated notes of contrasting character, the musical interpretation that might be suggested by the title, the physical condition of the room, the age of the singers, the techniques available in the choral organization, and likes and dislikes of the performer or director.

The Importance of the Word

A well-written song is a beautiful union of poetry and music; the rhythm conforms to and accentuates the meter of the poetry; the curve of the melody traces the rise and fall of emotion in the text; the important words and syllables are brought out by the musical accent; the harmonic background in the accompaniment provides a sympathetic commentary, ranging from lightness and gaiety to somber drama; tempo and dynamics underscore the mood, changing with each shade of meaning. Therefore, in a well-written song, singers need only think of the meanings of words and it will be possible to do an excellent job of singing.

A good teacher will provide the students with many opportunities to sing "word paintings" of descriptive words in the lyrics. All songs have many of these descriptive words, and these "key" words must be discovered and sung with imagination, emotion, and intelligence. But many times students are drilled on accurate notes, dynamics, phrasing, breathing, tone quality, etc., and the director never gets around to checking whether the choir can define all the words or understand the true meaning of the song. How can singers be expected to create in sound and emotion the images the words intend if these students don't understand what they are singing? Following are some suggestions directors may use to help students comprehend the song being studied.

Have the students read the poem aloud, using the correct rhythm of the music. (This will help solve problems of rhythm, diction, style, phrasing, and the proper dynamics.)

Have one student read the poem to the class, or read the poem to the class yourself (to teach phrasing and meanings).

Define any words that may not be understood by the students. It may be necessary to explain true meanings of the poem, since many times they are somewhat obscure. Project the mood or the spirit of the song through this study of the text.

When words are Latin, explain that the Latin pronunciation of church Latin (or singing Latin) is different from the school Latin the students learn. It is more Italianized. If this is not done, students may think the teacher doesn't know the correct pronunciations, for example, "V" pronounced as V, not W; "ae" pronounced as $\bar{A}$, not $\bar{I}$, etc.

Teach the students to recognize what constitutes a *word phrase.* When students are talking or reading, they will pause momentarily at the conclusion of an idea, usually without giving it a thought. This pause is generally marked by a comma (half stop) at the end of a phrase or clause, and by a period (full stop) at the end of a sentence.

Help the students to realize that every word has a stressed syllable and that every sentence has a "key" word that needs to be emphasized in order to unlock the meaning of that phrase. Following is one suggested procedure that will help the students locate the most important word or words in each phrase and also the unimportant words and parts of words. Write some or all of the lyrics on the chalkboard before class. (If the director is not able to write the poem in advance, a student may be delegated to write the text on the board while the choir is engaged in other profitable activities.) With the text ready, the conductor will direct the group through the song. Then, before singing it again, the director will help the choir decide what words are not essential, and erase such words as "the," "of," etc. After it has been decided what words are the truly important words, the chorus will sing the song again with as little emphasis as possible on nonessential words and with as much feeling as possible on essential words. Then underline the parts of words that need to be accented, for example, *"build-*ing," not *"build-ing."* Finally, have the class sing the song once more, stressing only the important parts of important words. Do not twist the rhythm out of shape, but do bend it enough that those words and syllables that are truly necessary in the lyrics are stressed; linger on them at some sacrifice of time taken from unimportant words or syllables.

Insist that the singers in a large choral group breathe only at the ends of phrases, *unless* the phrase is so long that "staggered breathing" is necessary. Following are some rules that may be followed by the small ensemble or soloist who may occasionally find it necessary to breathe in the middle of a phrase.

When breath has to be so taken as to divide a phrase, the first note after renewal of breath should be delivered with the volume, intensity, and color that characterized the note preceding the breath.

When it is necessary to take a breath, steal enough time from the final note of the phrase to take a quick breath and sing the beginning note of the new phrase precisely on the beat.

If necessary, "breath *may be taken:* (a) Where the direction of a run changes. (b) Where the general direction of a run is interrupted by a skip. (c) After a syncopated note. (d) Where the construction of a (florid) passage permits, it is allowable to divide it by repeating the words".[5] (e) After a noun.

The singer in a choir must form a habit of breathing at each punctuation mark, even when there is no necessity to breathe. Neglecting to breathe will cause the vocalist to break the next phrase. When exceptions to this rule occur, discuss the reasons for the change with the singers, and perform the music with the proper phrasing.

Staggered breathing technique. A choir member must develop a special technique for carrying long phrases. A habit must be formed of catching a new breath before running low on air supply by interrupting any white note for an instant when it is thought the neighbor won't breathe. The singer's mouth forms the position for the vowel being sung, a quick inhalation occurs before the vowel left momentarily is resumed. The singer gradually softens the tone just before breathing, and the neighbor sings with enough power to balance the ensemble. Then the singer comes back in softly, with a gradual crescendo, while the neighbor fades. This maneuver takes expert teamwork with the neighboring singer, and the well-executed breath will be imperceptible to an audience. Staggered breathing is like walking out of the room and back in without anyone missing you. The singers must never use staggered breathing when they can carry the phrase musically and with control without breaking.

Stimulate the students' imagination so that "dark" is sung with dark tone quality, "light" with light quality, etc. Get the students to sing "word paintings." Challenge the students to sing a word or a phrase as a command, sympathetically, contemptuously, with a feeling of patriotism, with excitement, with love, with amazement, defiantly, encouragingly, happily, with condemnation, with grief or despair, with fear, with exultation, or with whatever is needed to express the song being studied. Awaken singers' imaginations by the use of figurative speech, e.g., "Let it settle like a bird in its nest," "Give it a velvety surface," etc.

---

[5] F.W. Wodell, *Choir and Chorus Conducting* (Bryn Mawr, Penna.: Theodore Presser Company, 1931), p. 86.

Stimulate the singers to assume facial expressions that mirror word meanings. If they do not, the effect is apt to appear ridiculous to the audience. Appeal to every singer to sell the song like a good "pop" singer, but without the gestures.

Words are not the only important element in interpretation. The beauty of the melodic line, the pulse of the rhythm, the thrills of dynamic changes, and the richness of the harmony are also involved in the creation of exciting music. Any of these ingredients treated separately may give real satisfaction to the performers. For example, a beautiful melody produced on a neutral vowel may give a feeling of musical creation to a singer, and the feeling of surge and rise and fall of the phrase are part of true interpretation. In some musical numbers the exotic rhythms or different harmonies present are the ingredients that stir the singer. The area of dynamics (thrilling pianissimos and throbbing fortissimos) can be one of the most effective areas of interpretative creativity and pleasure.

Melodic Phrases

Teach the students to recognize what constitutes a complete melodic phrase. To the uninitiated, music may seem to be a formless flow of sound. Actually it is constructed as carefully as a building, for which it is possible, with a blueprint, to tell its size, where every rafter will be placed, the location and size of the rooms, the materials and colors to be used, etc. Compare it to *writing*, which is built from phrases, sentences, paragraphs, and chapters. Incorrect phrasing in music is the equivalent of running sentences together in speech or writing and is symptomatic of confused thinking. Also, as is the case with sentences, phrases in music vary in length; some are short, others are long. If a phrase in a song is broken in the wrong place, its musical meaning is sacrificed.

The following rules are fundamental in teaching the pupils how to handle melodies.

Usually the completion of a phrase will be found precisely two or four measures after its inception. Four phrases constitute a *period*, and a *simple period* contains just eight measures. Sometimes the period will be shorter or longer, especially in contemporary music.

Take care that the patterns of design, such as the swell, do not occur with mathematical regularity, or the effect will be mechanical.

The important notes in melody are those that cannot be dispensed with and still have the melody sound complete and satisfying. They usually occur on the beginning of a beat. An exception occurs in syncopated forms of music. These notes should receive emphasis, stress, or accent.

Embellishments or ornamental notes should be delivered without emphasis, lighter or softer than the principal notes. (See some exceptions in Chapter 10.)

A short note must be delivered with the same care as a long note.

Where a clearly defined melody appears in some voice or voices, the remaining parts supplying merely the harmonic basis, the shading should be managed so as to bring the melody parts into sufficient prominence to make the theme easily discernible.

In polyphonic music, all parts are of equal importance. Successive announcements by different voices of one subject must be delivered with like power or shading.

It is usually possible to effect a compromise that permits the preservation of the flow of the melody, even when the words demand frequent breaks in the melody line. By means of skillful enunciation, articulation, accentuation, and emphasis, the meaning of the words can be made clear.

Teaching Tempo Rules

The normal tempo can never be the result of arbitrary rules, and depends upon neither the composer nor the performer. In fact, the true tempo of a composition is the tempo that results from its actual structure. In general, a lighthearted dance requires a brisk tempo, a stately march goes at a moderate rate of speed, a song of sorrow is slow. Changes of mood require corresponding changes in tempo.

Music has a ceaseless alternation between movement and rest. Between the points of rest, the movement must be compelling, inexorable.

Too fast a tempo makes correct delivery of runs difficult. Runs will sound faster if delivered cleanly than they will if taken at a faster tempo and "smeared."

Full time value should be given to final chords of a number.

The greater the number of performers and the larger the auditorium, the slower should be the pace adopted, within reasonable limits. This is to give clearness to the delivery and time for the music to reach and properly impress all hearers.

Sudden changes from a slow to a quick tempo, or vice versa, without good reason, are very objectionable.

When changes of harmony are frequent, the pace must usually be slower than where the chord does not change for several beats.

The tempo must be slow enough to permit the full development of the melodic beauty of all the parts. The tempo must not be taken so fast that singers do not have time to enunciate and sound clearly every word and note.

When there are frequent changes of key, meter, or rhythm, the tempo ordinarily must be relatively slow. In general, the more complicated and crowded with details the music, the slower the tempo.

Piano passages are not necessarily taken any more slowly than preceding loud passages. *Forte* passages are not necessarily taken any faster than preceding soft passages.

In rapid passages, the tone should gradually decrease in volume as the speed of the notes increases.

In cross-rhythms let each individual rhythm be well-defined while preserving the swing of the whole.

Use Exciting Dynamic Variations

A knowledge of the style of a piece is necessary in deciding its dynamic range. A bold, violent text, telling of heroic deeds, may demand more intense dynamics than one describing a peaceful, woodland scene. "A mood of triumph calls for brilliant sonority and volume. Sadness needs subtle shading within a more subdued range of volume. The emotional meaning of the music imposes the proper dynamic scheme."[6] Different periods in history used various ideas of ff, etc. Bach's and Handel's dynamics were not as extreme as they are today. Folksongs, popular songs, spirituals, or broadway show songs all call for differences in dynamics and styles. When music is interpreted with the correct style and with the right dynamic variations, the singers' and the listeners' interest will be intensified. With middle school, junior high, and high school voices, use an extreme *soft* limit. If the valleys are deep enough, the hills will seem like mountains. Don't let the voice force.

Always go from somewhere to somewhere, rising directly or indirectly to some rousing climax, or toning down to some equally effective point of repose. Have an ideal at which to aim. Remember to apply this principle also with a long note; *do* something with it.

In choral work, the confidence and strength with which an extreme effect is produced carry success with them. Failure to go "all the way" will cause the desired effect to sound like a mistake. Get rid of the amateur's fear of overdoing. To do the effect enough to project properly to an audience will usually seem very exaggerated to the inexperienced singer.

"Regard the swell as the basis of the beautiful in music, and the chief source of all effective expression."[7]

"When a composer repeats an idea, its delivery should ordinarily be varied. Ascending imitation will usually call for greater force."[8] The only reason for repeating a word or phrase is to give more emphasis than would be possible by saying it only once. Sometimes a repetition of an idea is effective when delivered piano, contrasting with a preceding forte.

Generally, a soft phrase should have a crescendo of at least two dynamics and then a decrescendo back to piano to avoid monotony.

Emphasis may be helped by observing the following:

[6] E.J. Stringham, *Listening to Music Creatively* (2nd ed.; Englewood Cliffs, N.J.: Prentice-Hall, Inc., 1959), p. 25.

[7] H. Coward, *Choral Technique and Interpretation* (New York: H.W. Gray Co., 1940), p. 93.

[8] Wodell, *Choir and Chorus Conducting*, p. 92.

1. Secure variety by accenting. Care must be taken not to get a monotonous rhythm.
2. Do not accent a note merely because it is taken by a skip from a lower note.
3. Do not overaccent the last note of a phrase.
4. In case of a group of notes (or two notes) slurred together, the first note gets the accent.
5. Attack all syncopated notes and other irregular rhythms with firmness.
6. The first notes of triplets should be well-defined.
7. Frequently a note, by reason of its being a discord, prepared or unprepared, or a resisting harmony note, requires special emphasis.

Learn to produce a crescendo and diminuendo gradually. Most singers can increase their volume steadily enough; however, all but accomplished singers collapse the tone when the director signals for decrescendo. To graphically illustrate this lack of control, and ultimately to learn more control of dynamics, the director should draw this chart on the chalkboard and point to the dynamic changes, or have a student do it. Practice with this chart will help the students to be able to perform a decrescendo smoothly. Seeing these gradations visually assists in concepts of volume (for example, the approximate loudness of *mf* may be discovered and practiced).

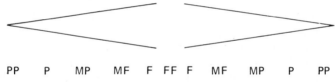

PP   P   MP   MF   F FF F   MF   MP   P   PP

Dynamic markings that a person should know are:[9]

Pianissimo (pp)—very soft. (*-issimo* means "very.") More than two *p*'s accentuate the fact that a passage should be performed with extreme softness. When this occurs in the music, move *ppp* or *pppp* into the place of *pp* on the chart, since it is impossible to get softer than *pianissimo*. This has the effect of adding more gradations to the dynamic chart (see below).

PPPP	PPP	PP	P	MP	MF	F	FF	FFF	FFFF
	PPP	PP	P	MP	MF	F	FF	FFF	
	1	2	3	4	5	6	7	8	

pp   p   mp   mf   f   ff

[9] Some directors assign a number to a dynamic level (see the dynamic chart). They say that asking a group for a dynamic level of 1 or 5 is more meaningful to the students than asking for *ppp* or *mf*.

Piano (p)—soft.

Mezzo-piano (mp)—medium soft. (*Mezzo* means "medium.")

Mezzo-forte (mf)—medium loud.

Forte (f)—loud.

Fortissimo (ff)—very loud. More than two *f*'s emphasize the extreme loudness. Move *fff* or *ffff* *into the place of ff* on the chart, since it is impossible to get louder than *fortissimo*. This has the effect of adding more gradations to the dynamic chart.

Sforzando (sfz, sf)—attack the tone with great force.

Note: Break the habit of slowing down whenever the volume is diminished or of singing louder whenever the speed increases.

Climaxes

Have choir members find all climaxes in the song. A correctly constructed song must be in proportion. It should not have its climax at the beginning; it should develop an idea or mood and reach its climax near the end. To sing with expression, the singers must emphasize some notes in even the softest passage, while in a *forte* passage some notes should be softer in relation to the others. There is one most important note in every phrase and it must be emphasized. Likewise, there is one master phrase that constitutes the climax or emotional high peak of the piece, and it must be brought into strong contrast with the rest of the number.

When, at the end of a *ff* number, still more power is wanted, the emphatic accent produces the desired effect.

If the music, as it grows louder, also increases in speed, there will be a marked accumulation of forward driving power, which helps in the building of climaxes.

Conversely, the *ritardando* is frequently used in conjunction with the *descrescendo* to produce the fadeout or dying away effect often desired at the ends of compositions.

"Sometimes an effect of great breadth and power is obtained by delivering an ascending and crescendo passage with a gradual decrease of speed."[10]

The climax must be reached by well-ordered and consistent steps. It must as a rule, be treated with breadth, dignity, and power and be held sufficiently long to be impressive, and it must not degenerate in power or intensity.

Never treat a note, a phrase, or a movement in an isolated manner, but let it be considered in relation to the whole movement, cantata, or oratorio. Learn to think in "musical continents."

[10] Wodell, *Choir and Chorus Conducting*, p. 79.

Quick-Moving Madrigals and Ballets with "Fa-La" Choruses

Interest is in the consonants and not in the vowels. Have the singers overenunciate consonant sounds. The "pull" is not very useful in that type of music; in fact, there is usually *no pull* off the beat pattern. The students should have the sensation of bouncing out of consonants and beat points. There is almost a feeling of accent on each word and immediate bouncing out of the accent. As a rehearsal technique, use "pm-pm-pm"[11] on each syllable to obtain the kind of feeling typical to this kind of music. Use a smaller and higher beat pattern, light and flexible, bouncing beat points; spit out consonants and the emphasis on the words. Good enunciation in a fast number may be attained by beginning at a very slow speed and singing very accurately, clicking consonants extra hard and gradually increasing the speed with each repetition until the desired speed is attained, continuing with the feeling of precision and clicked consonants.

"Pop" Music

Popular music "swings" and has style similarities to the quick-moving madrigal. For example, "pm" will help obtain rhythmical precision. The light style and the importance of the consonants are imperative for good performance, but the vowels are more important. One notable difference is that the "pop" or "show-tune" music (also the Negro spiritual and work song) swings in $\frac{12}{8}$ instead of in $\frac{4}{4}$. For example, sing the following line from a traditional arrangement in $\frac{4}{4}$; then sing the same arrangement in $\frac{12}{8}$.

[11] Ivan Kortkamp, *Advanced Choir,* p. 82.

Notice how much better it swings? Don't change rhythms, pitches, or dynamics unless there is a very good reason for doing so. When altering rhythm, such as in a certain arrangement of a song, explain to the class why the rhythm is being changed ("to make it swing," etc.).

Another rule or rehearsal procedure that is applicable to this example is: Have parts bump pitch changes, especially in a rhythmical number or when singing an $\overline{oo}$, ah, or humming part. The alto, tenor, and bass parts should "punch" each chord change in the previous example to help the feeling of precision and the rhythmic motion of the song and in order to clearly hear each chord change. It must be a *subtle* push or feeling of pressure, however. The conductor must also *anticipate* the syncopation in both melody and underparts with hand motion, body, and facial expression. Without the anticipation, the singers will not arrive on the syncopated note on time. (Use "pm" if the rhythm still doesn't swing.)

The Conducting of Eighteenth-Century Recitative

The point where vocal style varies most widely from instrumental is in the *recitative*. Recitative is characterized by freedom from strict form, being oratorical rather than melodic in its phrasing. It may appear in either accompanied or unaccompanied form. In the delivery of unaccompanied recitative it is especially important that the first thought be given to the text. The music is altogether a secondary consideration. The phrases have more of the nature of impassioned speech, emphasizing the intelligent and interested interpretation of the text. However, the recitative is still sung. It should be rendered musically, with musical accent and emphasis kept intact. The important point is, "What is said in singing, and not what is sung in the saying."[12]

The orchestral accompaniment is likely to consist of only one chord to a measure, and the conductor will customarily direct only the beginning of each measure with a downbeat. It is essential that a preparatory beat be given before each downbeat, so the orchestra may be prepared for the initial beat of each new measure. The instrumentalists must be given a decisive downbeat on every measure. Whenever the accompaniment contains more than one chord to a measure, the other notes should be conducted, but the director must allow the soloist the privilege of "bending" the tempo to fit the words. The conductor's tempo must adjust to that of the soloist. Regardless of the way the dominant and tonic chords are written in the score, when they are employed in the final phrase of a section they are ordinarily played *after* the soloist has finished. There are very few exceptions to the rule. Usually, whenever a musical phrase ends with two tones on the same pitch, an *appoggiatura* is employed. Either replace the pitch of the first of the two notes with a repetition of the note just before it or substitute a passing note appoggiatura. For example:

[12] W.J. Henderson, *The Art of Singing* (New York: The Dial Press, Inc., 1938), p. 145.

will be sung either

or

usually the latter. If a keyboard instrument accompanies the soloists, the director need not conduct.

If possible, before conducting a work, study the recitatives with an authority on oratorio or opera. When the authority is not available, use a recording by professional artists or reputable university organizations and follow the interpretation of the recording artists.

Techniques that Help a Teacher Study a New Score

Even if the teacher has done a good job of planning an efficient rehearsal, starts the class promptly, has the roll checked efficiently, has the order of rehearsal on the chalkboard before class starts, has an excellent, quick way of getting music into students' hands at the very beginning of class, has planned for good ear training exercises and vocalises to use, and has selected fine music for the class period, he or she still may be unable to hear the harmonies well enough to detect mistakes when the singers make them. The inexperienced conductor needs some ways, before rehearsal, to hear and learn the harmonies and rhythms of any new songs. Experimentation with the following techniques should result in discovery of one or two that work best:

Listen to available recordings and study the score simultaneously.

Play through the number several times, rolling the chords in arpeggios from the bass to the soprano without attention to rhythm. Work with the chord structure until positive that any voice line that is missing, flat, or sharp may be immediately detected. (Experiment by moving inner parts up or down to hear how the altered chords sound.)

Play the chords and listen to them with a voice part missing.

The director will sing each line until it can be sung accurately without the piano. This means that if he is a tenor, he will need to sing soprano, bass, and alto in whatever octave will work most effectively. When the conductor goes into rehearsal able to sing all voice-lines, deviations in pitch are more likely to be detected.

Sing each part while playing the other parts of the chords, or, lacking this much piano skill, play the full chord. The conductor must read from the score, not the piano part, in order to attain the skills of immediate recognition of proper octaves in the voice (especially the vocal tenor C clefs), of the position of voice-lines on the page and awareness of voice leadings, and of scanning the page vertically and reading the notes, words, markings, and music.

Use a metronome to improve rhythmic conceptions of a number.

If an organ is available, it will be much easier to hear the legato harmonies on it than on a piano. If a piano must be used, strike the complete chord on each voice change so the full harmony may be heard.

Many times holding the first chord until the tonality is heard will help the reading of the entire number. Always get the first chord in tune before continuing with the song. The singers cannot possibly sing the second chord in tune if the first chord is out of tune. Yet it is surprising how many times the young conductor, especially the conductor who has sung only soprano all her life, will be blissfully ignorant of the out-of-tuneness of a chord or even of a voice missing or in the wrong octave or a third up or down (especially male voices). One solution to this rehearsal problem is the next suggestion.

Hold each chord (unrhythmically) until it is tuned up, then move to the next chord. Make corrections, if needed, without resorting to the piano for assistance. If pitch reassurance is required, have the accompanist *roll* each chord from the bottom to the top, after the choir has sung it. Listen to each pitch to hear if all of the voices on that part are in tune. (This technique will get extremely monotonous if pursued through an entire song. Go through a phrase, or two phrases at most, then go ahead and sing in the regular manner.)

When the conductor hears a wrong chord (whether on the first chord or on a later one), the hand must be kept moving upward while the chord is analyzed and a decision made on who and what is wrong. Then release the chord and tell the group what to do. Too many times this writer has seen a conductor stop the choir and say, "There's something wrong with that chord." Then the conductor proceeds to try one part after another until the culprit is finally discovered. How much better it is for the director to hold the chord until he "hears" that the basses are flat,[13] then he can cut off the chord and say, "Basses, you are flat. The note is just one half step down from the previous one." This type of problem could very well be approached creatively if the teacher *knows* what is wrong. The entire choir might be asked, "Do you know why we stopped?" This gives students the opportunity to use their judgment and gives the teacher a good chance to teach something about the music theory.

Hold the final chord of a musical phrase and correct any intonation problems that are present. However, start the next phrase *on time*. A real weakness in the musicianship of the average choral director is a strong tendency to hold ending chords so long that the next phrase cannot be started in time to avoid disturbing the rhythmic movement of the number being performed. By all means *do* "tune-up" final chords, and even do it

---

[13] If the director still can't hear what is wrong with the chord, having the accompanist roll the chord while the choir sustains it will help the conductor identify pitches as they relate to voice parts.

unrhythmically, if necessary, in rehearsal, but don't get so in a habit of doing it that the performance is without rhythm.

Ear training exercises used at the beginning of the period for the benefit of the choir will tune up the conductor's ears even more quickly.

Study the section on intonation in Chapter 5 until at least some of the most obvious reasons for a group running into pitch difficulty are discovered. Learn to anticipate the flatting on half steps, the third of the chord or scale not being sung high enough, the sagging of pitch on descending scales or downward jumps, and so on.

The Accompanist

A student accompanist should be used whenever possible. The director who plays the piano well will find it easier and more comfortable to do the accompanying. Do not succumb to that temptation for the following reasons:

1. The conductor will direct and listen much more efficiently away from the piano.
2. The conductor has a responsibility to further the pianistic and musical development of the piano students by providing some training in accompaniment.
3. The conductor, through the training of accompanists, assures the school of an adequate supply of competent accompanists in the future.

If there is more than one good accompanist in a class, assign certain songs to certain accompanists, in order to give more students the experience of accompanying *and* singing (good accompanists sometimes are given no opportunity to learn to sing).

The requirements for a good accompanist are excellent musicianship, ability to follow, and even anticipate, the conductor's directions, ability to sight-read, ability to transpose, and ability to adapt quickly to the unexpected. The accompanist should also have previous experience. Since all of these qualities are seldom found in a student, the director must train him or her to some degree of the required proficiencies. Give instruction to the prospective accompanist on:

Studying words. The accompanist helps to convey the meaning by knowing the words and word meanings thoroughly.

Playing parts from an open score. Much of choral accompanying consists in "playing parts," until the musical number becomes known to the choir. The accompanist also learns to follow voice leadings, etc., better through this technique. (The tenor should be played the octave down, unless it is played in octaves.)

Giving pitches. Train the accompanist to be alert and to anticipate the director's wishes in regard to giving pitches.

Playing firmly and with confidence. Beginning pianists are liable to play timidly and weakly. Insist on accuracy, especially in the playing of parts.

The warm-up procedures. Be sure the accompanist is throughly familiar with any warm-ups you plan to use.

It will be necessary for the director to work with the accompanist outside class. If she is taking piano privately, enlist the aid of the private teacher. Unless she is a very good sight-reader, give her the numbers well in advance, and check to be sure she can do them proficiently before using them. (Sight-reading may sometimes be done *if* everyone understands the accompanist is also sight-reading.) In case of almost total student incompetence, consider the use of two pianists, one playing bass, and the other treble.

BOOKS CONTAINING GOOD CHORAL MUSIC LISTS

BURNSWORTH, CHARLES C., *Choral Music for Women's Voices: An Annotated Bibliography of Recommended Works.* Metuchen, N.J.: Scarecrow Press, 1968.

COMMITTEE ON CONTEMPORARY MUSIC, *Contemporary Music: A Suggested List for High Schools and Colleges.* Music Educators National Conference, 1964.

GARRETSON, ROBERT, *Conducting Choral Music* (5th ed.). Boston: Allyn and Bacon, Inc., 1980.

HAWKINS, MARGARET, *An Annotated Inventory of Distinctive Choral Literature for Performance at the High School Level* (Monograph No. 2). Ann Arbor, Mich.: American Choral Directors Association, 1966.

KNAPP, MERRILL, *Selected List of Music for Men's Voices.* Princeton University Press, 1952.

LAMB, GORDON H., *Choral Techniques* (2nd ed.). Dubuque, Iowa: Wm. C. Brown Co., Pub., 1979.

LOCKE, ARTHUR, and CHARLES FASSETT, *Selected List of Choruses for Women's Voices* (3rd ed.). Smith College, 1964.

NEIDIG, KENNETH L., and JOHN W. JENNINGS, *Choral Director's Guide.* West Nyack, N.Y.: Parker Publishing Co., Inc. 1967.

ROBERTS, KENNETH, *A Checklist of Twentieth-Century Choral Music for Male Voices.* Detroit, Mich.: Information Coordinators, 1970.

Selective Music Lists. Washington, D.C.: National Interscholastic Music Activities Commission of the MENC. Get the latest ones available. (See also state lists.)

ULRICH, HOMER, *A Survey of Choral Music.* New York: Harcourt Brace Jovanovich, Inc., 1973. (Not a list, but many music suggestions.)

(Investigate the Drinker Library of Choral Music [Free Library of Philadelphia, Logan Square, Philadelphia] as a source of music rental and as an especially good source for Bach.)

SELECTED BIBLIOGRAPHY

BESSOM, M.E., A.M. TATARUNIS, and SAMUEL L. FORCUCCI, *Teaching Music in Today's Secondary Schools* (2nd ed.). New York: Holt, Rinehart and Winston, 1980.

BOYD, JACK, *Rehearsal Guide for the Choral Director*. Champaigne, Ill.: Mark Foster Music Co., 1976.

DECKER, HAROLD, and JULIUS HERFORD, eds., *Choral Conducting: A Symposium*. New York: Appleton-Century-Crofts, 1973.

GARRETSON, ROBERT L., *Conducting Choral Music* (5th ed.). Boston, Mass.: Allyn and Bacon, Inc., 1980.

HILLIS, MARGARET, *At Rehearsals*. New York: American Choral Foundation, 1969.

HOFFER, CHARLES R., *Teaching Music in the Secondary Schools* (2nd ed.). Belmont, Calif.: Wadsworth Publishing Co., 1973.

LAMB, GORDON H., *Choral Techniques* (2nd ed.). Dubuque, Iowa: Wm. C. Brown Co., Publishers, 1979.

——, ed., *Guide for the Beginning Choral Director*. American Choral Directors Association, 1972.

NEIDIG, KENNETH, and JOHN JENNINGS, eds., *Choral Director's Guide*. West Nyack, N.Y.: Parker Publishing, Inc., 1967.

PFAUTSCH, LLOYD, *Mental Warmups for the Choral Conductor*. New York: Lawson-Gould/Gould G. Schirmer, 1969.

ROBINSON, RAY and ALLEN WINOLD, *The Choral Experience*. New York: Harper's College Press, 1976.

SINGLETON, IRA C., and SIMON V. ANDERSON, *Music in Secondary Schools* (2nd ed.). Boston: Allyn and Bacon, Inc., 1969.

SOMMARY, JOHANNES, "What the Orchestral Musician Expects of the Choral Conductor," *The Choral Journal*, February 1974, pp. 11–12.

VAN CAMP, LEONARD, *Warmups for Minds, Ears, and Voices*. New York: Lawson-Gould Music Publishers, Inc., 1973.

WHITLOCK, RUTH H.S., "The Design and Evaluation of Study Materials for Integrating Musical Information into the Choral Rehearsal," *Unpublished doctoral dissertation*, School of Music, NTSU, 1981.

——, *Choral Insights*. Park Ridge, Ill.: Neil A. Kjos Music Co., 1982.

10

Style and
Musical Traditions

If the students are to develop musical taste and basic musicality, style[1] must be incorporated into the music class. Knowledge of and sensitivity to style and musical tradition help to organize all of the musical elements into a cohesive whole. Without an understanding of style, the student learns only unrelated "parts"—pitches, dynamics, tone color, etc.—out of meaningful context with the music. With "style," all of these elements fuse into meaning, with music logically related to art and the other humanities. The teacher who teaches musical style through performance will find that in order to guide students into aesthetic experiences and make them knowledgeable about the structure of music, high quality literature must be chosen from the various styles. Cheap, trivial literature obviously can-

[1] Style can mean a multitude of things. Webster defines *style* as a distinctive or characteristic mode of presentation, construction, or execution in any art. According to the *Harvard Brief Dictionary of Music*, it may mean a characteristic manner of composition in reference to the treatment of melody, harmony, rhythm, and the other musical elements. The same source also states that the term may denote the characteristic language of composers, of types of composition, of mediums of performance, or of periods.

not be used for the teaching of style or for the development of the musical concepts that lead a student to the possession of musical taste and discrimination. Authentic examples of jazz and folk music are not ruled out, for the student must be exposed to all important stylistic influences. This approach to teaching will require better preparation and more musicianship from the teacher, but it can only result in improved instruction.

This chapter serves a vital function for the general music class, also. The brief history of music, in addition to providing a general background of information for students and teacher, contains a number of ideas for teaching about historical innovations ranging from the rhythmic modes to polytonality. The helps concerning notation, tone color, dynamics, and other musical elements presented in a historical context will be of assistance in the listening program as well as in performance.

The old masters left very few indications of the manner in which they desired their compositions to be performed. An educated guess may be made if the period and country in which the composer lived and composed are known.

It needs to be recognized that any sort of generalization concerning historical style will necessarily be deficient in some respect. Even though Tomas Luis de Victoria was a student of Palestrina, he wrote in a more personal vein than did his master. A composer's later works are frequently significantly different from his less mature works. A certain piece may be written because of a specific wish or by commission. If a composer has written anything of significance, the individual style and techniques should be compared with those of contemporaries to decide in which important ways it is different. The composer writing early in a historical period will write differently, probably, from one writing toward the end of the period. Some composers were far in advance of their time, and some were still writing in the style of the preceding period. Some traveled, and, therefore, the national characteristics of two or more countries color their compositions.

It is your responsibility as a conductor to be acquainted with the traditional way or ways in which a number is performed, even though you may elect to conduct it in another way. (If you depart too far from tradition, you usually lay yourself open to justifiable criticism from other musicians.) Imagine Bach sung in the style of a modern popular number, a folksong sung like an operatic number, or a sentimental Tchaikovsky number performed with the clarity and transparency of a Haydn or Mozart song. It may be desirable for a choir of 100–300 to experience the singing of a madrigal, but it will never achieve the true delicacy and intimacy that is inherent in the madrigal style; likewise, a choir of twenty youngsters can never manage to sing Stravinsky's *Symphony of Psalms* with the power and fullness that an audience has every right to expect.

After the director has learned as much as possible about the music to be performed, a decision must be made about what would be the most musical performance that can be managed with the resources at hand. It may not always be possible to have all the correct instruments for a Baroque number, female sopranos may need to be substituted for boy sopranos, the number of singers may differ somewhat from the desired number, etc. But the conductor *can* obtain a flexibility of tone and interpretation that will relate properly to the period, composer, and music being performed (and this is far better than an unmusical performance by the "correct" instruments and voices). The conductor must be careful that a passion for a certain type of tone quality does not make a travesty of style and period. The big, dark-sounding choir sounds good on a big modern number, but sounds wooden on a madrigal or even on a bouncy spiritual. The conductor can, logically, compromise by having his choir sing *most* of its numbers in the style that fits the preferred tone quality, with a sprinkling of other compositions sung in a correctly stylized manner.

Since this chapter presents only the barest outline of the individual style of each composer and of historical trends, the reader will need to refer to other sources for greater detail. Basic, inexpensive paperback sources that are full of excellent information are Frederick Dorian's *History of Music in Performance* (New York: W. W. Norton & Company, Inc., 1966) and Thurston Dart's *Interpretation of Music* (London: Hutchinson University Library, 1954). The most complete book on style, although expensive enough that the conductor may wish to have it purchased by the school library, is Robert Donington's *The Interpretation of Early Music* (London: Faber & Faber Ltd., 1963). Other inexpensive basic sources are *The Harvard Brief Dictionary of Music* (Cambridge, Mass.: Copyright © 1960, by the President and Fellows of Harvard College) and Westrup's and Harrison's *The New College Encyclopedia of Music* (New York: W. W. Norton & Company, Inc., 1960). A tremendous amount of insight may be gained through the extensive articles written by Edward P. Menerth, Jr., published in five issues of the *Music Educators Journal* between April–May, 1966, and January, 1967. *The Choral Journal* contains helpful information in each issue, and a series of articles by Allen Lannom was excellent. Other fine sources are the books in the Prentice-Hall History of Music Series (edited by H. Wiley Hitchcock); Richard L. Crocker's *A History of Musical Style* (New York: McGraw-Hill Book Company, 1966); Allen Winold's *Elements of Musical Understanding* (Englewood Cliffs, N.J.: Prentice-Hall, Inc., 1966); J. J. Quantz's *On Playing the Flute*, translated by E. E. Reilly (New York: The Free Press, 1966); The Eastman Outline Series published by Levis Music Stores in Rochester, New York; Donald J. Grout's *A History of Western Music*, shorter edition (New York: W. W. Norton & Company, Inc., 1964); O. Strunk's *Source Reading in Music History* (New York: W. W. Norton & Company, Inc., 1952); Theodore Baker's *Biographical Dictionary of Musicians*, 5th edition (New York:

G. Schirmer, Inc., 1958); and George Grove's *Dictionary of Music and Musicians*, 5th edition (New York: St. Martin's Press, Inc., 1954). This list is by no means complete. See the bibliography at the end of the chapter for additional suggestions.

The *Harvard Brief Dictionary of Music* suggests that the harmonic development of Western music be divided into three epochs: monophonic (from the beginnings until c. A.D. 1300), polyphonic (c. 800–c. 1750), and homophonic (c. 1600 to the present). Although this way of classifying musical history may be helpful, it becomes immediately apparent that the epochs are oversimplified. A clearer way to present the periods might be to point out that the monophonic period existed as the sole influence until about 800; and although polyphony began to make itself felt at that time and became increasingly important, monophonic music continued as the principal influence until about 1400. The polyphonic period (hastened through the impact of Ars nova, c. 1300) became the principal influence about 1400 and reached its peak about 1600, although much of its finest music was written in the first half of the seventeenth century, including the music of Bach and Handel who composed until about 1750. The fifteenth century is noted for its great development of sacred music (Mass and motet); and secular vocal and instrumental compositions such as the madrigal and toccata rose to prominence during the sixteenth century. The *Nuove musiche* (c. 1600) caused a temporary lessening of the influence of polyphonic music, for the opera, the cantata, the oratorio, and instrumental works brought about a renewed emphasis on monophonic music and a new emphasis on homophonic music. Around 1750, the instrumental and dynamic developments of the Mannheim School led to the full acceptance of homophony that continued until the present century. Debussy's development of impressionism and his use of the whole-tone scale in the 1890s were the first indications of a quickly growing reaction against Romanticism. The twentieth century has seen both the renewal of all the earlier forms (with some changes, e.g., neoclassicism) and experimentation with many new forms. Jazz has become increasingly important.

PRE-RENAISSANCE (550 B.C.–A.D. 1400)

Even though the first real flowering of music occurred during the Renaissance, music groups perform a great deal of music based upon Pre-Renaissance developments (folk tunes based on the pentatonic scale, the modes, solmization, descants, and so forth). During the centuries preceding Renaissance, music developed through various influences, some of which are described below.

The *pentatonic scale* contains five tones. The most common form may be represented by C D F G A, the third and seventh notes being omitted from the well-known diatonic seven-note scale. This scale can be seen most easily by playing the five black notes on the piano. "Auld Lang Syne" and "Comin' Through the Rye" may be used as examples. Some form of the pentatonic scale is used frequently in the traditional music of Africa, Japan, China, Polynesia, the American Indian, the Celts, and the Scots. (The scale of Bali and Java cannot be played on the piano keyboard.) The scale is being used a great deal in the elementary school and even in the junior high school as a natural way to begin some improvisation and basic harmonic concepts. The Orff and Kodaly methods have brought about this new emphasis. (Chapter 6 has more information concerning methods used.)

Pythagoras accomplished his systemization of the scale (c. 550 B.C.) through the use of the one-stringed instrument, the monochord. He discovered that the notes of the octave could be found by means of the perfect fifth and perfect fourth. (This important scale is discussed in Chapter 5.)

The Greek genera had three modes, of which the diatonic is the most important. Other modes are the chromatic and enharmonic. *The church modes* are based on the Greek modes. St. Ambrose (333–397) is given credit for the first uniform system of intoning the mass (the four authentic modes). Pope Gregory the Great (590–604) systematized the modal system and developed the Schola Cantorum at Rome in order to scatter the organized church service throughout Christendom by means of members of this singing school. The so-called Gregorian chants evolved into an established system of plainchant and plainsong by the eighth century. The sequences and tropes (ninth to twelfth century) were interesting additions to the chant. Word and music are beautifully blended. Rhythmic groups consist of two's and three's mixed together rather than of steadily recurring groups of *either* two's or three's as in the conventional music of the modern period. While singers should stress the beginning of each group, the accent should be very light. A group of three has fifty percent more length than a group of two. Conducting is usually done by *arsis* and *thesis*. Arsis refers to the lifting motion of the hand on the weak beat; *thesis* refers to the downward motion of the hand on the strong part of the phrase.

Neumes were characters placed above and below the syllables of the song text to indicate the rising and falling of the voice, a system that served as an aid to memory rather than an exact means of recording music. Around 1000, music was notated by locating the neumes on, below, or above F, which was represented by a line drawn in red. A yellow line placed on the C above the red line was the second improvement in this system of notation.

Guido d'Arezzo (990–1050) established the use of the *four-line staff.* Some historians credit Guido with the invention of the F clef. He is most often remembered for his invention of a system of *solmization.* For an understanding of the modern movable and fixed *do* systems, refer to Chapter 6.

Hucbald (840–930) was one of the first to write about music in two parts. He wrote about *Organum, Cantus Firmus* (melody), and another line a fifth above or a fourth below moving in parallel motion. By the eleventh and twelfth century, descant developed—two parts, with more freedom of motion, i.e., one descending, the other ascending. One of the two parts was still called the cantus firmus. As more parts were added during the next three centuries, this system became known as *counterpoint*. By the twelfth century (some set it as late as the fourteenth) organum was expanded to include thirds and sixths (*Fauxbourdon*).

Feudalism during the eleventh and twelfth centuries created a need for performers. Out of this need the groups called *troubadours* (southern France), *trouveres* (northern France), and *Minnesingers* (Germany) developed their individual styles. These singers recorded many of their melodies in square notes on the four-line staff. Another of their contributions was the introduction and popularization of the rhyming poem in songs, shaping the musical phrases to conform with the poetry. Further systemization of the present-day scales occurred during this period.

Ars antiqua (Latin for "the old art") is the name given to music of the late twelfth century and of the entire thirteenth century. Perotinus (c. 1150–1220) and his colleagues composed organa and *clausulae* (a small part of a Gregorian chant employing one or two, occasionally three, contrapuntal voices with the entire section vocalized on a single syllable [*melisma*]). The clausulae were the immediate predecessors of the medieval motet, the main form of the thirteenth century. The *conductus* were also composed during this period and are important because they were the first free composition, independent of Gregorian chant. During the *Ars antiqua*, composition progressed from two-part writing to three- and sometimes four-part writing. The six rhythmic modes were established at this time.

Musica ficta, extemporized chromatic notes, in use for several centuries, became quite prominent about this time. The word *chromatic* comes from the Greek word *chroma* meaning "color." In medieval times, sharped and flatted tones were written in colored ink. The symbol for the sharp (♯) was originally a St. Andrew's cross.

The origin of the ♭ sign is the "soft" or rounded B . . . used in the Middle Ages to indicate the fourth degree of the hexachord beginning on F:

F   G   A   b   C   D

as opposed to the "hard" or square B . . . used to indicate the third degree of the hexachord beginning on G:

G   A   ♮   C   D   E

The use of the natural sign (♮) to contradict either a ♯ or a ♭ was not normal until the 18th cent.[2] Before that time the ♭ was used to contradict a ♯, as well as to lower the pitch of an uninflected note (i.e., one without ♯ or ♭).[3]

Franco (thirteenth century?) is credited with having invented the *Franconian System of Notation*, which was systematic means of notating triple rhythms. According to Franco, the triple time was called perfect because it "hath its name from the Blessed Trinity which is pure and true perfection." This is why monks in the medieval days held it to be the best rhythm to be used for church music.

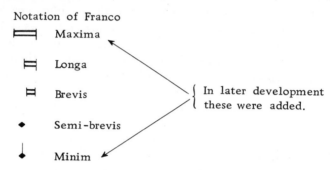

Notated Duple Rhythm Notation's introduction into manuscript music is ascribed to Phillipus de Vitry (c. 1290–1361). De Vitry reorganized notation so that duple and triple notation became equally important. He also applied free isorhythm to the upper parts as well as to the tenor. He wrote *Ars nova* (Latin for "the new art") and introduced the semiminima, fusa, and semifusa.

	Old Notation	Modern Notation	Old Form Names	English Names	American Names
Franco	▭		maxima		
	▭	▭	longa	long	
	▭	▭ or ‖◌‖	brevis	breve	
	◇	○	semibrevis	semibreve	whole
	↓	♩	minima	minim	half
Devitry	↓	♩	semiminima	crotchet	quarter
	♪	♪	fusa	quaver	eighth
	♪	♪	semifusa	semiquaver	sixteenth

[2] The obvious origin of the ♮ sign is the hard B.

[3] Westrup and Harrison, *The New College Encyclopedia of Music* (New York: W. W. Norton & Company, Inc., 1960), p. 247. Originally published as *Collins Encyclopedia of Music*—London and Glasgow.

Time signatures and notations were somewhat standardized by around 1600. The time signature could signify either Perfect (a triple metric scheme) or Imperfect (duple). There were four Prolations. *Modus Major* with the symbol 'Maxima' had a time signature in which Perfect = 3 longas and Imperfect = 2 longas. *Modus Minor* with symbol 'Longa' had a time signature in which Perfect = 3 breves, Imperfect = 2 breves. *Tempus* with the symbol 'Brevis' had a time signature in which Perfect = 3 semibreves, Imperfect = 2 semibreves. *Prolatio* with symbol 'Semibrevis' had a time signature in which Perfect = 3 minima, Imperfect = 2 minima. When this music is transcribed, usually the brevis is reduced to a half note, the semibrevis to a quarter note, the minima to an eighth note, and the semi-minima to a sixteenth note.

Until about 1600, *tactus* (the basic beat) set by the speed of the human pulse (usually M.M. 50–60, about one beat per second) set the tempi. The beat must stay relatively steady other than through changes brought about through shorter or longer notes or changes of time signature. French music during the Renaissance will tend to be faster than Italian, varying up to a tactus of 80. Italian secular music should also be sung faster than 50–60. The authority Quantz, in 1752, urged adoption of the faster speed. Music must *move*, so if it doesn't, use a greater speed. Tactus remained an influential factor until, and even beyond, the invention of the metronome around 1800. Some authorities say the tactus for around 1200 was the *longa* ◫, for the thirteenth century was the *brevis* ▭ , for the fourteenth to the sixteenth centuries was the *semibrevis* ○ , for 1550 to 1650 was the *minima* ♩, for the seventeenth century was the *semiminima* ♩ , for the nineteenth century was the *fusa* ♪, then a return to the modern quarter note (semiminima) ♩ during the twentieth century. Converted into modern terms, the singer will need to sing the thirteenth century brevis at the speed of a quarter note.

The discussion of *Ars nova* cannot be complete without mentioning Machaut (c. 1300–77) of France, under whom the motet became much larger and more complex structurally. Machaut's *Messe Notre Dame* was the first complete setting of the Mass. He also composed much secular polyphony. Landini in Italy developed the *ballata*. The development of the five-line staff during the fourteenth century, the invention of printing (1450), and the first printing of music (c. 1500) contributed immeasurably to the development of music notation.

RENAISSANCE PERIOD (1400-1600)

Tone Quality

It should be remembered that the high parts were only sung by boys during the Renaissance. Therefore, the sound of a boys' choir should be kept in mind when a choir sings this music. Extreme vibrato and big, mature sounds must be avoided, especially in the treble parts. The singer of this time was an amateur, and the big operatic voice of the twentieth century was unknown, although there is some evidence that it was starting to develop. Whatever instruments were available were used to double voice parts at the unison or the octave, or to substitute for any or all of the voices. The instruments were usually viols, gambas, lutes, recorders, or the harpsichord. (However, many other instruments such as trombone, flute, guitars, and krummhorns were in use. The first true violins were built between 1550 and 1611; Amati came in this time.) Instruments were played without vibrato, so it is easily seen that big voice vibratos would not blend into the tonal texture. The case against vibrato offered by Renaissance instrumental quality is reinforced by the knowledge that the horizontal lines of the compositions *must* be heard since each line is important in itself, and large vibratos will obscure the vocal lines of the polyphony.

Junior high and high school voices will sing Renaissance music with little or no modification. The tone must be alive and free and full. The ideal tone quality for this music is *not* breathy or a thin, pinched straight tone (even though Dart offers convincing proof of the singers' strained expressions with throat and face muscles tight, which resulted in a nasal, reedy tone; obviously, this kind of singing will not only result in unaesthetic sound, it will be detrimental to the students' voices). Even the mature high school voice will qualify for good singing of Renaissance music if a rolling, free tone is employed and not an uncontrolled vibrato without a pitch center. A bright, forward tone must be cultivated; a dark, overly mature dramatic placement of tone must be avoided. The college age cultivated mature voice will need to be carefully controlled but should still use a live, free tone with subdued dynamics and without a throbbing vibrato. The singer should use the same weight of tone quality he would employ in the singing of a folksong.

Dynamics

The first known mention of dynamics were the words *pian à forte* in Giovanni Gabrieli's work, *Sacrae Symphoniae* (1597). Dynamic markings of any kind were unknown until this time. Although bar lines existed in tablatures, they had no relation to metrical accent and existed only for the practical purpose of helping singers keep their place in the music. Dynamic contrasts were much more subtle than the ones currently employed. Certain devices were used, however, to obtain contrasts. Words must be made clear in this music, and the natural accentuation of the text must be stressed; in most of the music of this period, each individual voice line must make complete musical sense standing alone. A singer will unconsciously increase his volume as the line rises and decrease volume as the line lowers. The tonic accent (the highest note receives the most weight), which is discussed in more detail in Chapter 8, is always important in the interpretation of Renaissance music. The agogic accent (the longest note receives the most weight), also discussed more fully in Chapter 8, must be observed with care. Ordinarily the tonic and agogic accents will correspond with the natural word accent in well-written music. Other contrasts are made by doubling voices, adding or subtracting instrumental parts, alternating polyphonic and homophonic sections, and exploitation of various voice groupings with varying timbres (high vs. low sounds and thick vs. thin). Discords are strong (the suspension is the most important expressive dissonance), preparations and resolutions are weak. The ascending passing note is not accented, but the descending passing note may be either accented or not, depending upon the word. Sing Renaissance music flexibly as in a plainsong, with unimportant words and series of repeated notes de-emphasized and important melodic figures and words and entering voices emphasized. Menerth[4] emphasizes the importance of hearing the leading tones in the Landini and Burgundian cadences. When a pedal point occurs in a final cadence in early sixteenth-century music, the sustained tone(s) must be heard clearly while the other voices hover around it before settling. Grove's *Dictionary of Music and Musicians* and Rosamund Harding's *Origins of Musical Time and Expression* (1938) are excellent sources of additional information.

Tempo

The earliest instances of tempo variability occur in solo music as early as 1535. Luis de Milan (1536) and Adriano Banchieri (1611) were some of the first to use tempo marks. However, tempo marks were not generally used and were not necessary since the notation itself gave the speed (see the previous treatment of *tactus*).

Harmony, Scales, and Keys

Many facts about the progress of harmony, scales, and keys have been and will be presented in this chapter. There will be no attempt here to present a detailed summary of scale development from ancient scales to the eight authentic and plagal modes, through the changes brought about by *Musica ficta*, which resulted in four additional modes and led to major (Ionian) and minor (Aeolian) scales by about 1600. *Keys* are not pertinent until the advent of the major and minor scale. Harmony is traced briefly in this text through unisons, octaves, organum, counterpoint, and figured bass to vertical harmonies.

Polyphonic Church Music

The Renaissance is sometimes called the "Golden Age" of *a cappella* music. *A cappella* at this time in history referred to the *place* at which the music was to be sung and the *purpose* the music was to serve, rather than

[4] Edward F. Menerth, Jr., "Singing in Style Renaissance," Copyright © *Music Educators Journal* (April-May, 1966), p. 58. Reprinted with permission.

the *style* of performance. *A cappella* translated means "for use in the chapel." The European chapel is a room in a house, or part of a church, set aside for the most serious occasions. Consequently, *a cappella* refers to music for use in a religious situation, with or without accompaniment. Most of the music of this period is polyphonic, and frequently some of the voice parts were probably played on instruments. Although instruments were not excluded by Palestrina, the unaccompanied way of singing was preferred and exploited in depth by him.

The fewest number of voices needed for most sixteenth-century full choral services was from twelve to sixteen. The upper limit varied, since it depended upon the wealth of the proprietor of the choir and how much money he could spare to support its members. For festive occasions, large groups of singers and players might be recruited, but even then the numbers would ordinarily be modest compared to the modern large choir. If the twentieth-century director decides to employ masses of singers on each voice part, it will cause many problems as the attempt is made to maintain blend and clarity within the sectional lines in this horizontal polyphonic music.

The Masses and motets of the Renaissance were universal, objective, and impersonal. The music is ordinarily modal. However, toward the end of the Renaissance the modality moves toward tonality, and there is a tendency for cadences to end with the *tierce de Picardie* (a major third used in the final chord of a piece of music in the minor mode). Previous to the sixteenth century, the ending chord usually did not have a third. Whatever the mode, it usually *did* have a major third in the concluding chord in the sixteenth century. Up through Palestrina's time, the contrapuntal relationships are usually composed of unisons, fifths, octaves, and major or minor thirds or sixths. The music is essentially step-wise in the way it moves, with one harmony to a beat. Consonances are skipped to and from, dissonances are approached or left by a step. There are frequent imitations and augmentations. Arsis and thesis is a factor, since much of the music is modal, with typical groupings of two or three notes to a syllable. The melisma is melodic, but is likely to have more freedom and ornamentation than chant does.

Responsorial and antiphonal singing continued throughout the Renaissance and should be employed where appropriate. There was a great amount of fine music written for double and multiple choirs that is being increasingly used by fine high school and college choirs today. Sixteen to twenty-four voice Masses are not rare. Tallis (c. 1505–85) composed a number for eight five-part choirs involving forty voice lines; Benevoli (1605–72) wrote a Mass requiring fifty-three voices. The peak of this influence was reached in the Venetian school of composers, influenced by the architecture of the cathedral of St. Marks, which was built in the shape of a Greek cross. In 1527 Adrian Willaert started this kind of writing in earnest, and Giovanni Gabrieli and Monteverdi developed antiphonal singing to a still greater degree. Palestrina, di Lasso, Richard Farrant, Christopher Tye, Lotti, Caldara, Andrea Gabrieli (Giovanni's uncle), and even Heinrich Schuetz came under this influence. Among the outstanding choral pieces written are G. Gabrieli's *Jubilate Deo*, Monteverdi's *Jubilate Deo* and *In Ecclesiis*, Farrant's "Lord, for Thy Tender Mercies' Sake," Tye's "O Come, Ye Servants of the Lord," Palestrina's *Stabat Mater*, and di Lasso's "Echo Song" (nonreligious).

Chorale

The Lutheran (Protestant) chorale began about 1517. Martin Luther instituted congregational singing in order to carry out his belief in every person's right to communicate directly with God. Luther arranged simple tunes with the assistance of leading composers of his time. The material and text sources were adapted from Catholic hymns, translated into German, taken from plainsong or secular folksongs of the day or newly composed. At first these hymns were sung in unaccompanied unison by everyone. Then, extra parts, written in contrapuntal style, were performed by the choir while the church members sang the melody. Later the chords moved together homophonically, and the melody was transferred to the soprano. After 1600 the organ replaced the choir in the accompanying parts (with instrumental interludes between verses). Johann Volpar published three books in 1524 (only the melodies were given, with a text). About 1530, King Henry VIII caused a new music service in harmonic style to be written for the Anglican Church (*Sarum Rite*). Lucas Osiander set some of the melodies in four parts with the melody in the upper voice in 1586. All Protestant groups eventually adopted the chorale style for congregational use. The peak of chorale writing was reached with J.S. Bach.

Madrigal

There are two types of madrigal, both originating in Italy. Fourteenth-century madrigal was a short part song in two or three parts. The texts present a vivid panorama of Renaissance thought and feelings. Usually the term *madrigal* is associated with the kind of music that emerged in 1530 through Flemish composers who were residing in Italy, for example, Verdelot and Arcadelt. A familiar melody was used as the principal theme or cantus firmus, and many other voices were employed in counterpoint in a combination of equal melodies with no subordinate parts. The *chansons* (the secular counterpart of the sacred polyphonic motet) and the madrigal (a secular composition in a somewhat lighter style) were sometimes played on instruments instead of being sung. These pieces were sometimes performed only on instruments or with the instruments playing all the parts except the melody, which the voice sang (this latter practice helped to initiate the solo song with accompaniment). There was no concept of public performance at this time. All performance was in the home, with family members and perhaps neighbors gathered around a table singing or playing instruments that happened to be available. There was no formal direction. This is music for a small ensemble, usually one or two performers to a part.

The harmony was not conceived in a chordal way by the composers, but it was composed through maintaining certain intervals from other notes, starting with the cantus firmus. At first there was just the octave and the fifth, then major and minor thirds, and finally major and minor sixths. The resultant harmony has many V chords going to IV chords in this music. During the sixteenth century there is no example in a composer's own handwriting of a score form. The tenor line was handed to the tenor, the soprano score to the soprano, and so forth. The conception, then, is totally horizontal, and the placement of bar lines in the music is very likely to put stress on the wrong words and on the wrong agogic and tonic accents in some of the voice lines. Syncopation is very rare. If there is a feeling of syncopation in the way the music is being performed, it is probably being sung incorrectly. Modern methods of notating sixteenth-century rhythm and accent are: regular recurring bar lines with no accents indicated, regular recurring bar lines with accents indicated, changing time signatures, and irregular recurring dotted bar lines. The more recent the edition, the more apt it is to have been edited correctly.

It was 1588 when *Musica Transalpina (Music from Across the Alps)* was published in England, and this book inaugurated the beginning of English madrigal writing. A dancelike song written in a simplified madrigal style, with a homophonic beginning and a polyphonic "fa la" refrain, became popular in England. It is a ballet if it has a "fa la" refrain. Well-known examples are Morley's "Now is the Month of Maying" and "Shoot, False Love, I Care Not." English madrigal writing ceased by 1640, and the Renaissance came to a close in England with the English (Elizabethan) School and its leading exponents, Byrd, Morley, Dowland, Wilbye, Weelkes, and Gibbons.

Italian madrigal writing ceased about 1610 or 1615 because of the popularity of opera. The final great names in the Italian group are Marenzio, Gesualdo, and Monteverdi. Monteverdi belongs partially in the Baroque period (he has been called the great transition composer). Monteverdi's music must be sung with intensely passionate feeling. Following are some of the principal composers of the Renaissance, arranged chronologically, with some of their larger form choral works.

Renaissance Period (c. 1400–1600)

John Dunstable	England	c. 1370–1453
Gilles Binchois	Belgium	c. 1400–1460
Guillaume Dufay	Belgium	c. 1400–1474

	Johannes Okeghem	Belgium	c. 1420–1495
	Jakob Obrecht	Netherlands	c. 1430–1505
	Pierre de La Rue	Belgium	c. 1430–1518
	Heinrich Isaak	Belgium	c. 1450–1517
		Missa Carminum	
	Josquin Des Prez	Belgium	c. 1450–1521
	Jean Mouton	France	c. 1470–1522
	Adrian Willaert	Belgium	c. 1480–1562
	Martin Luther	Germany	c. 1483–1546
	Cristobal Morales	Spain	c. 1500–1553
	Thomas Tallis	England	c. 1505–1585
3	Jacob Arcadelt	Belgium	c. 1510–1567
	Andrea Gabrieli	Italy	c. 1510–1586
		Missa "Pater Peccavi"	
1, 3, 5	Giovanni Pierluigi da Palestrina	Palestrina, Italy	c. 1525–1594
		Magnificat; Missa Brevis; Missa Papae Marcelli; Missa Veni Sponsa Christe; Stabat Mater	
	Claude Le Jeune	France	c. 1528–1600
3	Richard Farrant	England	c. 1530–1580
	Guillaume Costeley	France	c. 1531–1606
1, 4	Orlando di Lasso (Lassus)	Belgium	c. 1532–1594
		Missa "Puisque j'ay Perdu"; Lamentations of Jeremiah	
2, 4	William Byrd	England	c. 1543–1623
		Mass for Four Voices; Mass for Five Voices	
3, 5	Tomas Luis de Victoria	Spain	c. 1549–1611
		Missa Dominicalis; O Magnum Mysterium; O Quam Gloriosum	
	Jacobus Gallus (Jacob Handl)	Austria (now Yugoslavia)	c. 1550–91
4	Orazio Vecchi	Italy	c. 1550–1605
4	Luca Marenzio	Italy	c. 1553–99
		(madrigals)	
2	Robert Johnson	England	c. 1555–1625
	Giovanni Gastoldi	Italy	c. 1556–1622
1, 2, 4	Thomas Morley	England	c. 1557–1603
	Don Carlos Gesualdo	Italy	c. 1560–1613
		(madrigals)	
	John Dowland	Ireland	c. 1562–1626
1, 4	John Wilbye	England	c. 1574–1638
2, 4	Thomas Weelkes	England	c. 1575–1623
2	Thomas Ford	England	c. 1580–1648
1, 3, 4	Orlando Gibbons	England	c. 1583–1625

The following books have music of some of the composers listed above (see code):

1. *The A Cappella Chorus Book.* Edited by Dr. F. Melius Christiansen and Noble Cain. Bryn Mawr, Penna.: Oliver Ditson Co., 1932.
2. *The Junior A Cappella Chorus Book.* Edited by Olaf C. Christiansen and Carol M. Pitts. Bryn Mawr, Penna.: Oliver Ditson Co., 1932.
3. *The Concord Anthem Book*, Series No. 13. Compiled and edited by Archibald T. Davison and Henry Wilder Foote. Boston: E. C. Schirmer Music Co., 1922.
4. *The A Cappella Singer.* Edited by H. Clough-Leighter. Boston: E. C. Schirmer Music Co., 1964.
5. *Master Choruses.* Selected by Hugh Ross, John Smallman, and H. Alexander Matthews. Bryn Mawr, Penna.: Oliver Ditson Co., 1933.

The Renaissance to Baroque Series, edited by Lehman Engel and published by Harold Flammer, Inc., contains choral music of many of these composers. There are five volumes: *French-Netherland Music*, *Italian Music*, *English Music*, *German Music*, and *Spanish Music*.

BAROQUE PERIOD (1600–1750)

Dynamics

Expression marks are either lacking or extremely sparse in pre-1750 music. Crescendo and decrescendo were employed principally in *messa di voce* (vocal crescendo and decrescendo on single sustained notes instead of equal sustaining on longer tones). *Tempo rubato* should be repressed or used to a very limited degree. Ritardandos, for instance, were taken care of by the Baroque composer through the lengthening of note values, making unnecessary the *ritard.* sign. Although *tempo rubato* was described in some detail by Frescobaldi in 1635, it is not pertinent until after it was written about in 1723 by Francesco Tosi, then in only a very limited application. Some exceptions to the rule are noteworthy. Caccini, influenced by the monodic style of the early Baroque, used music with subtly shaded expressions marked into the music in his preface to his collection of airs, *Nuove Musiche* (c. 1601). Francois Couperin made use of some expression markings from 1713 to 1730. Indications of dynamics appeared in early years of the seventeenth century, used principally to indicate contrasts in volume. Some kind of indications for forte and piano became essential in the seventeenth century because a great amount of the music had contrasting bodies of sound (echo effects with voices, instruments vs. voices, brasses and voices vs. strings and voices, etc.). Giovanni Gabrieli and Banchieri wrote the earliest music that uses the terms *forte* and *piano*, dating from about 1600. In 1638, Mazzochi said that everyone knew the terms *forte, piano, echo,* and *trill.* Our contemporary signs for *crescendo* and *diminuendo* appeared in 1739. However, crescendos and diminuendos were known and used on long phrases throughout the seventeenth century by indicating the varying stages of loudness (forte, piano, pianissimo *or* loud, soft, softer). Although a forte passage will generally be followed by a piano passage, with little crescendo or decrescendo, some people feel that the Baroque composer made his expression by block dynamic contrasts (terraced dynamics). The influence of the Mannheim School brought crescendo and decrescendo into fairly common usage by about 1750.

Bach's choirs were composed of three to four singers to a part—usually no more than twelve singers to eighteen instrumentalists. There were always at least as many players as choir members. Some of Handel's choirs ran into hundreds. Carl Philipp Emanuel Bach's choirs reached about 500.

Music became metered and measured during this period. Whenever metrical accent is employed, weak beats always lead into the following strong beats, i.e., two goes to three and four goes to one in $\frac{4}{4}$ time:

Another rule is that the smaller note value tends to lead to a longer note value: ( ). A note that is repeated is phrased,

a feeling of note grouping occurs whenever there is a shift in pitch direction,

and adjectives and articles tend to lead to the following noun (the Lord). There is also a relationship between strong and weak measures that is important to interpretation. When the harmony of one measure is sustained into the next measure,

the second measure becomes weak. Also, when a strong chord in a measure is followed by a weaker chord in the next measure, the second measure is weaker. Strong chords will be produced by agogic or tonic accents, modulations, dissonances, or less common chords of the period (seventh chords, altered chords, Neapolitan sixths, and so forth). Primary dissonances (usually a suspension or appoggiatura) ordinarily fall on the strong beat, and are stressed either dynamically or agogically or both (see F. Dorian's *The History of Music in Performance* and T. Dart's *The Inter-*

pretation of Music for specific treatment). Suspensions probably provide the most important expressive dissonance in polyphonic choral literature, and the appoggiatura is the most important one in solo vocal music. Passing tones, anticipations, escape tones, upper and lower neighbor-tones, and free neighbor-tones are some of the secondary dissonances. These dissonances are usually less than half a beat in duration and are functionally ornamental. Ordinarily they are performed on the weak part of the beat and are sung lightly and sometimes more quickly than their note value indicates. Other contrasts are provided through low vs. high, and so on, as in Renaissance music.

Notation

The dotted eighth and sixteenth and the eighth followed by two sixteenths are frequently performed by extending the longer note somewhat more than its exact value and shortening the smaller notes accordingly. This procedure tends to result in double-dotted eighths and thirty-seconds. An exception to this practice occurs in Italian style (including music of Handel and Bach), especially in compound triple time. Dotted rhythms conform to the basic swing music; for example, ♩. ♪ ♩. ♪ sung over a basic swing of ♩♩♩ ♩♩♩ is sung as ♩ ♪♩ ♪ .

When a number of triplets occur, the first note of a triplet landing on a strong beat is sometimes held a little longer. In a sequence of sixteenth notes, the first note on each beat or on a strong beat is held slightly longer than its note value. *Pointer* (prolonging strong beats at the expense of weak beats) results in sixteenths in $\frac{4}{4}$ and eighths in $\frac{3}{4}$ (these exceptions only) sung as though dotted; for example, |$\frac{4}{4}$| ♪♪♪♪ is sung ♩. ♪♪. ♪ and |$\frac{3}{4}$| ♪♪ is sung ♩. ♪ . Muffat in 1695 says that |$\frac{3}{2}$| ♪ ♪ (Allegro) is sung as ♪· ♪ and |$\frac{12}{8}$| ♪♪ (Adagio) is sung ♩·♩ . French treatment of *notes inegales* used the above treatment consistently. Farther south (in Italy, for example) musicians preferred the opposite treatment and shortened the first and third notes while lengthening the second and fourth. Dots over a string of notes in the French style means that they are performed with equal length (not that they are staccato), e.g., ♩♩♩♩ = ♩♩♩♩ .

However, ♩♩ ♩♩ is sung as ♪♩. ♪♩. . The use of the wedge-shaped staccato has already been treated in a previous chapter. The *thorough bass (figured bass)* was a very successful musical shorthand used throughout this period. A number indicated the chord to be used, as it is in the piano part of a modern jazz score, and the filling in of the chord was improvised at the discretion of the performer. *Ground bass (basso ostinato)* was also very prominent, especially during the early part of this period. The continuo part and the vocal bass line usually coincided. In chorales, the continuo was usually played by the organ and one or more other instruments, normally the cello, violone, or bassoon. The harpsichord and other keyboard instruments of the period were used frequently in other music of the period (the pianoforte, invented about 1710 by Christofori, began to replace the clavichord and harpsichord).

Instrumental Music

All Baroque vocal music had an instrumental accompaniment. The rise of the importance of instruments to equal rank with the voice almost eliminated the a cappella style, and polyphonic writing yielded to homophonic. Melodic writing became influenced by and dependent upon instrumental usage, resulting in the use of chromatic tones and big jumps in the melody line. The keyboard instrument was involved all the time in a continuo part. Up until middle Baroque, orchestration was of no concern (although Gabrieli published *Sacrae Symphoniae* in 1597 with instruments scored independent of vocal parts, and Monteverdi made great strides in this area, including the first use of tremolo in the strings). Contrast in weight was accomplished by adding more instruments or by alternating solo voices and the entire group. Since individual instrumental colors were not sought, parts tended to be doubled; for example, the viola usually played the bass part up an octave. Until Johann Stamitz (1717–57) of the famed Mannheim School of the pre-Classic period, most of the instruments could be played in first position. The Mannheim composer took the instruments out of first position, developed the long crescendo and decrescendo, brought about greater contrasts, used and developed instrumental colors, got the bow off the strings for the first time (flying bow technique), instigated the Mannheim Rocket (arpeggiated figure upward), and made other improvements that led to the full development of the modern symphony orchestra. No full symphony scores were written until Beethoven and later.

Tempo

The tempo of Baroque music is deliberate and temperate. Even quick tempi should be sung at a somewhat restricted speed. However, the rhythm is dynamic and driving—steady, never ceasing. Banchieri (c. 1600) wrote music using *allegro, adagio,* and *presto.* Towards the close of the seventeenth century *largo, adagio, allegro,* and *presto* were adopted in Italy and slowly came into general use. Seventeenth- and eighteenth-century *presto* meant only "quick"; Mozart used the term in its twentieth-century sense ("very fast"). When *andante* came into usage, it was considered to have a fair amount of movement until the nineteenth century, when it became known as a slow speed (Brahms, however, considered it a faster tempo). Dart's book[6] reproduces tempo tables by Purcell (1696) and L'Affilard (1694). Purcell's table lists C = slow, ¢ = a little faster, 𝄇 = brisk and airy, 2 = brisk and airy, $\frac{3}{4}$ = slow, 3 = faster, $\frac{3}{2}$ and $\frac{3}{8}$ = very slow (except the hornpipe), $\frac{6}{4}$ and $\frac{6}{8}$, = brisk. Quantz[7] lists the following tempos for C : *presto, allegro assai* = minim = 80; *allegro moderato, vivace* = minim = 60; *allegretto* = crotchet = 80: *adagio contabile* = crotchet = 40; *adagio assai* = crotchet = 20. In ¢ all these speeds are doubled. The tempi of Bach's music should be interpreted somewhere between these two charts. Information about the fermata is given in Chapter 8.

Harmony

Text was more important than form early in the period. There was emphasis on expression and emotion, a type of Romanticism, and there was a great deal of "word painting." Tone quality of the singers became much warmer, with wider dynamics. Modality changed to universal usage of the major and minor scales. When the composer wished to employ a minor key in a composition, he used the melodic minor if the melody line was the main consideration and the harmonic minor when his concern was the vertical harmony. It was not until 1729 that Rameau discovered the fact that the chord could be inverted. Virtuosity was demanded of many of the vocal performers, with long runs and roulades, ornamentation and improvisation. Form consisted of the elaboration of a theme until its development was completed. Harmony was not completely dependent upon the melodic lines; and modulations, altered chords, and deceptive cadences came into being. Development of the oratorio, the opera, the cantata, Masses for multiple groups, the aria, the recitative (which is performed *freely*—see Chapter 9), the passion, and the real beginnings of the art song took place. Instrumental forms such as the concerto, the fugue, the suite, variations, the sonata, the passacaglia, the chorale prelude, the rondeau, the toccata, and the chaconne developed. The music is commanding, imposing, dignified, and expansive in style. A rebellion against this form occurred during the Rococo (1725–75). Art and music of the Rococo period are very ornate, decorative, and elegant as well as subjective. Following are some of the principal composers of this period, arranged chronologically, with some of their larger form choral works (see Chapter 9 for some suggestions on conducting eighteenth-century recitative).

[6] Thurston Dart, *The Interpretation of Music* (London: Hutchinson University Library, 1954), p. 84.

[7] *Ibid.*, p. 98.

Baroque Period (c. 1600–1750)

Giulio Caccini	Italy	c. 1546–1618
Giovanni Gabrieli	Italy	c. 1557–1612
	(*Sacrae Symphoniae*)	
	(known for his chromaticism)	
Jacopo Peri	Italy	c. 1561–1663
	(first opera)	
3 Hans Leo Hassler	Germany	1564–1612
Claudio Monteverdi	Italy	1567–1643
	(madrigal) *Vespro Della Beata Vergine, Magnificat*	
1, 2 Michael Praetorius	Germany	c. 1571–1621
	Geistlicho Tricinium	
Girolamo Frescobaldi	Italy	1583–1644
Melchior Teschner	Austria	1584–1635
Heinrich Schutz	Germany	1585–1672
	Christmas Story, Nativity, Requiem, St. John Passion, St. Matthew Passion	
Johann Hermann Schein	Germany	1586–1630
Samuel Scheidt	Germany	1587–1654
Johann Cruger	Prussia, Germany	1598–1662
2, 5 John Bennet	England	1599–1614
Pietro Cavalli	Italy	1602–1676
	Il Giudizio Universale	
Heinrich Albert	Germany	1604–1651
Giacomo Carissimi	Italy	c. 1605–1674
Matthew Locke	England	c. 1630–1677
2 Jean Baptiste Lully	Italy	1632–1687
	Te Deum	
Deitrich Buxtehude	Denmark	c. 1637–1707
(Best known as a "German" composer)	*Alles Was Ihr Tut, Was Mich Auf Dieser Welt Betrübt, Magnificat, Missa Brevis*	
Johann Pachelbel	Germany	1653–1707
	Magnificat in C	
Giuseppe Pitoni	Italy	1657–1743
1, 2, 3, 5 Henry Purcell	England	1659–1695
Alessandro Scarlatti	Italy	1659–1725
	Motetto da Requiem, St. John Passion	
3 Antonio Lotti	Italy	1667–1740
Antonio Vivaldi	Italy	c. 1675–1743
	Gloria in D, Beatus Vir, Juditha Triumphans	
Georg Philipp Telemann	Germany	1681–1767
Jean Philippe Rameau	France	1683–1764

(cont.)

1, 3, 4 Johann Sebastian Bach	Germany *Cantata No. 4, Christmas Oratorio, "Jesu, Priceless Treasure," Mass in b minor, The Passion according to St. John, The Passion according to St. Matthew*, and many more —over 200 cantatas	1685–1750
Domenico Scarlatti	Italy	1685–1757
3, 4 George Friedrich Handel	Germany *Belshazzar, Israel in Egypt, Joshua, Judas Maccabeus, Messiah, Saul, Samson, Solomon*	1685–1759
2 William Hayes	England	1706–1777
4 Giovanni Battista Pergolesi	Italy *Stabat Mater*	1710–1736

The following books have music of some of the Baroque composers (see code):

1. *The A Cappella Chorus Book*
2. *The Junior A Cappella Chorus Book*
3. *The Concord Anthem Book*
4. *Master Choruses*
5. *The A Cappella Singer*

CLASSIC PERIOD (1750–1825)

During much of the eighteenth century there existed four styles of performance and composition. The French and Italian have already been discussed in connection with the Baroque period. The distinctive German style used at times by J.S. Bach and others of his contemporaries and predecessors had no special idiosyncrasies of performance styles or notation and so presents few problems. The artificial *style galant* has been mentioned briefly in the discussion of the Rococo and will be discussed more fully here. In addition to these styles, music was written specifically for the *theater* or the *church* or the *chamber*, and should be sung differently in each of these mediums. The style for the theater was lively and full of contrasts, the church style was solemn and moving, and chamber style was polished and delicate style. All of these instructions apply to the Baroque as well as to the pre-Classic period.

Galant Style

Style galant rose from the superficiality and frivolity of the French Court, although its influence may be seen in the writings of composers of all countries (even J. S. Bach). The height of this style was from about

1740–80, and the books of C.P.E. Bach, Quantz, and Leopold Mozart are the sources of authority on how this music is to be played or sung. This style is also intimately linked with *empfindsamer stil*, which was a sentimentally expressive style of "music from the heart." Carl Philipp Emanuel Bach and the Mannheim School probably exerted the greatest influence. In this music, the range of dynamics is extravagant and is constantly changing. The phrases are shorter than in Baroque music and contain much variation. Chromatic notes are sung *forte*, followed immediately by a *diminuendo*, main notes are sung strongly, and the lesser notes immediately following them drop suddenly to *piano*. The music moves toward the emotional peak of the music, a sighing cadence (Mannheim sigh or pathetic cadence). This may be described as a strong accent on a dissonant note followed by resolution on the weak beat. Pauses and irregularities of rhythm occur. The first note of the music begins *pp* and the final note fades into silence.

Classic Style

All of these influences, including *Sturm und Drang*, led into a period where the head ruled rather than the heart. Form became more important than text. Figured bass and continuo disappeared except in music written for the church and in oratorio. Instead of requiring improvisation, the music was written with many of the instructions in it, detailed enough that even the amateur musician could follow them. Principal melody must receive the major share of attention in interpretation; counterpoint and harmony are subservient. As a result, little a cappella music is available from this period. There is a breadth and continuity of style, and most of the music is bright and cheerful. However, phrases are shorter and more supple with occasional changes of tempo and rests (*general pauses*, sometimes complete silence for a measure or more). Allegros must not be performed so fast that they sound rushed and insecure. Eighths and sixteenths are sung slightly spaced, but not staccato. Moving parts must sound as unbroken as possible without actually being slurred. The markings are more delicate and precise than in the Baroque, and dynamics of all kinds are used. Haydn, Mozart, and Beethoven, the three outstanding composers of this period, will be discussed briefly in the following section.

Haydn and Mozart

Haydn's style begins as a late Baroque and progresses into a mature classical style. The conductor who does justice to either Haydn or Mozart must study each composer separately, for there are many important differences between them. For example, Haydn has the orchestra double the vocal lines (and also uses dynamic accents) when he wishes to emphasize them. Mozart's chromaticism is fundamental to both melodic and harmonic style, and emphasis or de-emphasis of a single note will influence an entire phrase. There are, however, enough points of commonality to deserve mention. Both use regular phrases, and their music is rhythmic (although Mozart is one of the first to use *tempo rubato* well). There are many runs, which must sound light and clean. The music performance must have *clarity* (cleanness of execution, a delicacy in basic style, and precision of attack). The music tends to sound easy, and *must* sound easy to be performed well. Watch out for the many key changes that are expressed by means of accidentals. There is a great variety of dynamics. Dynamics can be of the *block* type with no anticipation of the coming dynamic change. In such cases, there must be immediate change without using crescendo and diminuendo. Whenever there are two consecutive and identical segments and the initial measure is *forte*, the second measure should probably have a contrasting dynamic.

Beethoven

Beethoven constitutes a bridge between Classicism and succeeding Romanticism. His style is still elegant and formal, but his music has a great deal more power than Haydn's or Mozart's. The long crescendo and decrescendo are an integral part of Beethoven's style, and a greater range of dynamic changes are used than previous composers have employed. The staccato dot marking becomes important in Beethoven's music. He was the first composer to use metronomic markings, although he did not completely agree with their use. A number of reputable authorities feel that Beethoven did not take the time to check on his metronome markings carefully, so many of his markings were too fast.

Following are some of the principal composers of this period, arranged chronologically, with some of their larger form choral works.

Classic Period (1750–1825)

Christoph Willibald von Gluck	Germany	1714–1787
2, 4 Franz Joseph Haydn	Austria *The Creation, Missa Brevis in F, Missa St. JoAnnis in de Deo, Nelson Mass, The Seasons*	1732–1809
William Billings	United States (The first important American composer, known especially for his "fuging tunes")	1746–1800
2, 3, 4 Dimitri S. Bortniansky	Ukraine	1751–1825
Nicola A. Zingarelli	Italy	1752–1837
2, 4 Wolfgang Amadeus Mozart	Austria *Davidde Penitente Dixit et Magnificat, Exsultate,*	1756–1791

	Jubilate Mass in C (Coronation), Mass in c minor ("The Great"), Missa Brevis in F, The Missa Brevis in B, Requiem	
Luigi Cherubini	Italy	1760–1842
	Requiem in C, Mass in C	
3 Thomas Attwood	England	1765–1838
John Wall Callcott	England	1766–1821
3 Ludwig van Beethoven	Rhineland	1770–1827
	Missa Solemnis in D, Op. 123, Mount of Olives, Op. 85, Mass in C	

The following books have music of some of the classic composers (see code):

1. *The A Cappella Chorus Book*
2. *The Junior A Cappella Chorus Book*
3. *The Concord Anthem Book*
4. *Master Choruses*

ROMANTIC PERIOD (1820-1900)

This period was ushered in by a rebellion against the emphasis on form during the Classic period. During this period writers were attempting to find new ways to express themselves and to reveal their individuality. Music of the Romantic period appeals strongly to the emotions and the imagination. Moods change rapidly and frequently during songs, causing extravagant changes in tempo and dynamics to occur. Tempo, style, and dynamics are some of the main ways mood can be expressed in music. The markings *accelerando* and *ritardando* are more commonly used, and *tempo rubato* becomes indispensable. The chromatic scale is used a great deal with the diatonic scale. The composer thought in terms of vertical mass. Romantic music was fundamentally vocal in character. Composers even tried to make the instruments sing. One of the important developments of this period was the flowering of the art song. Schubert alone composed about six hundred solo songs. Introduced by Beethoven, the music of this period consists of the works of Weber, Wagner, Brahms, Mendelssohn, Schumann, Chopin, Liszt, and others.

Nationalism

The Romantic period corresponds roughly to the historical period of nationalistic expansion. The strong nationalistic movement in music began at this time and has continued until the present. Musical style is affected by nationalism in a number of ways. The subject matter of the music may reflect patriotism, the dominant religion, the native countryside, and the customs of the people. Each country has its own rhythmic variety and instruments. There is a tendency to use the minor scales and modes that are characteristic of the folk music of the country, but many times major and minor are intermixed. Melody must follow the textual demands, so the accents in the language will influence rhythm and meter. Tone quality will also be affected by the vowel and consonant sounds in the language. The extent and kind of emotionality of the people is a key to the correct interpretation of the music.

Although the conductor must study each composer's music specifically before he directs it, a few generalized essential characteristics of national schools may be helpful. The *Italian* school is noted for its beautiful melodies with smooth voice leadings. Melody and beauty of tone are more important than word meanings or harmony. Most of the music has embellishments of melody, rhythmic lilt, and vitality of movement. Music of the *French* school is light and fluid, with the text clear and distinct. Declamatory style is used commonly. The music tends not to show great emotion, but word meanings are more important than melody. In music of the *German* school, the melody is important principally because it is a vehicle for the poem. The songs have a feeling of strength and solidity with vigorous, regular rhythms and warm, rich, solid harmonies. The word is extremely important in the *English* school. It must be delivered in a clear and distinct (almost understated) manner. The melody is direct and straightforward, and is based on the harmony. Although the music is usually calm, the rhythms are fresh and vigorous. Most of the music of the *Russian* school is modal. Duple and triple meters are used freely in the same song. Rhythm (rhythmic tension is usually present) and harmony are more important than counterpoint. The harmony is solid and rich but is likely to be extravagant. The word is dramatized.

Following are some of the principal composers of this period, arranged chronologically, with some of their larger form choral works.

Romantic Period (1820–1900)

	Karl Maria von Weber	Germany	1786–1826
		Mass No. 1 in G	
	Giacomo Meyerbeer	Germany	1791–1864
	Gioacchino Rossini	Italy	1792–1868
		Stabat Mater	
	Lowell Mason	United States	1792–1872
1	Robert L. de Pearsall	England	1795–1856
4	Franz Schubert	Austria	1797–1828
		Mass in G, Mass in A♭	
	Gaetano Donizetti	Italy	1797–1848
	Alexis F. Lvov	Russia	1798–1870
	Sir John Goss	England	1800–1880

	Vincenzo Bellini	Italy	1801–1835
4	Adolphe Adam	France	1803–1856
	Hector Berlioz	France	1803–1869
		L'Enfance du Christ, Op. 25, *Te Deum*, Op. 22, *Requiem*, Op. 5	
	M.I. Glinka	Russia	1804–1857
3, 4	Felix Mendelssohn	Germany	1809–1847
		42nd Psalm, *Christus*, *Elijah*, *St. Paul*, *Hear My Prayer*, *Hymn of Praise*	
	Frédéric François Chopin	Poland	1810–1849
	Robert Schumann	Germany	1810–1856
3	Samuel Sebastian Wesley	England	1810–1876
	Franz Liszt	Hungary	1811–1886
		Missa Choralis	
	Richard Wagner	Germany	1813–1883
	Giuseppe Verdi	Italy	1813–1901
		Te Deum, *Requiem*	
	Robert Franz	Germany	1815–1892
4	Charles Francois Gounod	France	1818–1893
		Gallia, *The Redemption*, *Messe Solemnelle*, etc.	
	Jacques Offenbach	France	1819–1880
	Franz Abt	Germany	1819–1885
	Louis Lewandowski	Poland	1821–1904
4	Cesar Franck	Belgium	1822–1890
		The Beatitudes	
	Peter Cornelius	Germany	1824–1874
	Bedřich Smetana	Germany	1824–1884
	Anton Bruckner	Austria	1824–1896
		Mass No. 1 in d minor, *Mass No. 3 in f minor*, *Te Deum*, *Mass No. 2 in e minor*	
	Johann Strauss, II	Austria	1825–1899
	Stephen Collins Foster	United States	1826–1864
2, 5	Francois Auguste Gevaert	Belgium	1828–1908
1, 4	Johannes Brahms	Germany	1833–1897
		German Requiem, Op. 45, *Triumphal Hymn*	
	Alexander Borodin	Russia	1834–1887
5	Cesar Antonovitch Cui	Russia	1835–1918
	Camille Saint-Saëns	France	1835–1921
		The Deluge, *Christmas Oratorio*	
	Léo Delibes	France	1836–1891
	Alfred Robert Gaul	England	1837–1913
		The Holy City	*(cont.)*

	Theodore Dubois	France	1837–1924
		The Seven Last Words of Christ	
4	Georges Bizet	France	1838–1875
	Modest P. Moussorgsky	Russia	1839–1881
1, 3, 4	Peter Ilich Tchaikovsky	Russia	1840–1893
	John Stainer	England	1840–1901
		The Crucifixion, The Daughter of Jairus	
4	Antonin Dvořák	Bohemia	1841–1904
		Stabat Mater, Op. 58	
3	Arthur Sullivan	England	1842–1900
	Jules Massenet	France	1842–1908
	Edvard Grieg	Norway	1843–1907
1	Nikolai A. Rimsky-Korsakov	Russia	1844–1908
	Gabriel Urbain Fauré	France	1845–1924
		Requiem, Op. 48	
2	Alexander Arkhangelsky	Russia	1846–1924
	Henri Duparc	France	1848–1933
	M.M. Ivanoff	Russia	1849–1927
4	George Henschel	Scotland	1850–1934
	Hugo Jungst	Germany	1853–1923
1, 3, 4	Alexander A. Kopylov	Russia	1854–1911
	Engelbert Humperdinck	Germany	1854–1921
	Leos Janáček	Hungary	1854–1928
		Slavonic Mass	
	Ernest Chausson	France	1855–1899
	Sergei I. Taneyev	Russia	1856–1915
3	A.D. Kastalsky	Russia	1856–1926
	Edward Elgar	England	1857–1934
	Ruggiero Leoncavallo	Italy	1858–1919
	Giacomo Puccini	Italy	1858–1924
	Harry Rowe Shelley	United States	1858–1947
	Reginald De Koven	United States	1859–1920
4	Mikhail M. Ippolitov-Ivanov	Russia	1859–1935
	Hugo Wolf	Austria	1860–1903
3	A. S. Arensky	Russia	1861–1906
	Edward MacDowell	United States	1861–1908
	Pietro Mascagni	Italy	1863–1945
	Richard Strauss	Austria	1864–1949
	Alexander T. Gretchaninov	Russia	1864–1956
1, 2	Jean Sibelius	Finland	1865–1957
	Vassili S. Kalinnikov	Russia	1866–1901
	Henry Burleigh	United States	1866–1949
	Enrique Granados	Spain	1867–1916
	Mrs. H. H. A. Beach	United States	1867–1944
	T. Tertius Noble	England	1867–1953
	Grainville Bantock	England	1868–1946
	Henry Hadley	United States	1871–1937
	F. Melius Christiansen	Norway	1871–1955

1, 3, 4	Sergei V. Rachmaninoff	Russia	1873–1943
		The Bells	
	Hugh Robertson	Scotland	1874–1952
	Samuel Coleridge- Taylor	England	1875–1912
	Nikolai D. Leontovich	Russia	1877–1921
	Paul G. Tschesnokov	Russia	1877–1944

The following books have some of the above composers' works (see code):

1. *The A Cappella Chorus Book*
2. *The Junior A Cappella Chorus Book*
3. *The Concord Anthem Book*
4. *Master Choruses*
5. *The A Cappella Singer*

MODERN (CONTEMPORARY) PERIOD (1875–   )

Although many conductors follow Nietzsche's admonition to interpret the old masters subjectively (i.e., if Bach had lived today he would have used different instruments, vocal tone color, more emotionalism, and so forth), the significant trend in modern interpretation is toward historical accuracy in the musical score, the instruments used, and the interpretation. The element of pitch, however, *may* be altered. Mozart's pitch was approximately one half step lower, and the pitch in Palestrina's time might have been even lower (which means the tessituras of some songs are too high when those songs are performed using the original pitches with the modern 440–444 vibrations). Further implications of the influence of pitch on singing are discussed more fully in Chapter 5.

Nationalistic influences in contemporary music are shown through approaching folksong in the spirit of scientific research and separating the authentic peasant music (primitivism) from watered-down versions. Other nationalistic trends are displayed through harsh dissonances, percussive rhythms, archaic modes, machine music, and music portraying the hectic pace of city life. Americans are discovering they can be proud of their musical heritage, and teachers are beginning to teach this interesting music in the schools. Recorded versions of choral pieces by recognized conductors have made many model performances of all types of music for the educator to study, and they are a fine source of information. Some wariness needs to be exerted, however. It is necessary to know if the performance is subjective or objective, and only knowledge about the conductor will give this information. The tone quality may be a model for a professional group but will require modification for a school group. The tempo will not necessarily be accurate, for the conductor may need to speed up or slow down a little to conform to the size of the record (TV and radio broadcasts have a necessity to conform to a time schedule). Unless the record player is made to the most exacting standards, the speed may deviate. Finally, the studio technician may have altered the dynamics on the recording or broadcast.

The Scale

1900–1925 was the greatest period of change in the evolution of the scale in modern times. Debussy helped to break down the old system of tonality with innovations such as the whole-tone scale, which does not end with the finality of the diatonic scale. (Regular vocalization in the choral rehearsal using the whole-tone scale will help the students' performing ability; also the use of simple tunes such as "Frere Jacques" sung in the whole-tone scale will be interesting and helpful.) Another technique involves polytonality, which is the use of two or more scales or keys at the same time. Darius Milhaud is probably its leading exponent. (A well-known song sung in two keys simultaneously will demonstrate the kind of sound.) Schoenberg and his followers developed the technique of serialism out of the chromatic scale. Serialism, also called tone row or twelve-tone scale, uses the twelve chromatic notes within an octave consecutively, in an order predetermined by the composer. These twelve tones are also used in inversion (upside down), retrograde (backwards), and in retrograde inversion (upside down and backwards).

Used by permission of Belmont Music Publishers, Los Angeles, California 90049.

Furthermore, the composer may treat the notes sequentially, in variation, with octave displacement, with melodic fragmentation, chordally, or in augmentation or diminution. All of these principles may be performed by the students, and it is shown easily through the use of resonator bells as suggested in Chapter 6. All kinds of modern innovations have ensued, such as experiments with the quarter-tone piano by Alois Haba and with the third tones (old Arabian system) by Busoni. *Sprechstimme* (tone-speech) is found in Schoenberg's *Gurre-Lieder* (1900–1911) and, in a more elaborated form, in his Pierrot Lunaire (1912). Schoenberg gave notational symbols for speech without pitch, whispered, with closed mouth, with glottal attack, and with approximate pitch. Alban Berg added speech on pitch to this repertoire. *Musique concrete* widened the possibilities to every imaginable variation, for example, tone moving from open to closed and back, modifications of vowels and consonants, grunts, moans, hissing, whistling, finger snapping, thigh slapping, hand clapping, and so on. Melodies are based on an instrumental conception, with wide leaps and dissonant passages (although composers are now reaching back into the past and using modality and other of the older forms, usually combined with complex harmonies or rhythms). The choral group will need to be drilled regularly on ear training and vocal exercises on all the major and minor intervals from a second through the seventh, as well as on the 1-3-5 exercises needed for traditional harmony. The conductor will probably find that students will be more at home in contemporary music than he or she will, since this is *their* music.

Harmony

Dissonance is quite common in the harmony, and the music tends to move from tension to tension instead of resolving as it would in the music of previous times. Although there is still some homophonic music being written, counterpoint, or linear music, is the rule. Many unusual chordal structures are being used. Chords built on tertian harmony may go from simple 1-3-5 chords to extremely dissonant elevenths and thirteenths. Other principal types of chords are whole-tone chords, tone clusters (based on seconds), chords formed from tone row, bitonal chords, and chords based on fourths. The conductor and the singers will need to obtain their pitch orientation through the lowest note in the chord, which tends to serve as the chord root in the absence of one, and through sonorities that occur frequently. Attempting to analyze or sing with the traditional harmonic progressions in mind will end only in confusion. (Jazz still tends to be based on I-II-IV-V chords with added sixths, sevenths, and ninths while improvisation occurs against this set harmonic background. New sounds are being influenced by medieval and Classical church music, and by the symphonic sound of Stan Kenton's Neophonic music.)

Rhythm

Strong rhythmic movement is characteristic of the emotional tone of the twentieth century. Emotion tends to be replaced by motion; and although melody is sometimes important, rhythm is *always* important and is the unifying foundation for contemporary musical complexities. Some of the principal rhythmic innovations are multimeter (rapidly changing meter, e.g., 2/4, 3/4, 3/16), polymeter (two or more meters sounding at the same time, e.g.,

polyrhythm (two or more completely contrasting rhythmic patterns employed together), e.g.,

and unusual meters in unlimited variety. Choral music is beginning to use the unconventional notation of electronic music, expressed in precise measurements of duration. Some composers still adhere strictly to the natural stresses of speech rhythm, while other composers use words for euphony instead of meanings ("Let It Be Forgotten" by Mechem and "Weepe O Mine Eyes" by H. Stevens). Jazz (see a discussion of this aspect in Chapter 8) is usually written in simple meter but has a feeling of compound meter when it is performed. Some of the jazz rhythms are described in Chapter 9. Progressive jazz resembles contemporary non-jazz music. Implications for music rehearsing are that all kinds of rhythmic patterns must be taught regularly and related to song literature until the singers develop a keen sense of rhythmic accuracy.

Twentieth-Century Composers (1875–   )

Claude Debussy	France	1862–1918
	The Blessed Damozel,	
	L'Enfant Prodigue	
Frederick Delius	England	1862–1934
	Mass of Life	
Erik Satie	France	1866–1925
	Mass for the Poor	
Ralph Vaughan Williams	England	1872–1958
	Mass in g minor,	
	Santa Civitas, Thanksgiving	
	for Victory	
Clarence Dickinson	United States	1873–
Gustav von Holst	England	1874–1934
Arnold Schoenberg	Austria	1874–1951
Charles Ives	United States	1874–1954
Maurice Ravel	France	1875–1937

Martin Shaw	England	1875–1943
John Alden Carpenter	United States	1876–1951
Ernest Bloch	Switzerland	1880–1959
	Sacred Service	
Healey Willan	England	1880–
Béla Bartók	Transylvania	1881–1945
	Cantata Profana	
Zoltán Kodály	Hungary	1882–1967
	Psalmus Hungaricus,	
	Te Deum	
Igor Stravinsky	Russia	1882–
	Les Noces, Oedipus	
	Rex, Persephone, Symphony	
	of Psalms	
Charles T. Griffes	United States	1884–1920
Wallingford Riegger	United States	1885–1961
Konstantin N. Shvedov	Russia	1886–
Heitor Villa-Lobos	Brazil	1887–1959
Ernst Toch	Austria	1887–1964
Joseph W. Clokey	United States	1890–
	When the Christ	
	Child Came	
Sergei Prokofieff	Russia	1891–1953
	Alexander Nevsky	
Arthur Honegger	France	1892–1955
	Christmas Cantata,	
	King David, Jeanne d'Arc	
	au Bucher	
Darius Milhaud	France	1892–
	Miracles of Faith	
Carl F. Mueller	United States	1892–
John Jacob Niles	United States	1892–
Douglas Moore	United States	1893–
Paul Hindemith	Germany	1895–1963
	Requiem	
Albert Hay Malotte	United States	1895–
Leo Sowerby	United States	1895–1968
Carl Orff	Germany	1895–
	Carmina Burana,	
	Catulli Carmina, Trionfo	
	di Afrodite	
Howard Hanson	United States	1896–
	Song of Democracy,	
	Drum Taps	
Richard Kountz	United States	1896–1950
Jaromir Weinbergen	Czechoslovakia	1896–
Virgil Thomson	United States	1896–
Alexander Tansman	Poland	1897–
	Isaiah, the Prophet	
George Gershwin	United States	1898–1937
Roy Harris	United States	1898–
Hugh Ross	England	1898–
Francis Poulenc	France	1899–1963
	Stabat Mater	*(cont.)*

Carlos Chavez	Mexico	1899–
Randall Thompson	United States	1899–
	Testament of	
	Freedom, Mass of the	
	Holy Spirit, Peaceable	
	Kingdom	
Eric Thiman	England	1900–
Kurt Weill	Germany	1900–1950
Aaron Copland	United States	1900–
	In the Beginning	
Otto Luening	United States	1900–
Jean Berger	Germany	1901–
	Brasilian Psalm	
Olaf C. Christiansen	United States	1901–
Harry Robert Wilson	United States	1901–1968
	Upon This Rock	
Edmund Rubbra	England	1901–
	Missa in Honorem	
	Sancti Dominicti	
William Walton	England	1902–
	Belshazzar's Feast,	
	Te Deum, In Honour	
	of the City of London	
Paul Creston	United States	1906–
	Isaiah's Prophesy	
Normand Lockwood	United States	1906–
Dmitri Shostakovich	Russia	1906–
	Song of the Forest	
Miklos Rozsa	Hungary	1907–
	To Everything	
	There Is a Season	
Samuel Barber	United States	1910–
	Prayer of Kierkegaard, Op. 30	
William Howard	United States	1910–
Schuman	*A Free Song,*	
	This is Our Time	
Franz Reizenstein	Germany	1911–
	Voices of Night	
Gian-Carlo Menotti	Italy	1911–
Benjamin Britten	England	1913–
	Ceremony of Carols,	
	Op. 28	
Norman Dello Joio	United States	1913–
	Psalm of David	
Gardner Read	United States	1913–
Irving Fine	United States	1914–1962
	The Choral	
	New Yorker	
Cecil Effinger	United States	1914–
Vincent Persichetti	United States	1915–
Leonard Bernstein	United States	1918–

Lukas Foss	Germany	1922–
	Parable of Death,	
	Psalms	
Daniel Pinkham	United States	1923–

BIBLIOGRAPHY

APEL, WILLI, *Harvard Dictionary of Music* (Revised and enlarged). Cambridge, Mass.: Harvard University Press, 1969.

APPLETON, JON J., and RONALD C. PERERA, eds., *The Development of Electronic Music*. Englewood Cliffs, N.J.: Prentice-Hall, Inc., 1975.

BAKER, THEODORE, *Baker's Biographical Dictionary of Musicians* (5th ed.), ed. N. Slonimsky. New York: G. Schirmer, Inc., 1958.

BERNSTEIN, M., and M. PICKER, *An Introduction to Music* (3rd ed.). Englewood Cliffs, N.J.: Prentice-Hall, Inc., 1966.

CROCKER, RICHARD L. *A History of Musical Style*. New York: McGraw-Hill Book Company, 1966.

DART, THURSTON, *Interpretation of Music* (Rev. ed.) London: Hutchinson University Library, 1960.

DECKER, HAROLD A., and JULIUS HERFORD, *Choral Conducting: A Symposium*. Englewood Cliffs, N.J.: Prentice-Hall, Inc., 1973.

DONINGTON, ROBERT, *The Interpretation of Early Music*. London: Faber and Faber, Ltd., 1963.

DORIAN, FREDERICK, *History of Music in Performance*. New York: W.W. Norton and Company, Inc., 1966.

GROUT, DONALD J., *A History of Western Music*. New York: W.W. Norton and Company, Inc., 1964.

GROVE, GEORGE, *Dictionary of Music and Musicians* (5th ed.). New York: St. Martin's Press, Inc., 1954.

HABERLEN, JOHN, "Microrhythms: The Key to Vitalizing Renaissance Music," *Choral Journal* XIII (November, 1972), pp. 11–14.

HITCHCOCK, H. WILEY, ed., *Prentice-Hall History of Music Series*. Englewood Cliffs, N.J.: Prentice-Hall, Inc.

LaRUE, JAN, *Guidelines for Style Analysis*. New York: W.W. Norton and Company, Inc., 1970.

OSTRANSKY, LEROY, *Perspectives on Music*. Englewood Cliffs, N.J.: Prentice-Hall, Inc., 1963.

ROBINSON, RAY, and ALLEN WINOLD, *The Choral Experience*. New York: Harper's College Press, 1976.

RUSSCOL, HERBERT, *The Liberation of Sound: An Introduction to Electronic Music*. Englewood Cliffs, N.J.: Prentice-Hall, Inc., 1972.

SACHS, CURT, *Our Musical Heritage: A Short History of Music* (2nd ed.). Englewood Cliffs, N.J.: Prentice-Hall, Inc., 1955.

SCHOLES, PERCY A., *The Oxford Companion to Music* (9th ed.). London: Oxford University Press, 1955.

STRUNK, OLIVER, *Source Readings in Music History*. New York: W.W. Norton and Company, Inc., 1952.

WINOLD, ALLEN, *Elements of Musical Understanding*. Englewood Cliffs, N.J.: Prentice-Hall, Inc., 1966.

11

Performances

A choir should perform at least once a semester, preferably more. One to three paid concerts and one to five free concerts are a good average number per year. A choir must perform as frequently as it can concertize with polish and finesse. Preparing for performances maintains interest and keeps the choir members in the mood for work. A group that performs very little or not at all is usually a dying organization, because the desire for perfection and feelings of accomplishment and organizational pride are not aroused.

There are four initial steps to take whenever performances are to be presented. These steps will be discussed in the next few paragraphs.

IN-SCHOOL PERFORMANCES

The director and school administration must cooperatively determine the number and types of free and paid programs to schedule each semester for the students and the public. Various educational experiences may be gained through concerts, festivals, contests, operas or operettas, Broadway shows, variety shows, and pageants. Experiences may also be attained through assembly programs, clinics, all-state chorus, recital programs, exchange concerts, special trips or tours, appearances before service organizations or churches, TV broadcasts, radio programs, solo ensemble programs, and guest conductor concerts. Keep in mind that part of the obligation of performing organizations is to "exist as laboratory groups to provide educational experiences for their members and for the school as a whole."[1] Music teachers have an obligation to furnish music for school assemblies, festivals, pageants, baccalaureate, and commencement. Another obligation is to assist with programs integrated with other areas, such as physical education (folk music, square dancing) and home economics (style shows). The director needs to have some music prepared for Thanksgiving, Christmas, Easter, religious services, and patriotic programs.

OUT-OF-SCHOOL PERFORMANCES

Out-of-school performances by musical organizations must be fully discussed by the music teacher and administrators prior to making commitments. Decisions concerning out-of-school performance by school music organizations and soloists should take into account the size of the group involved, the effect on the school program, the travel involved, the finances (whether paid by the school or raised by the students), and the instructional benefits to be derived by students and teachers including opportunities for gifted students and broadening experiences for all students. Try to arrange student activities so that performances do not interfere with classes, and *always* obtain administrative permission for student absences from school even when the absences occur during study halls. Do not accept an engagement *for* the students, since one of the ensemble may have planned to be out of town or needs that time to prepare for exams. Make sure homework and class assignments are arranged for or completed before students miss a class.

Programs for PTAS, service clubs, women's clubs, and other organizations are usually performed by small ensembles and soloists rather than large groups, and are not ordinarily scheduled more than two to four weeks ahead. The program may even be scheduled as late as the day of performance if the situation is an emergency, the students have a program ready, and the administration and students wish to oblige. Don't, however, permit the emergency situations to become too frequent. Clubs sometimes take advantage of the schools and call them only after some

[1] *Music in General Education*, Ernst and Gary, eds. (Washington, D.C.: MENC, 1965), p. 206.

other program has fallen through. The music teacher wants and needs public appearances for the soloists and groups, but not to the point of their exploitation. The teacher should be present at these appearances to lend moral support. No person or group should represent the school unless music is well selected and ready for public performance. Don't allow students to sing inadequately prepared numbers simply because they are tired of singing their well-prepared numbers. Even though the audience is very small, every public appearance is important.

An excellent idea for giving soloists and small ensembles experience is to use a class period on alternate weeks for performance by these individuals. These performances will give the performers an audience (the choir) and will help greatly in the development of a solo and ensemble program in the school. The Modern Music Master Club, described in Chapter 1, is another way to encourage soloists and ensembles. Insist upon strict attendance at rehearsals by members of the small group; make it an honor to be selected. (See the suggestion in Chapter 3 for keeping an ensemble record.)

THE SCHOOL CALENDAR

The third consideration must be the reservation of the auditorium for dress rehearsals and concerts. Make reservations for the entire school year on the school calendar (which is usually kept in the principal's office). Space these projects as evenly as possible. Avoid, if possible, any conflicts with end-of-semester exams, athletic events, church choir practices and programs, nights that stores are open in the city, and city events that might take some parents from the audience. With a large production involving many students, consider having three dress rehearsals instead of two. Rehearse the first half of the show the first night, the second half of the show the second night, and the entire production the third night. This will give more economy of time for rehearsal than even three full rehearsals; and although the stage and lighting crews will need to be there all three times, many students will only need to come twice.

PROGRAM BUILDING

The fourth step, after the kind of program and the date have been settled, is the building of that program. The following paragraphs briefly consider some items that require consideration regardless of the kind of program that is being organized.

The program must have educational as well as entertainment value, and the needs of the school and community must be considered. Usually concerts should reflect the total music program and should grow out of the music class and class activities. The presentation must be dignified, unless a section is deliberately undignified by plan of organization. The abilities of students must be considered and utilized, but not exploited. An audience must understand the purpose of the performance in general terms of the music program's objectives, including the fact that performance is necessary for growth. The instructor must be sure the soloist or the group is thoroughly prepared for the appearance, so the students and school will not be embarrassed by failure. However, a teacher cannot wait until a beginning group (or more advanced group) has reached perfection. They must perform very well according to the level of their maturity and experience, and the audience must be informed what experience the group has. General music classes may be presented to parent groups. Parents will be interested in materials and techniques used in teaching the class or in class projects or units completed.

There must be a consideration of whether music will be accompanied by brass band, orchestra, piano, or in a variety of ways. When a pianist is used, give the accompanist an advance opportunity to play the piano that will be used in the performance. Be sure the pianist can see all the director's motions clearly. Also be sure the piano is placed so the soloist or the group can hear it well (this might require the use of a microphone at the sound board when a very large group or an acoustically dead stage is involved). The accompanist's hands remain on the keyboard as a signal to the audience that there must be no applause between numbers of a song cycle or other connected group (or until the director's hands drop at the conclusion of a number). Whenever an instrumental group of any size is used with a vocal soloist or a vocal group, be sure that both groups know their parts perfectly before they are combined for rehearsal. No matter how diligently the director works to obtain pure vowels and vigorously articulated consonants, the audience will still be unable to understand all of the words unless microphones are used. Instruments cover up voices. The conductor can help the audience to understand the words by printing the words on the program, by being sure the vocalists use beautifully clear diction, and by using microphones. It may be necessary to reduce the number of instruments on a part; for example, for a soloist in an opera, cut the orchestra and use the piano only; with a big voice, use two first violins, two seconds, etc.; with a small group, use two first violins, etc.; when a large group is used, use full orchestra, but it may be necessary to modify the dynamics. When the instruments play alone, use full orchestration and full dynamics. Arrange the chorus so that at least part of it is as close to the audience as the orchestra is. It will be still better if the chorus is in front of the orchestra, but this is usually not possible.

There must be a consideration of the audience's endurance and span of attention. Most programs should not exceed one hour and fifteen minutes to one hour and a half. Be sure to include applause and entrances and exits in the program's total length. A program must not last longer than the audience can endure. It is a real compliment to a program when the audience leaves the auditorium audibly wishing the program had lasted longer. It is no compliment when the audience is heard to remark, "That was a fine program, but it was too long."

Planning the General Program

There are many reasons why a director may choose to produce a program or a variety show instead of an opera or Broadway show. The entire music department may be used, while fifty or sixty is about the maximum number of students a director would dare use in an operetta. When all the students have a chance to sing in a production, they have a far greater interest in its success. A variety show or a program can be produced with far less money and much more assurance of making a profit (which may be reason enough for doing this kind of program); and the many parents, relatives, and friends of the additional students will ensure a large audience. An administrative reason for doing this kind of program is that it may be rehearsed within the regular class period time except for final dress rehearsals, while operas require many extracurricular rehearsals. Many instructors do not use Broadway shows and operettas because so much of the music is inferior or even vocally damaging to the performers. The program format permits the director to choose the best music his singers are capable of polishing. Also, the program may be built around the best musical talent in the school; whereas there are nearly always some characters required by the opera score that force the directors to select good actors who can't sing, good singers who can't act, or good singers who don't fit a role physically. When a main character in an opera has to be dropped, the show may be in difficulty even when there is a system of understudies. A number or two may be dropped from a concert or variety show, if someone decides to be temperamental or becomes seriously ill, without serious consequences to the show's success.

Plan the overall arrangement of the program carefully. Following are some basic plans which may be used or modified.

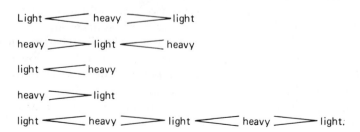

When more than one organization is in the program, take care that each group in the sequence is a complete unit in itself. For example, see that the male chorus segment is related to the central theme of the show but has unity and variety of its own. This facilitates rehearsal since the male chorus part in the program can be completely rehearsed and polished in the classroom. Use music that will allow the group to warm up at the beginning of its section of the program (but be sure the number used also has audience appeal). Do not mix sacred and secular or serious and humorous songs within the same group unless there is a sound reason for it. The final number in a unit must be climactic and memorable.

It is not enough to simply pick a number of selections. Each selection must be interesting enough in itself to hold the audience's attention and must also be so related to the other numbers that the evolving program possesses *variety* and *contrast* at the same time that it stays faithful to a central theme or idea. Variety and contrast may be provided through changing moods, rhythms, tempi, and lengths of numbers. The keys must not be too unrelated, but must not be the same. Good variety and contrast may be obtained even while adhering to a central theme or related themes. Thus, a program may be built around classes of songs, for example, folk music of various countries, music of the space age, college songs, sailor songs, marine songs, or songs depicting colors or moods. Songs of summer, fall, spring, and winter, are easily obtainable. A fascinating and educational program is to show the development of the scale, harmony, rhythm, or any of the other musical elements. Composed music of various styles and periods of musical history will provide a good theme (one often used for recital-type programs). Some related ideas to be considered are presentation of the music of a country or depiction of the history of a city or country in song. The life of a composer will provide a focus for a show. Another way to introduce the music is through a TV or radio show, night club, style show, or dream. Shawnee Press has some excellent ideas. Have at least one group of songs which the audience will know and love. Don't hesitate to use some good show tunes, if they fit into the program.

It is important to time each number carefully. Vocal numbers usually average about three minutes in length, so the conductor probably can safely place five or six songs to a group and figure it will last fifteen to eighteen minutes with applause and announcements.

The opening and closing numbers of a program must be done well and must be effective and memorable. A powerful opener will make an audience sit up and take notice. Characteristics to look for in the opening number are vigorous rhythms, a high dynamic level, and impressively massive and full sounds. It must *not* be the most difficult number on the program. Wait until the performers are warmed up (but not tired and not quite so overly excited as they are apt to be at the very beginning of a program). Usually the final number of the opening group will be the ideal place to put that difficult big number. Keep in mind, however, that numbers that tax a choir (soloist or ensemble) to its utmost are likely to be dangerous to use at all in a public performance. The number that closes a program must not be too difficult and should have vigorous rhythms, high dynamic levels, and impressively massive sounds. If several groups participate in the program, use them all in a joint number. This provides a thrilling climax that will erase to some extent the memory of any mishaps that may have occurred earlier in the program.

A planned sequence is essential to keep a program moving. An arrangement similar to the following is one effective plan:

Group A—full choir
Group B—small ensemble(s) or solo(s)
Group C—full mixed choir or women's or men's chorus
Group D—small ensemble(s) or solo(s)
Group E—full chorus or mass chorus.

If only two musical groups are performing, the simplest procedure is to program an intermission between the two to allow for adequate time to shift scenes. In a concert using only one large performing group, the logical arrangement is to have the big choir remain on the stage, and to have the soloists and small ensembles move forward out of the group to perform. Shifts would be too numerous to program when three or more organizations are involved. Using the arrangement suggested above will enable the curtains to close and small ensembles or soloists to perform *in front* of the curtain while another large group forms *behind* the curtain. Unless this type of sequence is used, much time may be wasted by entrances and exits and the show will not be smooth. These waits are tiring to an audience.

A good beginning and a powerful conclusion to the total program are imperative. When several organizations are performing on the program, be careful to avoid programming a mediocre group immediately following a strong one. Instead, use instrumental groups or soloists, and vocal groups or soloists for variety. Comments by the director, student lines, or choral speaking can provide variety.

The endurance of the participants must be a consideration. Before the programs are printed, go through the program exactly as planned with no avoidable pauses. Immaturity may cause the students to become fatigued and not do as well as they are capable of doing. Difficulties will be avoided when all vocal soloists sing in the first part of the program before they become overtired. A soloist will appreciate not having to "give all" in the ensemble number just before a solo. Program the solo *before* a difficult ensemble number that requires the soloist's full participation. It is advisable to place the heavy portion of the music in the first half of the program and taper off with music which is lighter and of shorter length. This will counteract the natural tendency of the singers to tire. The audience will also be on the road to fatigue by this time and will appreciate the "lift."

Planning the Musical Show

There are a number of excellent reasons for doing an opera or a Broadway show instead of some other type of program. Students are enthusiastic about a Broadway show, so the director who is struggling to build up a weak vocal department may elect to use this means to motivate the students. The show is a natural outgrowth of our own culture and contains the vital elements of good music and good theater. The well-known show has unlimited promotional possibilities, which will probably allow the school to at least meet expenses. Since the entire school needs to cooperate in order to put on a successful show, this type of program becomes a social and integrating agency for the departments as they work toward a common goal. Young people have a natural interest in expressing themselves through singing and acting, and this craving is satisfied only through the musical show.

The first step must be the selection of a show that fits the facilities and talents available in the school. The three primary agents who handle musical comedies are: Tams-Witmark Music Library, Inc., 560 Lexington Ave., New York, N.Y. 10022; The Rodgers and Hammerstein Repertory, 120 East 56th Street, New York, N.Y. 10022; and Music Theatre International, 119 West 57th Street, New York, N.Y. 10019. They will be happy to forward catalogues and on-approval scores upon request.

When the music arrives, the director and selection committee must first examine it for possible production difficulties. The size of the available stage and the amount of space in the wings may prohibit the choice of some shows. Other considerations must be the elaborateness of the scenery, the number of scenery changes, the properties called for, and the lighting and special effects that are necessary. The historical period represented along with the type and elaborateness of the costumes required by principals and chorus may make the cost unrealistic. The number of costume changes may pose additional problems to the production.

Another important consideration must be the suitability of the subject matter and the language used in the libretto to the interests of the students and community. Most shows require both cutting and editing, and obvious difficulty in achieving either or both will be a factor in determining which show is chosen. The principal acting parts called for must be studied carefully, weighing the number of male and female parts, character parts, and personalities against known qualities of prospective actors. The music must be good enough to be worth the time that will be spent on it. There is nothing better than Gilbert and Sullivan for high school groups, but the director may need to sell these operas to his students and to the community. Excellent high school groups can handle chamber operas such as *Amahl and the Night Visitors* by Menotti, *The Lowland Sea* by Wilder, and *Down in the Valley* by Weill. These operas contain some very nice choral work. Victor Herbert and Sigmund Romberg light operas tend to be a little bit passé at the present time, although they contain many beautiful melodies. Also, most of them require a good tenor, which is not always available in high school. The soprano parts tend to be quite demanding. Of the Broadway shows, *Li'l Abner*, *South Pacific*, and *Good News* have been used in high schools with good success. *The King and I* is the most wholesome Rodgers and Hammerstein show and doesn't require much cutting. Many of the shows, such as *Annie Get Your Gun*, do not have enough good choral work in them for a director to consider them. However, there is good choral work in *Brigadoon*, *Showboat*, *Oklahoma*, and the revision of *Fortune Teller* by Don Wilson. Most of the soprano solos in the Rodgers and Hammerstein repertory are quite low. The soprano will need to belt the songs in chest voice in order to be heard, which is apt to cause register break problems before the show is over. A lower voice may be used; but since this voice is usually not as well-developed in high school as the soprano, the director may feel that it will not show the public the school's best talent. So the director has a choice to make concerning the music styles and ranges of voice, but this choice may be limited by the student talent that is available for leading roles. The number of choral pieces in the show, their difficulty, and the number of students and choral organizations the director wishes to employ in the choruses are determining factors. If both men's and women's choruses are required, some smaller schools will not have enough young men to make a convincing presentation. The difficulty of the orchestra or piano parts must be kept in view. The type and intricacy of the dances, the availability of a teacher, and the dancing experience of the students must be taken into account.

Since cost is an important factor, the director needs to know what materials will be furnished, along with the rental and royalty. The *music and dialogue* comprise one piano conductor score for use by the conductor. Orchestra scores are not available for musical comedies and operettas. Music and dialogue is shipped usually one month prior to performance. Some companies like Tams-Witmark ship three months prior to performance. If more time is needed for this material or additional conductor's scores are desired, an extra rental charge is made. One *prompt book*, containing the complete dialogue, is furnished. Additional prompt books carry an extra fee. A *Stage Manager's Guide* can be obtained at extra cost. This is a combined prompt book, vocal score containing plots, stage directions, diagrams of situations, groupings, and all details of stage business. A book of the *choreography plots* is not always available, but it may be obtained for certain musicals by paying an additional fee. An example is

Oklahoma, which has complete directions for all the dances. It is necessary, however, to have someone familiar with dance terminology to interpret these dances. Twenty-five *chorus books* are provided. The soprano and alto parts may be combined in a separate book, the tenor and bass in another; or in many cases they are combined into one book. Additional chorus parts carry an extra fee. In some instances the *vocal scores* are provided for the singing characters; however, most of the time it is necessary to purchase all vocal scores. It is necessary to buy the vocal scores of any Rodgers and Hammerstein musical. The best place to purchase these scores is from the Music Exchange, 109 West 48th Street, New York, N.Y. 10036, or Chappell & Co., Inc., 609 Fifth Avenue, New York, N.Y. 10017. *Dialogue parts* for the speaking characters are provided. *Orchestra parts* include one stand of each of the wind parts and two stands of first violin, plus one stand each of second violin, viola, cello, and bass. Orchestra parts are not shipped with the rehearsal material, but are sent one month prior to the date of the performance. If they are needed for a longer time, an extra rental charge is made. Extra orchestra parts may also be rented. The rentee pays all express and mail charges on packages both ways. The rentee also pays all telegrams or phone calls pertaining to the rental and shipment of material. The *royalty* cost is somewhat dependent upon the size of the auditorium, the price of the tickets, the number of performances, and the dates. Rights to radio broadcast or to telecast are not included in the royalty fee. To sum up the costs, the director must add up the royalty cost, rental costs of orchestrations, the cost of scores, costume, lights, property, and scenery costs, estimated advertising costs, and the printing costs of the tickets and programs. After the show has been selected, a budget must be set up for administrative approval. After it has been received, the director may then order and receive the music from the selected show.

GENERAL INFORMATION PERTINENT TO PROGRAMS

Tryouts

Before tryouts, teach selected solos from the show to the whole chorus to develop enthusiasm and discover new talent. Announce the tryouts early and make the music and speaking parts available to be studied. Use a selection committee composed of the dramatics teacher, an English teacher, an interested teacher, the home economics teacher, and at least one man, preferably a coach. Watch for new personalities, voices, and musicianship. During the tryouts the committee should consider each candidate on the basis of singing and speaking voice, imagination and flair for dramatics, suitability for the part, and dependability and cooperation.

It may be advisable to select some understudies or two complete casts. Announce the cast and post it on the bulletin board immediately.

Production Chart

General Director (usually the vocal teacher)	Music, in the charge of the conductor	Chorus / Soloists / Accompanists / Orchestra
	Stage and action, in the charge of the stage manager and committee	Chorus / Carpenter (shop man) / Scenery crew / Costumes (Home Ec.) / Property man
	Dialogue coach and dramatic coach if available, otherwise the director is responsible	Dance director / Principals and chorus
	Business manager (may have to be the music director also)	Finances / Advertising committee / Publicity committee / Tickets committee, program / Stage manager

Student Committees

Students can aid greatly in the production of shows. Students, *with supervision*, can do the majority of costuming, lighting, and scenery. Even though music teachers are more apt to do the script writing, grouping, and movement, students can also do much of this work. Dramatics usually needs to be handled by a speech teacher or by the music teacher, although the student can assist by being student director. Committees are appointed for each special occasion, and all members of the music department are expected to serve on the committee that fits and uses their talents most efficiently.

The *ticket sales committee* organizes the advance ticket sales. There must be a very reliable and intelligent student as the chairman. All tickets are numbered and checked out by the chairman to members of the committee by number. Members of the committee record the numbers of the tickets as they check them out to class members. This accuracy and the use of numbers will protect everyone against ticket loss. Class members give unsold tickets and money back only to the committee member who checked them out to them. All committee members check unsold tickets and money back to the chairman. The director must not accept money. With the multitude of other details that must be attended to, the conductor may sometimes neglect to give students credit for turning in their money and tickets.

The *stage crew* builds any scenery or anything that must be built, sets up the stage for performances, and handles all scenery changes during rehearsals and shows. The *properties committee* arranges for any materials that are small enough to be carried and is in charge of putting them in the correct place during dress rehearsals and performances. The *scenery committee* is in charge of any art work needed, except posters. It takes charge of painting scenery and of similar projects. The *poster committee* makes and distributes the posters and takes them down after the show. The *costume committee* arranges for the costumes. It rents, makes, buys, or suggests to the students what can be done to provide costumes from their own resources. It also does the fitting of the costumes. The *make-up committee* puts on make-up at the dress rehearsals and shows. It also arranges for all make-up, tissues, and other materials to be there in sufficient quantity. The *ad sales committee* sells the ads for the printed programs to help bear the expense of printing. The *ushering committee* functions only at the program. It needs a good chairman who very carefully explains to the ushers where they work, how the seats are numbered, and the importance of being quick and courteous to the patrons, and who will move around at the program to see that everything is taken care of properly. The *choreography committee* is in charge of any dancing. If a professional choreographer is hired, the cost is likely to be almost prohibitive. The *typing and mimeographing committee* takes care of the typing and mimeographing of scripts, light cue sheets, curtain cue instruction, instructions for scenery and property cues, mimeographed brochures for out-of-town advertising of the show, and the program draft for the printers. A *script writing committee* is employed by some directors. After a theme has been chosen and music selected, try using a script written by students. They will usually be surprisingly clever and original. It is advisable to have recommendations by the students and English faculty for good writers. An English teacher can usually be persuaded to assist the students. The *publicity committee* writes publicity stories for the school newspaper, the local town paper, the local radio station, and the ads, arranges for pictures, and distributes mimeographed or postcard publicity. The *program committee* helps the director set up the program style and what will appear on the program. The *lights and curtains* are usually handled by the dramatics teacher and dramatics class. This committee needs a great deal of rehearsal with the show, since it can make or break the effectiveness of any theatrical effects. Two dependable student *runners* have scripts and summon the individuals and groups from supervised rooms to the stage one number ahead. The *student director* helps with dramatics, group movements, prompting, etc. This is a very important position whenever a show is to be presented.

Publicity Details

The junior and senior high school should be responsible for sending the news through the mail to the respective media, for example, radio stations, TV stations, and the local newspaper. Also, a copy of each news story should be mailed to the Office of Public Relations for the purpose of filing and also one to the superintendent's office. Any story of the utmost importance may be taken directly to the media for release.

─────── News Story Form ───────

The Inverted Pyramid

Include all important facts in the lead sentence. If possible, answer: who? when? where? what? how? and why? Next list facts of secondary importance, then give details of least importance. The first paragraph should be a capsule form of the article.

Prepare the copy for the news media by typing and double spacing it on 8½″ × 11″ paper. Go four spaces down and at the right number each page. Four additional spaces down write the following information:

Guideline: (a statement giving the main idea of the article).
Ex.: Walnut High Installs Modern Music Masters Officers.

By: your name and school. After the byline, leave about eight spaces for headlines. It is not necessary to write headlines since most newspaper staffs prefer to do their own. If the article is longer than one page, include the guideline on each page. At the end of the article write "End." Be careful to spell all names correctly, use active instead of passive verbs, write short paragraphs, and avoid editorializing. News stories should contain only statements of fact or the quoted opinions of others.

When a program is being advertised in a news story, be sure to include the following essential information.[2] First give the nature of the program. Advertise it as an *all-school* project, not just as a Music Department project. Second, list the performing organizations and soloists. Emphasize the large organizations as the main feature, but also spell the names of soloists correctly and give them credit. Third, state the place, date, and hour. Fourth, give the admission price if there is one. The paper may not be willing to print the price, however. Fifth, if tickets are being sold, state where they may be procured. If a picture is used, it should tell a story, be simple, and have significant meaning to the observer. Newspapers will prefer a human interest picture of a soloist or small group rather than a picture of the choir. Some authors feel that it is not fair to the newspapers

---

[2] This same essential information should be used for posters, handbills, ads, radio and TV announcements, and tickets.

(or even ethical) to ask them for free advertising without buying some advertising space as well. The music teacher who buys newspaper ads becomes unpopular with radio and TV men unless advertising is bought from them. Probably the best course lies in asking all the mediums for advertising as a "public service" and not buying ads from any.

News is found everywhere in the school system. There is never a scarcity of it. For every story published, a dozen more could be written containing important information. A checklist, like the following, indicates sources from which stories may be drawn. Daily reference to the checklist will lead to better copy and broader coverage.

Music curriculum study changes

New instructional materials, equipment, or robes

Drives and campaigns for robes or other materials or equipment

Academic achievement, scholarships, awards, and special honors of choir members

Special Music Department projects

Donations to charity or worthy projects by the Music Department

Services to the community and participation in community affairs

School music club activities

Musical programs, graduation exercise numbers, pageants, festivals, and clinics

Various contests, preparation for and results of

Successes of alumni in the music field

Visits by musical celebrities, clinicians, etc.

The music director's offices in professional organizations, appointment as a delegate to a national convention, or books and articles written

Other good ways to publicize a show are through posters, having religious programs announced in churches, and publishing a list of future programs on each printed program. Handbills are costly and do not appear to pay for themselves through increased gate receipts. With an alumni list, some schools have fine success with postcards (however, postcards may cost a great deal of money and result in very little increase in the size of the audience). Try a fifteen minute skit of the "best" of the show for a school assembly. If the show is good, many students and parents will be attracted. Involve as many students as possible in most programs. This is the best possible advertising. *Always advertise a program*, whether it is free or not. An advance ticket sale on pay programs not only is good advertising, but oddly enough will promote a much larger audience than will a free progam. Send programs and tickets to the administration and school board for all entertainments. It is very good business for the music director to invite these important people. Also invite persons in the school and community who are particularly interested in music and persons who *should become* more interested in the work of the department.

Printed Programs

The printed programs must be attractive in appearance and be available to all the performers and audience. Even with the great improvements in the mimeographing process, the printed program is still neater and more professional looking. Cost may be a factor, especially when no admission is charged. Even in that case advertising may be sold to help pay the expenses, or some firm may be willing to underwrite the printing. Usually, program printing may be considered part of the expense of a production. A four-page program is likely to be preferable. The first page must have an attractive, eye-catching design and general information. Play up other people's names and the school; the conductor must play down his or her own credits. If a show is used, the names of the author and composer of the work must be given, and most companies also require a line stating that the opera or musical comedy is produced by arrangement with, and the music and dialogue furnished by . . . . Place any program notes and names of numbers and composers on the two center pages. The songs should be arranged in systematic groups. Publish the names of all singers and officers of organizations on the final page. Give proper credit to all departments, teachers, the administration, the custodians, firms for the loan of furniture and other props, and all who in any way assisted. The teacher must personally check the proof of the program to be sure that the format is good and that all titles, composers' names, and other words are spelled correctly, *particularly students' names.* An attractive program has a definite favorable effect on the audience and makes a souvenir of importance for student scrapbooks. Rental companies require one copy of the printed program.

Attractive Staging

Attractive staging will greatly enhance the effectiveness of any kind of program. Good staging creates visual appeal. The principal factors of good staging are grouping, lighting, individual and group costuming, scenic effects, and movement and choreography.

Grouping may be by section, in quartet seating, or with vocal and instrumental forces intermingled. One of the best ways to group is to use a "scene," employing costumes, scenery, and lighting to add interest.

Be sure to use enough light that the audience can see faces. Parents like to see the faces of their sons and daughters. That's the only reason why many of them came to the program. Be sure there are enough ambers and reds so that the faces of the singers do not look washed out. It may be necessary to erect temporary spot lights in order to eliminate shadows. Spotlights work more effectively than either borders or footlights; footlights are the least satisfactory of the three kinds of lighting. It may be necessary to experiment with the lighting to find the particular level of lighting and color that will bring out the colors of the robes and costumes or create certain effects. Variety of lighting will add to the attractiveness of any program. Be sure to have adequate replacements for spotlight bulbs and gelatins; they often go bad at the most inconvenient times. With a formal program, it is usually desirable to leave the houselights on, but lowered, so the audience can see its programs and the soloist or choir can see the audience response. Ordinarily, for any kind of program, use a lower illumination for the audience.

A choral group actually seems to sing better when dressed in some type of uniform or costume. The visual unity seems to give tonal unity. The dress of a group should be suitable for the kind of music being performed. It should even form a setting that enhances the music. Whenever possible, use a costume that the school or students already possess. Be careful to not eliminate members who cannot afford to buy new clothes. Whenever the group is involved, avoid colors that are too bright, white shoes, shoes that need polishing, hair ribbons, floppy earrings, or anything that calls attention to individuals at the expense of uniformity. *Robes* are suitable for serious and religious music, but incongruous when a choral organization is singing popular, light, or funny songs. An appropriate uniform for a large massed chorus (festival, oratorio, or clinic) is for the young women to wear dark skirts with white blouses and the young men to wear dark slacks with white shirts and dark four-in-hand ties. Inexpensive dresses may be made from the same pattern, a uniform height from the floor, for young women in mixed choirs or women's choruses. Other possibilities are sweaters and skirts or buying or making skirts and blouses. For a spring concert, a women's chorus looks fresh and pretty with varying pastel shades of dresses they already own. Evening dresses are excellent when used in conjunction with the proper setting and music. Young ladies must wear hose unless the script calls for bare legs. Have them wear dark-colored dress shoes with a moderate heel. Moderate heels will be safer and will not clomp so loudly as they march onto the risers or across the floor. If it is necessary to have high heels, have soloists and the singers in the first row wear them and the appearance will be that of everyone wearing them. Young women will sing better, more securely and strongly, if they don't have to wear high heels. Also, high heels sap vitality if worn for any length of time. Jackets may be made for young men in mixed choirs or male choruses. Identical slacks and sweaters may be purchased. Similar shirts will add uniformity to appearance; for example, loud shirts will fit well into a square dance scene. Dark suits will present a reasonably uniform look. Always have the men wear dark shoes and socks.

Cyclorama curtains may be used effectively for scenic effects. It may be possible to use some standard flats without change for some of the scenes. When it is necessary to make new sets, they may be constructed with cheesecloth and glue stretched on a frame, then painted. An easier solution is to cover the sets with heavy paper and paint the paper. There are limitless possibilities to the way corrugated boxes may be used. Masking tape is the best way to designate the positions of scenery, the curtain line, the microphone area, the positions of the choirs, and positions of props. Use properties owned by the school whenever possible. Arrange for other properties to be made or to be loaned by parents or merchants. Instead of having many complete scene changes, try to use one basic elaborate set with other scenes created by suggestion. Use three to five stage entrances for a production.

In order to discuss movement and choreography, it is necessary to show the stage areas and eight basic body positions. Stage areas:

UR	URC	UC	ULC	UL
R	RC	C	LC	L
DR	DRC	DC	DLC	DL

AUDIENCE

The abbreviations stand for: up right, up right center, up center, up left center, up left, right, right center, center, left center, left, down right, down right center, down center, down left center, and down left. The eight basic body positions are:

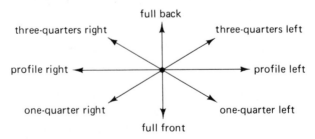

AUDIENCE

A little additional basic stage terminology may be helpful. *Stage right* is the actor's right as he or she stands on the stage facing the audience.

The meaning of *stage left* is obvious. *Downstage* or *below* is toward the audience, *upstage* or *above* is away from the audience. (An actor who walks *below* a piece of furniture walks between the furniture and the audience; an actor who walks *above* a piece of furniture walks between the furniture and the upstage wall of the setting.) *In* is toward the center of the stage; *out* is away from the center. The *cross* is a movement from one area to another. In writing, it is usually abbreviated by X. *Blocking* is the term applied to the process of working out the actor's movements and positions during rehearsal.

The director must know some of the basic principles of movement on a stage. Even if not in charge of the dramatics, the director will be involved in coaching after the dramatics teacher has done the blocking. Actors must move on the shortest line and avoid backward movement. The speaking character should be the moving character, and only one character should move at a time. The lead-off on the cross is made with the upstage foot and is generally made in front of the stationary actor unless the actor is seated. The actor should arrive at the destination prior to the end of the line. If movement precedes the line, the line will be emphasized. If movement follows the line, the movement will be emphasized. Teach singers and actors to stand still unless involved in a definite move. A standing position should usually be taken with the upstage foot slightly ahead of the downstage foot. Teach the singers and actors to gesture with full movements above the waist line, getting their elbows out and away from their bodies. Any turns on the stage should usually be made toward the audience. Unless the singers and actors are told to play to the audience, they must keep their attention on the stage. Every movement on the stage must serve a purpose. If an actor or singer cannot justify a specific movement or gesture, it must be omitted.

Plan movement on the stage. Have the groups change, spread out, and so on to create audience interest. Block the chorus on the stage the same for each number. The chorus must know the songs before blocking takes place. Number the students (1, 2, 3) for entrances, crosses, gestures, and other movements. Have the singers always use the same entrances and exits. The more detailed planning the teacher does in the chorus rehearsal time, and the earlier, the better. Play the principals, soloists, small ensembles, and chorus as far forward as possible on the stage as they can be well-lighted. In most auditoriums this will give more sense of immediacy and impact to the tone that the audience experiences. Singing from far back on a large stage will sound like a radio playing in the next room. Even if the sound is pretty, there is no thrill to it.

When there is formal singing on risers, be sure everyone knows how to get on and off stage. If there is a curtain, it is usually better to have everyone in place before it is opened, everyone must remain motionless until it is closed. When marching on in full view of the audience it looks best to have the first row come in first and remain standing in front of the risers to shield the entrance of the remainder of the choir. Have the last row come in second, then the next to last row, and so on. When leaving, the first row steps forward and remains standing to screen the other rows as they leave. The second row will leave first, etc. The director may wish to signal the moving down of each row together.

WORK SCHEDULE FOR PERFORMANCE

Modify this time schedule according to need.

Three Months Before Performance

The time required for the total production depends upon the local situation and the type of performance. The cast and chorus may work on the show all the way from one month to three months, depending upon how concentrated the rehearsal can be. To have a well-polished show, around ninety hours of rehearsal are usually required. About thirty hours of rehearsal are required per hour of performance. Work the principal singers (or cast) and chorus separately. Use the regular, scheduled music hours for rehearsals if possible. It is possible to use after- or before-school time or nights for extra rehearsals that will be necessary. Decisions should be made on the times. Find out about the availability of the stage and of floor areas about the size of the stage, for example, the music room, home economics room, and gym. Schedule the available areas.

Ten Weeks Before Performance

Have the first meeting of the complete cast and production crew. Distribute the story of the plot and simple sketch of the sets. Also, distribute copies of the complete rehearsal schedule. Give out typed or mimeographed sheets with complete details and instructions for singers, players, stage crew, lighting crew, and all others connected with the performance. Call for memory work immediately; *scare* the students into memorizing. Set deadlines for the completion of the learning of specific portions of the dialogue and music. Everything must be rehearsed.

Two Months Before Performance

Order costumes, properties, and scenery without delay. Personally check and inventory costumes on arrival. Plan the publicity and begin the posters and news releases. Prepare the printed program and get it to the printer. Have it back from the printer at least three weeks before the performance. Arrange for the printing of the tickets and order them (numbered consecutively). With the faculty business manager, plan the ticket sale and arrange for faculty members to sell tickets at the door.

One Month Before Performance

Begin selling the tickets. The make-up must be ordered if there is none available locally. Paramount Theatrical Supplies, 32 West 20th Street, New York, N.Y. 10011, is an excellent source. Better yet, borrow make-up from the high school dramatics department, with its permission, and have it bill the vocal music department. Have the costumes made or have a firm commitment on the time the rental costumes will arrive. The making of costumes can be a project of the home economics department or of a student committee. Some directors ask mothers to make costumes. Parents may be willing to buy a costume if it can be adapted afterwards to serve a useful function in the student's wardrobe. Another possibility is for the school to buy costumes and keep them. Lighting and sound effects must be ready, and the stage crew must rehearse with the cast for the month previous to the show. Technical rehearsals with the stage and lighting crews are not only important, but essential for a smooth show. The lighting crew should be headed by a faculty member, preferably the dramatics teacher. Lighting may be vastly improved by someone who knows wiring. Sound effects may be attained through tape or disc recordings. Write Lyon–Healy, 243 S. Wabash Ave., Chicago, Illinois 60604, for a special list of sound effect records. Have the staging, scenery, and properties arranged for a month before the program.

Two to Four Weeks Before Performance

Have the scenery in place and rehearse with it for two to three weeks, if possible. Sometimes it is not feasible to tie up a stage that long. Have the properties ready and use them as soon as possible; however, they *must* be used in the dress rehearsals. Plan the details of housing and supervising the groups when they are not on stage. Make arrangements at least two or three weeks in advance for dressing rooms, a place to leave coats, a warm-up room, and the exact faculty personnel who will assist backstage. Whenever more than one group is involved, it is necessary to enlist the aid of faculty members to supervise the halls, backstage, in rest rooms, and in the dressing rooms assigned to students. A teacher should stay with a group until it goes on stage and should meet it when its part is completed. Arrange for ushers, ticket collectors, and after-performance clean-up. Put all instruments used in the concert into the best of condition. If possible, arrange for the piano to be tuned on the day of the program. *One week before the performance* mail out complimentary tickets and programs, check the stage equipment and public address system, and check to see that all small props have been secured.

Not Later than the Rehearsal
Just Before the Final Rehearsal

Time the complete performance carefully to be positive that the original estimates have allowed adequate time for all scene and costume changes. Critically look and listen to all acts (dances, ensembles, soloists, action, etc.). Make final corrections and cuts. Rehearse any rough spots until they are polished. Plan and rehearse encores (if they are used), curtain calls, and other acknowledgement of applause. The make-up schedule should be posted and announced before this rehearsal. Have the chorus and principals put on their own basic make-up to save time and trouble. Students need a chance to become at ease with their make-up and costumes, for mustaches, longer skirts, etc. may be difficult to maneuver without practice. The other students also must become accustomed to the changed appearances so they can stay "in character" the night of the big show. Check the costumes and make-up carefully and make any necessary corrections. All properties must be in use. Have all tickets and money turned in to the ticket sales committee. Set this deadline and insist that it be observed.

Final Rehearsal

The final rehearsal must be held where the performance will take place. This enables the conductor to make certain that the performers become accustomed to the acoustics, lighting effects, curtains, and the moving of properties and scenery. Practice going on and off the stage and on and off the risers. The performers must rehearse and know the exact order of performance. Check to be sure the performers can hear the piano or orchestra well enough to retain pitch. The soloists must know how to adjust the microphone and the proper singing distance from it. Practice the ways of acknowledging applause. Soloists must be rehearsed until they can bow gracefully. The director must have the mimeographed instructions handed out to each member at the start of the rehearsal. Give final instructions concerning the dress for the performance. The group must be reminded of the meeting time and location, what doors to use in arriving and leaving, and where to put wraps the evening of the performance. Also, remind the students that they should not eat or drink anything just before or during the show. Review the order of the selections. Rehearse the choir by singing a phrase or two of each song as a reminder and clean up any weak spots. The conductor must do some listening from the back of the performance hall to determine blend, balance, precision, enunciation, and general effects. Keep in mind that when the auditorium is empty, reverberation will be greater than with an audience. Allow the group time to ask questions. Instructions are seldom as clear to students as they seem to the director.

Just Before the Performance

The conductor must arrive at least an hour before the performance to check that everything has been done and is still in place. The auditorium should be checked to see that all the lights are turned on properly, the ventilation is adequate, the ticket sellers and ticket takers are ready, the printed programs are at hand, and the ushers are in place and the reserved section marked off. Backstage and onstage, check to see that the stage crew is ready. While there, see if the stage setting and properties are in place. Don't neglect to check the conductor's podium and stand, also the placement of the flowers. Be sure that anyone who does any work on the stage in sight of the audience is appropriately dressed (not doing this is a good way to introduce humor into the program, if that is what is wanted). Check to see if the lighting, sound, and curtains crews are ready. Test the onstage lighting, spotlights, sound effects, and public address system. Be sure the microphones are placed correctly. Check on the prompters, the student director, and the student runners. Instrumental soloists must be tuned to the onstage piano. See if the chorus, leads, and dancers are properly costumed, properly made-up, and ready. The faculty members who are supervising backstage and in dressing rooms must be on duty. In the warm-up rehearsal room, distribute music if any is used and check attendance. The conductor must be calm, or appear to be. A smile and a relaxed appearance will have a calming effect on the group. Warm up each choir and refresh memories. The director must make a careful final check of all the music, both the order of selections and pages, before placing it on the stand for the performance.

THE PERFORMANCE

Ushers

The ushers create a favorable or unfavorable first impression of the program. When ushers are properly dressed for the kind of program and are courteous and friendly, proudly welcoming the audience to an enjoyable evening, they set the mood for the program. The ushers must know their business and usher the audience into the correct seats quickly and efficiently. The ushers must see that the doors are closed before a number begins and that no one enters until the number is ended. Ushers should be instructed to seat people only between numbers, or programs should be marked for the ushers telling them what two or three places in the program latecomers may be admitted and ushered to their seats.

Backstage Deportment

The student must stay completely away from the stage, the lights, the microphones, and the curtains during rehearsals or programs. The stage crew needs to be efficient in handling curtains, lights, microphones, equipment, and scenery, and cannot be if a student is in its way. Curtains are very expensive and will become soiled even by touching them. Be careful that no one walks behind the cyclorama when it is down, since it will ripple and the audience can tell that someone is walking back of it. Students must never run backstage, for invariably things are knocked over or wrecked. Do not allow talking or loud whispering backstage at any time (especially when a large group is involved) since it will distract the attention of the spectators from the program. If it is necessary that a student be close to any microphones, extra care must be taken not to make any noise.

Stage Deportment for the Choir

Choir members must be courteous and conduct themselves impeccably anytime they represent the school. This refers to offstage remarks and conduct as well as to the strictest attention paid to the director onstage. Eyes must not move from the director from the first piano chord until the director's hands are lowered at the end of the final piano chord, although good facial expression is essential. Excellent deportment is even more important than how well the choir sings (audiences hear partly through their eyes); but the choir that gives complete attention to its director will also sing infinitely better. To work a posture miracle on choir entrances, have each student draw in a deep breath, hold it, and walk briskly into place on the stage.

Stage Deportment for the Conductor

The conductor should be the last person to come on stage. The chorus should be in place and ready to sing, the accompanist ready at the piano. Walk on briskly and confidently. Wait until the audience is quiet, and be sure singers are poised and ready to go before beginning. Acknowledge applause graciously. Give the choir and accompanist credit by stepping to one side and including them with a sweep of the arm.

After the Performance

Have a clean-up committee operate immediately after the show (unless it is a weekend and the students can come the following day to straighten up). See that all costumes, properties, equipment, rented music, and so on are returned promptly. Send thank-you letters to everyone who assisted in any way. Congratulate the students for the part they played in making the show a success. Deposit the money immediately. Pay all bills immediately. Prepare a business report for the school administration.

SUGGESTIONS FOR TELEVISING
STUDENT PRODUCTIONS³

Goals of educational television productions are fourfold: keeping the public informed on what is taught and how it is taught in the public schools; presenting a balanced picture of the range of educational activities in today's schools; making a large contribution toward fulfillment of the school system's obligation of providing adult education offerings by television; and providing students with an acquaintance with television, a mass-communication medium that will play a definite part in the world in which they are being trained to lead useful lives. Subjects are selected on the basis of adaptability to television, the contribution to the general goals of the system's educational TV programs, and viewer-interest value. Types of shows are talent programs, classroom shows, or discussion programs.

Plain clothing shows up better than figured clothing, and medium shades are better than dark or light shades. Dangle earrings or bracelets are often distracting. Have the student perform without glasses, if possible. However, this point is not so important that the glasses should be removed at the expense of the production's smoothness.

Be sure to specify all properties needed on the Television Program Recommendation Form or send in a supplemental list at least a week in advance of the production. Properties needed from the school should be tagged with the name of the school and with the time and date of the show on which they are to be used. Be sure to bring wide chalk and clean erasers if the script demands the use of the blackboard.

Effective use of visual aids will brighten up a program. Be sure that all printing is done boldly since TV cameras do not pick up fine details. List all visual aids planned in the Television Program Recommendation Form, and add others only after receiving approval of the public relations office. Bring all visual aids to the studio, and be sure to arrive in time to have lighting arranged on the materials. Effective visual aids are: flannelgraphs, still photographs (semi-matte finish only), 16 mm movies, 35 mm slides, placards, live objects, bulletin boards, charts, graphs, maps, posters, exhibits, and models. Only films and slides produced outside the public schools must be cleared with producers.

All live or recorded music must be cleared. All music that is to be used on the show must be listed on the Television Program Recommendation

³ Except for visual implications, this information may be used for radio broadcasting.

Form. Include the name of the composition, composer, publisher, and the length of time it runs. Studios can reproduce either disc or tape recordings.

Name tags will be used only on panel programs. The tags should be dark red on light blue backgrounds and folded so they stand on the table in front of the person being identified. Cards should show first name, last name, grade level, and school.

Prepare the continuity for all programs, including the script for openings and closings. Ordinarily, do not use script for the body of the program. It is best to avoid memorization in television production. Time the various parts of the outline of the program in order to keep the studio timetable when telecasting.

Time the production as closely as possible, but it is always convenient to have a closing activity that may be cut or stretched upon signal from the producer. Have the last five minutes the least important part of the show so in case the production runs long it won't spoil its effectiveness. Have extra music for the end of the program in case the show moves too fast. In a thirty-minute program, plan a solid program of twenty-five minutes. Commercials before and after the program will usually take one minute. The announcer will take approximately two minutes to open and close the show. The twenty-five minutes of solid programing will probably take two extra minutes.

Usually, rehearsals in the studios may be arranged a week in advance of the production, but actual rehearsals should be within a day or two of the program's presentation. One major goal of a rehearsal is to allow students time in the studio to do sightseeing, so that the studio will not attract strange glances from them on the night of production.

A television studio is much like a three-ring circus most of the time. The important thing to remember is to adapt to the situation as quickly as possible. Be very quiet all of the time, and be very careful not to walk in front of a live camera. (*Note:* A live camera can be detected from a dead one by two small red lights that flash when a camera is telecasting.) When on camera, help the camera operator by calling people by name first and then addressing the question to them second. When talking to the viewers, look directly into the lens of the camera bearing the red lights and address the camera as though it were a person. Never look at the monitor set, the producer, or people off the set. Speak clearly and do not talk toward the floor, since the audio boom is above. When much of a program is close up, avoid excessively vigorous movements.

Watch the producer (near a live camera) when the program is nearing completion. Finger cues will be given to indicate the number of minutes remaining. If the producer motions as if pulling taffy, it means to stretch it out. If the motion is a cranking motion, hurry it up and wind up quickly. If the motion resembles cutting the throat, it means the show must be cut off promptly. After the show is concluded, stay in place quietly until the producer indicates the camera is off.

Public Information Office

Radio and Television Program Recommendation

Name_____   Title _____

Department _____   School _____

Number of students to be used: _____ Boys   _____ Girls

Names and grades of students: _____

(If not all from same   _____
school, also list name   _____
of school for each)   _____

_____

_____

_____

_____

_____

_____

Title of Subject: _____

Purpose: _____

Brief description or outline of program:

Music needed (live or recorded: list title, composer, publisher, length):

Films or slides needed (list title, producer, source):

Other visual aids planned:

Other properties:

(Use additional sheet if necessary.)

CONTESTS AND FESTIVALS

Reasons for Contests

The contest encourages competitive spirit and selects the best performer or performance. It trains students in poise and self-confidence. Students have an opportunity to hear and see other organizations and soloists perform and to compare them with their own efforts. It gives the teacher and students the benefit of the criticisms of experts. Strengths and weaknesses are pointed out by the judges. These criticisms may raise the standards if taken seriously. The contest gives the students a definite goal of "perfection" that allows the director an excuse to polish more than the students might ordinarily permit without becoming rebellious and restless. This permits the conductor to insist upon a high performance standard. In addition to being an incentive for thorough preparation, it is a spur to the director to secure the authoritative interpretations. In cases where the students and the community are not interested in good music, contests give the teacher an opportunity to develop those musical tastes. Also, if the contest reveals the fact that robes or equipment are inferior, community and school pride will attempt to rectify the situation before the next contest. Students reap the social benefits of a trip. The trip may be a motivating factor for students belonging to the organization.

Defects in the Contest

If contestants and groups do not receive a high rating, the teacher's job may be placed in jeopardy. Many of the smaller school systems have felt compelled to spend an undue amount of time on the contest numbers. When this is done, students are robbed of many musical opportunities and experiences. (This director may be too shortsighted to realize that the organizations will be *better* prepared if they sing much more music and are taught musicianship and sight-reading.) Judges, unfortunately, do not always give enough constructive criticism. Because of the tight bus schedules, many times students have only enough time to perform and then go home immediately. This does not allow these students the opportunity to hear other organizations and soloists and to compare them with their own. The expenses of the participation fees and transportation become almost prohibitive in some instances when the distances are great. It is hard to justify spending that much money, when buying music and equipment would seem to do so much more good for the music department. There are many heartaches for soloists, ensembles, groups, and even the director. The contest brings glory for the winners, disgrace for the losers, and bitterness engendered by rivalry.

A Few Considerations for Contests

Show judges what the soloists, ensembles, or choir *can* do, not what they can't do. Don't use "old saws" for a contest. Judges may be prejudiced against, or just tired of, these worn-out songs. Also, avoid a poor translation or a poorly arranged song. Analyze a group or soloist carefully against the criteria and song lists that are valid in your state. Self-criticism is the best possible preparation for a contest (or concert). Give all organizations the opportunity to perform in at least one concert before they go to contest. Have an elimination contest in the local school to give soloists and small ensembles experience under pressure. Find out from the principal what the school policies have been concerning participation in contests. Work out the financial needs and proper procedures with the principal. Know the rules and deadlines of the contest. Above all, don't be late in entering. Contact the contest chairman in plenty of time. Arrange for the transportation, sleeping accommodations, and any necessary meals well in advance. A month and a half to two months is not too soon. Try to use as many good accompanists as are available to avoid conflicts at the contest. Be sure the accompanists have worked with the soloists or group enough to do a good job. Have the music properly numbered and labelled for use by the judges.

Festivals and Clinics

Participation in a festival involves cooperation between two or more musical groups within the city or county, or in close proximity. Usually an excellent guest conductor is brought in to inspire the groups with new suggestions or old suggestions in a new dress. The music should be preselected and must be carefully prepared, either memorized or to the point of memorization. The learning and socializing benefits of a festival or clinic are tremendous. It promotes friendliness between members of the participating groups, with emphasis on cooperation rather than on rivalry. The host director must have all organizational details carefully planned—seating, meals, social occasions, etc. The host director is also responsible for meeting and briefing the guest conductor and is in charge of introductions. Students get a real thrill from mass performance participation. Most of the strain and tension of competition is eliminated, and there is more opportunity to enjoy music for music's sake.

Trips

When trips are necessary, decisions must be made about the kind of transportation that will be used. Whenever trips are made, all modes of transportation except train and plane will always leave from and return to the sidewalk nearest to the music room door. In order to save confusion in other parts of the school building, a student will enter and leave only from the music room door and will not go to the locker unless special permission is received. Funds may be obtained from money-making projects, school district allotments, private donations by private individuals or clubs, or from the student's own funds. Housing may be arranged at college dormitories, motels and hotels, or private homes. Private homes should be used, if possible, since they are much easier to supervise. Clothing will be limited to one small suitcase (or none if not overnight), plus robes or uniforms and equipment. Parents or other teachers will be the chaperones. One man for ten male students or one women for ten female students is a reasonable ratio for an extended tour. Use one chaperone per private car or one chaperone per bus when on a one-day trip.

SUGGESTED READINGS
FOR MUSICAL SHOW PRODUCTION

BALK, H. WESLEY,   *Singing-Actor: Training for Musical Theatre*. Minneapolis, Minn.: University of Minnesota Press, 1977.

ENGEL, LEHMAN,   *Planning and Producing the Musical Show*. New York: Crown Publishers, Inc., 1957.

FRANKLIN, MIRIAM,   *Rehearsal: The Principles and Practice of Acting for the Stage* (4th ed.). Englewood Cliffs, N.J.: Prentice-Hall, Inc., 1963.

GOLDOVSKY, BORIS,   *Bringing Opera to Life*. Englewood Cliffs, N.J.: Prentice-Hall, Inc., 1968.

WHITE, ROBERT C.,   "The High School Musical—Accentuate the Musical and Eliminate the Voice Abuse," *Music Educators Journal* 64:9 (May, 1978), pp. 27–33.

Appendix: Applying for a Teaching Position

GENERAL HINTS

Be sure all your papers in the Placement Office are up to date. Keep your confidential papers together, and send all programs, reviews, and honors to the Placement officer or the Dean's office. Keep any honors and additional courses up to date even after you start teaching. As a courtesy, be sure to *ask* each teacher for a recommendation. If the teacher hesitates, probably better not use that instructor as a reference.

You may also wish to sign up with a commercial placement bureau, particularly if you want to teach in a part of the country far removed from where you are attending school. If the job is secured by this means, of course, there will be a percentage of your first year's salary charged by the agency, usually five percent.

It is permissible to write a letter asking the hiring official to put your name on file in case of a future opening. (This is only when you wish to teach in a particular school. Letters must not be mimeographed and sent to *many* schools in this manner.) You must not apply for a specific job in a small system while that job is still occupied by a teacher. In a large city system like Dallas, where many positions may open up every year, ordinarily you should apply to the system, rather than for a particular job. Apply to the hiring official of the school. Be sure you know who the official is and the correct title. In the absence of reliable information, consult the *State Public School Directory*, which will contain the titles and jobs of public officials. Tell the official how you discovered the job to be open. Do not misstate your qualifications. If you do, you may be asked to teach something in which you have little experience or knowledge, and as a consequence you will have much less chance for success than in areas where you are well-prepared. Do not apply for a position that has qualifications you cannot meet.

Do not continue to look for another job after you have verbally committed yourself to a job. If it becomes necessary to break a contract, you must get permission *from the school* to break it. Most schools will not allow you to break a contract after August 1st. If the move represents a real advancement or a large increase in salary, most schools will be very willing to release you from contract up until August. You shouldn't ask to be released if the difference is small. Remember, usually it is to your advantage to stay in a school for at least two years. Teachers who move every year and constantly break contracts very quickly get a bad name. If you decide you don't want a position, it is not professional to spread the word to your friends about the school, unless the school requests you to do so.

PHONE

Many times a phone call or a telegram to the hiring official immediately upon hearing of the vacancy stating your interest in the job is the most effective way to tell your prospective employer that you are interested enough in the position to spend some money in order to secure it. In that phone call, specify: how you were advised of the job; the job for which you are applying; a very brief statement of your educational qualifications; and your willingness to write a letter, fill out any application forms, or come for an interview. Be sure to address the hiring official by the correct title.

THE LETTER

The letter is usually the hiring official's first impression of you, unless you have sent a telegram or have phoned. Use a quality bond stationery. Type it, unless the school has requested a hand-written letter. If you write it, write legibly in blue or black ink. Don't ditto or mimeograph letters and send them. Also, don't send a letter which has a lot of erasures or strike-overs on it. It makes it appear that you are either a careless individual or that you didn't care enough about the job to type the letter again and make it neat. Proofread the letter before sending it. Use *correct English.* If your English is poor, get a friend to proofread the letter for you, or pay someone to do it. The hiring official will be apt to discard any letter that uses poor English and spelling. Write on only one side of the paper.

The *letter contents* should reflect care, courtesy, intelligence, train-ing, and personality. Put yourself in the place of the superintendent. Try to visualize the situation, the community, and the needs of the job. Ask yourself what you have to offer that would fit you into that situation. Ask yourself, also, what you would like to know about yourself were the condi-tions reversed and you were doing the selecting. Then, with those things in mind, write the letter. Always use the hiring official's correct title. In the first paragraph state the job for which you are applying, and indicate how you were advised of the job. In the second paragraph give a very brief statement of your educational qualifications. In the third paragraph state that you are willing to fill out any application forms, come for interviews, etc. Sign the letter in blue or black ink. Send a self-addressed stamped envelope for reply, but don't call attention to this obvious fact in the letter. Send a picture with your letter. Keep a carbon copy of every letter you send out to keep you in the clear on commercial placement office charges.

APPLICATION FORM

Send a picture. The application form will usually ask, "What is the minimum salary you will accept?" Write "open." Do not commit yourself to a minimum. Their minimums may be higher than your minimum, in which case you would be cheating yourself of the difference. Their minimum, conversely, might be just fifty dollars or some such trifling sum lower than yours, and you would probably be willing to take the lesser amount.

INTERVIEW

Go alone to the interview. However, it is a good plan to bring your spouse along to the school if you are married. Some hiring officials will not hire you until they have seen and talked to your spouse.

Be *on time.* Look the official squarely in the eye. Wait for an offer to shake hands and then shake hands firmly. (Women may not need to shake hands.) Wait for the official's invitation to be seated. Be careful of your posture, especially while seated. State your business and immediately say, "I'm Miss or Mr. So-and-So." Let the potential employer direct the interview. Be friendly and smile. Know how many hours of music and how many hours in your minors you have taken. Have them on the tip of your tongue and know exactly what courses. You will probably be asked your philosophy of education. Have this carefully thought out. Be prepared to say something about your hobbies. Have some things to ask him if he gives you an opportunity. You have every right to ask questions about instructional equipment, facilities, clubs to sponsor, what the school policies are on discipline, living conditions in the town, and salary (and if there is a salary scale, where you fit on it). Questions may also be asked about sick leave, tenure, chances for promotion, required donations, policies concerning field trips, the grouping of students, homerooms, and what you will be teaching. The applicant should obtain information about the district's music program: how much time is allowed for music in the elementary school and who teaches it, how much music is required in junior high school or middle school, and the past strength of the senior high vocal and instrumental departments.

Don't drag out the interview. Get out, and thank the interviewer for his or her time. After the interview, all you can do is wait. However, if something new has arisen that may have a bearing on the job, you may use this as an excuse to contact the hiring official again.

On the following page is a suggested outline which you may use in preparing a Summary Sheet to be used in applying for positions. Such a Summary Sheet is valuable in that a great deal of information about the candidate can be listed without writing a lengthy letter to each prospective employer.

Summary Sheet

Personal data:

    Name:
    Born:
    Height:
    Weight:
    Health:

Photograph

Marital status:

    Qualifications of wife or husband:
    Children:

Teaching fields:

Training:

Performance capabilities:

Professional activities:

Campus activities:

Member of organizations:

Academic honors:

Military service:

Experience:

Recommendations:

Primary interest areas in which I would like to teach

    Music: i.e.,   instrumental
                     vocal
                     Music Literature or History
                     theory, etc.

    Other: i.e.,   education, etc.

Where possible attach printed programs in which you
have performed.

Index

A

A capella, 287–88
Accents, 225–27
    agogic, 226
    dynamic, 227
    marcato, 227–28
    metric, 226–27
    tonic, 225–26
    word, 226
Accidentals, 110
Accompanist:
    rehearsal technique for, 275–76
    student, 26
Acoustics, pitch and, 103
Agogic accent, 226
Alto-Tenor Plan, 181
Amati, Andrea, 286
Ambrose, St., 282

American Academy of Teachers of
    Singing, 65–66
Annual reports, 49
Articulation, 227–29
Assistant teacher, 4–5
Atmospheric conditions, pitch and,
    103
Attendance records, 48
Automatizing devices, 44
Awards, 48

B

Bach, Carl Philipp Emanuel, 293,
    299
Bach, Johann Sebastian, 293, 294,
    296, 298–99
Backstage deportment, 334

S

Sacrae Symphoniae (Gabrieli), 286, 295
Scale, 108–12
  equal-tempered, 108, 109–10
  flatting, 110–12
  intonation, 108–12
  just, 108
  modern (contemporary), 306–7
  natural, 108
  pentatonic, 281
  Pythagorean, 108, 109–10
  Renaissance, 287
  teaching, through keyboard experiences, 141–43
Scheduling:
  difficulties in, 14
  for performance, 330–33
  recommendations for, 8–13
Schoenberg, Arnold, 306, 307, 308
School calendar, 314
Scores:
  closed, 174–75
  memorizing, 229–30
  obtaining concept of, 256–57
  open, 174–75
  presenting new, 256
  studying new, 273–75
Scott, Richard, 138, 139. *See also* Vandre, Carl W.
Seating arrangements, 27–35
Secretary, student, 26
Section leader, student, 27
Seventh grade singers, 174–75
Sight-reading, 127–58
  for contests, 155–57
  and establishing harmonic familiarity, 149–55
  and establishing melodic patterns, 140–49
  hand signals, 129–30
  Orff instruments, 129, 130
  and resonator bells, 130–31
  rhythms, 131–40
    bodily movements, 137
    one-beat patterns, 132–37
    rests, 138
    rhythmic patterns, 139–40
    two-beat patterns, 132–37
    Vandre's concept of, 138–39

verbal devices, 138–39
Singers:
  gaining attention of, 221–22
  inaccurate, 114–16
  organizing, 15–35
  untuned, 114–16
Singing Movement, 67
Socialized person, 245–46
Society for the Preservation and Encouragement of Barbershop Quartet Singing in America (SPEBSQUA), 176
Solo voice class, 9–11
Speaking voice, 21
Stage deportment, 334
Staging, 326–30
Stamitz, Johann, 295
Standardized tests, 15–16
Student committees, 322–23
Student officers, 26–27
Student organization, 185–86
Student recruitment, 5–6
Student self-control, 239
Student-teacher rapport, 240–41
Style, 278–311
  Baroque, 292–98
    composers, 297–98
    dynamics, 292–94
    harmony, 296
    instrumental music, 295
    notation, 294–95
    tempo, 295–96
  classic, 298–301
    Beethoven, 300
    composers, 300–301
    galant style, 298–99
    Haydn, 299–300
    Mozart, 299–300
    style, 299
  modern (contemporary), 305–11
    composers, 308–11
    harmony, 307
    rhythm, 307–8
    scale, 306–7
  pre-Renaissance, 281–85
  Renaissance, 285–92
    chorale, 289
    composers, 290–91
    dynamics, 286–87
    harmony, 287
    keys, 287

Vocal palette of colors, 123
Voice:
    care and development of, 65–66
    changing, 178–83
    high school, 19–21
    junior high school, 16–19
    speaking, 21
    test for, 16–25
Vowels, 80–89
    modification, 122–23

W

Women's chorus, seating arrange-
    ment of, 30–32
Word accent, 226
Word phrase, 264
Words, importance of, 263–66
Worn musical groove, 112–13
Written tests, 16